War, Strategy, and Maritime Power

War, Strategy, and Maritime Power

Edited by
B. Mitchell Simpson III

RUTGERS UNIVERSITY PRESS
New Brunswick, New Jersey

Library of Congress Cataloging in Publication Data
Main entry under title:

War, strategy, and maritime power.

CONTENTS: Editor's introduction.—The nature and purpose of war: Knox,
B.M.W. Herodotus, Thucydides, and the problem of power. Turner, G.B. The nature
of war. Hart, B. H. L. The objective in war. Gibbs, N.H. Clausewitz on the moral
forces in war. [etc.]
  Includes index.
    1. War—Addresses, essays, lectures. 2. Strategy—Addresses, essays, lectures. 3. Sea
power—Addresses, essays, lectures. 4. United States—Armed Forces—Addresses,
essays, lectures.
I. Simpson, Benjamin Mitchell, 1932-
U21.2.W38   359'.009   77-3247
ISBN 0-8135-0842-8

The thoughts and opinions expressed in these essays are those of the respective
contributors and are not necessarily those of the Navy Department or of the Naval
War College.

Contents

Acknowledgments   vii

Editor's Introduction   ix

I. THE NATURE AND PURPOSE OF WAR

Herodotus, Thucydides, and the
   Problem of Power   *Bernard M. W. Knox*   3
The Nature of War   *Gordon B. Turner*   21
The Objective in War   *Sir Basil H. Liddell Hart*   31
Clausewitz on the Moral Forces
   in War   *Norman H. Gibbs*   49

II. STRATEGY: THE COMPREHENSIVE DIRECTION OF POWER

New Thoughts on Strategy   *Herbert Rosinski*   63
The Basic Elements of Strategy   *Henry E. Eccles*   67
The Origins of Maritime Strategy
  and the Development of Seapower
                        James A. Field, Jr.   77
Mahan on Use of the Sea   *William Reitzel*   95

III. WAR AND MARITIME POWER IN THE
    TECHNOLOGICAL REVOLUTION

Technology and Strategy   *John Hattendorf*   111
National Interest in Imperial
    German Foreign Policy: Bismarck, William II, and
    the Road to World War I   *Norman Rich*   139
Links between World Wars I and II
                            Martin Blumenson   159
Seapower in World Wars I and II
                            Stephen E. Ambrose   175

IV. POLITICS AND STRATEGY IN THE NUCLEAR
    ERA

The Rearming of Germany 1950-1954:
    A Linchpin in the Political
    Evolution of Europe   *B. Mitchell Simpson III*   199
Suez 1956: Some Military Lessons
                            Henry E. Eccles   221
The Cold War: Some Lessons for
    Policymakers   *John Lewis Gaddis*   251
The Evolution of American Nuclear
    Thought   *Robert L. Pfaltzgraff, Jr.*   271
The Future of United States Development
    Assistance in the Insurgency Environment
                            Allan E. Goodman   283
The Decline and Fall of the
    Joint Chiefs of Staff   *William A. Hamilton III*   295
United States Military Roles in a Period
    of Resource Scarcity   *John M. Lee*   325
Index   351

Acknowledgments

A compiler of a collection of essays and lectures depends upon the courtesy and cooperation of the contributors. I am particularly grateful to all of them for their kind permission to include their work in this collection, and especially to Lady Kathleen Liddell Hart for permission to include Sir Basil Liddell Hart's lecture. The promptness with which they responded to requests for review and revision eased my task considerably. Indeed, my most difficult task was selecting only nineteen out of the many excellent lectures and essays available.

I owe a particular debt of gratitude to Rear Admiral Henry E. Eccles, USN (Retired). There is hardly anyone who has attended or has been associated with the Naval War College over a period of nearly thirty years who has not been influenced by him. His advice, assistance, comments, and example have been invaluable to me.

I wish to express my thanks to Admiral Stansfield Turner, USN, former President of the Naval War College, and to his successor, Vice Admiral Julien J. LeBourgeois, USN, who gave their personal encouragement for this collection and official permission to use material that had already appeared in the *Naval War College Review* or been otherwise presented at the Naval War College.

I gratefully acknowledge permission to quote copyrighted extracts from Atheneum Publishers for *A Very Personal Presidency* by Hugh Sidey; from Harper & Row, Publishers, Inc., for Theodore Sorenson, *Kennedy;* from Houghton Mifflin Company and Andre Deutsch Limited for Arthur Schlesinger, *A Thousand Days;* from Penguin Books, Ltd., for Rex Warner's translation of Thucydides, *The Peloponnesian War;* from Random House, Inc., for two lines from W. H. Auden, "Spain, 1937"; and from Hartmut Pogge von Strandman for *Die Erforderlichkeit des Unmöglichen.* Finally, many thanks are due to the members of the Naval War College staff and library staff who assisted me in a multitude of ways.

Editor's Introduction

Ever since its founding by Stephen B. Luce in 1884, the Naval War College at Newport, Rhode Island, has been devoted to a continuing examination of the broader aspects of the nature and use of military force. The focus is on the role that U.S. military forces play in furthering our national interests.

The students at the Naval War College are selected officers of the U.S. Navy, Army, Air Force, Marine Corps, Coast Guard, Foreign Service, and Civil Service as well as naval officers from about forty foreign countries. They are men and women who have held positions of responsibility, including the command of ships or troops, and whose future careers make it likely they will advise senior civilian authorities as to the military implications of political decisions, and the structure and employment of their nation's military forces.

During the ten-month course, speakers of widely varied backgrounds and experience are brought to the College to deliver a series of lectures designed to stimulate the individual student to think for himself, to analyze contemporary problems as they relate to national policy and to evaluate the effectiveness of military power in achieving national objectives. The stimulation these lectures provide is translated into education for the students in their seminars, and in their own written essays, study, and reflection.

The nineteen essays in this collection were selected from lectures delivered or essays published between 1952 and 1974, most of which have appeared in the *Naval War College Review*. In reviewing the material I found it deals with four broad areas: the nature and purpose of war; theories of strategy and their underlying concepts; war and maritime power in the 20th century through the end of World War II; and politics and strategy in the nuclear era. The collection has been, therefore, divided into those four broad areas.

Today voices are raised against the maintenance and use of military force. This view ignores the lessons of history, which contain ample proof that there are times when the use of force is not only suitable but essential in the defense of a nation's interests. Decisions concerning peace and war are among the most important that a state makes, and history has shown repeatedly the importance of using military power wisely. The Peloponnesian wars demonstrate how the failure of a nation and its leadership to understand the nature of war and its effect on society can lead a nation to disaster. More recently, failure to understand the relationship between national policy and strategy led to the commitment of the U.S. armed forces to objectives that could not be achieved.

From the seventeenth century to the present day, the preservation of freedom in Great Britain and the United States has depended to an important degree upon the development and effective use of maritime power—the power that accrues to an island nation or to a transoceanic continental nation from a predominance upon the sea and upon the ability to use the sea for broad political purposes as well as to achieve specific military objectives.

The development of nuclear fission has been followed by its adaptation in the form of power and armament on seagoing vessels, and there is no reason to believe that maritime power will decline in importance in the foreseeable future. The tremendous increase in the number of vessels in the navy of the Soviet Union suggests that it is vital for the citizens of this nation, its policymakers, and its military to understand the nature of strategy and the importance of the effective use of maritime power to help achieve our national objectives and thus contribute to our continued existence as a free and independent nation.

The essays collected here suggest ways of looking at the multifaceted relationship of maritime power and national interests in a world in which conflict is a frequent element. They are representative of some of the most incisive thinking on this topic and, in both their method and content, they illustrate the perennial concerns of policymakers.

B. MITCHELL SIMPSON III

Newport, R.I.

I. The Nature and Purpose of War

Herodotus, Thucydides, and the Problem of Power

Bernard M. W. Knox

Editor's note: *War was a normal aspect of life to the Greeks of the fifth century* B.C. *Both Herodotus and Thucydides were concerned with recording and analyzing it. Thucydides' account of the Peloponnesian War is not only military history, it illustrates the multitudinous ways in which war affects society and in particular how war and inadequate statesmanship brought about the downfall of democratic Athens.*

Bernard M. W. Knox is director of the Center for Hellenic Studies in Washington, D.C., and author of The Heroic Temper *and* Oedipus at Thebes.

The Greek word *historie* gave us our word *history,* but its original meaning was less precise. It meant "enquiry," "research," and it came to have its present meaning "research into the past" because it was the word used by the first historian, Herodotus of Halicarnassus, to characterize his own work. His book, which deals with the wars between the Greeks and the Persians in the opening decades of the fifth century B.C., is the product of the questions he asked; of the visits he made to cities, temples, and battlefields; of his insatiable curiosity about the past not only of the Greeks but also of the foreign, especially the Eastern, nations with whom they came into contact.

His "history" has an immense scope. It describes not only the Persian invasions of Greece in 490 and 480 B.C., but also everything that led up to them; he ranges far back into the past—in the case

3

of Egypt, thousands of years back. His work is enlivened at every turn by fascinating stories about people, places, and customs; one sometimes has the impression that he was not too much concerned about whether the story was true, so long as it was good. He often gives two or three different versions of one event and declines to choose between them; sometimes he will tell a story that he finds hard to believe. "It is my duty," he says at one point, "to report what people say, but I am not required to believe it." As he approaches his own time, his history becomes more reliable (but remains just as fascinating); and Thucydides, in the next generation, though he does not mention Herodotus by name, pays him the compliment of starting exactly where Herodotus left off: the flashback on the foundation of Athenian seapower in Thucydides, Book I, begins exactly at the point where Herodotus' narrative ends.[1]

With Thucydides, however, we enter an entirely different world of thought and feeling. Unlike Herodotus, he is a child of the intellectual revolution; its achievements and also its limitations are reflected everywhere in his work. The charm and endless fascination of Herodotus' stories and his digressions about everything that aroused his interest—the crocodiles in Egypt, the strange sexual arrangements of the Lydians—all this is deliberately avoided. "It may well be," said Thucydides, "that my history will seem less easy to read because of the absence in it of a romantic element." He is quite right. It is less easy to read. But the sacrifice is justified. His purpose was "to be judged useful by those who want to understand clearly the events which happened in the past and which, human nature being what it is, will at some time or other and in much the same way be repeated in the future." And in this he was successful. The events themselves, compared to other wars, especially our own, were small scale. But the profound analysis to which Thucydides subjected them has made them a working model of the dynamics of war and policy for all succeeding generations. He has produced, as he promised, "a piece of writing designed to last forever."

Unlike Herodotus, who wrote of the events of the far and immediate past (he was six years old in 478 B.C., the date at which his history ends), Thucydides wrote the history of his own time, contemporary history. For earlier times Herodotus had to rely on local traditions, many of them obviously mythical; his history of the Persian wars was based on the accounts of old men who had fought the war in their youth or on the stories their sons remembered hearing from their fathers. Thucydides, on the other hand, fought in his war as a general, or rather an admiral, and could talk to others who had fought it or were still fighting it. He could compare eyewitness accounts, and, unlike Herodotus, he was only interested in them as a means of establishing the truth; he does not report "what they say," no matter how good a story it might have made, but what in his judgment actually happened. The eyewitness accounts, he says, he "checked with as much thoroughness as possible." And the truth, as we all know, is often less spectacular than what the people who fought the battle remember, or claim to remember, long afterwards.

His sources, with the exception of the digression in Book I where he reconstructs the "probable" history of early Greece, were contemporary. He drew, first of all, on his own observation and participation; he probably listened to the speeches of Pericles which he reports in Books I and II, and he was active as a naval commander in the north, where he lost the city of Amphipolis to the Spartan, Brasidas. Second, he utilized eyewitness accounts, and since he was exiled for twenty years because of his failure in the north he was able to talk to participants on both sides. Third, he consulted official documents, but these were very rare. Treaties, for example, were inscribed on blocks of stone, and he gives us the texts of some of these; but the paperwork which we associate with war did not yet exist. And last, he reports speeches made at important discussions of policy during the course of the war.

This last item, the speeches, calls for some comment. Nobody today, writing a history of the war in Vietnam, would give too much space to the speeches of Presidents Johnson and Nixon and still less to those of President Thieu. The policies governing the war are not hammered out in public speeches; the speeches are merely justifications (sometimes cover stories) for the real bases of policy which are to be found, if they can be found, in secret memoranda, diplomatic documents, and government position papers. In fifth-century Greece, however, and above all in democratic Athens, it was in public speeches that policy was made. The statesman had to persuade an assembly of his fellow citizens that his proposal was to their interest and also likely to be successful; in the decision to sail to Sicily the speech of Alcibiades undoubtedly was a crucial factor, just as Thucydides reports. The speeches of Greek political leaders were not just an important source, they were essential items in Thucydides' account of the events of the war.

But, as he admits, they were a problem for the historian. They were not recorded, taken down in shorthand, nor even published (it was not until the next century that statesmen circulated their public speeches in book form). Thucydides has to rely on memory, his own for the speeches of Pericles and the debates between the Corcyreans and Corinthians in Athens, and other people's memories for speeches in Sparta and elsewhere.

It is true, of course, that in Greek civilization, where literacy was a comparatively recent phenomenon, people's memories were much more reliable than ours. Nevertheless, Thucydides had to admit his limitations here. "I have found it difficult to remember the precise words used in the speeches which I listened to myself and my various informants have experienced the same difficulty." So he compromised. "My method has been, while keeping as closely as possible to the general sense of the words that were actually used, to make the speakers say what, in my opinion, was called for by each situation." What this method enabled him to do was to present, in addition to phrases he remembered, the political and military background of the action under debate, the conflicting opinions, the alternative courses of action—all the material which a modern historian presents editorially as his own analysis.

Some of the speeches fall at times to a level of obvious generalization that tempts one to think Thucydides might better have used the modern method of so-called objective presentation. Nevertheless, most of them combine "what was called for by the situation" with a dramatic personality which clearly reflects the actual speaker. And in the greatest of them—the Corinthians' contrast between Athenian dynamic activism and Spartan conservative isolationism, Pericles' funeral speech with its celebration of Athens' free institutions and cultural magnificence—the method Thucydides has invented for his re-creation of the speeches presents intellectual analysis expressed with a passion and a dramatic immediacy which have never been equaled.

From these sources he constructed an account of the war so reasonable, so clear, and, on the surface, so unemotional that it seems to have been written by the pen of a recording angel. He was acclaimed by the historians of the nineteenth century, who were attempting to write history scientifically, as their predecessor, their great example. He was for them the first scientific, objective historian. Today, of course, we realize that there is no such thing as scientific, objective history; the historian is part of the process he attempts to record, or a result of it. Thucydides does have his blind spots and his prejudices. He does not very often express a personal opinion or judgment, but in his treatment of Cleon, for example, he is not exactly fair. Cleon was certainly the most violent of the Athenians (we have other sources to confirm this judgment), but he was not a fool or a coward, and Thucydides presents him as one in the debates over Phyos and in the battle at Amphipolis.

Even when a historian does not express his own opinion, his emphasis and his judgment of what is important will be clear from his selection. Select he must; there is too much data—there was too much even for Thucydides, in an age before the invention of paperwork. Some things have to be left out, some treated in summary fashion, while others are emphasized or presented in full detail. In Thucydides' case it was only too clear what interested him above all other things, indeed to the exclusion of almost everything else. It was war. "Thucydides the Athenian"—this is how the book begins—"wrote the history of the war between the Peloponnesians and the Athenians, how they fought against each other ...," and there is practically nothing in his history which is not directly relevant to that subject. It is particularly appropriate for the Naval War College to devote some time to him for he is the only great historian I can think of who concentrates rigidly and exclusively on the dynamics, the methods, the causes, and results of war between sovereign states.

This exclusive emphasis is all the more remarkable since the Athens in which he lived was one of the most intellectually and artistically creative cities the world has ever seen. In his lifetime the great tragedies of Sophocles and Euripides, as well as the comedies of Aristophanes, were staged in Athens; the Parthenon was built, and its great frieze cut in marble; Athenian potters and painters produced masterpieces which are the jewels of our museums; the philosophers worked out an atomic theory of the constitution of matter; the Sophists revolutionized political, moral, and social theory. Yet of all this there is not one word in Thucydides except some extremely faint allusions in Pericles' funeral speech. If Thucydides' history were the only document that his century had left us, we could never have guessed what a brilliant cultural life the city possessed. What was important to Thucydides was Athenian power, and power for him was expressed in terms of a capacity to make war. We can be sure he admired the tragedies of Sophocles, but they were not, for his purposes, relevant.

This preoccupation with war and the power to make it is present throughout; it is even the guiding thread of his brilliant reconstruction of early Greek history in the introductory chapters. In the second half of the fifth century the idea of viewing human history as progress was in the air. Protagoras wrote a history of man's conquest of nature and advance to civilized communal liv-

ing; in the Hippocratic collections we have a text which describes
human progress from the doctor's point of view, the advance from
savage to civilized diet, the discovery of disease and its treatment.
What Thucydides presents us with is a history of Greece in which
progress is measured in terms of military and naval power. At
first there is nothing but poverty, disorganization, constant migration. Then the first light in the dark: Minos, king of Crete, organized a navy, suppressed piracy, and founded a sea empire. Agamem-
non led the united Greeks against Troy, but the expedition was
not as important as Homer would have us believe; lacking reserves
and supplies, the Greeks were forced to dissipate their military
power in cattle raids and piracy. The Trojan War was followed
by more confusion, migration, emigration, colonization. But soon
progress begins again. "The Corinthians are supposed to have been
the first to have adopted more modern methods of ship-building";
they built a fleet, put down piracy. Later the Ionians were a great
naval power, then Polycrates of Samos, the Phocaeans.... But
these navies did not possess triremes, fast maneuverable warships.
These were used first by the Sicilians; then Themistocles persuaded the Athenians to build a fleet of them. Thus Athenian naval
power came into being. After the defeat of the Persians, Athens
built up her empire, which in turn set the stage for Thucydides'
subject, the Peloponnesian War, the greatest war of all. It is the
high point of a history of Greece conceived in terms of the growth
of naval and military power.

This exclusive concentration on war is not just a reflection of
the fact that Thucydides was himself a general officer in the war,
and it does not mean that he was what some people today would
call a militarist, if not a warmonger. He is simply taking for granted what most of his fellow Greeks took for granted, that war was
a perfectly normal aspect of human life. Their whole history is
one of constant war: small repetitive struggles between neighbor-
ing cities over borderlands, larger clashes between alliances of cities
with common interests, and the great war against the Persian in-
vader in which, characteristically, some Greek cities were neutral,
and some even fought on the Persian side. A modern historian,
A. R. Burn, has entitled his short history of ancient Greece *The
Warring States of Greece,* and that is a very good title. The Greeks
accepted war as inevitable. Even their Utopias, *The Republic* of
Plato, the perfect state of Aristotle, make full provisions for military training and defense. They would have regarded the maxim
of Clausewitz, "War is the continuation of politics by other
means," as so obvious that it did not need to be said. War was

the most concentrated expression of those competitive values the Greeks so valued in their dramatic festivals and in their athletic contests; and to them as to Thucydides it was a function of human nature, that basic "nature" which the sophistic teachers opposed to conventional law. War revealed human nature in its naked form —in the heights of courage and endurance to which it could rise and in the depths of cruelty and degradation to which it could sink. It is in these terms, of war as a crucible in which the elements of human nature are refined and revealed, that Thucydides speaks, both of the men who died heroically in defense of their country— "The consummation," says Pericles, "which has overtaken these men shows us the meaning of manliness in its first revelation and in its final proof,"—and also of the hideous carnage at Corcyra—"in peace and prosperity, cities and individuals alike follow higher standards. ... But war is a violent teacher; in depriving them of the power of easily satisfying their daily wants it brings most people's minds down to the level of their actual circumstances."

This human nature, which Thucydides claims will always behave in the same way in similar circumstances, is described and analyzed in purely secular terms. Homeric man lived in a world full of gods ready at any moment to encourage, warn, threaten, or mislead, but in Thucydides' vision of the human condition there is no divine governing will, no cosmic justice, not even a nameless destiny. Man is alone and, as far as he can see, master of his own fate. With power and foresight there seems to be no reason why he cannot mold events to his own liking. This is the underlying assumption of Pericles' three speeches in which he assures the Athenians that with the right policy they cannot lose the war.

This is a new vision of man's place in the universe; Herodotus saw things differently. Everywhere in his work we are confronted with prophecies made by divine voices, the oracles, and in Herodotus they always turn out to be right even though human beings may not understand them correctly until it is too late. In Thucydides such prophecies are mentioned where they have a psychological effect on those who believe in them (that, after all, is a fact), but it is clear that Thucydides did not. "For those who put their faith in oracles," he says, "here is one solitary instance of their being proved accurate"; he refers to the prophecies which had been in circulation to the effect that the war would last twenty-seven years. The irony of this is that only Thucydides thought it did; his contemporaries and later historians too thought of it as two separate wars, the first lasting ten years, the second eight, with a period of peace in between. Only Thucydides saw that the so-

called Peace of Nicias was really a continuation of the war. Equally characteristic is his acid comment on the oracle which was supposed to have predicted the plague. "A Dorian war will come,"
it said, "and a plague with it." But there had been another version
in circulation which, with one vowel slightly different (*limos* instead of *loimos*) predicted a famine. Since the war brought with
it a plague, everyone was convinced that what the gods had said
was *loimos,* a plague. "But," said Thucydides, "if we get another
war with the Peloponnesians and it brings a famine, everybody
will claim that the oracle said *limos,* famine."

In Herodotus these oracular voices are the expression of a universal justice which in the rise and fall of individuals and states
sees that in the end everything is paid for. It so happens that
at one particular point the histories written by the two men inter-
sect, and the contrast between their attitudes to the event is re-
vealing. Herodotus tells how in the opening stages of the great
Persian wars the Persian king sent heralds to Sparta demanding
earth and water, the usual tokens of submission. The Spartans
threw the heralds into a well and told them to get earth and
water there; their deaths were a violation of the custom of nations,
for heralds, as ambassadors, were sacrosanct. The Spartans later
found that because of the anger of the long dead hero Talthybius—
the patron saint, so to speak, of heralds—their sacrifices were refused. They got the point; they asked for two volunteers to go
to the Persian king to offer themselves in exchange for his heralds,
and two men at once volunteered. Their names were Spercheius
and Boulis. But when they got to Persia, the king refused to kill
them; he would not act like the Spartans, he said, and he would
not let them get off so lightly. So Spercheius and Boulis came
home and lived out the rest of their lives. But, says Herodotus,
the anger of Talthybius was not appeased. It fell sixty years later
on their sons Aneristus and Nicolaus who, many years later, were
sent by the Spartans to the Persian king to ask for help against
Athens in the Peloponnesian War. They were betrayed to the Athenians in north Greece and put to death. "This seems to me,"
says Herodotus,

one of the most plain proofs of divine power. Justice, of course,
required that retribution should fall on ambassadors, but that
it should fall exactly on the sons of the men who went up to
the Persian King, this seems to me quite plainly to be the work
of the gods.[2]

Thucydides also records the capture of the two Spartan envoys to Persia. "At the end of the same summer, an embassy consisting of Aristeus from Corinth, Aneristus, Nicolaus, and Stratodemus from Sparta, Timagoras from Tegea, and a man from Argos called Pollis ... was on its way to Asia. ...." Herodotus' two men, Aneristus and Nicolaus, are there all right, but they are part of a group of six, and Aristeus of Corinth is in command. Thucydides tells how they were handed over to the Athenians as the result of Athenian intrigue with the king of Macedon; when they arrived in Athens

> the Athenians, fearing that Aristeus, who had done them much harm already, might do more if he remained alive, put them all to death without a trial.... They did this in retaliation for the way the Spartans had been behaving—putting to death all the Athenian and allied traders they captured at sea.[3]

We know that Thucydides had read Herodotus; he must have realized that he was describing the same incident, but in his account he does not even bother to correct his predecessor, still less to argue with him; he does not even refer to him. The execution of these two Spartans, which for Herodotus was such a firm proof of divine justice, is treated as a detail incidental to the really important matter, the execution of Aristeus of Corinth.

Herodotus' view of the incident may not seem too comforting: gods who exact punishment from the sons whose fathers had escaped it (through no fault of their own) are not exactly merciful gods—they may even seem vindictive. Yet there is an element of comfort in the story: even though the justice of the gods is harsh, there is a justice, and this gives meaning to whatever happens. It is all part of a pattern which we may not understand, but which gives some meaning to our lives and, above all, our deaths. The fate of the two Spartan ambassadors, as Herodotus presents it, is a detail in a pattern of order imposed by the gods; it makes a kind of sense and has a certain dignity. But in Thucydides it simply happened. There is no particular reason for it except that the two men were unlucky to be caught at that time and in that company.

Thucydides proclaimed that his history lacks "a romantic element." It also lacks any religious feeling. There is no heaven above to judge, encourage, or punish; no pattern ordained by divine providence; only the conflicting wills of human beings organized in sovereign states locked in unremitting struggle. In this empty universe things can happen which have no explanation, no possible justification. They are, in fact, pure accidents, and when they are also hideous calamities, the fact that they are meaningless makes them almost too much for the human mind to accept. Thucydides goes out of his way to describe one such incident, one which had no effect on the war one way or the other.

Athens had sent for some Thracian savages to hire as mercenaries. They arrived too late to sail with Demosthenes to Sicily, so they were sent home with an Athenian commander in charge and a roving commission to do some damage to Athens' enemies on the way. This commander attacked the city of Mycalessus, but his Thracians got out of hand. They began slaughtering the inhabitants; they went berserk, in fact, and killed men, women, children, farm animals, and everything they saw. Particularly horrible was the assault on the boys' school where they killed all the children. "It was a small city," says Thucydides, "but in the disaster ... its people suffered calamities as pitiable as any which took place during the war." Nobody wanted it to happen this way. There was no rhyme or reason for it. It was an utterly meaningless event.

It is precisely because Thucydides had no religious view, no mystical sense of destiny or divine justice at work in human history, that he can observe without preconceptions and analyze so mercilessly that human nature which, he suggests repeatedly, will always be the same. The mainspring of human nature in action, as he sees it, is the will to power, to dominate others, and in the actions of states this will expresses itself as politics and war. "It is a general and necessary law of nature," says the Athenian negotiators to the Melians, "to rule wherever one can. This is not a law that we made ourselves; we found it already in existence and we shall leave it to exist forever for those who come after us." In his examination of the operation of this law, Thucydides presents us with a number of analyses of power politics in action which have been admired and studied ever since as the purest distillation of political experience.

Among them is the famous Melian dialog in Book V. The Athenians bring overwhelming force against a small neutral island and then sit down at the negotiating table. They want no words wasted. "If we have met here for any other purpose than to look facts in the face ... there is no point in going on with the discussion ....We will use no fine phrases." They do not attempt to justify their actions with the usual appeals— "a great mass of words that nobody believes"—and they do not want to hear similar arguments from the other side. "You should try to get what it is possible for you to get, taking into consideration what we both really think." And then this terrible but true statement: "when these matters are discussed by practical people, the standard of justice depends on the equality of power to compel." The United States and the Soviet Union may discuss the justice of their claims against each other, but in the case of the Soviet Union and Czechoslovakia or the United States and, say, Santo Domingo, such discussion is irrelevant. In fact, "the strong do what they may, and the weak accept what they must."

The Melians reply that even in such a case there is a need for fair play, for the superior power may be itself one day defeated. "This is a principle which affects you as much as anybody since your own fall would be visited by the most terrible vengeance ...." This warning is countered by a cynical but cogent argument. "We are not afraid," say the Athenians, "of being conquered by a power which rules over others as Sparta does .... You can leave it to us to face the risks involved." And they are right. When Athens fell at last, she was deprived of her fleet, her fortifications, her empire, and her democratic regime, but she was not destroyed; she did not suffer the massacre and enslavement she had decreed for Mitylene and actually inflicted on Melos and Scione. The Corinthians and the Thebans wanted to raze Athens to the ground, but Sparta would not allow it; not for love of Athens, but because the destruction would have made Thebes and Corinth too powerful, created a power vacuum Sparta was not ready to fill. Furthermore, Sparta, which had won the war with Persian help, now had to face the problem of Persian pressure in the Aegean. After World War II there were many who wanted to destroy Germany and Japan as states, but we did no such thing. On the contrary, we built them up. We needed them against our former allies, Russia and China.

The Melians then ask simply to be allowed the privilege of neutrality, but the answer is negative. Melos is an island, and a neutral island cannot be tolerated by a naval empire. "Our subjects would regard it as a sign of weakness in us." We can translate that into our own terms: "our credibility is at stake." And so it goes on. The Melians appeal to the chances of battle, their hope to save themselves, but the Athenians reject hopes as foolish. They appeal to the gods, but the Athenians claim the gods as power politicians like themselves. The Melians proclaim their reliance on Sparta, but they are told that no help will come from that quarter, and indeed it did not—as no help came from the European democracies to the Spanish Republic or the Czechs, for, as the Athenians say, "good will shown by the party that is asking for help does not mean security ... what is looked for is a positive preponderance of power." So the Melians went down fighting, and when the city fell the men were slaughtered, the women and children sold into slavery.

Equally penetrating is Thucydides' analysis of the appalling cruelties which accompanied revolution and civil war in Corcyra. Revolutions were not rare in ancient Greece, but this one and the many which followed it were made more brutal by the presence of the war which invited foreign intervention. "The consequent slavery was the cause of many calamities, as happens and always will happen while human nature is what it is, though, as different circumstances arise, the general rule will exhibit some variety." The collapse of law and moral standards was accompanied by a process of corruption in the language men spoke: "to fit in with the change of events, words too had to change their usual meanings. A thoughtless act of aggression was now regarded as the courage one would expect to find in a party member: any idea of moderation was just an attempt to disguise one's unmanly character." We know this phenomenon very well. George Orwell (who apparently did not realize that Thucydides had anticipated him) satirized the perversion of language for political ends in his chapter on "Newspeak" in his novel *1984,* but the process has continued undeterred. The half of Germany which calls itself the Democratic German Republic is the one ruled by Communist dictatorship, and the "peace-loving nations" are the members of the Warsaw Pact; to come closer home, the word *pacification* is used to describe some activities of ours in Vietnam which have very little to do with peace, and George Orwell would have taken off his hat to the unnamed genius in the Air Force who thought up "preplanned protective reaction."

In these same chapters on Corcyra, Thucydides gives us a lucid analysis of the aftermath of successful revolution; once the safeguards of rule by law have been destroyed, the revolutionaries themselves fall victim to the furies they have unleashed. In the struggle for power among the victors,

> those who were least remarkable for intelligence showed the greatest powers of survival. Such people recognized their own deficiencies and the superior intelligence of the opponents; fearing that they might lose a debate or find themselves out-maneuvered in intrigue by their quick-witted enemies, they boldly

launched straight into action; while their opponents, over-confi-
dent ... were the more easily destroyed ....[4]

Truer words were never spoken. In the French Revolution, Danton, the great orator who had roused France to drive out the invaders and whose impassioned oratory dominated the revolutionary Convention, did not imagine that he could be overthrown
by a pettyfogging lawyer, a poor speaker, a pedantic schoolteacher
named Robespierre—but it was Robespierre who sent Danton and
his friends to the guillotine. Leon Trotsky, the fiery speaker, the
brilliant writer, the organizer of the first Red army, the companion
of Lenin, had no fear of the crude Georgian peasant who called
himself Stalin, but Stalin drove him out of Russia and many years
later engineered his murder in Mexico City. The whole passage
in Thucydides is the most probing analysis of the effects of violent
revolution and civil war ever made; here, if nowhere else, Thucydides justifies his claim to be useful forever.

Armed with this power of surgical analysis and with a fierce
devotion to the truth, Thucydides wrote the history of the war
which began with Athens at the height of her economic and naval
power and ended twenty-seven years later in her total defeat. In
the opening books, especially in the speeches of Pericles, he
prepares the stage for what seems to be the inevitable victory of
Athens. She is invulnerable at home because of the long walls
which connected city and harbor—"if only we were an island,"
says Pericles—and the walls in effect made her so. Her resources
in money, ships, and trained naval personnel were infinitely superi-
or to those of her enemies. In order to win she had only to stand
pat; the war was an attempt to destroy the Athenian empire, but
it could never succeed as long as Athens retained control of the
sea. All she had to do was to avoid large-scale battles on land
and refrain from any attempts to extend the empire. If these two
restrictions were observed, the war was bound to end in a stalemate, and since the enemy had begun the war as a challenge to
the status quo, a stalemate would be an Athenian victory. Such
a policy would require great discipline (the Athenians would have
to watch the enemy burn their farms), but in Pericles they had
a leader who could hold them to it. Yet Athens lost the war. Something was wrong with Pericles' calculations. Why did Athens lose?

Thucydides never poses the question in quite those terms, but
his answer to it emerges from his narrative. In Pericles' first speech
the strategy is outlined, a calculation of resources made; a supreme
confidence is expressed—Athens cannot lose if it follows the Peri-

clean guidelines. A warning note, however, is sounded in the speech of the Spartan king Archidamus as his troops invade Attica. "There is much," he says, "that is unpredictable in war." Pericles was soon to learn that lesson himself. No amount of calculation and preparation can foresee the accidents and combinations of circumstances that war is liable to produce. Pericles had foreseen the Spartan invasion and the destruction of the Athenian crops but not the plague which caused such havoc in the overcrowded city. He admits this in his last speech. "When things happen suddenly, unexpectedly, and against all calculations, it takes the heart out of a man; and this has certainly happened to you," he tells the Athenians, "with the plague coming on top of everything else." The plague dealt a terrible blow to Athenian manpower and morale; but it did something even more damaging, it killed Pericles. And his death opened the way for new leaders who made the mistakes he had feared—involvement in land battles (at Delium and later at Mantinea) and expeditions to enlarge the empire (the disastrous expedition to Sicily). This last mistake came at a time when, strictly speaking, Athens had won the war. When peace was made in 421, she had, it is true, sustained heavy losses in the plague and in the unnecessary land engagement at Delium; she had also lost her subject cities in the north to a Spartan captain of genius, Brasidas, but she had captured, at Pylos, enough Spartan soldiers and officers to induce Sparta to sue for terms. And after all, this was, as Pericles foresaw, the way the war would end. The war was a challenge to Athens' rule over the empire; if the enemy settled for less, he admitted failure. With the return to something like the status quo, a dynamic Athens was now free to build her resources to the level, or above it, of her position in 431.

But the Athenians not only proceeded to engage Sparta in an infantry battle at Mantinea (which they lost); they also gambled their whole fleet and the bulk of their fighting manpower on an attempt to take over Sicily, a place they could hardly expect to hold even if they conquered it.

The fault then lay in the leadership, and this raises the question of Athenian democracy and Thucydides' attitude toward it. Pericles' funeral speech, of course, is one of the great documents of Western democratic ideals. But when Thucydides pays his tribute to Pericles after describing his death, he says something rather disturbing. "In what was nominally a democracy, power was really in the hands of the first citizen." True, Pericles had to be reelected to the board of generals each year, but he managed to do so for a period of some fifteen years before his death in 429, and he did it without flattering the people or playing on their prejudices. "He was so highly respected," says Thucydides, "that he was able to speak angrily to them and to contradict them." His successors, however, had no such personal authority. They had to adopt "methods of demagoguery which resulted in their losing control over the actual conduct of affairs." This loss of control by the successors of Pericles resulted in the disastrous abandonment of his strategy; they were unable, unlike him, "to respect the liberty of the people and at the same time hold them in check."

The trouble with Athenian democracy was, of course, that it was a direct democracy. The modern slogan we hear so often from our radical left, "All power to the people," exactly describes it. Policy was decided in an assembly which any citizen could attend; clever orators could play on passions and fears to promote their own interests, as Alcibiades did in his advocacy of the expedition of Sicily. In the last years of the war (Thucydides did not live long enough to describe this incident, though he must have known about it) the admirals at the battle of Arginusae, who in the turmoil of a successful naval engagement failed to rescue the crews of their wrecked ships before a gale made it impossible, were recalled, tried before an assembly whipped up to a rage by their political opponents, and condemned to death. When Thucydides puts into the mouth of Alcibiades at Sparta the statement that democracy is a system which is "generally recognized as absurd," one cannot help feeling, with all due allowance made for the slipperiness of Alcibiades and for the fact that he was addressing a Spartan audience, that Thucydides may have been to some extent in agreement. Periclean democracy was one thing; it was almost like our own democracy in that it had a powerful executive capable of a consistent policy; but the democracy which was to be dominated by Cleon and led to catastrophe by Alcibiades was quite another. In fact, in Book VIII, where Thucydides describes the antidemocratic revolution in Athens which followed the disaster in Sicily, he says of its final phase (an assembly restricted to five thousand property-owning citizens) that "during the first period of this new regime, the Athenians appeared to have had a better government than ever before, at least in my time." For once Thucydides seems to have been in agreement with that Cleon he so despised; Cleon in the debate over Mitylene had said, "A democracy is incapable of governing an empire."

What did Thucydides think of the empire? I, for one, have no doubt that he thought the empire, ruled with tact and wisdom as it was under Pericles, was the justified reward of Athens' crusade against Persia and of her creative energy and administrative skill. He gives a great deal of emphasis to the claim that Athens under Pericles governed her subjects with moderation and benevolence. There is a ring of truth in the words he puts into the mouth of the Athenian representative to the Congress in Sparta before the war. "Those who really deserve praise," he says, "are the people who, while human enough to enjoy power, nevertheless pay more attention to justice than they are compelled to do by their situation. Certainly we think that if anyone else was in our position it would soon be evident whether we act with moderation or not." He goes on to explain that the subject allies complain that lawsuits involving Athenians and allied citizens are tried in Athens, but, as he points out, the fact that the cases are tried at all is unusual. Other imperial powers do not bother with such things. "Our subjects, on the other hand, are used to being treated as equals; consequently, when they are disappointed in what they think right and suffer even the smallest disadvantage . . . they cease to feel grateful to us for all the advantages we have left them." In Pericles' funeral speech there is a sentence that points in the same direction—the liberal handling of the allies, and their treatment as equals, except insofar as the basic matter of foreign policy is concerned. "We obey the laws," says Pericles, "especially those which are for the protection of the oppressed and those unwritten laws which it is an acknowledged shame to break." But even if Athens' claim to rule with a benevolent despotism which distinguished it from all other ruling powers were to be rejected, the empire, as Thucydides clearly realized, was Athens' only guarantee of security. "It may have been wrong to take it," said Pericles, "it is certainly dangerous to give it up."

Nevertheless it is also clear that Thucydides would have repudiated the reckless doctrine of permanent expansion preached by Alcibiades:

> And it is not possible for us to calculate, like housekeepers, exactly how much empire we want to have. The fact is that we have reached a stage where we are forced to plan new conquests and forced to hold on to what we have got, because there is a danger that we ourselves may fall under the power of others unless others are in our power.[5]

This doctrine of limitless expansion was proclaimed in Alcibiades' speech in favor of the Sicilian expedition, the fundamental and fateful departure from Periclean strategy.

Thucydides' attitude toward Cleon's imperial policy is harder to define. There is no doubt that he hated and despised Cleon as a vulgar mob-orator and violent demagog, but it is remarkable that he attributes to him a description of the Athenian empire which must be a deliberate repetition of a phrase of Pericles. "You hold your empire as an absolute power," they both say; *tyrannis* is the Greek word, a dictatorship, an absolute rule established and maintained by force. Pericles, I feel sure, would not have proposed the slaughter of the male population of Mitylene, but I suspect that if he had been obliged to defend his position against Cleon, he would have used the same line of argument as Diodotus—an appeal, not to humanity, but to Athenian interests. So it is not easy to assess Thucydides' attitude to the Melian dialog. Would his beloved Pericles have spoken like that? One finds it hard to believe. But he would have recognized the logic of the position. Power over others may be disguised, it may be gently used, it may be beneficial to those who are ruled, it may even be in the interests of humanity at large; but in the last analysis it rests on superior force.

Many historians, great ones among them, have seen Thucydides' history as a repudiation of Athenian imperialism as a whole. He does not specifically condemn it, of course, but a case can be made (and a good one has been) to show that in his dramatic arrangement and emphasis (the cynicism of the Melian dialog followed immediately by the Sicilian expedition, for example), he is suggesting that Athens had transgressed the moral law and now has to pay the penalty; that, in other words, even though Thucydides excludes divine providence or justice from the world, he still sees a moral law operating which punishes all excess; that his mood after all is not so different from that of Herodotus and the tragic poets. And some critics have gone further to see in his work a condemnation of all power over others in any form and at any time as leading inevitably to the same results.

On the other hand, some students of his work take the opposite extreme and feel that he is simply an analyst of power who believes that, in power relationships, morality of any kind is irrelevant. This view has recently been put forward in a brilliant book by A. G. Woodhead, *Thucydides and the Nature of Power;* he sums up Thucydides' concern as "power described and illustrated as the object of effort, held and retained by those who have it, envied and hated by those who do not have it, but in itself characterless and without moral content."

My own view is that the truth is somewhere in between. Thucydides, it seems to me, felt deeply that the Athens of Pericles, as described in the funeral speech, was a superior form of society which deserved its preeminent position and was justified in fighting to retain it. It ruled its empire with moderation and gave its subjects much in return for the independence of action it took away. I think that one can even read between the lines a belief that Greece would only be saved from perpetual internecine war by the emergence of a predominant unifying power and that Athens, under Pericles, was uniquely fitted for that role. But the failure of statesmanship, after Pericles' death, left Athenian democracy in the hands of leaders who ruled the empire with the mailed fist without the velvet glove and who launched Athens on a course of mad adventurism.

His history, then, is in a sense a tragedy, but the tragedy for him is that Athens lost the war. The sense of waste and loss which his writing conveys is, to my mind, best summed up in the English poet Auden's epitaph on the defeat of the Spanish republic:

History, to the defeated
May say Alas but cannot help or pardon.[6]

NOTES

Based on a lecture delivered at the Naval War College, September 1972.

1. See Thucydides, *The Peloponnesian War,* trans. Rex Warner, ed. (Baltimore: Penguin Books, 1954).

2. Herodotus, *The Persian Wars,* bk. VII, chap. 137, trans. by B.M.W. Knox.

3. Thucydides, *The Peloponnesian War,* bk. II, chap. 67, translated and condensed by B.M.W. Knox.

4. Thucydides, *The Peloponnesian War,* trans. Rex Warner (Hammondsworth: Penguin Books, 1971), bk. III, chap. 5, pp. 210-11.

5. Ibid., bk. VI, chap. 2, p. 379.

6. W.H. Auden, "Spain 1937" in *The Collected Poetry of W.H. Auden,* (New York: Random House, 1945) p. 181.

The Nature of War

Gordon B. Turner

Editor's Note: *In the years immediately following World War II it was widely believed that the next war would be an all-out total war. The North Korean invasion of South Korea showed that the United States could indeed become involved in and wage a limited war. Gordon B. Turner spoke to an audience for whom the Korean War was a recent combat experience.*

Professor Turner is vice-president of the American Council of Learned Societies and editor of A History of Military Affairs in Western Society Since the Eighteenth Century. *With Richard Challener, he edited* National Security in the Nuclear Age.

Military affairs and civil affairs are so intimately enmeshed, indeed the relationship between war and society is such a close one, that to think of war solely in terms of its military aspects is not only misleading but may lead to dangerous miscalculations. It is not too much to say that the nature of war hinges upon the nature of society. And this is so precisely because the objectives of war are political in nature, the composition of military forces is dependent upon ideals and limitations of civilian life, and the strategical, tactical, and logistical principles are determined in large measure by political, scientific, and economic factors.

History provides us with many examples of this phenomenon, but the clearest and most concise one is that provided by the sudden shift from the eighteenth- to the nineteenth-century forms of war. This change from limited to unlimited war coincided with the transition from dynastic to national structures of government, and was a direct consequence of the French Revolution.

21

In the eighteenth century the way of life of Western Europe was sufficiently homogeneous that it is possible to speak of the European military system as a unit. Warfare in that era was characterized by moderation and precision. It was mechanical and rational. Battles were avoided rather than sought, and a victory was seldom pushed to the point of complete destruction of the enemy forces. Defense predominated over the offense, and military targets were primarily supply lines, magazines, and the fortifications that defended them rather than the enemy's main army itself. The direct assault was scorned in favor of complicated maneuvers. A partial explanation of the limited nature of warfare in the eighteenth century doubtless lies in matters purely military, but the basic reasons must be sought in other fields. They are to be found in the social composition and military structure of the armies, in the limited political purposes of war, and in the economic milieu in which the wars were fought.

One principle, indeed, above all others shaped the military forces of Western Europe in the eighteenth century. It was expressed explicitly by French and Prussian military experts, and was implicit in British, Spanish, and Austrian thought. The guiding principle was this, and I quote from the French minister of war, the Comte de Saint Germain: "It would undoubtedly be desirable, if we could create an army of dependable and specially selected men of the best type. But in order to make an army, we must not destroy the nation; it would be destruction to a nation if it were deprived of its best elements. As things are, the army must inevitably consist of the scum of the people and of all those for whom society has no use. We must therefore rely on military discipline to purify and mold the mass of corruption and turn it into something useful."

You will note that Germain says: "as things are," the army must consist of the scum and the unproductive. He was referring to the fact that Western civilization was just coming into a period of productive expansion but that it had not yet reached the machine age, and that skilled labor was in great demand. He was quite correct in saying that if the productive labor force had been conscripted for nonproductive military purposes, the nation's economy would have suffered. In the preceding century Western Europe had been scorched by a series of highly destructive wars, and thus when the economy was just beginning to revive and expand under the impulse of overseas commercial ventures and the Industrial Revolution, skilled labor was necessarily scarce. The guiding principle of Europe's eighteenth-century military system was, therefore, to have a strong army without injuring the productive forces of the nation.

This rule applied with equal validity to both officers and enlisted men. On the continent the higher ranks in the armed forces were apportioned among the nobles, who received the top-echelon commands as their prescriptive right. To say that they were unproductive is no exaggeration. It was not at all uncommon, except in Prussia, for a nobleman to be commissioned at birth, and to spend his time idling with the women of the court, and debauching himself into a fat old age. Although some officers were able, it was inevitable that many were worthless, having been commissioned from the riffraff of the aristocracy just as the privates were shanghaied from the offscourings of the proletariat. The armies of Europe were not, of course, without some capable and resourceful generals, but court intrigue kept them out of responsible commands.

Destined for a military career almost from birth, the officers had a magnificent opportunity to learn their trade. Great care was taken to see that they were properly educated. Those wealthy enough to buy their way into the top ranks soon learned the advantages of employing the finest tailor, the best perfumer, the most splendid carriages, and the most expensive liveries in town. They learned that it was expected of them to gamble a great deal, to dance often, and to be seen frequently at the theater. Then they were ready to fight. These officers lived in the army very much as they had at court, accompanied by their carriages and their cooks. Loath to give up the comforts of society, they were certain to obtain an elaborate field kit before entering upon any campaign. This might well consist of a coach, a coupé and a berlin, half a dozen mules with gorgeous trappings, and a host of footmen and grooms in colorful liveries. It was not unknown for French generals to entertain as many as two hundred guests for dinner right in the midst of an active campaign.

This situation, of course, had profound effects upon the mobility of the army. No army could move far or fast with such cumbersome baggage trains when road networks were few and of inferior quality. When officers thought so much of their comforts as to cause the quartermaster-general to mobilize the resources of an entire city to provide for them, as was often the case, it is not surprising that battles were few and campaigns were indecisive.

This relative rareness of battles and inconclusiveness of wars was not, of course, the result of the structure of the officer corps alone. The conditions which made for the predominance of the defensive in war can be understood only in light of the whole social,

political, and economic pattern of the time. We must take the
enlisted man into consideration in seeking to explain the moderation of eighteenth-century warfare. Recruited either from abroad
or from the economically useless segments of the population, the
common soldier was thoroughly undependable. He enlisted ordinarily only for the most compelling reasons, such as the lure of
food and drink held out by recruiting officers. And if sufficient
men could not be procured in this way, kidnapping was practiced,
and criminals and murderers were given the opportunity to exchange the sure death of prison pestholes for a chance to survive
upon the field of battle.

Armies so constituted had to take extraordinary precautions
against desertion, and tactics were planned with this in mind.
Marching during the night and camping in forests had to be avoided. Tight formations were the rule, and open fields were the preferred battlegrounds. Soldiers, who were held in the utmost contempt by their officers and scorned by the civilian populace, felt
neither loyalty to the army nor patriotism to the state. A general
who was rash enough to let his men spread out in the advance
or who ordered them to assault with the bayonet, could expect
that a large portion of his troops would either go over to the enemy
or, not wanting to die, would simply fade away. For this reason,
the advance was slow. Frequent halts were called in order to close
ranks; and battles were broken off before decisive action could
be taken.

So much for tactics.

The system of supply was similarly affected by the type of soldiers employed. Foraging was strictly prohibited. No army could
live off the land when civilians and soldiers were filled with loath-
ing for one another. A soldier who everywhere read signs posted
on public buildings and garden walls which read "No dogs, prosti-
tutes, or soldiers allowed" could not be expected to treat civilians
with respect or courtesy. Under these conditions a centralized ra-
tion system had to be established in order to restrict pillage and
destruction of the countryside and to keep a check upon desertion.
The magazine system was established for this purpose. Grain and
flour were stored in magazines to be used to supply the troops
in time of war, and these storage houses were placed according
to strategic determinations along existing lines of communication.
This system in its turn determined the strategy of any major campaign, for all armies were tied to their magazines, and hot pursuit
of a defeated enemy was impossible to undertake.

This formal, deliberate, not to say leisurely, way of conducting campaigns in the eighteenth century may seem incomprehensible to the twentieth century mind, bred as it is on total wars waged for national survival, but it fitted in very nicely with the objectives of eighteenth-century wars. Western Europe had by that time reached a stage of relative political stability. The vicious and bitterly contested religious wars of the seventeenth century were over. The normal form of government was absolutely monarchy, and wars were fought generally for some minor economic advantage or national aggrandizement with strictly limited objectives. The moderation with which eighteenth century warfare was conducted was the result, therefore, not only of the social composition of the armies, but of the economic and political requirements that the civil life must not be disrupted.

Moreover, for two reasons the monarchs of the old regime could not have waged total war even if they had wanted to do so. The first reason: wars in the eighteenth century were wars between rulers and not between peoples. The common man had no stake in them, no motive for fighting, and, hence, the human resources pool was limited either to vagrants or mercenaries. The second reason: under the dynastic form of state the monarch was in a precarious position with respect to the aristocracy. No matter how absolute the king's power might be in theory, sizable privileges had to be extended to the nobles in order to keep them in line, and these privileges ordinarily took the form of tax exemption and a monopoly on the commissioned ranks in the army. In other words, the monarchs of the dynastic state could not draw on the full material resources of their nations because their powers of taxation were restricted. Total war implies the utilization of all resources, both human and material, and this the governments of the eighteenth century simply could not do. So the wars of the eighteenth century were limited. They were fought with limited means for limited objectives.

All this was changed after 1789. The national wars in the period from 1792 to 1815 were characterized by mass armies, by lightning operations, and by total destruction. They marked a turning point between a type of conflict which had its origins in the early sixteenth century and the type with which we are familiar today— that is, they marked the shift from limited to unlimited war.

Back of the sweeping transition from moderation to total destruction lay the French Revolution. The military revolution, in other words, was at bottom a political revolution which fused the government with the governed and gave the people a feeling of participation in the state and a sense of loyalty in fighting for its cause. At the same time the government, which now governed in the name of the people, could tap the human and material resources of the nation in a way that a monarch isolated from his subjects had never been able to do. The potential wealth and military manpower of France could now be developed for the first time. With the nobility stripped of its privileges of tax exemption and monopoly of the officer corps, and with the mass of the people raised to the status of citizen, the government found itself for the first time in possession of the two elements essential for the waging of total war. First, it could create a war economy which could bring all the physical wealth to bear on the national war effort. Second, it could introduce the principle of universal military service which produced an army with national self-consciousness.

The new national state thus at at one stroke solved the two major problems which had limited the actions of the dynastic states. The manpower problem was licked by the ease with which mass armies could be raised; and a strategy of mobility and annihilation could be invoked because the citizen-soldier was willing to endure the discomforts of a limited supply train, because he was capable of being trusted as a scout and a skirmisher, and because he was zealous in the destruction of the enemies of Revolutionary France.

These qualities of the new citizen-soldier in their turn produced a revolution in logistics and in tactics. It was now possible to supply the French armies by requisitions rather than by magazines. These requisitions might be made directly by the state upon the national economy, or they might be made by the army on the people of the French countryside. Then, once the army had advanced beyond the borders of France, severe levies could be made upon the enemy in the form of military equipment or in the plunder of foreign treasuries. No longer were civilians immune from military devastation. *This* was something new.

Finally, it was possible to revolutionize tactics because patriot soldiers could be thrown into battle and allowed to act on their own initiative, deployed as skirmishers, firing and taking cover as individuals.

I mentioned a moment ago a change from moderation to unlimited, total, destructive warfare. The French government, as a result of the French Revolution, could reach directly down to the individual and assess both his person and his property for military duty. This made total war possible, but did it make it inevitable? What was the reason for the new concept of ruthlessness? Why unlimited objectives in war?

It was in the first place the civilian government, and not the military establishment, which called for unlimited war and which started the large-scale consumption of soldiers. For the civilian government, the strategic objective of the foreign wars was essentially the same as that of the civil war at home; that is, the complete annihilation of all enemies of the state to insure the survival of the state and to protect the gains of the Revolution.

In order to secure as many voluntary enlistments as possible, and to give courage and a common purpose to untrained troops, propaganda techniques were extensively developed and employed by the government on an impressive scale. Propaganda had of course been used before, but its use as a weapon of war against the enemy was new, and the recognition of it as an indispensable tool for the raising and inspiring of mass armies can safely be called an element distinctive to the new military system of the national state. Citizen-soldiers marching to war singing the "Marseillaise" and carrying revolutionary ideas to all parts of Europe were something new under the European sun. Groups of French soldiers mingled with the enemy declaiming the brotherhood of man, and singing the praises of liberty and equality. In short, this was ideological warfare, and out of it grew the cry for victory—total victory—and nothing less than total victory.

Here, then, we have for the first time the two prerequisites of unlimited war: unlimited means and unlimited objectives. And for the next 150 years it was these factors which were to determine the nature of war. Once the nations—that is, the governments and the people—had the *ability* and the *will* to fight on to the point of exhaustion, their military leaders organized their units and framed their strategy with this in mind. In other words, as the nature of society changed, as science and industry produced new and more deadly weapons, and as the objectives of war reached new heights, the nature of war changed to conform.

There is nothing rigid about the nature of war. It is as flexible and as dynamic as society itself. If the governments of the world do not learn and apply this simple dictum, if they fail to limit their objectives in international affairs, or if they remain so suspicious and distrustful of one another as to prevent effective limitation of weapons of mass destruction, then war can and will destroy society as we know it today. The world has the ability to save itself, but the path to national security is not an easy one.

Indeed, it is made much more difficult by the conviction that is widely held, and incorrectly maintained, that war "is an act of violence pushed to the utmost bounds." This maxim, laid down by Carl von Clausewitz after an intensive study of the Napoleonic wars, unfortunately caught the imagination of the world's statesmen and soldiers so vividly that even today, when we have the means to destroy ourselves, it is commonly believed that the objective of war is victory—unconditional victory. This simply is not so.

The objective of war is political in nature, not military; the objective of war is whatever the belligerent powers determine at any given moment. It may be to compel unconditional surrender as it was in World War II. It may be merely to prevent complete defeat—to string the war out until the enemy is willing to negotiate or compromise some of his initial objectives. It may be simply to ensure a potential enemy's neutrality in future wars, as was Bismarck's objective in the Austro-Prussian conflict. Or, indeed, the objectives themselves may be flexible and may change during the course of the war as was the case in Korea. In that instance the initial aim of the United Nations was restricted to forcing the North Koreans back to their own boundaries in order to demonstrate that the United Nations would not condone aggression. It was not until after the Inchon landing that the objective was officially altered by the United Nations to the unification of all Korea by means of a drive north to the Yalu. The objective of that war never did become total military victory over the Chinese Communists.

The road back to limited wars will not be an easy one in the face of the Clausewitzian dictum that war is an act of violence carried to the extreme. The fact that Clausewitz understood the nature of war better perhaps than we do today, the fact that he knew perfectly well that war is not an isolated act divorced from social life, and that many factors can work to modify its philosophical definition as an act of extreme violence—these facts are too often forgotten today. The Clausewitzian definition has been misunderstood by many historians and professional soldiers and this makes the task of limiting wars more difficult.

But this is not the only obstacle. It has long been the conviction of Americans that war must be fought à outrance. They incline to be impatient with delays. When war begins, though the United States may be unprepared for it, they look for an immediate offensive and will accept nothing less than total victory. They like to do things in a big way not only in the realm of civil life but in wars as well. Now I do not condemn this attitude—far from it. It is probable that without this vigorous spirit our past war efforts would have been less successful. But the idea that we have always

imposed our will upon enemies, that we have always compelled
unconditional surrender, is not true; and the belief that we must
do so in the future is a dangerous doctrine in the nuclear age.

Again I say, the nature of war is flexible, and for our salvation
we must keep this in mind. If our military leaders, under the influence of Clausewitz or under pressure from the government and
the people, lay their plans *solely* and *exclusively* on the historical
assumption that we must wage all-out war, the United States may
find itself faced with the embarrassing alternative of having to
wage total nuclear war or no war at all. And, I might add, the
ill repute in which most Americans hold the Korean War, because
of its limited nature, makes the task of limiting our objectives
and formulating flexible plans for military action much more difficult.

Yet, in spite of the extreme dislike for the nature of the Korean
War, conflicts of this character may be our only means to escape
destruction under the conditions of nuclear holocaust. I think I
need say little about the consequences of an all-out thermonuclear
war in the future. We all know that when hydrogen bombs and
long-range bombers or guided missiles are in the hands of the Soviet Union in quantity, we shall not escape destruction if it comes
to total war between us. We know that the word *victory* in a war
of this nature is meaningless.

This, I believe, should be the starting point for our thinking.
If there can be no such thing as total victory in the traditional
sense of the word, if we must be destroyed in the process of achieving total victory, then we must reset our sights and define victory
in more limited terms. I am not of course suggesting that circumstances will never arise when we may have to resort to full-scale
thermonuclear war, and we must be prepared for it. I am suggesting that we change our attitude, that we alter our politico-military
policy and readjust our military planning so that an all-out war
is not the only solution we can advance for every emergency problem. Our sights must be set to avoid the big war, if at all compatible
with our interests. We must modify our objectives so that if resort
to war becomes necessary, we will not compel our opponents and
ourselves to reach beyond the realm of limited conflict.

NOTE

Based on a lecture delivered at the Naval War College in 1955.

The Objective in War

Sir Basil H. Liddell Hart

Editor's Note: *Together with J. F. C. Fuller, Sir Basil H. Liddell Hart is best known as the leading British proponent of armored tank warfare before World War II. He was the author of some thirty books, including* Strategy—The Indirect Approach.

In considering this subject, we must be clear about the distinction between the political objective and the military objective. The two are different but not separate, for nations do not wage war for war's sake, but in pursuance of policy. The military objective is only the means to a political end. Hence, the military objective should be governed by the political objective, and serve it faithfully, subject to the basic condition that policy does not demand what is militarily—that is, practically—impossible. Thus, any study of the problem ought to begin and end with the question of policy.

The term *objective,* although common usage, is not really a good one. It has a physical and geographical sense—and thus tends to confuse thought. It would be better to speak of "the object" when dealing with the purpose of policy, and of "the military aim" when dealing with the way that forces are directed in the service of policy. The object in war is a better state of peace—even if only from your own point of view. Hence, it is essential to conduct war with constant regard to the peace you desire. That applies both to aggressor nations who seek expansion and to peaceful nations who only fight for self-preservation—although their views of what is meant by a better state of peace are very different.

History shows that gaining military victory is not in itself equivalent to gaining the object of policy. Victory, in the true sense, implies that a nation's prospect after the war is better than if it had not gone to war. But, as most of the thinking about war has been done by men of the military profession, there has been a very natural tendency to lose sight of the basic national object, and identify it with the military aim. In consequence, whenever war has broken out, policy has too often been governed by the military aim—and this has been regarded as an end in itself, instead of as merely a means to the end.

The ill effects have gone further, for, by losing sight of the proper relationship between the object and the military aim—between policy and strategy—the military aim became distorted, and oversimplified. For a true understanding of the problem, essentially complex, it is necessary to know the background of military thought on this subject during the past two centuries, and to realize how conceptions have evolved. For more than a century the prime canon of military doctrine has been that "the destruction of the enemy's main forces on the battlefield" constituted the only true aim in war. That was universally accepted, engraved in all military manuals, and taught in all staff colleges. If any statesman ventured to doubt whether it fitted the national object in all circumstances, he was regarded as blasphemously violating holy writ —as can be seen in studying the official records and the memoirs of the military heads of the warring nations—particularly in and after World War I.

So absolute a rule would have astonished the great commanders and teachers of war theory in ages prior to the nineteenth century. For they had recognized the practical necessity and wisdom of adapting aims to limitations of strength and policy.

I

The rule acquired its dogmatic rigidity largely through the posthumous influence of Clausewitz and his books upon the minds of Prussian soldiers, particularly Moltke—and thence more widely through the impact that their victories in 1866 and 1870 made upon the armies of the world, which copied so many features of the Prussian system. Thus, it is of vital importance to examine his theories.

As so often happens, Clausewitz' disciples carried his teaching to an extreme which their master had not intended. Misinterpretation has been the common fate of most prophets and thinkers in every sphere. Devout but uncomprehending disciples have been more damaging to the original conception than even its prejudiced and purblind opponents.

It must be admitted, however, that Clausewitz invited misinterpretation more than most. A student of Kant, at second hand,
he had acquired a philosophical mode of expression without developing a truly philosophical mind. His theory of war was expounded
in a way too abstract and involved for ordinary soldier-minds, essentially concrete, to follow the course of his argument—which
often turned back from the direction in which it was apparently
leading. Impressed, yet befogged, they grasped at his vivid leading
phrases—seeing only their surface meaning, and missing the deeper
current of his thought.

Clausewitz' greatest contribution to the theory of war was in
emphasizing the psychological factors. Raising his voice against
the geometrical school of strategy then fashionable, he showed
that the human spirit was infinitely more important than operational lines and angles. He discussed the effect of danger and fa-
tigue, the value of boldness and determination, with deep understanding.

It was his errors, however, which had the greater effect on the
subsequent course of history. He was too continental in outlook
to understand the meaning of seapower. And, on the very threshold
of the mechanical age, Clausewitz was led to declare his "conviction that superiority in numbers becomes every day more decisive."
Such a "commandment" gave reinforcement to the instinctive con-
servatism of soldiers in resisting the possibilities of the new form
of superiority which mechanical invention increasingly offered. It
also gave a powerful impulse to the universal extension and permanent establishment of the method of conscription—as a simple way
of providing the greatest possible numbers.

This, by its disregard for psychological suitability, meant that
armies became much more liable to panic, and sudden collapse.
The earlier method, however unsystematic, had at least tended
to ensure that the forces were composed of good "fighting animals."

Clausewitz contributed no new or strikingly progressive ideas
to tactics or strategy. He was a codifying thinker, rather than
a creative or dynamic one. He had no such revolutionary effect
on warfare as the theory of the "divisional system" produced in
the eighteenth century or the theory of "armored mobility" in the
twentieth. But, in seeking to formulate the experience of the Napoleonic wars, the emphasis he put on certain retrograde features
helped to cause what might be termed a "revolution in reverse"
back toward tribal warfare.

In defining the military aim, Clausewitz was carried away by his passion for pure logic:

> The aim of all action in war is to disarm the enemy, and we shall now show that this, theoretically, at least, is indispensable.
> If our opponent is to be made to comply with our will, we must place him in a situation which is more oppressive to him than the sacrifice we demand; but the disadvantages of this position must naturally not be of a transitory nature, at least in appearance; otherwise the enemy, instead of yielding, will hold out in the hope of a change for the better. Every change in this position which is produced by a continuation of the war should therefore be a change for the worse. The worst condition in which a belligerent can be placed is that of being completely disarmed. If, therefore, the enemy is to be reduced to submission ... he must either be positively disarmed or placed in such a position that he is threatened with it. From this it follows that the complete disarming or overthrow of the enemy ... must always be the aim of warfare.[1]

The influence of Kant can be perceived in Clausewitz' dualism of thought—he believed in a perfect (military) world of ideals while recognizing a temporal world in which these could only be imperfectly fulfilled. He was capable of distinguishing between what was militarily ideal and what he described as "a modification in the reality." He wrote:

> Thus reasoning in the abstract, the mind cannot stop short of an extreme. . . . But everything takes a different shape when we pass from abstractions to reality.[2]
> This object of war in the abstract ... the disarming of the enemy, is rarely attained in practice and is not a condition necessary to peace.[3]

Clausewitz' tendency to the extreme is shown, again, in his discussion of battle as a means to the end of war. He opened with the startling assertion—"There is only one single means—it is the fight."[4] He justified this by a long argument to show that in every form of military activity "the idea of fighting must necessarily be at the foundation." Having elaborately proved what most people would be ready to accept without argument, Clausewitz said:

... the object of a combat is not always the destruction of the enemy's forces ... its object can often be attained as well without the combat taking place at all. ...[5]

Moreover, Clausewitz recognized that:

... the waste of our own military forces must, *ceteris paribus,* always be greater the more our aim is directed upon the destruction of the enemy's power.

"The danger lies in this, that the greater efficacy which we seek recoils on ourselves, and therefore has worse consequences in case we fail of success.[6]

Out of his own mouth, Clausewitz here gave a prophetic verdict upon the consequences of following his own gospel in World Wars I and II.

Not one reader in a hundred was likely to follow the subtlety of his logic or to preserve a true balance amid such philosophical jugglery. But everyone could catch such ringing phrases as—

"We have only one means in war—the battle."[7]

"... The bloody solution of the crisis, the effort for the destruction of the enemy's forces, is the first-born son of war."[8]

"Only great and general battles can produce great results."[9]

"Let us not hear of generals who conquer without bloodshed."[10]

By the reiteration of such phrases, Clausewitz blurred the outlines of his philosophy, already indistinct, and made it into a mere marching refrain—a Prussian Marseillaise which inflamed the blood and intoxicated the mind. In transfusion it became a doctrine fit to form corporals, not generals, for by making battle appear the only "real warlike activity," his gospel deprived strategy of its laurels, and reduced the art of war to the mechanics of mass slaughter. Moreover, it incited generals to seek battle at the first opportunity, instead of creating an advantageous opportunity.

Clausewitz contributed to the subsequent decay of generalship when in an oft-quoted passage he wrote—

Now, philanthropists may easily imagine that there is a skillful method of disarming and overcoming the enemy without great bloodshed, and that this is the proper tendency of the Art of War.... it is an error which must be extirpated.[11]

It is obvious that when he wrote this he did not pause to reflect that what he decried had been regarded as the proper aim of generalship by all the masters of the art of war—including Napoleon himself. Clausewitz' phrase would henceforth be used by countless blunderers to excuse, and even to justify, their futile squandering of life in bull-headed assaults.

The danger was increased because of the way he constantly dwelt on the decisive importance of a numerical superiority. With deeper penetration, he pointed out in one passage that surprise lies "at the foundation of all undertakings, for without it the preponderance at the decisive point is not properly conceivable."[12] But his disciples, struck by his more frequent emphasis on "numbers," came to regard mere mass as the simple recipe for victory.

Even worse was the effect of his theoretical exposition, and exaltation, of the idea of "absolute" warfare—in proclaiming that the road to success was through the unlimited application of force. Thereby, a doctrine which began by defining war as only "a continuation of state policy by other means" led to the contradictory end of making policy the slave of strategy—and bad strategy at that.

The trend was fostered, above all, by his dictum that—

... to introduce into the philosophy of war a principle of moderation would be an absurdity.... War is an act of violence pushed to its utmost bounds.[13]

That declaration has served as a foundation for the extravagant absurdity of modern total warfare. His principle of force without limit and without calculation of costs fits, and is only fit for, a hate-maddened mob. It is the negation of statesmanship and of intelligent strategy—which seeks to serve the ends of policy.

If war be a continuation of policy, as Clausewitz had elsewhere declared, it must necessarily be conducted with a view to postwar benefit. A state which expends its strength to the point of exhaustion bankrupts its own policy. That hard truth of experience, which has been brought home to us after victory in 1918 and 1945, had been well appreciated two centuries earlier—in "the age of reason."

A long series of mutually exhausting and devastating wars, above all the Thirty Years War, had brought statesmen by the eighteenth century to realize the necessity, when engaged in war, of curbing both their ambitions and their passions in the interest of their purpose. This realization tended to produce a tacit limitation of warfare—an avoidance of excesses which might damage after-the-war prospects. On the other hand, it made them more ready to negotiate a peace if and when victory came to appear dubious of achievement. Their ambitions and passions frequently carried them too far, so that the return to peace found their countries weakened rather than strengthened—but they had learnt to stop short of national exhaustion.

Clausewitz himself had qualified his principle of "utmost force" by the admission that—

> ... the political object, as the original motive of the war, will be the standard for determining both the aim of the military force and also the amount of effort to be made.[14]

Still more significant was a reflective passage in which he remarked that to pursue the logical extreme entailed that—

> ... the means would lose all relation to the end, and in most cases this aim at an extreme effort would be wrecked by the opposing weight of forces within itself.[15]

His classic work *On War* was the product of twelve years' intensive thought; if its author had lived to spend a longer time in thinking about war, he might have reached wiser and clearer conclusions. As his thinking progressed, he was being led towards a different view—penetrating deeper. Unhappily, the process was cut short by his death from cholera in 1830. It was only after his death that his writings on war were published, by his widow. They were found in a number of sealed packets, bearing the significant and prophetic note—

> Should the work be interrupted by my death, then what is found can only be called a mass of conceptions not brought into form ... open to endless misconceptions.[16]

Much of the harm might have been avoided but for that fatal cholera germ, for there are significant indications that in the gradual evolution of his thought he had reached a point where he was about to drop his original concept of "absolute war," and revise his whole theory on more common-sense lines—when death intervened. In consequence, the way was left open to "endless misconceptions" far in excess of his anticipation — for the universal adoption of the theory of unlimited war has gone far to wreck civilization. The teachings of Clausewitz, taken without understanding, largely influenced both the causation and the character of World War I. Thereby it led on, all too logically, to World War II.

II

The course and effects of the First World War provided ample cause to doubt the validity of Clausewitz' theory, at least as interpreted by his successors. On land, innumerable battles were fought without ever producing the decisive results expected of them. But the responsible leaders were slow to adopt their aim to circumstances or to develop new means to make the aim more possible. Instead of facing the problem, they pressed theory to a suicidal extreme, draining their own strength beyond the safety limit, in pursuit of an ideal of complete victory by battle which was never fulfilled.

That one side ultimately collapsed was due more to emptiness of stomach, produced by the economic pressure of seapower, than to loss of blood—although the blood which was lost in the abortive German offensives of 1918, and the loss of spirit in consequence of their palpable failure to gain the victory, hastened the collapse. If this provided the opposing nations with the semblance of victory, their efforts to win it cost them such a price, in moral and physical exhaustion, that they, the seeming victors, were left incapable of consolidating their position.

It became evident there was something wrong with the theory, or at least with its application—alike on the planes of tactics, strategy, and policy. The appalling losses suffered in vain pursuit of the "ideal" objective, and the postwar exhaustion of the nominal victors, showed that a thorough reexamination of the whole problem of the object and aim was needed.

Besides these negative factors, there were also several positive reasons to prompt a fresh enquiry. One was the decisive part that seapower had played, without any decisive battle at sea, in producing the enemy's collapse by economic pressure. That raised the question of whether Britain, in particular, had not made a basic mistake in departing from her traditional strategy and devoting so much of her effort, at such terrific cost to herself, to the prolonged attempt to win a decisive victory on land.

Two other reasons arose from new factors. The development of air forces offered the possibility of striking at the enemy's economic and moral centers without having first to achieve "the destruction of the enemy's main forces on the battlefield." Airpower might attain a direct end by indirect means—hopping over opposition instead of overthrowing it. At the same time, the combined development of the patrol motor and the caterpillar track opened up a prospect of developing mechanized land forces of high mobility. This, in turn, foreshadowed a newly enlarged possibility of producing the collapse of "the enemy's main forces" without a serious battle—by cutting their supply lines, dislocating their control system, or producing paralysis by the sheer nerve-shock of deep penetration into their rear.

Mechanized land forces of this new kind might also provide—like airpower, though in a lesser degree—the possibility of striking directly at the heart and nerve system of the opposing country. While air mobility could achieve such direct strokes by an overhead form of indirect approach, tank mobility might achieve them by indirect approach on the ground avoiding the "obstacle" of the opposing army.

To illustrate the point by a board-game analogy with chess—air mobility introduced a knight's move, and tank mobility a queen's move, into warfare. This analogy does not, of course, express their respective values, for an air force combined the vaulting power of the knight's move with the all-ways flexibility of the queen's move. On the other hand, a mechanized ground force, though it lacked vaulting power, could remain in occupation of the "square" it gained.

These new air and land developments were bound to have a profound influence on the military aim and choice of objectives in future war. They increased the capacity of applying military action against civil objectives, economic and moral, while making it more powerful in effect. They also increased the "range" of military action against military objectives, making it easier to overthrow an opposing "body"—such as an army—by paralyzing some of its vital organs instead of having to destroy it physically and as a whole by hard fighting.

To nullify opposition by paralyzing the power to oppose is far better economy of force than actual destruction of opposition, which is always a more prolonged process and more costly to the victor. Airpower promised new scope for producing such paralysis of armed opposition—besides its capacity to evade opposition and strike at civil objectives in the enemy country. The sum effect of the advent of this multiplied mobility, both on the ground and in the air, was to increase the power and importance of strategy relatively to tactics.

The higher commanders of the future would have the prospect of achieving decisive results much more by movement than by fighting, compared with their predecessors. While the value of winning a decisive battle would not disappear, and the chances of doing so would actually be increased by the new powers of mobility, even such a battle would have less of the traditional battle form. It would become more like the natural completion of a strategic maneuver. *Battle* is really a misnomer for such a consecutive operation.

Unfortunately, those who were at the head of the armies after World War I were slow to recognize the need of a fresh definition of the military aim in the light of changed conditions and war instruments. Unfortunately, also, those who were at the head of the air forces were too exclusively concerned to assert their independence, and thus concentrated too narrowly on exploiting the possibilities of striking at civil objectives—without regard either to its limitations or to its detrimental results. Filled with a natural enthusiasm for the new service to which they belonged, they were excessively confident that it could produce either the speedy moral collapse of the opposing people or the economic stranglehold of seapower in an intensified form and with a much more quickly decisive effect.

When the next war came, the handful of new land forces of a mechanized kind that had been created amply fulfilled the claims that had been made for them, and for their decisive effect if employed for long-range strokes at strategic objectives. A mere six divisions of this kind were largely instrumental in producing the collapse of Poland within a few weeks. A mere ten such divisions virtually decided the so-called Battle of France before the main mass of the German army had even come into action—and made the collapse of all the Western countries an almost inevitable sequel. This conquest of the West was completed in barely a month's campaign, with amazingly small cost to the victor. Indeed, the "bloodshed" all around was very slight, and in the decisive phase trifling, by any Clausewitzian standard.

While this sweeping victory was attained by action against objectives of a military nature, it was mainly through action of a maneuver form—strategic more than tactical. Moreover, the effect of cutting the opposing armies' communications, and dislocating their control system, in the deeply penetrating drive, is hard to distinguish from its accompanying effect in shaking the people's morale and disrupting civic organization. So it could be termed, at least in part, a proof of the new effectiveness of operating against civil objectives.

Similar reflections apply to the even swifter conquest of the Balkans in April 1941—which once again demonstrated the paralyzing effect of the new instruments and their strategic application. *Battle* was insignificant in comparison, and *destruction* palpably an inappropriate term for the way that the decision was achieved.

When it came to the invasion of Russia, a somewhat different method was tried. Many of the German generals—particularly Halder, the chief of the General Staff—complained of Hitler's tendency to aim at economic rather than military objectives. But analysis of the operational orders and of their own evidence does not bear out the charge. While Hitler was inclined to think that the economic aim would be more effective, it is clear that in the crucial period of the 1941 campaign he conformed to the General Staff's preference for fighting battles. The pursuit of this aim did not prove decisive, although it produced several great victories in which immense forces of the enemy were destroyed. Whether concentration on economic objectives would have been more decisive remains an open question.

But in reflection some of the ablest of the German generals consider that the best chance of defeating Soviet Russia was lost by aiming to win battles in the "classical" way, instead of driving through as fast as possible to the moral-cum-economic objectives offered by Moscow and Leningrad—as Guderian, the leading exponent of the new school of mechanical mobile warfare, wished to do. On this key question, Hitler had sided with the orthodox school.

In the series of swift German conquests, the air force combined with the mechanized elements of the land forces in producing the paralysis and moral disintegration of the opposing forces and of the nations behind. Its effect was terrific, and must be reckoned fully as important as that of the Panzer forces. The two are inseparable in any valuation of the elements that created the new style of lightning warfare—the blitzkrieg.

Even greater was the contribution that the British and American air forces made, later in the war, to the success of the Allied armies and navies. It was due to the air forces, above all, that the Allied invasion of the Continent became possible in the first place, and then an assured advance to victory. By their action against military objectives—particularly communications—they had a decisively crippling effect on the ability of the German armies to counter the Allied moves.

The Air Staffs, however, never showed the same eagerness to conduct operations of this kind as they did to pursue independent operations against "civil" objectives—the attack on the industrial centers of the opposing country. Its purpose, as conceived, was to combine a direct economic and moral effect on the opposing nation, in the belief that it would prove more decisive, and more quickly decisive, than cooperative action against the enemy's armed forces. Although the Air Staffs termed this *strategic bombing,* the term was really a misnomer, for such an aim and action lie in the sphere of grand strategy. It would be more correctly defined as *grand strategic bombing,* or, if that seems too cumbrous a term, as *industrial bombing,* a term which covers moral as well as economic effect.

The actual effect which this kind of bombing achieved as a contribution to victory is very difficult to assess, despite much detailed investigation. The estimation of the data is confused by partisan assessments—both by those who favored industrial bombing, and by those who opposed it on various grounds. Apart from the fog thus created, a correct assessment is handicapped and made almost impossible by the amount of imponderabilia in the data—even more than in the evidence about any other form of military action. But it seems fairly certain, even in a reasonably favorable view of its effects, that they were less decisive than the action of air forces against strategic objectives—in the military sphere. In any case, they were much less clearly decisive. It is also clear that, stage by stage throughout the war, the results fell far short of what was being claimed for this kind of action by those who were conducting it. Still clearer is the extremely detrimental effect of industrial bombing on the postwar situation. Beyond the immense scale of devastation, hard to repair, are the less obvious but probably more lasting social and moral effects. This kind of action inevitably produces a deepening danger to the relatively shallow foundations of civilized life. That common danger is now immensely increased by the advent of the atomic bomb. Here we are brought to the fundamental difference between strategy and grand strategy.

The function of grand strategy is to coordinate and direct all the resources of a nation toward the attainment of the political object of the war—the goal defined by national policy. Whereas strategy is only concerned with the problem of winning military victory, grand strategy must take the longer view—for its problem is the winning of the peace.

Such an order of thought is not a matter of "putting the cart before the horse," but of being clear where the horse and cart are going. Air action against an object that is primarily "civil" is action on the plane of grand strategy. It is called into question on that very account. By the test of its own nature, it is seen to be an unsound objective. It would be an unwise choice as a military aim even if its ability to decide a war were more conclusively proved, or at least more clearly demonstrated, than it actually has been.

III

In trying to revise any theory and readjust it for better balance, it is a help to have a background of study in the subject—as long as one is willing to modify one's conclusions. I was, so far as I know, the first student of war after 1914-18 to make a reexamination of the prevailing doctrines, derived from Clausewitz, about the objective in war. After calling it in question in a number of articles in the military journals, I dealt with it more fully in *Paris, or The Future of War, 1925.*

This little book began with a criticism of the way that the orthodox aim, "the destruction of the enemy's main forces on the battlefield," had been pursued in World War I—pointing out its indecisive and exhausting results. It then went on to argue the advantages of the "moral objective," showing—

1. How armored forces might deliver a decisive blow against "the Achilles heel of the enemy army—the communications and command centers which form its nerve system";

2. How air forces, besides cooperating in this strategic action, might also strike with decisive effect directly at "a nation's nerve system," its "static civil centers" of industry.

The General Staff prescribed the book for the study of the officers of the first Experimental Mechanized Force when this was formed two years later. The Air Staff, less surprisingly, made still fuller use of it—there was then a lack of textbooks on air strategy, and it fitted the developing trend of their views on the subject. The chief of the Air Staff distributed copies of it to his fellow Chiefs of Staff.

What I have said now is thus a revision, after prolonged reflection, of what I wrote a quarter of a century ago—and an avowal of error over part of the thesis. It shows how, in correcting the balance, one is apt to tilt it too far the other way. T. E. Lawrence observed in a letter he wrote me in 1928:

The logical system of Clausewitz is too complete. It leads a-stray his disciples—those of them, at least, who would rather fight with their arms than with their legs .... You, at present, are trying (with very little help from those whose business it is to think upon their profession) to put the balance straight after the orgy of the last war. When you succeed (about 1945) your sheep will pass your bounds of discretion, and have to be chivied back by some later strategist. Back and forward we go.

In 1925 I myself went too far in arguing the advantages of the air stroke at civil objectives—though I did qualify this by emphasizing the importance of executing it in such a way as to inflict

the least possible permanent injury, for the enemy of today is the customer of the morrow and the ally of the future.

My belief then was that

a decisive air attack would inflict less total damage and constitute less of a drain on the defeated country's recuperative power than a prolonged war of the existing type.

In further study I came to realize that an air attack on industrial centers was unlikely to have an immediately decisive effect, and more likely to produce another prolonged war of attrition in a fresh form—with perhaps less killing but more devastation than the 1914-18 form.

But when one began to point this out, one soon found that the Air Staff was far less receptive to the revised conclusion than to the original conclusions! They continued to cherish faith in a speedy decision, and when war experience compelled them to relinquish it, they pinned their faith instead to industrial attrition —as fervently as the General Staff of the last war had done to manpower attrition.

Nevertheless, a realization of the drawbacks and evils of taking the civil fabric as the objective does not mean the restoration of "battle" in the old sense as the objective. The drawbacks of that Clausewitzian formula were amply shown in World War I. In contrast, World War II demonstrated the advantages and new potentialities of indirect, or strategic, action against a military objective —amply confirming what had been forecast in that respect. Even in the past such action had been effectively exploited by some of the "Great Captains," despite the limitations of their instruments. But now, with the help of new instruments, it proved still more decisive—despite the increased strength of tactical resistance.

The new mobility produced a flexibility, in varying the directive of thrust and threat, which "disarmed" such resistance.

The time has come for a fresh revision of the doctrine of the objective, or military aim, in the light of recent experience and present conditions. It is much to be desired that it should be undertaken on a Combined Service basis, to produce an agreed solution— for there is a dangerous discordance of doctrine at present. The outlines of a revised theory fitted to present conditions and knowledge have emerged, I hope, in the course of this discussion of the subject.

The key idea is *strategic operation* rather than *battle*—an old term that has outlived its suitability and utility. Battles may still occur, but should not be regarded as the objective itself.

To repeat an earlier conclusion that was strikingly vindicated in World War II—

the true aim is not so much to seek battle as to seek a strategic situation so advantageous that if it does not of itself produce the decision, its continuation by a battle is sure to achieve this.

IV

While grand strategy should control strategy, its principles often run counter to those which prevail in the field of strategy. For that very reason, however, it is desirable to include here some indication of the deeper conclusions to which a study of grand strategy leads.

If you concentrate exclusively on victory, with no thought for the after-effect, you may be too exhausted to profit by the peace, while it is almost certain that the peace will be a bad one, containing the germs of another war. This is a lesson supported by abundant experience.

The risks become greater still in any war that is waged by a coalition. For in such a case a too complete victory inevitably complicates the problem of making a just and wise peace settlement. Where there is no longer the counterbalance of an opposing force to control the appetites of the victors, there is no check on the conflict of views and interests between the parties to the alliance. The divergence is then apt to become so acute as to turn the comradeship of common danger into the hostility of mutual dissatisfaction—so that the ally of one war becomes the enemy in the next.

Another conclusion which develops from the study of grand strategy (national war policy), against the background of history, is the practical necessity of adapting the general theory of strategy to the nature of a nation's fundamental policy. There is an essential difference of aim, and must be a consequent difference of appropriate method, between an "acquisitive" and a "conservative" State. In the light of this difference it becomes clear that the pure theory of strategy best fits the case of a State that is primarily concerned with conquest. It has to be modified if it is to serve the true purpose of a nation that is content with its existing territorial bounds, and primarily concerned to preserve its security and maintain its way of life.

The acquisitive State, inherently unsatisfied, needs to gain victory in order to gain its object—and must therefore court greater risks in the attempt. The conservative State can achieve its object by merely inducing the aggressor to drop his attempt at conquest—by convincing him that "the game is not worth the candle." Its victory is, in a real sense, attained by foiling the other side's bid for victory. Indeed, in attempting more it may defeat its own purpose—by exhausting itself so much that it is unable to resist other enemies or the internal effects of overstrain. Self-exhaustion in war has killed more States than any foreign assailant.

Weighing these factors of the problem, it can be seen that the problem of a conservative State is to find the type of strategy that is suited to fulfill its inherently more limited object in the most strength-conserving war—so as to ensure its future as well as its present. At first glance, it might seem that pure defense would be the most economical method; but this implies static defense—and historical experience warns us that this is a dangerously brittle method on which to rely.

Economy of force and deterrent effect are best combined in the defensive-offensive method, based on high mobility that carries the power of quick riposte. The East Roman Empire was a case where such an actively "conservative" strategy had been carefully thought out, as a basis of war policy—a fact which goes far to explain its unrivalled span of existence.

Another example, more instinctive than reasoned, is provided by the strategy, based on seapower, that England practiced in her wars from the sixteenth to the nineteenth century. The value of it was shown by the way that her strength kept pace with her growth, while all her rivals broke down in turn through self-exhaustion in war—traceable to their immoderate desire for the immediate satisfaction of outright victory.

It is folly to imagine that the aggressive types, whether individuals or nations, can be bought off—or, in modern language, "appeased"—since the payment of danegeld stimulates a demand for more danegeld. But they can be curbed. Their very belief in force makes them more susceptible to the deterrent effect of a formidable opposing force. This forms an adequate check except against pure fanaticism—a fanaticism that is unmixed with acquisitiveness.

While it is hard to make a real peace with the predatory types, it is easier to induce them to accept a state of truce, and far less exhausting than an attempt to crush them, whereby they are, like all types of mankind, infused with the courage of desperation. The experience of history brings ample evidence that the downfall of civilized states tends to come not from the direct assaults of foes but from internal decay, combined with the consequences of exhaustion in war. A state of suspense is trying—it has often led nations as well as individuals to commit suicide because they were unable to bear it. But it is better than to reach exhaustion in pursuit of the mirage of victory. Moreover, a truce to actual hostilities enables a recovery and development of strength, while the need for vigilance helps to keep a nation "on its toes."

Peaceful nations are apt, however, to court unnecessary danger, because when once aroused, they are more inclined to proceed to extremes than predatory nations, for the latter, making war as a means of gain, are usually more ready to call it off when they find an opponent too strong to be easily overcome.

It is the reluctant fighter, impelled by motion and not by calculation, who tends to press a fight to the bitter end. Thereby he too often defeats his own end, even if he does not produce his own direct defeat.

NOTES

Based on a lecture delivered at the Naval War College, September 1952

1. Carl von Clausewitz, *On War,* (London: Kegan, Paul, Trench, Truber & Co., Ltd., 1911) 3 vols., bk. I, chap. I, sec. 4, pp. 4-5.
2. Ibid., bk. I, chap. 1, sec. 6, pp. 6-7.
3. Ibid., bk. I, chap. 2, p. 29.
4. Ibid., bk. I, chap. 2, p. 36.
5. Ibid., bk. I, chap. 2, p. 39.
6. Ibid., bk. I, chap. 2, p. 42.
7. Ibid., bk. I, chap. 2, p. 39.
8. Ibid., bk. I, chap. 2, p. 45.
9. Ibid., bk. IV, chap. 11, p. 285.
10. Ibid., bk. IV, chap. 11, p. 288.
11. Ibid., bk. I, chap. 1, sec. 3, p. 2.

12. Ibid., bk. III, chap. 9, p. 199.
13. Ibid., bk. I, chap. 1, sec. 3, p. 3-4.
14. Ibid., bk. I, sec. 11, p. 11.
15. Ibid., bk. VIII, chap. 3 (B), vol. 3, p. 88.
16. Ibid., Author's Notice, p. xxv.

Clausewitz on the Moral Forces in War

Norman H. Gibbs

Editor's Note: *Norman Gibbs is Chichele Professor of the History of War at All Souls College, Oxford. He is the author of* Origins of the Committee of Imperial Defense, Grand Strategy in the Second World War, Vol. 1 Rearmament Policy *and is a contributor to* The Cambridge Modern History.

Clausewitz is deeply concerned with why men fight, what it is that makes wars emerge and develop as they do, and what general factors contribute to victory and defeat. However, the writing and discussion about Clausewitz' book *On War* which has taken place during the past thirty years or so has been to a large extent about his argument that "war is an extension of policy by other means." It is undoubtedly an argument basic to his whole concept of the nature of wars that actually occur as distinct from any theoretical concept of war; or, to use his own words, an argument which helps explain the contract between real war on the one hand and absolute or ideal war on the other. But the view of war as an extension of policy was no discovery by Clausewitz, as I think he would have been the first to admit. And we do him an injustice by stopping, as I think we do too often, at that point. He has something else, equally important, to say and that is about the importance of the moral forces in war.

This is one of those points at which Clausewitz goes in a new direction, and in following which he is concerned to analyze, among other things, the importance of the concept of ideology in war.

But first a proviso. I think we can narrow the meaning of the word *ideology* and its usefulness for our purpose too much. Ideologies are not only political creeds. To be of full value in the analysis of warfare, or indeed any other part of social analysis, ideology should be seen as something more comprehensive than simply political doctrine; something which, operating in the hearts and minds of men, moves them and inspires them to action. It is, of course, true that that "something" can often be identified with political doctrine, and that such doctrine can be a contributory cause of war. Nonetheless, as I have already said, I think it would be wrong for us to limit the meaning of the word *ideology* to political doctrine, and I would argue that Clausewitz himself adopts a looser interpretation when dealing with warfare in general and the period of war between 1792 and 1815 in particular. In this context he uses the phrase *moral forces* though I think we would now delete *moral* and substitute *psychological*.

To Clausewitz and to many of his contemporaries, warfare in their own time had become revolutionary in two senses; not only had it stemmed, politically, from the revolution in France, it was also conducted, militarily, in a new and sometimes startling way. In their view, warfare in the eighteenth century had settled down into a static condition which made it of limited value politically. Even the major countries of continental Europe operated with relatively small armies compared to those commanded by Napoleon. These small armies moved about as single, often cumbersome, units accepting without serious question severe restrictions upon their mobility. For example, although a good deal of road and canal improvement was going on in some countries of Western Europe during the eighteenth century, the conduct of war did not become more mobile and far-reaching. Generals tended to restrict their operations to fixed lines determined by prepared depots and generally slow movement and, by limiting methods, to limit results. In other words, the wars of the eighteenth century were limited both in the facilities and resources employed in them and in their political purposes. And Clausewitz on more than one occasion wrote contemptuously of the attitudes and beliefs which produced such a state of affairs.

However, despite all this, changes in thinking were going on in the generation before 1789 and new ideas about warfare—as about so much else—were most apparent in France. There, writers were advocating and professional soldiers were implementing many technical changes such as improvements in artillery, and the adoption of the division as a smaller tactical unit composed of all arms which made possible both greater concentration of firepower and greater mobility and flexibility in the use of armies. Others went beyond technical considerations of this kind and, applying the new ideas about government and society—as exemplified in Rousseau's *Social Contract*—to the business of making war, argued that if political and social structures could be radically changed then so, also, could man's ability to use organized force for political purposes. The best-known of these writers was a French nobleman, the Comte de Guibert, who produced a substantial work in the 1770s called *A General Essay on Tactics.*

"What," Guibert wrote, "can be the result today of our wars? The States have neither treasures nor superfluous population. Their expenditure, even in peace, is in excess of their revenues. Yet they declare war. They take the field with armies which they can neither recruit nor pay. Victors and vanquished are both soon exhausted. The mass of the national debts increase. Credit falls. Money grows scarce. Fleets are at a loss for sailors and armies for soldiers. The ministers on both sides feel that it is time to negotiate. Peace is made. A few colonies or provinces change masters. Often the source of the quarrels is not dried up, and each side sits on its shattered remains while it tries to pay its debts and to sharpen its weapons.

"But suppose there should arise in Europe a people endowed with energy, with genius, with resources, with government; a people which combined the virtues of austerity with a national militia and which added to them a fixed plan of aggrandizement, which never lost sight of this system; which, as it would know how to make war at small cost and subsist on its victories, would not be compelled to lay down its arms by calculations of finance. We should see that people subdue its neighbors, and upset our feeble constitutions as the north wind bends the frail reeds."[1]

These were the ideas which the French increasingly put into practice with the outbreak of war in 1792, and which the other nations of Europe—Prussia among them—subsequently learned from the French. And you will notice that Guibert is just as much concerned with the spirit or attitude of mind of the military as with their weapons and logistic systems.

The French Revolution broke out in 1789, and it soon became clear that the monarchy and the whole social and economic order in France were threatened. In 1792 Prussian and Austrian armies invaded France to stop the revolution and restore the monarchy to its former position. In response to this danger the Terror and the rule of the Committee of Public Safety developed in France in 1793, in an attempt to weed out traitors and strengthen the resolve of French citizens. Then, faced with the need for ever-increasing numbers of troops, the Revolutionary government issued its most important statement of military policy and belief—the decree announcing the *levée en masse*—or conscription. The French army had faced disruption in the first two or three years, partly because of the emigration of aristocrat officers and partly because of indiscipline in the absence of effective central authority. The danger from external enemies was too great to tolerate that situation any longer. What was needed was a great national army to fight for the nation's survival. And so the Revolutionary government, through the *levée en masse,* announced that political liberty and military duty were to go hand in hand. Thus was proclaimed the concept of the "nation in arms." The people would fight because they were fighting for themselves, not for a king or an aristocracy. They now had a stake in their own country and a corresponding duty to protect it. On 23 August 1793, it was announced that:

> From this moment until that in which every enemy shall have been driven out of the territories of the Republic, every Frenchman is permanently under requisition for service with the armies. The young men will go out and fight; the married men will manufacture weapons and transport stores. The women will make tents and clothing and nurse in the hospitals; the children will scrape lint from old linen. The aged will betake themselves to the public squares, there to raise the courage of the warriors and to preach hatred against kings and in favor of the unity of the Republic. The levée will be a general levée.... Unmarried citizens and childless widowers between the ages of eighteen and twenty-five will be the first to march.... The battalions we raise in each District will be gathered round a banner bearing this inscription: "This, the French Nation Has Risen Against Tyrants."[2]

Inspired by their beliefs the new armies of France swept across Europe. It is difficult for us to understand, given modern means of transport and communication, quite what a phenomenon the armies led by the generals of the Revolution, and then by Napoleon, were. To those who welcomed them they were the bearers of a new gospel. To those who feared them they were a scourge. These were larger armies than Europe had seen before, and they traveled farther and faster. Whereas generals, previously, had fought with armies of sixty to seventy thousand men, Napoleon often commanded armies of a quarter of a million. Moreover, he depended for success on surprise combined with accurate timing and was prepared to go right across Europe to get the battlefield he wanted. In 1805, for example, Napoleon led his army from Boulogne to Ulm on the Danube in ten days, arriving at the right place at the right time. This was lightning, blitzkrieg warfare of a kind modern Europe had never previously experienced. As Clausewitz himself put it, those who had expected the traditional kind of warfare in 1792-93 were taken completely by surprise,

> ... such a force as no one had any conception of made its appearance. War had again suddenly become an affair of the people, and that of a people numbering thirty millions, every one of whom regarded himself as a citizen of the State.[3] ... By this participation of the people in the War instead of a Cabinet and an Army, a whole nation with its natural weight came into the scale.... After all this was perfected by the hand of Bonaparte, this military power, based on the strength of the whole nation, marched over Europe, smashing everything in pieces so surely and certainly, that where it only encountered the old-fashioned Armies, the result was not doubtful for a moment.[4]

You will notice that Clausewitz is not concerned with inequalities arising from an arms race. In stressing, as he does, the commitment of the whole nation to war he is concerned—as so much of his work demonstrates—with moral or psychological forces. And in this his own experience was critically important. Of all the campaigns Napoleon fought, and of all the peace treaties he imposed, by far the most successful campaign and by far the harshest treaty were those against Prussia at the battle of Jena and in the subsequent Treaty of Tilsit. Until 1806, when the Prussians were handsomely defeated at the battles of Jena and Auerstedt, they considered themselves the foremost military nation in Europe; they had behind them a tradition of military success going back to the Great Elector of the midseventeenth century and culminating in the reign of Frederick the Great. How could they have been beaten by the French so easily and so completely? That shock, moreover, was made only more profound by the harsh terms of the Treaty of Tilsit drawn up in the summer of 1807, a treaty which, incidentally, was simply imposed on Prussia by an alliance between France and Russia with the Prussian government helpless in between. By the terms of that treaty Prussia lost half of her territory including the most prosperous parts of it; her armies were reduced by four-fifths; and she was compelled to close all her ports to trade with England as part of the Continental System. This was total war and unconditional surrender, all happening within the space of a few months.

Clausewitz, in common with many other Prussians, was profoundly shocked by what had happened. Professional and patriotic pride were hurt. Shock, however, soon turned into determination to find how and why matters had gone so wrong and to search for a remedy; and it was this search which led to the period of political, social, and economic, and military reform in Prussia from 1808 guided by Stein and Scharnhorst.

The reformers' explanation of what had happened and their suggested remedies were roughly as follows. The old Prussian army reflected Prussian society and government. Only aristocrats could be officers. The rank and file were recruited from the streets and the fields and, although then highly trained, were treated like the scum their officers believed them to be. How could such men— without rights, without dignity, without education or possessions— be expected to fight for a government in which they played no part and for policies which they did not understand and perhaps would not have agreed with even had they understood them? In France, on the other hand, the Revolution had given Frenchmen a voice in their own government (or so it seemed), a belief in their leaders, and a sense of fighting to defend what properly belonged to them. The reasons for their victory were to a great extent psychological or moral ones. Therefore, if Prussian armies were to wipe out the disgrace of defeat, then Prussian government and society, too, must be reformed as those in France had been. Liberty and responsibility would go hand in hand and men would fight for what they believed in.

What happened was that Prussians began to expound the concept of the "nation in arms" even more explicitly than the French had done. There were some political and social reforms and a corresponding degree of reform within the army as well. The result, as Clausewitz and others saw it, was that, with the widespread reaction against Napoleon in 1813 "in Germany, Prussia rose up the first, made the War a National Cause, and without either money or credit and with a population reduced one-half, took the field with an Army twice as strong as that of 1806."[5]

Against this background let us now turn back to Clausewitz' general exposition of the place of moral or psychological forces in war. And first let me make it clear that Clausewitz was always correct in his reading of history. He saw the events of his own time—as most of us do—through tinted spectacles; he was sometimes biased and even sentimental. But, in effect, he was saying no more in relation to the events of his own time than the French writer, Georges Sorel, has said in general, i.e., that all great social movements find a driving force in a body of images or myths. It is the existence of the driving force which matters.

In Clausewitz' analysis, war—as a concept—is identified with violence, and violence naturally tends to extremes. Or, in his own words, "war is an act of violence intended to compel our opponent to fulfill our will" and is in fact "an act of violence pushed to its utmost bounds."[6] Looked at in this theoretical way then, it follows that the overthrow or even the extermination of the enemy must always be the aim of warfare. But these are logical propositions, not an accurate description of the real world.

Reasoning in the abstract [writes Clausewitz], the mind cannot stop short of an extreme because it has to deal with an extreme, with a conflict of forces left to themselves, and obeying no other but their own inner laws. If we should seek to deduce from the pure conception of war an absolute point for the aim which we shall propose and for the means which we shall apply, this constant reciprocal action would involve us in extremes, which would be nothing but a play of ideas produced by an almost invisible train of logical subtleties.

If adhering closely to the absolute, we try to avoid all difficulties by a stroke of the pen, and insist with logical strictness that in every case the extreme must be the object, and the utmost effort must be exerted in that direction, such a stroke of the pen would be a mere paper law, not by any means adapted to the real world.... But everything takes a different shape when we pass from abstraction to reality.[7]

In Clausewitz' view there are two reasons why real wars, wars which actually take place, are different from—in the sense of being less extreme than—ideal or absolute war. The first is the political context or purpose of actual wars. Given this context, we are concerned not with a blind force risking uncontrolled to total destruction, but "a calculation of probability based on definite persons and relations." Or, as Clausewitz puts it in more detail:

The smaller the sacrifice we demand from our opponent, the smaller, it may be expected, will be the means of resistance which he will employ; but the smaller his preparation, the smaller will ours require to be. Further, the smaller our political

object, the less value we shall set upon it, and the more easily
shall we be induced to give it up altogether.

Thus, therefore, the political object, as the original motive
of the War, will be the standard for determining both the aim
of the military force and also the amount of effort to be made.[8]

This, as I suggested earlier, is the part of Clausewitz with which
we are most familiar. But a few pages later he goes on to argue
that a realistic theory of war

... must also take into account the human element; it must
accord a place to courage, to boldness, even to rashness. The
Act of War has to deal with living and with moral forces, the
consequence of which is that it can never attain the absolute
and positive.[9]

In other words, those two factors, political and psychological,
work—at least to a great extent—in the same direction. And looked
at from that direction it is reasonable to claim that Clausewitz'
whole book is an argument about limited war. But, having said
that, it is important to remember that these same two factors,
within the overall limits of real war, also produce all the variations
between a skirmish or border incident on the one hand and world
war on the other. To quote Clausewitz again—

The greater and more powerful the motives of a War, the
more it affects the whole existence of a people. The more violent
the excitement which precedes the War, by so much the nearer
will the War approach to its abstract form, so much the more
will it be directed to the destruction of the enemy....[10]

Moreover, Clausewitz was persuaded that the Revolutionary
and Napoleonic wars, because of the great political interests and
deep-rooted psychological forces engaged in them, had approached
nearer than ever before to the absolute or extreme. Or, in language
more familiar in our own time, that he and his contemporaries
had witnessed the nearest approach thus far to total war. And
the basic cause of that phenomenon "was the participation of the
people in this great affair of State."

Primarily in Books I and VIII of his work *On War,* but repeatedly elsewhere, Clausewitz returns to his theme of war as a continuation of policy. And, equally frequently, he returns to the theme
of the importance of the moral and psychological forces. For exam-

ple, when in Book I he writes of ends and means in war, Clausewitz lists as one of his basic considerations—i.e., in addition to destruction of armies and annexation of territory—the "gradual exhaustion of the physical powers and of the will by the long continuance of exertion." The willpower of combatants figures repeatedly. In the long chapters on defense and attack the psychological aspects of both forms are ranked as highly as the purely physical or material ones. Defense is argued to be the stronger form of war partly because of the moral reassurance of beginning the fight on one's own chosen ground and partly because of the psychological exhilaration of being able to go over to attack from defense encouraged by the thought that the enemy has been held and one's own efforts have thus far succeeded.

> During the twelve hours' rest [Clausewitz writes], which usually succeeds a day's work, what a difference there is between the situation of the defender in his chosen, well-known, and prepared position, and that of the assailant occupying a bivouac into which—like a blind man—he has groped his way ... when the defender is close to his fortresses and supplies, whilst the situation of the assailant, on the other hand, is like that of a bird on a tree.[11]

Likewise, looked at from the other side, a successful attack depends upon a superiority of forces, both moral and physical.

Again, in a long chapter entitled "The Genius for War," Clausewitz is almost exclusively concerned with such qualities as presence of mind, strength of character, the calculations of the trained intellect, arguing that as war progresses from the actions of half-civilized tribes to those of organized political communities, so the powers of the understanding and the soul increasingly predominate. And all this is developed at considerable length in Book III, entitled "Of Strategy in General." Early on in that book Clausewitz claims that—

> ... the moral forces are amongst the most important subjects in War. They form the spirit which permeates the whole being of War. These forces fasten themselves and with the greatest affinity on to the Will which puts in motion and guides the whole mass of powers, uniting with it as it were in one stream because this is a moral force itself.[12]

Then follows an analysis of what he considers the chief moral forces—boldness, perseverance, national feeling, the military virtue of an army, the talents of the commander. And he also includes a chapter on "The Surprise" as an element of strategy on the ground that the surprise is "to be regarded as a substantive principle in itself on account of its moral effect."[13]

The evidence I have pointed to is merely a selection of what could be produced to support my argument that Clausewitz is just as much concerned with the importance of the moral forces in war as he is with his other much more familiar argument that war is a continuation of policy by other means. What I want to do finally is to suggest two conclusions arising from this. When contrasted with other writers who have written about the place of warfare in society, Clausewitz is sometimes described as a rationalist. It is true that, unlike many ancient and medieval writers, he pays no attention to cyclical theories of human behavior and human institutions, nor does he regard war as a natural phenomenon like an earthquake or a flood. His explanation of war as a political act with a political purpose certainly implies a rational approach. War is something which, broadly speaking, has cause and effect. But he does not stop there. War, he repeatedly reminds us, is characterized by chance more so than other human activities. It cannot all be calculated to the last decimal point. It involves living and reacting forces, the result of which is that any "seeking and striving after laws like those which may be developed out of the dead material world could not but lead to constant errors." And of all the factors in war which defy the making of laws the most important are the moral or psychological ones. "They will escape from all book analysis," he tells us, "for they will neither be brought into numbers nor into classes, and require to be both seen and felt."[14]

Secondly, Clausewitz is sometimes labeled as the prophet of the vast armies of the twentieth century and the belief that more men, machines, and ammunition are bound to win. Sir Basil Liddell Hart, for example, called him the Mahdi of Mass. Clausewitz certainly did scoff at what he considered the fancy theories of some of his predecessors, and he also argued that "the first rule is therefore to enter the field with an Army as strong as possible." Would any general not do so? But if you look at Book III, "On Strategy," you will find that he deals with numbers after moral forces; he then follows on with a chapter on "The Surprise," a factor which he argues is as important as numerical superiority. Surprise leads to confusion and broken courage, and out of these arise defeat even for the side which may possess more men and machines.

Finally, far from being a militant, Clausewitz had a clear under-standing of the limits of the value of war as an instrument of policy. If later generations of Germans thought and acted other-wise—Bismarck certainly did not—then the fault was theirs through mistakes in interpretation if Clausewitz was their textbook. And in his own more critical view of the value of war for political pur-poses, Clausewitz' appreciation of the importance of moral forces in war played a vital part.

NOTES

Based on a lecture delivered at the Naval War College in September 1972.

1. Comte de Guibert, "Essai général de tactique" in *Oeuvres militaires du comte de Guibert* (Paris: Chez Magimel, 1803), vol. I, pp. 15-16.

2. F. A. Aulard, *Recueil des Actes du Comité de Salut Public* (Paris: Imprimerie Nationale, 1893), vol. LX, pp. 72-73.

3. Carl von Clausewitz, *On War* (London: Kegan, Paul, Trench, Trubner & Co., Ltd., 1911), vol. 3, bk. VIII, chap. 3, p. 100.

4. Ibid., bk. VIII, chap. 3(b), p. 101.

5. Ibid., vol. 3, bk. VIII, chap. 3(b), p. 102.

6. Ibid., vol. 1, bk. I, chap. 1, passim.

7. Ibid., bk. I, chap. 1, pp. 6, 7.

8. Ibid., p. 11.

9. Ibid., p. 21.

10. Ibid., p. 23.

11. Ibid., vol. 3, bk. VII, chap. 2, p. 4.

12. Ibid., vol. 1, bk. III, chap. 3, p. 177.

13. Ibid., bk. III, chap. 9, p. 199.

14. Ibid., bk. III, chap. 3, p. 177.

II. Strategy: The Comprehensive Direction of Power

New Thoughts on Strategy

Herbert Rosinski

Editor's Note: *All too often there is a general lack of clarity among writers in the field of strategy. Much of the confusion can be attributed directly to a lack of sound, workable concepts. In 1955 Herbert Rosinski discussed this conceptual problem with the chief of staff and the president of the Naval War College. "New Thoughts on Strategy" is a memorandum based on those conversations.*

In 1936 in the face of Nazi persecution, Dr. Rosinski left his post as lecturer on military and naval affairs at the German Naval Staff College and went to England. A. Lawrence Lowell called him to the United States in 1940 to lecture in Boston. Until his death in 1962 he was an itinerant scholar holding such positions as Carnegie Fellow, member of the Institute for Advanced Study at Princeton, consultant to the Army War College, Naval War College, the Brookings Institution, and the Council on Foreign Relations. He wrote The German Army *and* Power and Human Destiny, *among other works in English and German.*

For the past 150 years there has been a continuous effort to arrive at satisfactory and illuminating definitions of strategy and tactics. This effort has so far been greatly hampered by the fact that the definitions have been verbal enumerations rather than analytical definitions. The situation is further complicated by the widely differing meanings of the terms as used in the German and Russian as opposed to the French, British, and American schools of military thought.

As a result of the work done on my paper on "The Evolution of Warfare and Strategy,"[1] the following definition is suggested as a formulation which bridges the gap between these two schools of thought and brings into better perspective and focus the ideas of the military thinkers of the past 150 years. *Strategy is the comprehensive direction of power; tactics is its immediate application.*

This definition requires the recognition that there is much more to strategy than mere direction of action. It is a type of direction which takes into account the multitude of possible enemy counteractions, and thus it becomes a means of control. It is this element of control which is the essence of strategy: control being the element which differentiates true strategic action from a haphazard of improvisations.

Thus strategy, in contrast to haphazard action, is that direction of action which aims at the control of a field of activity be it military, social, or even intellectual. It must be comprehensive in order to control every possible counteraction or factor.

Therefore, except where there is absolutely overwhelming superiority, strategy must be selective in order to achieve economy of force. Comprehensive control of a field of action means a concentration upon those minimum key lines of action or key positions from which the entire field can be positively controlled. This is well illustrated by the concept of control or command of a sea area.

This concept of strategy as a comprehensive control has the advantage that it applies equally to the offensive and to the defensive. On the offensive, the aim of strategy is to break down the enemy's control while simultaneously preventing him from interfering with our attack. On the defensive, strategy similarly seeks to constrain the enemy attack to such a form and degree that while the defense may be forced back, it still maintains control of its actions and avoids collapse. As long as it can manage to do so, as long as it can continue to parry all decisive thrusts of the enemy, it may suffer a series of defeats but it will still be a coherent strategy and avoid wholesale catastrophe.

In this sense a discussion of the strategy of the three services can best be analyzed in terms of their differing capacities for such comprehensive control. Control is easiest in land warfare, has always been more difficult in naval strategy, is still more difficult in the field of air warfare, and is most difficult in that of the combined strategy of all three forces.

This definition has the advantage that it can be transposed from the military field in which it originated to any of the other fields to which, in the course of the year, it has been increasingly applied by analogy, such as, for instance, the strategy and tactics of science.

This definition has the further advantage that tactics very simply is defined as the immediate action beyond which comprehensive control of the entire field is not necessary.

NOTES

Originally published in Henry E. Eccles, ed., *Military Concepts and Philosophy* (New Brunswick: Rutgers University Press, 1965), pp. 46-47.

1. Edited by William Reitzel and published in 1972 by the Naval War College as "The Evolution of War and the Conduct of Strategic Thinking" for course use.

The Basic Elements of Strategy

Henry E. Eccles

Editor's Note: *Using Herbert Rosinski's "New Thoughts on Strategy" as his reference point, Rear Admiral Eccles elaborates the concept of strategy as comprehensive control.*

In thirty years of active duty Admiral Eccles had extensive sea duty, including command of a battleship. Since his retirement in 1952, he has written and lectured extensively on military theory, strategy, and logistics. He is the author of Military Concepts and Philosophy. *Currently, he is a consultant to the president, Naval War College.*

I

Strategy can be discussed from two perspectives—that of the student of strategy, who is unhampered by deadlines and free from adherence to any particular formulation or authority other than that imposed by intellectual rigor; and that of the executive authority, who must formulate specific national and military strategic policies and plans. This latter activity must always be done within a specified time and must always be both responsible and authoritative. For the purpose of this essay, I will discuss the first point of view, emphasizing the nature and structure of strategy while choosing to omit both the methods and considerations used in reaching strategic decisions, and the critique of specific strategic policies and plans. Unless one is willing to confine discussion of the subject to some specific aspect of the general concept, discussion often tends to dissolve into lamentations and confusing speculative arguments rather than constructive analysis.

In dealing with this subject, I ask that the reader bear in mind that when one has executive responsibility for the formulation of an operative strategy, little time or energy can be devoted to developing constructive military theory or concepts. One must decide on the basis of one's basic assumptions, one's view of current facts, and on the fundamental concepts one has already developed. Assumptions and current facts, of course, vary greatly according to circumstances, but concepts, if well thought out, have much greater endurance.

In his book *Strategy*, Liddell Hart devoted the last forty pages to the theory of strategy and to grand strategy. Here, in developing "a new dwelling-house for strategic thought," he discussed the ideas of Clausewitz and Moltke. He defined strategy as "the art of distributing and applying military means to fulfill the ends of policy." He noted that strategy is concerned with the effect of military action, not solely with the movement of forces. To him the actual dispositions for and control of forces is "tactics." He added an important qualification, "The two categories, although convenient for discussion, can never be truly divided into separate compartments because each not only influences, but merges into the other."[1]

This analysis does not differ in its essentials from Rosinski's statement that strategy is the comprehensive direction of power and that tactics is its immediate application. Liddell Hart concludes this important passage by relating tactics and strategy to grand strategy, strategy, policy, and objectives. In so doing, he places them all in a clear perspective:

As tactics is an application of strategy on a lower plane, so strategy is an application on a lower plane of "grand strategy." While practically synonymous with the policy which guides the conduct of war, as distinct from the more fundamental policy which should govern its object, the term *grand strategy* serves to bring out the sense of "policy in execution." For the role of grand strategy—high strategy—is to coordinate and direct all the resources of a nation, or band of nations, toward the political object of the war—the goal defined by fundamental policy.[2]

The element of policy Liddell Hart stressed was clearly brought out in the Naval War College publication, *Sound Military Decision,* which emphasizes the necessary relationship between policy and strategy and between the civil and military leaders:

Understanding between the civil representatives of the State and the leaders of the armed forces is manifestly essential to the coordination of national policy with the power to enforce it. While military strategy may determine whether the aims of policy are possible of attainment, policy may, beforehand, determine largely the success or failure of military strategy. Therefore, it behooves policy to ensure not only that military strategy pursue appropriate aims, but that the work of strategy be allotted adequate power, and be undertaken under the most favorable conditions.[3]

These thoughts, together with the Rosinski concept of strategy as the art of control, provide the foundation for the conceptual unity and coherence so essential to military theory.

II

Many discussions of strategy suffer from the semantic confusion arising from the two commonly used meanings of the word *strategic*. The first meaning evolves from defining strategy as the art and science of using political, economic, psychological, and military forces of a nation to support national policy. Thus, in this sense, *strategic* refers to the plan or scheme for such use.

The second meaning defines *strategic* action as the physical destruction of an enemy's warmaking capacity. This second meaning refers primarily to economic, agricultural, and military targets. Although the term *strategic* is widely used in this sense, such use only serves to confuse its users, as well as their readers and listeners. Such use leads to the fallacy of equating strategy with destruction. The essence of strategy is control, that is, to establish control. Obviously, destruction is not a *sine qua non* for the establishment of control. The important thing is to realize that strategy seeks to establish control, not necessarily to destroy.

The Rosinski concept of "comprehensive control" has certain specific implications of tremendous importance. In particular, it establishes the primacy of strategy in the conduct of national affairs as opposed to emphasis on destruction that is implicit in any "weapon strategy." The idea that the weapon should determine the strategy to be used is based on the implied assumption that strategy and destruction are synonymous. This is simply not true. Naturally, strategy will be influenced by the availability of weapons, but strategy should use destruction only when there is no other way of gaining or exercising control. The concentration of thought on control naturally leads to a reexamination and better understanding of the objectives whose attainment is the purpose of the attempt to exercise control.

The concept of continuing control prepares the mind for shifting the emphasis from weapon to weapon or from tool to tool in accordance with changing situations or with the changing capabilities or application of the weapon or weapon systems involved. Thus, the intellectual concept of strategy as "comprehensive control" naturally leads to the intellectual concept of flexibility. But "flexibility" itself must be understood lest it degenerate into mere hesitancy, uncertainty, and vacillation. The essence of true flexibility lies in the continuing clear appreciation of the aim, the purposes, the objective.

Strategy is always concerned with objectives. But merely to state the objective is not enough: the objective must be analyzed. The mere statement of an objective can easily degenerate into a rigid and dangerous slogan. The analysis should not only clarify the purpose for which action is to be taken, it must also show what constitutes a satisfactory attainment of the objective. Here we encounter one of the chief problems of strategic thinking. How are the objectives influenced by the course of events? How does one distinguish steadfast adherence to a firm purpose from dogmatic pursuit of an outworn or irrelevant objective? In modern conflict, objectives are multiple and seem to have a hierarchy of major and minor, immediate and ultimate.

But since plans, once prepared, frequently have great and dangerous momentum, the running estimate of the situation must involve an alertness to changes and particularly to the reactions of the opponent which influence one's own objectives. Both political objectives and political control are essential elements of all strategy. This brings us squarely to the vital relation of strategy and tactics.

Edward Lasker, the chess grandmaster, made the following perceptive comment:

> ... Strategy sets down the whole of the problems which must be solved in war, in order to. attain the ultimate result aimed at; tactics solve such problems in various ways, and according to the conditions prevailing in the particular case. Sound strategy, when setting the task, must never lose sight of tactical practicability, and only a thorough knowledge of tactical resources makes correct strategy possible.[4]

This last description explains why the term *strategic doctrine* is so frequently a dangerous misnomer. Doctrine arises from repeated experience and is useful in dealing with recurring situations. Its purpose is to provide a good solution to the repeating problem to be applied almost automatically when a recognized situation occurs. It saves time and achieves instant understanding between unit commanders without the necessity for consultation or elaborate communications. It simplifies decision and facilitates coordination in action. It is an essential element of tactics, logistics, and communications, but has little, if any, application to strategy.

Bear in mind that most strategic problems seldom recur in such a manner that the tactical resources are so disposed as to make a doctrine applicable. There is, however, room for doctrine in the area of grand tactics.

Sound Military Decision again is useful in explaining fundamental relations:

> ... Tactics, unguided by strategy, might blindly make sacrifices merely to remain victor on a field of struggle. But strategy looks beyond, in order to make the gains of tactics accord with the strategic aim. Strategy and tactics are inseparable.
>
> It is thus the duty of tactics to ensure that its results are appropriate to the strategic aim, and the duty of strategy to place at the disposal of tactics the power appropriate to the results demanded.[5]

This latter consideration imposes upon strategy the requirement that the prescribed aim be possible of attainment with the power that can be made available.

Consequently, while the attainment of the aims of strategy generally depends upon the results gained by tactics, strategy is initially responsible for the success of tactics. It is therefore within the province of strategy to ensure that the attainment of tactical objectives furthers, exclusively, the aims of strategy and also that the tactical struggle be initiated under conditions favorable for the attainment of the designated objectives.

In military strategy the interweaving of logistical, tactical, and strategic considerations in the mind of a single responsible individual will always be an intuitive process based on professional experience and judgment. Both the logistical and tactical factors contain many quantitative aspects whose evaluation is subject to many modern analytical techniques.

In moving from purely military strategy to the level of national strategy, we have an increasing emphasis on economic and political considerations.

At the level of national strategy, political and economic factors, both international and domestic, are important. At this level, strategy, economics, and logistics tend to coalesce. Duncan Ballantine's comment on logistics is instructive:

> As the link between the war front and the home front the logistic process is at once the military element in the nation's economy and the economic element in its military operations. And upon the coherence that exists within the process itself depends the successful articulation of the productive and military efforts of a nation at war.[6]

The understanding of the interweaving of strategy-economics-logistics is enhanced by recognizing the two phases of logistics: producer and consumer.

At the level of national strategy, political factors, both international and domestic, are important. At this level, strategy, economics, and logistics tend to coalesce: with national and international economics—that is, producer logistics—limiting the forces one can create; and operational logistics—that is, consumer logistics—limiting the forces one can tactically employ. Strategic deployments involve both producer and consumer logistics. As an example, consider the concepts of prepositioning and all the controversies concerning the concepts for rapid overseas movement of army divisions, their supporting equipment and resupply.

Finally, the classic principle of military decision found in *Sound Military Decision* emphasizes this interweaving of integrated thought by testing each proposed course of action for:

Suitability—Will it accomplish the mission? Attain the objective? This involves both strategy and politics.

Feasibility—Can it be accomplished with the means available? This involves tactics, logistics, and economics.

Acceptability—Are the consequences as to cost acceptable? This involves politics, economics, and logistics.

III

Deterrence is certainly a very important aspect of strategy, but it by no means is the only element. But since it is a negative element, undue concentration on it may easily detract from the essential positive aspects of strategy. I believe, however, that its full implications have not been adequately understood.

Concepts of strategy and control must be examined in two major aspects. Strategy is the comprehensive direction of power to control situations and areas in order to attain objectives. Thus, we can examine the nature of the situations and areas that must be controlled in order to attain objectives, and the means and methods of the use of power in its various forms by which such control will be exercised.

We also must examine the means and the methods by which the power which is being used is itself controlled. The uncontrolled use of power can easily be both self-defeating and disastrous. This means strict political control of all military action must be exercised through the elaborate worldwide command control system made possible by modern electronics technology.

But the controlled use of force has a further vital implication first brought out by James E. King, Jr., in 1957:

> We must, in short, guarantee that only effectively limited hostilities can be rationally undertaken.
>
> Moreover, we must be prepared to fight limited actions ourselves. Otherwise we shall have made no advance beyond "massive retaliation," which tied our hands in conflicts involving less than our survival. And we must be prepared to lose limited actions. No limitations could survive our disposition to elevate every conflict in which our interests are affected to the level of total conflict with survival at stake.
>
> Armed conflict can be limited only if aimed at limited objectives and fought with limited means. If we or our enemy relax the limits on either objectives or means, survival *will* be at stake, whether the issue is worth it or not . . . .[7]

This, in effect, means that the level of tactical defeat which in the past has been acceptable in pursuit of a higher strategic objective has been raised. This in turn places greater burdens on all levels of command. Combat morale, which is the single most important element of combat effectiveness of the armed forces, must be maintained in spite of severe defeats suffered while refraining from the use of powerful and available weapons. This, in fact, is the hidden and heretofore unmentionable aspect of deterrence.

There is a further point: the commonly used distinction between strategic and nonstrategic war is, in fact, a semantic trap which can cause real trouble. In recognition of this, I would like to raise the following question: If one attacks the core industries and power and transportation facilities of a nation with high explosive rather than nuclear weapons, does that constitute "strategic war"? Or does the term *strategic war* apply only to the widespread use of atomic or thermonuclear weapons?

I submit that the use of the term *strategic war* is dangerous and may easily confuse us.

IV

The understanding of power and force and their effective use is critical to the understanding of strategy. Again we come to the basic problem of capabilities and limitations and through these to the problems of public, as well as military, discipline and morale. Discipline and morale are frequently taken for granted or else ignored in the writings of so-called military intellectuals.

Strategy becomes most complex when we try to relate concrete tangible military violence to the abstract intangible elements of national interests and national values. This is a necessary, if painful, process, for a strategy which is contrary to the values of the people of the nation concerned will not be successful. A strategy which does not serve the national interest is self-defeating. Yet, how do we define or describe national interests and national values in terms which provide a firm base for a sound strategy?

Obviously, this is a highly intuitive process which means that it is an individual matter in which opinions differ strongly. Here we find the major sources of those elements of paradox, contradiction, and equivocation which today are so apparent and so disturbing.

If our concepts of the nature and structure of strategy and its relation to the other elements of military thought and action are vague or confused, we will inevitably further compound our troubles. Plato's Lament, as expressed in *The Republic,* Book V, is still pertinent:

Until philosophers are kings, or the kings and princes of this world have the spirit and power of philosophy, and political greatness and wisdom meet in one, and those commoner natures who pursue either to the exclusion of the other are compelled to stand aside, cities will never have rest from their evils—no, nor the human race, as I believe—and then only will this our State have a possibility of life and behold the light of day.[8]

I have indicated the complexity of thought associated with the use of the word *strategy*. The word *strategy* can be properly used in a great variety of levels and contexts. In some contexts it is desirable to use a qualifying word or phrase to maintain semantic clarity. However, when any policy or plan of action, no matter how inconsequential, is labeled a "strategy" rather than simply a "policy" or a "plan," the meaning of the word *strategy* becomes degraded. I suspect that such usage may sometimes have its roots in the user's pretentiousness or subconscious desire to inflate rather trivial ideas by the use of a term which sounds important.

While it is useful and sometimes necessary to discuss strategy in isolation from its associated subjects in the art of war, such discussion does not give one an understanding of more than a small part of the strategy. Strategy in its full sense can be understood only when it is considered as part of an interwoven fabric of coherent military thought and theory. Such interweaving and coherence are enhanced by the use of the description that:

Strategy is the Comprehensive Direction of Power to Control Situations and Areas in Order to Attain Objectives.[9]

It is useful to meditate on the words *Comprehensive, Direction, Power, Control, Situations, Areas, Objectives.* As we so meditate, further ideas will occur.

Finally, I believe that the general quality of military education and, ultimately, military decision and action will be improved if the word *strategy* is used with respect and with semantic clarity. For if the word is carelessly used, the rigor and comprehensiveness of strategic thinking will be unnecessarily degraded.

If anyone thinks that this discussion has been on a too abstract or theoretical level, he should examine the two greatest specific political-military blunders of our times—the British action in Suez in 1956 and the United States Bay of Pigs episode in 1961. They contain vivid illustrations of the importance of the points that I have discussed.

NOTES

Originally published in the *Naval War College Review,* December 1971.

1. Basil H. Liddell Hart, *Strategy* (New York: Praeger, 1954), p. 335.
2. Ibid., pp. 335-36.
3. Naval War College, *Sound Military Decision* (Newport, R.I., 1942), p. 9.
4. Edward Lasker, *Chess Strategy* (New York: Dover, 1969), p. 17.
5. Naval War College, pp. 10-11.
6. Duncan S. Ballantine, *U.S. Naval Logistics in the Second World War* (Prince-

ton: Princeton University Press, 1947), p. 3.

7. James E. King, Jr., "Nuclear Plenty and Limited War," *Foreign Affairs,* January 1957, p. 256.

8. Plato, Jowett trans., *The Republic,* (New York: Colonial Press, 1901) p. 167.

9. See Henry E. Eccles, *Military Concepts and Philosophy,* (New Brunswick; Rutgers University Press, 1965), pp. 46, 257.

The Origins of Maritime Strategy and the Development of Seapower

James A. Field, Jr.

Editor's Note: *Professor Field spoke in 1954, when containment was an active American policy.*

Professor Field is Isaac C. Clothier Professor of History at Swarthmore College. He is the author of America and the Mediterranean World, 1776-1882.

In this discussion I propose first to consider very briefly the historical development of seapower, then to see how the classic interpretation of this phenomenon came to be made by Captain Mahan, an officer with little previous interest in these matters, who had by chance been invited to give a short course in an almshouse to officers of a navy then in a considerable state of disrepair. And finally to move on to a consideration of *maritime strategy* in a context both somewhat broader and also somewhat narrower than is usual: broader in that I propose to consider *strategy,* following the lessons of recent years, as not limited to periods of formal war; narrower in that I propose to concentrate wholly upon the maritime strategy of our own country. Perhaps if I had to choose a short title it would be "The Influence of History upon Seapower."

In a phrase which has gained a local immortality, an officer at the Naval War College once observed that "since man first sat astride a floating log, and propelled himself with the spatulate

foot of some long-defunct animal," seapower has been of continuing importance to mankind. While not disputing the validity of
so vivid a statement, I think we can for present purposes begin
at a somewhat later date, and deal only with those times in which
communities, rather than solitary paddlers, have concerned themselves with these things, and in which civilization has been so far
advanced that economic concerns—trade, or such more elementary
forms of exchange of goods as conquest, piracy, or abduction—have
provided a continuing incentive to maritime activity.

So far as the Western World is concerned, these qualifications
can serve to start us off with the city-states of Greece at the beginning of what someone has called the thalassic period of history.

Now *thalassic,* of course, is only a big word which means for
sea what *oceanic* means for ocean, but it is a Greek word. This
is appropriate in view of the nautical accomplishments of those
peoples, not only in the amphibious expedition against Troy and
the travels of Ulysses, but in trade, colonization, and the defense
of their rimland against the invading Persian hordes. Their civilization was brilliant and cosmopolitan, as have been a good many
maritime civilizations, but they failed—and this may be worth
noting—to solve their political problems. Overjealous attachment
to their independence on the part of the several states defeated
all efforts to match their cultural unity with a political one, and
the result was gradual decline.

Their successors, and ultimately on a far greater geographical
scale, were of course the Romans. They had great political gifts:
after unifying Italy they defeated the rival Carthaginian seapower
in the Punic wars and then, in the course of three centuries, succeeded in conquering and organizing the shores of the Mediterranean and all Europe south of central Britain and the Rhine-
Danube line. So great a structure was wholly dependent upon
communications. The Roman roads are of course deservedly
famous, and brought land transport to a peak not again reached
until the early nineteenth century. But I would argue that the
Mediterranean, the wet hole in this doughnut-shaped empire,
which facilitated not only the movement of legions but also the
feeding of Italy from African granaries, was the real basis of their
achievement.

But Rome, too, declined. Countless causes have been advanced
by countless historians, but I would suggest, without being dogmatic, that at least one central cause was corruption by success:
some failure of the will, some refusal to accept responsibilities on
the part of the ruling groups. Barbarian invaders—or, perhaps bet-

ter, barbarian immigrants—filtered down from the north and reached the shores of the Mediterranean. There, despite edicts or laws to the contrary, they succeeded in mastering the arts of shipbuilding and navigation and turned traders or pirates.

More important, because the immigrants arrived fighting and at a speed which precluded Romanization and assimilation, was the westward advance of Islam from the Arabian peninsula. Their first breakout gained the Arabs the great shipbuilding center at Alexandria, and within a generation of the death of Mohammed they had conquered Cyprus and had mounted a major expedition against Constantinople. These Moslem invasions permanently shattered the cultural and political unity of the Mediterranean. They greatly limited—for a time perhaps destroyed—the vital East-West trade. They forced the European frontier westward to an extent not seriously modified until the nineteenth century.

With the end of Roman peace there came some centuries of disruption and strife, of raiding and crusading. But the ideological conflict of Christian and Moslem should not be overestimated. It was not total or perpetual war. Sensible arrangements were often made for mutual profit. The Moslems were great traders, and opportunities for Europeans remained. We may instance the rise of the Republic of Venice which, strategically situated at the head of the Adriatic and at the foot of the trade routes to the north, grew rich on the products of the golden east and acknowledged the maritime base of her prosperity by an annual wedding ceremony between her political boss and the sea.

Nonetheless, the great revival which we term the Italian Renaissance was a last flash. With the discovery of the sea route to the Indies, the Mediterranean was destined to become a backwater. The age of discovery marks the end of the thalassic and the start of the oceanic period in the history of seapower.

There had, of course, been signs of maritime vigor in the western ocean long before the great discoveries of Portugal and Spain. Norsemen had sailed westward to Vinland. Other Norsemen, usually called Normans, had from the ninth century harried the coasts of Europe and had conquered Normandy, Sicily, and England. In the Baltic and in the North Sea there had developed important trading communities. The wool trade between England and Flanders foreshadowed the rise of Dutch and British seapower.

There had also been indications that the long period of European compression, the period which had seen Europe steadily on the defensive, was approaching an end, and that these rimlands, unable to push eastward by land, were about to enter a great phase of seaborne expansion. The increased knowledge of the Renaissance and the increased resources which followed on improved social organization permitted and indeed urged an organized effort in exploration. By the end of the fifteenth century Vasco da Gama and others had reached India by way of the Cape of Good Hope, while a somewhat less carefully planned effort by an Italian sailing under the flag of Spain to go east by heading west had resulted in the discovery of a new world.

Suddenly there were made available, for exploitation by the Europeans, immense areas of the world, some heavily populated and some largely vacant, some rich and some not. But all were accessible by sea, and in none were the inhabitants able to compete on even terms with the armaments of the Europeans. There consequently ensued three centuries of remarkable expansion, a period in which much of the history of the world revolves around European competition for control of these overseas areas and of their trade.

With the ensuing wars for empire we can deal only in the briefest of terms. Financed by American gold and silver, Spain threatened to dominate all Europe, and by so doing called into existence a coalition which permanently ended this possibility. The attempt to conquer England led to the defeat of the Armada by the technically superior English squadrons. The attempt to put down the Dutch was no more successful, but by forcing the Dutch to take to the sea it made that small nation for a time the dominant maritime power. The great age of the Dutch Republic and of Dutch cultural achievement was based on an extremely rapid expansion into both East and West Indies and on what was, for a time at least, by far the largest merchant marine in the world.

The dominance of Holland on the seas was brief, ending with the Anglo-Dutch wars of the later seventeenth century. The British, having effectively liquidated both Spanish and Dutch threats, found themselves faced with one still more formidable in that of France: competitor in India, competitor in North America, only a few miles away across the Channel, and by then the strongest power on the continent of Europe.

As to the outcome of this crisis, we need not remain long in suspense. The French overseas empire was liquidated in 1763, at the end of the Seven Years War, although a delayed price was to be paid for this when French maritime intervention led to the loss of the American colonies. The prospect of French domination of Europe was ended with the final defeat of Napoleon.

Such, in capsule form, was the history of the European

seapowers up to the time when the long peace of the nineteenth century descended. We should not be too chauvinistic or narrow, however. It is well to remember that there have been other seapowers outside our own Western tradition. The Chinese had developed the mariner's compass as early as the twelfth century, and their age of exploration preceded that of Europe by a century or so. In the early fifteenth century the great Admiral Cheng Ho reached Africa, and the claim has been made that other Chinese navigators gained the western shores of North America. Those who aspire to flag rank, however, may be grateful that our naval customs, traditions, and usage come from Western rather than Chinese sources, for to become an admiral in Ming dynasty China one had first of all to become a eunuch.

Now if you will accept this outline history of the West, at least for purposes of discussion, let me ask you to consider what the meaning of it all would have been to a nineteenth-century student. Quite obviously, I think it could have first been said that the record showed a succession of political units rising to more or less commanding position before giving way to their successors, and that somehow there seemed a relationship between prowess at sea and prominence in the general scheme of things. The precise nature of the relationship between exploitation of the seas and national power was perhaps a little more complex. But it would have seemed reasonable to say, as a first approximation, that strength at sea meant prosperity through trade and, other things being equal, the more prosperous the community the higher its cultural attainments and the greater its power.

If our enquirer should then have wished to push one step further, and to ascertain what factors in a community were important in permitting it to gain power at sea, he might well have produced a list of factors such as the six postulated by Mahan. These, you will remember, were geographical position, physical conformation, including climate and natural products, extent of territory, number of population, character of the people, character of the government and other institutions.

So far, so good, but once these general categories are established things become somewhat more complex. Changes in technology, slower then than now, could nonetheless seriously modify capabilities, as Medina Sidonia found out when he sailed his armada against England. The two principal strategic resources of the British, in the centuries of their rise to power, were their geographical location and the direction of the prevailing wind. These, taken together, facilitated blockade of continental ports and permitted

Mahan his famous phrase about the "far distant storm-beaten ships" that stood between Napoleon and the dominion of the world. What changes in this picture would come with steam, which blew in no prevailing direction? What changes, more particularly, had Britain not been well endowed with deposits of coal and iron?

Equally important, perhaps, was the way the requirements of policy governed the employment of its instruments. The Roman problem of policing a closed sea was one thing; the Viking custom of raiding coastal and river towns was another; the wars of national states for trade routes were different still. Each made very different demands upon the sailor, or at least upon the admiral. Lessons drawn from one set of conditions might not necessarily be valid for another. And this brings us to the captain Admiral Luce brought to Newport to lecture on these things.

Looking back in later life, Admiral Mahan described himself in 1884 as one who had "grown up in the atmosphere of the single cruiser, of commerce destroying, defensive warfare, and indifferent to battleships; an anti-imperialist, who for that reason looked upon Mr. Blaine as a dangerous man." This was the old American doctrine, yet the man who had grown up with the commerce destroyer was to become the most effective opponent of the *guerre de course;* the man who was indifferent to battleships was to be largely responsible for the biggest building programs in the history of the world. The anti-imperialist became the principal exponent of views which encouraged Germans and Japanese to demand their places in the sun, and which so directed a war for the independence of Cuba that it led, somewhat improbably, to the annexation of the Philippines. How did all of this happen? The answer is one we should all ponder. He read some books.

The summons to Newport to lecture at the Naval War College found Captain Mahan cruising off the west coast of South America. There, while awaiting his relief, he began his reading. At the English Club in Lima he discovered Mommsen's *History of Rome,* and it was Mommsen's account of Hannibal's invasion of Italy by the long march from Spain that first brought vividly to his mind the virtues of command of the sea.

Here was the fundamental insight. How it would be developed depended on further reading, and here three works were of supreme importance: first, *A History of the French Navy* by La Péyrouse-Bonfils; second, *A History of France* by Henri Martin, covering the seventeenth and eighteenth centuries (the same period that was to be dealt with in *The Influence of Sea Power Upon History*); third, the works of Jomini.

Now observe the hazards of book-learning. The source books are all continental European. The period under consideration is a restricted one, that of the Anglo-French wars for empire. It is the period of contending mercantilist autocracies, when international politics took the form of perpetual economic warfare, of restrictive economic policy, of struggle for colonial empire, of blockades and battle fleets. Two heroes emerge from the tale. On the one hand there was the Royal Navy, whose successes (and indeed also failures) "proved" the rightness of its intuitive policies. On the other hand there was Colbert, the great minister of Louis XIV, father of the French navy and organizer of the most rigidly directed state economy of the day who, even if he failed, at least had the right ideas. The ultimate goal of policy was, of course, predominant national power by means of command of the sea.

The great work, perhaps the most important "do-it-yourself" book published in the last hundred years, appeared in 1890 and had, as every one knows, colossal success—primarily in Great Britain, but with Germany, Japan, and the United States not far behind. In the light of its gospel, British wisdom was justified. By its message the kaiser was inspired, as were Theodore Roosevelt and some Japanese, and the course of naval activities for the next generation or so was largely defined. So far as the more remote American past was concerned, however, the effects were rather disheartening, and Truxton, Preble, Decatur, and the rest, while doubtless brave enough, now seemed to have been sadly misguided men. This attitude remains current in the works of many authorities who view the period of the Old Navy as one of almost willful neglect of obvious and available lessons.

It seems to me that there are two alternatives in a situation such as this. Either our early naval policy was wrong, and this is the orthodox opinion, or the standard of judgment applied to it was wrong. Since everybody takes the former view I propose to argue briefly for the latter.

One can take a first step in this direction by pointing out that Mahan's principal lesson—the emphasis on the importance of the battle fleet and on command of the sea—is most helpful to the dominant maritime power, and that weaker nations can find little comfort in it. In a way, it is a sophisticated statement of the old saw that "nothing succeeds like success." This, of course, accounts for the prevalence even after 1890 of other naval schools such as the *jeune école* in France, with their emphasis on the *guerre de course*. It could also account for our own naval history. I think, however, that there is more to it than this, and so I will suggest

that the doctrines of Mahan are basically un-American. This is
so because his doctrines are drawn from just what the colonists
revolted against—a society in which the state, and not the individual, is supreme.

Now this is perhaps not the generally accepted view. I think
most people, if asked what has traditionally distinguished the
American approach to the sea and to naval and maritime affairs,
would think first not of ideological matters but of technical ingenu-
ity, of willingness to innovate, and of skill in the development
of new instruments of navigation and warfare.

There is much to be said for this view. Evidence can be found
to support it in the Dahlgren gun, in Fulton's experiments in steam
propulsion, in the Humphreys frigates, and even earlier in the ingenious attack on British shipping at Philadelphia in 1777 by
means of mines floated downstream. Of this notable event the
best action report we have is a contemporary poem which suggests
quite clearly that such tactics had not been anticipated by General
Howe:

> Sir William he, snug as a flea,
> Lay all this time a-snoring;
> Nor dreamed of harm, as he lay warm,
> In bed with Mrs. Loring.

Overlooking for the moment the question of collaboration, we may
say that the rebels here gained both tactical and technical surprise.
This is certainly important. But while conceding the undeniable
importance of nuts and bolts, it is on the ideological rather than
the technical level that I propose to concentrate.

What are the consequences of the belief in the supremacy of
the individual—the consequences of the idea that all men have
certain inalienable rights that no government may subvert?

I think that we can say that the American Revolution was a
revolution in favor of the theory, and against the practice, of the
eighteenth century. It was not just a revolution for a change in
government, but part of a continuing effort for a change in the
nature of government, from big government to small, from master
to servant. It was part, if you wish, of the first serious effort to
make government wither away.

Too much government by the British brought revolution and
the Articles of Confederation. Too much government, or misgov-
ernment, by the several states under the Articles of Confederation
brought the Constitution with its manifold restrictions on state

powers. Fear of too much government under this new instrument led to the creation and adoption of the Bill of Rights, specifying areas which the general government was not to invade. Although it may seem a little remote, I think all of this had important implications for the American approach to the seas and the world beyond them, in a word for American maritime strategy. And since any armed force reflects the society which produces it, there were also important implications regarding the nature and the employ-ment of the navy.

Let us take a few of these implications. From the point of view that the state should serve and not dominate the citizen—from this idea of small government—there came a fear of standing armies and the executive warmaking power. You can see this in the insist-ence on state control of the militia forces, in the right of the citizen to bear arms, and in the early emphasis on privateering—on warfare, that is to say, conducted by the individual rather than the government. Hence, the reluctance to create a navy; hence, once the American navy was created, reluctance to build a battle fleet; hence, also, the long disinclination to establish any rank higher than that of captain.

In the related area of foreign affairs, this same hostility to the leviathan state can be plainly seen. To a considerable degree, the attempt to cut the English connection came from a desire to cut the link with Europe's wars. There was also the feeling that alli-ances, particularly with great powers, were dangerous, as shown by the reluctance, even during the Revolution when life depended upon it, to go beyond a commercial agreement with France. There was the effort to force upon Great Britain the limitations in the use of naval power inherent in the "free ships, free goods" view of international law. There was the view—not yet dead—that diplo-macy was just another word for skulduggery, and that all America needed abroad was consuls and commercial agents. This last you can see in the writings of Jefferson; you can see it also in the hundred years' delay in establishing the rank of ambassador.

In economic terms, the opposite of statism is individualism. Un-like Colbert and unlike the British Parliament, the colonists knew that in trade both parties profit. The Revolution was largely the result of resistance to measures restrictive of foreign trade. One consequence was a lasting bias against a protective tariff. Another was the fact that the American navy, wholly unlike the navy that Colbert created for France, was the result of individual rather than governmental aspirations. The first frigates were authorized to chastise the Barbary pirates, to open the Mediterranean to the commerce of American individuals and to redeem other Americans who were being held there in captivity. This concern for individual freedom, as well as for individual enterprise, is worth noting: Great Britain, with the strongest navy in the world, only freed her Algerine captives in 1816, and other European states lagged even farther behind.

Although Americans, for both ideological and practical reasons, were opposed to war as something that could threaten freedom both from without and from within, they coupled with this antipathy an acute awareness of the existence of conflict in human affairs. War, well described in the motto cast upon European cannon, was the *ultima ratio regum,* the final argument of kings. As a substitute for this costly and dangerous expedient, Americans relied upon economic pressure—the final argument of the individual—to undercut, if they could, opposed governmental structures by working on the interests of important individuals and pressure groups. Hence nonimportation during the Revolution and embargo during the Napoleonic wars, expedients not quite so silly as some later critics would have us believe; hence also a navy which, designed for police action against pirates, whether in Barbary or the West Indies or the Far East, was used in great power situations for commerce raiding, as with France in 1798 and Britain in 1812. To take on Tripoli or to destroy the ships of the Marseilles and London merchants was within our means, was consistent with our philosophy, and was, or at least ought to have been, effective. To take on the Royal Navy was not.

So much then for ideology as expressed in general attitudes. The question arises now: What did it mean in terms of policy? What were the consequences in general terms for American maritime strategy?

Here, first of all, a warning. Any ideology so opposed to the European state system as the one just described might be expected, and indeed has often been described, as one tending towards "isolationism." There is no question that distance made this heretical kind of practice possible, for distance was a tremendous insulator, but to call it isolationist overlooks two important factors: first of all, the universal nature of the ideology itself, which applies not merely to Americans but to all men; and, secondly, the vital importance to the colonies and to the young nation of an expanded trade.

I would suggest that a more fruitful way of looking at this business would be to consider it an internationalism of those of like interests, plus containment of those too far gone in sin to be redeemed. Or, to put it another way, isolation *of* rather than *from* Europe, with Europe being operatively rather than geographically defined as those great powers which were always broiling.

This idea of isolating Europe, as opposed to that of isolating ourselves, can be seen in our early history, in the efforts to break down the mercantilistic restrictions on European overseas possessions, and in our support, as in Latin America, of revolutions against the home country. The Monroe Doctrine is perhaps the best-known example of this attitude. In its original formulation the emphasis was on their staying out of here. Our staying out of there was largely pumped into it later.

There was originally no idea of going it alone. The Washington administration seriously considered collective action with Sweden and Denmark against British and French interference with maritime commerce. Even earlier, Jefferson (thought by some to have been a great isolationist) had proposed that we league ourselves with the smaller trading powers for common action against the Barbary pirates. Indeed, the unilateral action against Barbary which finally ensued can be seen, not only as reflecting the reluctance of honest freemen to pay tribute to these scoundrels, after the fashion of corrupt Europeans, but also as an effort to limit the power of the warlike European nations by depriving them of these unofficial allies. Benjamin Franklin's remark that "if there were no Algiers it would be worth England's while to build one," is well known.

The consequence, then, of this ideology was a foreign policy concerned with such things as the self-determination of peoples, small government, limitations on warmaking, international intercourse insofar as possible on the individual rather than the governmental level, and multilateral fostering of trade—all based on the belief that such a rational policy was conducive to the welfare not only of Americans but of all mankind. In the export and implementation of this worldview, an export possible only by sea, the navy played a central role, and the nature of the American experiment defined the nature of the navy. Since the aim was not command of the sea but freedom of the seas, the navy was less an instrument of war than an instrument of policy. It was, if one can use a somewhat singular expression, a navy of the Enlightenment.

If this analysis is kept in mind, and if the importance of policy as opposed to war is remembered, then it seems to me that the manifold activities of the Old Navy begin to make real sense. It was in the first instance a police force, engaged in the protection of maritime trade throughout the world. Given this function, and the lack after 1815 of any serious threat to the continental United States, the natural consequence was the organization of permanent overseas squadrons—Mediterranean, West Indies, Pacific, South Atlantic, and the rest. Overseas squadrons need base facilities and these, in the years before the Civil War, we obtained: in the Mediterranean at Port Mahon and at Spezia; in the Far East at Hong Kong and at Macao; on the west coast of South America, prior to the conquest of California, at Valparaiso and Callao.

Like many other institutions, the overseas squadrons survived their real period of usefulness, which ended with the post-Civil War collapse of the merchant marine. The survival of the squadrons accounts in large measure, in view of the lack of overseas coaling stations, for the much-ridiculed return to sail after the Civil War. Whether needed or not, whether we had any trade or not, these squadrons were maintained. In the 1880s domestic considerations were paramount, but in 1882, when the British bombardment of Alexandria set the stage for the occupation of Egypt, the first foreign troops to enter that burning town were not our imperialistic cousins but United States Marines.

Now not only was trade worth protecting; it was also fundamental, both to the existence of the American economy and also to the American idea of a world worth living in, that it be continually expanded. From this fact flowed the numerous negotiations of naval officers aimed at integrating new non-European areas—that is to say, nonmercantilistic, nonstatist, nonprotectionist areas— into the mutually profitable and civilizing network of maritime commerce.

This missionary purpose was fundamental, not only to the war with Tripoli, but to our negotiations with the other Barbary powers. It lay behind the efforts of Commodores Biddle, Crane, and Rodgers to make a commercial treaty with the sultan of Turkey. It governed the actions of Commodore Kearny in China in the 1840s. The opening of Japan, suggested as far back as 1815 by Commodore Porter, was accomplished by Perry with this purpose explicitly stated, as was that of Korea in the 1880s by Commodore Shufeldt. These were a lot of openings for a country of the second rank, and it is worth noting that these were all openings, rather than seizures, of territory. What was wanted was freedom of access, not control.

There are two other ways in which the Old Navy acted as an instrument of policy: one, as a scientific institution adding to the sum total of useful knowledge; the other, as forwarding in one way or another the cause of human liberty and the self-determination of peoples. As regards the former, one thinks at once of the important hydrographic work of Matthew Fontaine Maury and of the various exploring expeditions—the expedition to discover the source of the Amazon; the well-known Wilkes expedition of 1838-42; and saltiest of all, the United States Navy expedition, all members of which were pledged to abstinence from intoxicating drink, which accomplished in 1848 the first charting of the River Jordan and the Dead Sea.

In regard to the latter function—the forwarding of the cause of freedom—a number of events can be cited in which the navy, or people intimately connected with it, were involved. First of all, the modern-sounding question of arms aid to small nations to permit them to maintain their independence. In the 1830s the Turkish navy was rebuilt, after its destruction at the battle of Navarino, by two American naval constructors—Henry Eckford and Foster Rhodes—with continuing technical advice from our chargé d'affaires at Constantinople, Commodore David Porter. Aid to Turkey is no very new thing: two Turkish naval missions visited the United States prior to the Civil War.

In 1848-49 the Germans attempted to accomplish a constitutional federation. The effort ended in failure, but not before serious negotiations had been entered into for the employment of American naval officers to organize the planned new German navy. In the 1870s vessels of the navy of the khedive of Egypt were commanded by Annapolis graduates. The sultan of Zanzibar attempted to defend his possessions by creating a navy by the purchase of surplus Confederate warships from the United States. In 1880 negotiations concerning the improvement of the Chinese navy were held between Commodore Shufeldt and the Viceroy Li Hung-chang.

Distance made us safe, community of mutual aspiration made us trustworthy, our technical skills made us useful. For all of these reasons, then, American help was solicited by rulers of backward countries desiring to modernize and to defend their realms.

Nor was 1848, in Germany, the only time that we showed this interest in popular revolution. Individual Americans in the nineteenth century fought for freedom in almost any revolution one can name. But perhaps the most interesting incident, as showing the effects of ideology on naval officers, occurred in 1860 when Garibaldi's forces, bogged down in Sicily for lack of ammunition, were alleged to have been secretly and unofficially supplied with gunpowder from the magazine of a United States man-of-war.

So much for the old-time American maritime strategy. The basic idea of knitting together a rational world of peaceful development and advancing liberty was and still is a good one. But as usual, with the passing of time, circumstances seemed to alter cases. The world changed.

For one thing, it became clear that Americans had grossly overestimated the possibilities of reforming non-European societies, the possibilities, if you wish, of exporting Americanism to these regions. The cultures were resistant and the military strength of Europe posed a continual threat. Of the three non-Western nations—Turkey, Egypt, and Japan—which made serious efforts to modernize themselves in the course of the nineteenth century, only the last succeeded, protected as she was by her distance from the power centers of Europe.

The second basic assumption on which this old American policy rested—the idea that European great power civilization was hopelessly corrupt and had to be contained in the interests of progress beyond the seas—also required some modification. There had always been an ambiguity in the British position in this scheme of things. The British were the ancestral enemy, but they were also blood brothers and our most important partners in trade. They were one of the powers to be contained and yet, being the principal seapower, they were also a principal agent of European containment. As the peaceful century wore on and as the British went over increasingly to policies of free trade, they became increasingly, in deed if not in word, partners in the American enterprise.

Furthermore, as time went by, these European powers succeeded in reforming and democratizing themselves to an extent undreamed of by the Founding Fathers. Having thus made themselves more acceptable, in one sense at least, they then embarked on a new wave of imperialism which rapidly gobbled up all the remaining blank spaces on the map. By the end of the nineteenth century much had changed: it seemed that democratized or constitutional monarchies could be just as imperialistic as the old mercantilist ones of the century before, while forced-draft industrialization had brought with it a new mercantilist economy with state subsidies and tariff walls.

Nor had the United States entirely escaped this new era. Like the Italians, like the Germans, we too had our war of nationality. As is our custom, it was the biggest, best, and bloodiest war of all. As two important by-products of this Civil War came the disappearance of the merchant marine and the advent of a high tariff policy which, the result of wartime accident, came shortly to be considered the acme of Republican wisdom. In this sense we, too, went mercantilistic, while concentration on internal problems led to neglect of the seas and of what lay beyond them. These, and other factors, fostered a national inwardness, and one consequence was the period of naval decay. It was at this time—the 1870s and 1880s—that it came to be felt that the first qualification of a secretary of the navy was not to have seen salt water outside of a pork barrel.

It is worth noting that this post-Civil War trend toward isolation paralleled a trend in military technology which, for the first time, made isolation feasible. This, of course, was the coming of steam, for when the limited coal bunker replaced the limitless winds, the radius of action was gravely diminished. One can compare the freedom of action enjoyed by de Grasse during the Revolution with that of the unfortunate Admiral Cervera in 1898. The moral here for those who wished to play in these new mercantilist big leagues was to snatch colonies and bases faster than ever, and this, of course, was explicitly stated by Mahan. Indeed, even if we contend that he was un-American in the old-fashioned sense, we must concede that he was wholly in tune with his times.

In this context one can look at the new American navy and observe two things: first of all, in accordance with the new fashion, derived largely from Mahan, it became in short order a battleship navy; second, since nobody ever really faced up to the problem of defense of our Far Eastern possessions, it became, by virtue of limitations of bunkers as well as limitations of ideology, an isolationist one. This, indeed, was made explicit by the Congresses, who were pleased to appropriate money for what they called "seagoing coastline battleships," the idea being that if a captain were kept short on coal he would not involve this country in distant incidents with scoundrelly foreigners.

But while such a navy might be an effective instrument of war in, say, the Caribbean, it was not a very effective or flexible instrument of policy. Conflict, in this new period, came more and more to be considered in polar terms of war and peace; it is worth noting that the years of battleship-building were also the great years of the peace and arbitration movements. What this neomercantilist world meant in terms of naval operations can be simply seen in the contrast between the worldwide deployment of the American navy, in any peaceful year between 1815 and 1890, and Theodore Roosevelt's advice to his successor in the White House: "Never divide the fleet."

Yet in retrospect one may say the basic problems remained largely unchanged, if hidden from the eyes of contemporaries. If the peaceful, cooperative, trading, developing world that Americans had earlier envisaged was to remain even a possibility, the seas had to be kept free for people who were at least relatively inclined this way. It was always in a sense a question of "containment."

In the battlefleet era, from the rise of the German navy to the disappearance of that of Japan, the main problem from our side was to prevent the consolidation of the two ends of Eurasia by warlike powers whose ideas were cast in a different mold. The Caribbean question, although alarming for a time, was never a critical one, assuming the continued existence of the Royal Navy. One may grant that the purpose of containment was, from the American view, somewhat concealed in Monroeist ideology, but the real problem in both world wars was to keep Germany away from the Atlantic and to prevent an imperialist Japan from concentrating her hold on East Asia.

I think we now find ourselves in a third period, and here I find myself being a little un-American in postulating a sort of Hegelian thesis, antithesis, and synthesis.

In the first period—the period of the Old Navy—we had a policy: freedom of the seas, promotion of trade, the peaceful integration and betterment of mankind. The navy was an instrument of that policy. Our power was limited. We did not propose to fight major wars. Command of the sea, insofar as needful, we left to the British to provide, under such restrictions as we could impose through the development of international law.

During the second period—from the building of the New Navy down to the defeat of Japan—we had increasing power. Yet, for whatever reasons, our policy, once we got beyond the defense of our continental possessions, was never a very clear one. It seems that a world divided into many compartments is not an easy one for Americans to deal with intellectually. Increasingly in this period our navy became an instrument of war, useful in emergencies but inflexible in other times.

In the third period things have become mixed. We have great power, yet our policy has been developing rapidly along the old American lines. Now, to keep the freedom of the seas which knits this free world together, we exercise command of the sea. In nineteenth century terms I suppose you could say that our armed forces (no longer only the navy) perform the functions of both the Royal Navy and the United States Navy.

Eighteenth-century ideas of the brotherhood of man persist in this country to a remarkable degree. We have, of course, a very large government in terms of budgets, stenographers, and mimeograph machines. But in the essential point it remains small: it is to serve, not dominate, the individual. Even in some Republican circles it is now permissible to talk of tariff reduction and of promoting international trade, and the barriers between peoples are coming down in other ways.

The artificial and somewhat divisive concept of sovereignty, which the Founding Fathers so successfully concealed and dispersed in our Constitution, is again being concealed and dispersed by alliances and understandings. I think it is perhaps not wholly playing with words to point out that some units of our navy now fly the white ensign and that a good part of our merchant marine navigates under the flags of Panama, Liberia, Norway, and Greece.

Once again, as before the Civil War, the navy is an instrument of policy. Once again we have overseas bases. Underway replenishment has restored to the fleet the range and endurance of the sailing squadrons. Once again we support the less-developed nations, over the whole scale from the states of Western Europe down to the emerging societies of the Orient. We can and do contain the new broiling powers, but while doing so we should remember that this is not the sole end of policy. How, we should ask ourselves, while containing, can we best use our freedom of the seas to develop our better world?

Now all this has been, I am afraid, pretty ideological, and perhaps seems somewhat remote from reality. You may say that ideology is all very well as a means of rationalizing a policy, or of selling it to the electorate, but that the policy itself should be built on facts and not on words. In conclusion, therefore, I would like to submit a brief factual argument which will show, I think, that our present maritime strategy, in its broadest aspects, is almost unavoidable given the international facts of life; and that something very like it would be developing even if this country had not been born on a Fourth of July in the late eighteenth century, attended by a very literate corps of obstetricians who forced the thinking of that period deeply into the national subconscious.

The argument is that of an Englishman, Sir Eyre Crowe, who was for many years one of the important permanent members of the Foreign Office. Written prior to the First World War to describe the situation in his country, it is now remarkably applicable to ours. Crowe's argument, in brief, is a triple one: First of all, that in a very real sense the pervasiveness of maritime power makes the state supreme at sea, neighbor to all other maritime states, and as such likely to excite their hostile fear and combination. Air strength, of course, is relevant in this equation today. Second, that the danger of these combinations could only be averted if the national policy of the dominant naval power harmonized with the general aspirations of mankind and, more particularly, in a world of independent nations, with the interests of as many states as possible. Third, and in conclusion, that since the first concern of any state is the preservation of its independence, Great Britain in her own interest then, and we in our own interest now, must oppose any power which threatens to dictate to the weaker communities of the world.

If this is true, our national strategy is self-defined. Necessity and inclination alike press the same policy upon us. "Go it alone" has no meaning, and the inescapable problem is, as has always been, a double one: to hold the balance against the aggressor and, while containing him, to maintain what is by general consent a viable world outside.

NOTE

Based on a lecture delivered at the Naval War College in 1954.

Mahan on Use of the Sea

William Reitzel

Editor's Note: *William Reitzel is Professor Emeritus of Social Science at Haverford College. He is author of* Major Problems of United States Foreign Policy.

It is not easy to recapture Mahan's idea of maritime power. Although statesmen were supposed to have slept with his books under their pillows, the evidence is that they merely made extracts, summaries, and highly selective formulations of his views, using these chiefly to justify the role of a navy in relation to such national interests and policies as they wished to develop.

Mahan, taken as a whole, was not a thinker whose generalizations were of universal validity. Actually, once the skeleton of his concept was constructed, his preference was to persuade his fellow countrymen to action, applying his generalizations to the analysis of issues and situations of current liveliness. The climate of American opinion was highly receptive, combining as it did a feeling that the United States had a role to play in the world with diverse uncertainties about what that role was or should or could be.

Mahan, along with the bulk of his contemporaries, was exhilarated by the idea of the United States flexing its economic and political muscles in the world arena. He and they saw the country's economic maturation as both necessary and desirable and accepted as natural the implication that this might well involve conflict with other muscle flexers. The basis for acting on this conviction was, according to Mahan, an understanding and proper use of seapower.

The elaborate historical analysis on which this rested was, for the most part, confined to narrow professional circles. For the greater number of his contemporaries, civil and military, Mahan's views were used in fragmented, particular snippets. In the hands of the military, especially those of naval advocates, the selections tended to become formulas, repeated to justify claims that were no longer unhesitatingly accepted by Americans generally. The change can be succinctly illustrated by an exasperated remark of Secretary of War Stimson about ". . . the peculiar psychology of the Navy, which frequently seems to retire from the realm of logic into a dim religious world where Neptune is God, Mahan his prophet, and the U.S. Navy the only true church."[1]

The piecemeal use of Mahan still goes on. Its use, however, after three-quarters of a century, naturally raises the question of the real applicability of Mahan's concept to the present-day international scene. In order to provide a reliable basis for examining this question—if necessary, a basis for rewriting Mahan—the original full-dress thesis must be recovered, recaptured, one might say, from the accumulation of cliché-ridden formulas in which it is now expressed. Thus, the sole purpose of what follows is to get back to the original.

Mahan's methods make it difficult to do this with any assurance. Like many sweeping generalizations, his core idea was not reached after slow and painful research. It sprang from a sudden insight, which research was then brought in to confirm, organize, and expand. Mahan knew what he wanted to prove before he set about proving it.[2] Consequently, Mahan's history is deliberately selective.

A further difficulty is that he expands and develops his basic insight in a variety of contexts—seapower in peace, in diplomacy, in commercial competition, in imperial expansion, in armed conflict—and does not always make it clear in which context he is working at any particular moment. He applies his key generalization somewhat indiscriminately to specific international crises, to the role and policy of the United States, to the world in general. He moves from the present to the past, and back again, with a freedom of analogy that is indifferent to the critical changes that time may have brought about.

In spite of these hazards, a reconstruction is necessary. What follows is such a reconstruction. It is given either in Mahan's own words or in a close paraphrase. The structure has also been given a logical coherence. Except for these devices, the following is Mahan's concept of seapower.

I

The concept of seapower derives, in the last analysis, from Mahan's assumptions about man and society. One quotation is enough to set the tone.

Power, force, is a faculty of national life; one of those talents committed to nations ... no more than any other can it be carelessly or lightly abjured, without incurring the responsibility of one who buries in the earth that which was entrusted to him for use.[3]

The sea is to be considered in the glare of this "actual world." It is a common over which men can pass in all directions. It is a great medium of communication established by nature. But it is important only to the extent that men use it.

Man's interest in the sea, and hence the interest of nations, is almost wholly interest of carriage, that is, trade. Maritime commerce, in all ages, has been most fruitful of wealth. Wealth is a concrete expression of a nation's energy of life, material, and thinking. Given the relation between wealth and maritime commerce, the sea is inevitably the major arena of competition and conflict among nations aspiring to wealth and power.

The capacity to move freely on the sea oneself and to inhibit as need be a similar capacity in others is a critical consideration, for it is a fundamental truth that an ability to control movement on the sea is chief among the purely material elements determining the comparative power and prosperity of nations.

There are four basic requirements for desiring, achieving, and maintaining this freedom of movement. First, a nation must produce and exchange products. Second, shipping, the instrument of exchange, must be available. Third, colonies and bases—at any rate, nationally held points of safety—must be secured to enlarge and protect the operations of shipping. Fourth, armed force—a navy—must be available to guard and keep open communications between these points of safety and the home base.

Put another way, seapower is shipping, bases, and their supporting adjuncts. Seaforce is a navy.[4] When brought into being and kept in motion by national productivity, a system of maritime power exists. Recognition of these interdependent elements is the clue to understanding the policies and actions of nations that use the seas and for whom the use of the sea is vital to national life.

Any nation bordering on the sea can, in principle, aspire to develop a system of maritime power; but, on the evidence of history, only a few have achieved it in fact. Maritime states differ widely in respect to the characteristics that are definitive. These characteristics are geographical location, physical configuration, territorial expanse, size and nature of population, nature of the political system. The value of these characteristics is not absolute. They can and do change with time and circumstances. But, in a general sense,

—If a nation has easy access to the oceans of the world and is, as well, in a position to dominate major trade routes, it is in a position to develop maritime power; and,

—If its physical configuration provides harbors and puts a productive hinterland in easy touch with its sea frontiers, an impulse to develop maritime power naturally follows; and,

—If its territory is extensive or diversified, its population large and active, and its political structure encourages productive energy and gives it an outward thrust, an irresistible pressure to exploit the sea commercially and militarily demands and gets concrete expression in the form of seapower and seaforce.

In short, a true maritime state comes into being; and as long as time, circumstances, and faults of policy do not undermine its advantages, its maritime power increases and becomes its distinguishing feature. Maritime power, at this point, represents a tightly knit system of national activity critically meshed with the life and well-being of the nation.

Great Britain is the classical illustration. Throughout the eighteenth century it was the one nation that consistently earned its wealth in time of peace by seapower and in time of war ruled the sea by virtue of its seaforce. It spread its bases of maritime operation over the globe, bases that would have been valueless if seapower and seaforce had not combined to keep communications open. No one can fail to conclude that British maritime power was, by long odds, the dominating factor in that century of conflict.

The constant exercise of maritime power, however, cannot be equated with peace. Commercial interests, the foundation underlying any maritime country's vitality and power, may tend to deter war from fear of the presumed losses that war might bring, but from its very nature commerce is competitive and engenders conflict by fostering ambitions that lead to armed collision; for when a nation sends its merchant ships abroad, it naturally looks for positions upon which those ships can rest for trading, for supplies, or for refuge. From this follows the need for control, primarily a matter of ensuring communications, which, in turn, multiplies the number of positions needed for the effective exercise of control. Since this progression does not take place in an empty world, the upshot is that a nation's seapower cannot be brought to its full value except by the addition of seaforce.

A navy follows from the existence and needs of peaceful shipping. The extent to which a navy subsequently takes on functions unrelated to the protection of trade, shipping, and commercial communications is a matter to be considered separately. But it can be said in anticipation that if these acquired functions displace or weaken a navy's capacity to fulfill its primary historical role, the maritime power of a nation is correspondingly reduced.

The efficient use and control of sea movement is but one link in the chain of exchange by which wealth accumulates, but it is the central link, for it puts other nations under obligation to the wielder of maritime power. The end result of the sustained exercise of maritime power is a nation geared to the production and exchange of goods, conducting its commerce freely and safely with all continents, possessing a network of colonies and bases, a visible presence of power and force on the high seas and in the world's ports.

When this stage has been reached in the life of a nation, maritime power has become the basis of a system for the creation and expansion of national wealth and greatness. It is now essential to the life of the nation, and its maintenance and advancement are the major considerations of national policy. But the system is now one of immense size and complexity, as well as being extremely sensitive to interruption. It is in connection with the various possibilities and modes of interruption that we come to the navy, that is, to the addition of seaforce to seapower.

The basic relation of seaforce to seapower is simple and direct. The navy springs from the needs of merchant shipping. Though it would be theoretically possible to argue that if maritime commerce ceased to be essential to the life of the nation the navy could disappear, this conclusion is no longer practically tenable. The present realities of international life forbid it.

As things now stand, and have stood historically, the operations of seapower create competition, and competition is always capable of taking an armed form. A navy, accordingly, operates in peacetime to check inevitable disagreements from recklessly growing into armed clashes. At the same time, the necessary readiness to shift from the day-to-day work of deterring conflict to the occasional role of fighting a war has the effect of giving a navy a specialized life of its own with specialized requirements. This can, and sometimes has, tended to obscure the navy's fundamental relationship to seapower.

One must be clear. Navies do not exist merely to fight one another—to gain the sterile glory of fighting battles to win them. They do fight battles, but the purpose of the battle is to maintain maritime power. Thus it follows that in war a navy must aim first and always at depriving an opponent of sea movement in its broadest sense. This is not a matter of casual commerce destruction. It is a matter of strategically dominating superior maritime power.

A fully established maritime nation, if it is attentive to the conditions that dictate its policy, will aim at acquiring and maintaining that superiority in seaforce that enables it to project its seapower to the most distant quarters of the earth. In fact, it might well be argued that such a nation would be well advised to increase its navy above those arms more narrowly styled military.

Once a navy is developed, it begins to take on functions additional to the basic role for which it was created. It becomes an instrument of national policy in the broadest sense. When commerce expands a nation's contacts beyond its shores, a navy converts contacts into interests and consolidates interests as political influence. Statesmen, habituated to the concept and use of maritime power, find in a navy a means of forcible, yet beneficent, adjustment in international affairs, adjustments that would be impossible without the existence of seaforce.[5]

One should note in passing the case of a nation which, though not possessing seapower, nevertheless seeks to develop seaforce. Such a policy, in the absence of a significant seapower interest, inevitably produces the effect of planned aggression. The creation of such a force automatically makes its possessor an uncertain and threatening factor in international life. The policy cannot fail to stimulate vigorous defensive action in already developed maritime states, since it implies not commercial competition, but armed threat.

The essential structure of a system of maritime power can now be summed up. It rests upon a geographical location and a productive society. From this base springs seaborne trade and all its supporting agencies. This is seapower. The net of trade thus built up must then be protected. Seaforce becomes an integral part of the system. The navy, in turn, has its own requirements. These often include the acquisition of extracontinental territory. Such holdings frequently prove valuable as new markets or sources of raw materials, and then navy needs and seapower become reciprocal.

By this time the maritime system has become an intricate mesh of interlocked components, a system in which the parts must be kept in balance if the system is to function effectively and economically. If any one element gets out of balance—if seapower declines, if seaforce expands for reasons unconnected with seapower, if national productivity falters—the system either demands internal adjustment or it loses ground in the international arena. On the other hand, if the system as a whole acquires colonies and bases beyond what is required by the commercial activity of the nation, the expansion becomes a source of national weakness by entailing division of energy and resources in order to maintain communications that have become too complex.

II

The experience of Great Britain brought a new dimension into thinking about maritime policy. In support of Britain's maritime growth there was developed, first, a mobile navy; and, second, local posts along the great sea routes for use as naval bases. In the seas where there were no national possessions, the navy first depended upon friendly harbors, but the uncertainties of such dependence soon led to territorial acquisition. The results were so striking that, in our time, this pattern of expansion is being followed by all states with maritime aspirations.

It will be readily appreciated that the pattern has implicit in it the constant threat of conflict. Furthermore, commercial competition being now worldwide, the regions of potential conflict are now global. Communications on a global scale are inevitably maritime, and conflict over such communications can only mean sea war. This defines the essential task of the navy.

But, to perform this task, an opponent's navy must be dominated. This is the true object to be assailed on all occasions. While fixed positions are important, a fleet itself is the key position. A crushing defeat of a fleet means the ultimate dislocation of an entire system of maritime power, irrespective of the spot on the seas where the defeat is administered. With the elimination of opposing seaforce, the remaining elements of maritime power are wholly exposed to destruction. This is the foundation of control of the seas. From it follows the true objective—the sole end of naval war: to protect one's own commerce and to deprive an opponent of that great resource.

It is vital, in this connection, to disabuse American minds of their erroneous views of the function of a navy. These have historically been held to be: to defend American territory and to engage in commerce raiding. The defensive role was established as guarding coasts and harbors, and, by this measure, the demand was for many small ships, since tonnage put into large vessels could not be subdivided to cover all the points to be defended. The offensive role, commerce-raiding indulged in by individual ships, could not bring down an opponent that had and knew how to use maritime power. It could not be the taking of single ships, or even convoys, that would strike down the money power of such a nation; only overbearing seaforce, literally driving the enemy's flag from the sea, could achieve this end.

Such narrow views ignore a critical fact. Political status in the world, to which a productive nation must aspire, involves activities that imply conflict. The real question for Americans, in respect to a navy, is a clear judgment of the political status they wish their country to occupy, for this determines the character and size of their seaforce. If the United States were an aggressive nation and not simply a maritime state, the measure would be what it desired to accomplish by aggression. But, as a productive society with potential maritime power, the true measure becomes what Americans are willing, or not willing, to concede to other states in a world of commercial competition and potential armed conflict.

It is impossible, as one reviews the part played by maritime power in the history of the prosperity of nations, not to consider the implications for the United States.

The great civilized nations of the world now feel a strenuous impulse to find and establish markets outside their borders. This is leading to manifold annexations and naval agressions. The United States has, as yet, taken no part in this, though it constitutes a situation that adds immensely to American political and commercial anxieties. No one can ignore that seapower and seaforce play a leading part in these developments or that the United States, by its geographical position and by the expansive pressure of its industrial and commercial activity, must of necessity become a participant. Necessity, like a blind force of nature, is sure at last to overwhelm all that stands in the way of a movement of the nation toward acquiring a wider influence in the world.

When the United States is impelled to play its inevitable role in the world, it can no longer leave to one side the need for seapower and its essential adjunct, a navy. The commercial interests at stake are so great and the political considerations so uncertain that the desire to secure advantages leads countries that possess force into a dangerous temptation to use it. Force, when remote localities are concerned, means seaforce.

The development of maritime power by a state should not in itself be considered a threat, since maritime power is not aggressive. In fact, the interests of such a state are generally peaceful, since it acquires too great an interest beyond its shores to wish to expand by force. But the superior influence of such a state is a condition that must be competed for.

The march of events not in the United States alone but all over the world—political events, events economic and commercial—has brought about a necessity for active seapower and larger navies. Furthermore, a world in which other states press competitively to all corners of the globe is one in which it is highly improbable that the seas will ever again be exclusively dominated by a single nation. Unless the United States is prepared to maintain its interests in this kind of world, its people may find themselves excluded. It must either participate or be shut out from the essentials of national growth. It follows that upon the seas must be developed the means to sustain the requisite external policy, and the means are seapower defended by seaforce.

III

There were two basic assumptions by which Mahan viewed international life. The first was that it was a struggle for survival, with the best fitted coming out on top—what we would now call Social Darwinism. The second was that his historical evidence, drawn largely from the seventeenth and eighteenth centuries, provided a complete analogy with the situation of the late nineteenth and early twentieth centuries. The two assumptions reenforced each other and furnished a picture of the world to which the concept of maritime power was totally applicable.

Consequently, Mahan's thinking cannot be fully recreated without adding—again in his own words or by paraphrasing—his view of the world around him.

There is no region so remote or forsaken as not to be possessed by some human group. Many of these groups lack the capacity to organize themselves to hold what they possess. Civilized man— that is, modern, organized, and productive societies—needs and seeks space that he can control and use on his own terms. The chief feature of the present world is the extent to which feeble groups are pressed upon by strong groups.

This pressure is a natural force and, like all natural forces, takes the line of least resistance. When it comes upon a region rich in possibilities but unfruitful through the incapacity or negligence of those who dwell there, the incompetent race goes down before the persistent impact of the superior. The feeble may have a vast preponderance of numbers but, being disorganized, are helpless in the face of organized power backed by material prosperity. To this historically recurring situation is now added steam, which, applied to seapower and seaforce, has multiplied the points of contact between peoples and made proximity a significant characteristic of the times.

In these circumstances, enterprising commercial nations are not content to move patiently. Commercial activities are invariably followed by demands for settled government, for security of life and property. Productive nations proceed to control the centers of commerce they have opened, well aware that control is a powerful influence on the course and security of trade. And trade, as they envisage it, goes far beyond a question of bare existence. It is the source of national wealth and the measure of national importance.

It should be no cause for surprise that the competition for such great prizes results, not only in growing armaments, but in the increase of a national spirit of which armaments are but an expression. Artificial institutions of adjustment may serve to soften somewhat the competition of organized and powerful states, but they are not applicable to the relations of strong advanced peoples and weak backward peoples. The present stage of evolution is one in which enterprising nations will inevitably try to remedy impediments to their growth.

They can scarcely do otherwise. Their leading political interest is to provide and maintain outlets for the productive energies of their people. They will seek solutions by methods that are inherently combative. But, not merely do they confront societies that are resistive, even if feeble; they compete with each other for exclusive positions. Since the underlying spirit is one of domination, the possibility of military action is always present. The world is clearly in a state of transition, and some new order must evolve out of the chaos. But the order that emerges will be desirable and will be desirable and lasting only to the extent that the natural forces involved act freely and find their own equilibrium.

The power to act effectively in these circumstances is no mere accidental attribute. It is the natural concomitant of the qualities that have set advanced nations to expanding and that keep them in active motion. However, the relative ease with which they now deal with weaker opponents is not a permanent condition. The lesson they teach is one that can be learned. Present collisions are bound to become more frequent and more intense.

Since these confrontations are widely scattered and remote from the territories of advanced nations, the capacity to bring, first, influence and then force to bear, is the prerogative of nations that possess maritime power. In fact, this is the means by which they can compensate in distant places for their inferiority in numbers, their disadvantages of position, and their difficulties of communication. In short, this is an age in which maritime power fully predominates. With the extension of overseas commerce, the control and safety of maritime routes and positions have become the first aim of national foreign policies. Consequently, all advanced nations vigorously compete to develop the elements of maritime power.[6]

IV

In anticipation that someone may wish to analyze the applicability of Mahan to the contemporary scene, it will be useful to summarize the concept of maritime power in contemporary terms.

Maritime power is a comprehensive and complex system. In addition to certain attributes that belong to the system as a whole, maritime power contains two subsystems: seapower and seaforce (navy). Each of these subsystems has its specialized attributes. The whole, in its operation, reflects a national maritime policy, that is, maintaining and using maritime power systematically to support and advance national well-being under conditions of international competition.

In detail:

•MARITIME POWER, given the requisite geographical advantages and national will, is generated initially by an economic activity that produces surpluses for exchange. These surpluses must be disposed of and seaborne trade results. The process, however, requires institutional machinery—financing, insurance, exporters, importers, brokers, et cetera—and specialized industry—shipbuilding, ship repair, cargo handling, and the like—for its operation. Without such machinery in place and working smoothly, domestic and foreign markets cannot be developed, cargoes cannot be found, ships cannot be moved, and whatever maritime potential a nation may have cannot become a reality.

•SEAPOWER, given the initial impetus to develop maritime potential, is a specialized subsystem of sea movement. Its basic element is merchant ships (cargo carriers), but their effective use depends upon the buildup of the supporting facilities mentioned above. With these facilities systematically related and employed, seapower can be presumed to compete successfully in world commerce and even to absorb increasing shares of world markets and to gain greater access to raw materials needed by the nation's economic activities. The thesis is that the interplay between the national productive base of the maritime system and the sea movement capacity of seapower systems steadily adds to national wealth and influence, and the end product is maritime dominance. It is open to every variety of interference, from political and economic impediment to armed attack. It requires organized protection.

•SEAFORCE (NAVY), is a highly specialized subsystem geared primarily to the support and defense of seapower. The components of this subsystem need no detailed description here. It should be noted, however, that, like seapower, it has its own specialized shore-based requirements and that these are only to a limited extent interchangeable with those of the seapower system. Furthermore, as the special uses that could be made of seaforce came to be more fully appreciated, policymakers tended to give a lower priority to the primary and original function of seaforce—namely, the support and defense of seapower. The result in time was increasingly to equate the navy with the military elements of national power rather than to see it as a specialized subsystem of national maritime power.

In his view, a maritime power system was an integrated whole, working to forward a nation's position in the world. It worked as a stimulus to a nation's total capacity to produce, to distribute, and to influence in its favor the trend of international life. It used its seapower component offensively in commercial competition. It used its seaforce component defensively in a world of incipient conflict. Mahan's consistent reminder was that he was talking of a tightly knit system of institutions, facilities, commercial carriers, and naval fleets and that no one of these elements of the system could be allowed to become inadequate without the system losing its effectiveness.

NOTES

Originally published in the *Naval War College Review*, May-June 1973.

1. Henry L. Stimson and McGeorge Bundy, *On Active Service in Peace and War* (New York: Harper & Brothers, 1948), p. 506.

2. In 1884, then forty-four years old, Mahan sat in the library of the English Club in Lima. He was reading Theodor Mommsen's *History of Rome* (London: Richard Bentley, 1868). Puzzling over Hannibal's dramatic failure as a conqueror, "... there dawned upon me one of those concrete perceptions ..., that the control of the seas was an historical factor which has never been systematically appreciated and expounded. Once formulated consciously, this thought became the nucleus of my writing for twenty years to come."

3. Allan Westcott, *Mahan on Naval Warfare* (Boston: Little, Brown and Co., 1919), p. 344. The Chief of Mission at a Hague Conference reported on Mahan's contribution to discussion as follows: "... his views have effectually prevented any lapse into sentimentality. When he speaks, the millenium fades and this stern, severe actual world appears."

4. *Seaforce* is not Mahan's term. It is introduced in order to make more explicit Mahan's argument that maritime power is a system formed of distinct but inter-locked elements.

5. Mahan cites the Monroe Doctrine as a case in point. Here a comprehensive position was taken whose only guarantee was naval.

6. To illustrate the fact that Mahan's view was not unique but shared by many of his generation, compare Brooks Adams in his *American Economic Supremacy* (New York: Macmillan, 1900):

Towards 1890, a new period of instability opened. Civilization then seemed to have entered upon a fresh period of unrest, and the inference is that no condition of permanent tranquility can be reached until a new equipoise shall have been obtained.... Conflict will be between the maritime and non-maritime races, or between the rival merits of land and sea transport.

III. War and Maritime Power in the Technological Revolution

Technology and Strategy

John Hattendorf

Editor's Note: *John Hattendorf, a former lieutenant in the United States Navy, is now a doctoral candidate at Pembroke College, Oxford.*

Strategy has always accompanied war. At first it was primitive as man and his weapons were primitive. As social and political organization became more complex, war became more complex. Strategy became an art, necessary not only in war but also in peace as preparedness. Developing this theme, a speaker at the 1912 summer conference at the Naval War College continued:

> The prototype of the Navy, the solitary savage in his canoe, has developed into the modern Dreadnought with its intricate machinery of offense and defense, its thousand souls of diversified specialties, all of which to assure success must be instantly obedient to the mandate of a mastermind.[1]

While this imagery may have brought wry smiles to his audience, his remarks touched on a central issue of professional naval thought in the years between the Spanish-American War and America's entry into World War I. The revolution in ship construction, ordnance, and engineering had begun more than half a century before, but the navy, as a profession, did not immediately come to grips with the new technology. Its impact was deeper than merely providing weapons of greater destructive force or developing new tactics for armored steamships. At the turn of the century, many naval officers began to understand that the developments

111

in technology profoundly affected such broad areas as command and control, personnel training, leadership and morale, as well as the more obvious affairs of research and development, logistics, and tactics. Naval strategy became more than just the physical distribution of fleets. It became the art of comprehensively directing seaborne power. For those who practiced it, naval strategy more so than ever before involved an understanding of the capabilities and limitations of men as well as the machines with which they worked and lived.

Since the 1880s, the navy had advanced dramatically in technology. "The most obvious thing about a Navy," wrote Rear Admiral Bradley Fiske, "is its material: the ponderous battleship, the picturesque destroyers, the submarines, the intricate engines of multifarious types, the signal flags, the torpedo that costs $8,000, the gun that can sink a ship 10 miles away."[2] These were the things that had caught the public eye and had engrossed the attention of naval men. Many of the organizational, administrative, and personnel changes in this period were related to the problem of controlling and utilizing this new equipment.

The appearance of H.M.S. Dreadnought in 1906 relegated all previous battleships to a secondary position. As an archetype of later battleships, the new British ship had a main battery twice as powerful as any other ship in the world. During trials the turbine engines steamed 7,000 miles at an average of 17½ knots and sustained a maximum speed of 21.6 knots, far better than the performance of the ordinary reciprocating engines found in other navies. Dreadnought featured a number of epochal innovations which were soon imitated by navies around the world.[3] The battleship became the best-known and most controversial innovation in the period. In addition, both Britain and Germany developed the battle cruiser: a highspeed, heavy-gunned ship, built to outrun battleships and outgun conventional cruisers. Destroyers evolved from the light torpedo boats of the 1880s and 1890s. Pioneered by the Germans, the battle cruisers maintained their original function for torpedo attacks, but other armament was added. The destroyer soon became an important part of the fleet as an adjunct to the scouting line and a protection for capital ships.

Within the United States Navy, technological events moved rapidly to keep pace with foreign developments. The nation gained the reputation in 1898 as a naval power to be reckoned with. The navy's first submarine, U.S.S. *Holland,* commissioned in 1900, was soon followed by five more, slightly larger boats. Seeing their usefulness, European nations began to order them for their own navies. By 1914 there were forty-nine submarines in the United States fleet. The gasoline engine designed for the original *Holland*-type boats was replaced with the German Diesel engine developed in 1909. At about the same time, a perfected gyrocompass made possible sustained underwater navigation and more accurate torpedoes.

Eugene Ely made successful landings and takeoffs from improvised light decks on navy ships in 1910 and 1911. Also in 1911, Glenn Curtis developed and built the first seaplane. The following year Lieutenant T. G. Ellyson flew a plane launched from a compressed-air catapult, and Rear Admiral Fiske patented the first design for a torpedo plane. The first scouting flight by an airplane in a fleet exercise was made by Lieutenant J. H. Towers in 1913, and in 1914 aircraft were actually used by the navy for scouting and spotting in combat at Vera Cruz, Mexico.[4]

Naval guns grew from the 13-inch and 8-inch guns of *Kearsarge* and *Kentucky* to the *Maryland*'s 16-inch, 45-caliber guns. Fleet target practice was initiated on the Asiatic station in 1902, and significant procedural changes were made in fire control. Armor-piercing projectiles, improved propellants, and "carbonized" armor were introduced and were widely used.[5]

Other important events occurred in the field of communications. The first official radio message from a United States naval vessel was transmitted from U.S.S. *New York* in 1900. By 1904, twenty-four navy ships had been equipped with radio, and nineteen naval radio stations were established ashore. In May 1916 the commanding officer of the *New Hampshire,* while at sea off the Virginia capes, held a two-way conversation with the Secretary of the Navy in Washington and the commandant of the Mare Island Naval Ship Yard in California by using both radio and landlines. Later in the same year, a chain of high-powered naval radio stations was completed with the commissioning of the station at Cavite, Philippine Islands.[6]

In other areas the scope of the new naval technology ranged from water tube boilers, liquid oil fuel, electric logs, research into a cure for tuberculosis in naval hospitals, and a new compass card divided by degrees as well as points, to the feat of towing the floating drydock *Dewey* 13,089 miles from the East Coast to Olongapo in the Philippine Islands.

While the development of the navy's new technology was obvious and dramatic, its ramifications were more extensive than many observers suspected. Technology continued the rapid development which had begun in the early years of the nineteenth century;

the intellectual basis to control such complicated mechanisms was only beginning.

During the last three decades of the nineteenth century much thought was given to the implications of the new technology. In England the Colomb brothers began to examine the broad issue of what a navy should be designed to do. John Knox Laughton in 1874 proposed a "scientific" study of naval history for this purpose.[7] In America, Rear Admiral Stephen B. Luce founded the Naval War College in 1884 for the systematic study of warfare. Luce gathered around him a small, but promising, group of officers. They included French Chadwick, Bradley Fiske, Albert Gleaves, Caspar Goodrich, William McCarty Little, Alfred Thayer Mahan, William L. Rodgers, William S. Sims, Yates Stirling, and Henry C. Taylor. In addition to naval officers, he drew the New York lawyer and Naval Academy professor, J. R. Soley, the army's Tasker Bliss, and also Theodore Roosevelt. Those who gathered at Newport in the 1880s and 1890s were a unique and relatively unknown group of intellectuals and visionaries whose views were not widely shared in the naval service or in the nation.[8] Nevertheless, by the end of the Spanish American War, one of the officers, Captain Mahan, had achieved international renown. In a series of ten books published between 1890 and 1900, Mahan elaborated upon the concept of seapower as a basis for national policy. Using historical examples, he awakened a broad audience to the general purposes and capabilities of naval power in its broadest context. Within the naval service, Luce, Mahan, and their disciples at the Naval War College took a broad view of the profession and avoided a narrow, technical outlook. Mahan focused professional thought on the basic purpose and nature of a naval force. Unlike Great Britain's Sir Julian Corbett, he did not work out a carefully structured statement of maritime strategy. Instead, Mahan provided a necessary intellectual focus and also created a receptive audience for the men who developed and exercised strategic control of the sea.

Because he was the most prominent student of naval power in America, Mahan's work is particularly important in relation to the naval developments of his time. Today the reader of his works is struck by the fact that even in an age of dramatic technological change Mahan could seemingly ignore the complex problems of ordnance, engineering, and communications, all of which absorbed his fellow officers. This was precisely the point of the matter. As he wrote in the Introductory to *The Influence of Sea Power Upon History, 1660-1783,*

It is not therefore a vain expectation, as many think, to look for useful lessons in the history of sailing ships as well as in that of galleys. Both have their points of resemblance to the modern ship; both have also points of essential difference, which make it impossible to cite their experiences or models of action as tactical *precedents* to be followed. But a precedent is different from and less valuable than a principle. The former may be originally faulty, or may cease to apply through change of circumstances; the latter has its root in the essential nature of things. ... Conditions and weapons change; but to cope with the one or successfully wield the others, respect must be had to these constant teachings of history in the tactics of the battlefield, or in those wider operations of war which are comprised under the nave of strategy.[9]

While acknowledging that rapid developments in technology had vastly increased the scope and rapidity of naval operations, Mahan believed that, no matter what equipment was employed in fighting wars at sea, certain basic principles had remained changeless over the ages. These included the function and objectives of a navy in war, the establishment of supply depots and the maintenance of communications between advanced depots and home bases. These principles included consideration of the value of commerce destruction, as well as the necessity of controlling positions through which all traffic must pass. In Mahan's mind, changing technologies in different areas canceled out one another and left only basic issues with which naval men must always deal. Warfare is more an art than a science, and the principles and abstract general maxims which Mahan developed were not mathematical formulae invariably applied as "rules of war." As an "art," the principles of warfare, no matter how sound and generally held, are always subject to qualification when applied in specific situations. Mahan commented in a lecture at the Naval War College,

I must allude to the vast variety of motives, conditions of its age or surroundings which impel Art to its creation. For War these are found reproduced in the variety and changes of weapons from age to age, in the varying character of regions which are the scenes of war, in the temper and organization of the armies. . . .[10]

The man who developed the naval war game in the United States, Captain William McCarty Little, expressed the same concept when he bluntly but ungrammatically told War College students, "a principle applies when it applies and it don't apply when it don't apply."[11] Both men were underscoring the point that abstract strategic or tactical principles cannot be applied in real life. Application requires good judgment, which is based on an intuitive understanding of the spirit of the abstract principles.

Technological knowledge was an essential requirement in the formulation and exercise of naval strategy. An understanding of the tools employed was as important to the tactician engrossed in their use as it was to the strategist concerned primarily with goals and principles. McCarty Little expressed the close relationship between tactics and strategy when he noted,

> ... a fight without a mission, is action without purpose, muscle without brain. And this suggests what to some may seem a somewhat novel view of the difference between strategy and tactics, that is, the "inner" or fundamental distinction: strategy, war from the point of view of the one who has an object to attain, i.e., the planner; and the tactics, war from the point of view of the executor; or something like the distinction between the architect and the builder, the playwright and the actor.
>
> While the distinction between strategy and tactics is clear, yet when it comes down the line between the two, we find that they encroach somewhat upon each other's domain, each tending to overlap. This alone is sufficient to show that their movement of approach is from opposite sides. Strategy is the thought seeking its means of execution, and tactics is the means to carry out the desires of the thought.[12]

To his way of thinking, tactics was the servant of strategy. No tactical problem had meaning without a strategic setting. No strategy could develop successfully without reference to tactics.

The United States Navy was slow in creating an effective organization for implementing such ideas. Up to the 1880s no centralized planning or coordinating activity existed, other than the Office of the Secretary of the Navy. The chiefs of bureaus under the secretary tended to quarrel rather than to cooperate. They were characteristically more interested in their specialties than in efficient, central direction during wartime. The temporary changes in organization instituted by Secretary Gideon Welles and Assistant Secretary Gustavus Fox during the Civil War were quickly abandoned at the end of the war. Not until the 1880s was a successful attempt made to coordinate the activities of the bureau chiefs. The Office of Naval Intelligence was established in 1882 under the Bureau of Navigation and charged with the mission of gathering information in peace and war. Seven years later the Bureau of Navigation was given the additional responsibility of supervising the fleet.[13]

This increasing general awareness of the need for planning and coordination coincided with the establishment of the Naval War College and Admiral Luce's desire to *"raise naval warfare from the empirical stage to the dignity of a naval science."*[14] Luce's own writings on naval administration and organization stressed the need for an organization which could effectively control the navy in rapidly changing wartime conditions. Captain Henry C. Taylor, while president of the Naval War College from 1893 to 1896, instituted studies of the German General Staff, whose strategic planning had brought about the defeat of France in 1870. These studies resulted in recommendations to combine the functions of intelligence gathering, war planning, and general staff duties into a single coordinating body. These recommendations found little support in Washington. Prior to the Spanish-American War no effective coordinating body or war planning activity existed. In 1891 Mahan prepared "plans of operations in case of war with Great Britain" in conjunction with Secretary of the Navy Benjamin Tracy's "secret strategy board."[15] Five years later, Lieutenant William W. Kimball in the Office of Naval Intelligence prepared a general war plan for war against Spain. At nearly the same time, an *ad hoc* board appointed by the Secretary of the Navy also developed plans for war with Spain. Throughout this period, students at the Naval War College continued to deal with the problem of war with Spain in their solutions to the annual problems.[16] While these plans reflected some of Mahan's theories on blockades, supply routes, and Kimball's plan even foreshadowed Admiral Dewey's victory at Manila, none of them were backed by a comprehensive doctrine and supported by an administrative organization which would allow effective implementation. Nevertheless, these plans are interesting examples of the growing trend to see warfare on a broader scale. They are the earliest attempts to apply theory to practice.

Secretary of the Navy John D. Long established the General Board of the Navy on 13 March 1900. Conceived by Rear Admiral Henry C. Taylor as an organization which would eventually evolve into a general staff of the German type, the board consisted of the Admiral of the Navy, who acted as president, the chief of the Bureau of Navigation, the chief intelligence officer and his principal assistant, the president of the Naval War College and his principal assistant, and three other officers above the grade of lieutenant commander. The board's purpose was to "ensure the efficient preparation of the fleet in case of war and for the naval defense of the coast."[17] Specifically, Secretary Long wrote Admiral of the Navy George Dewey, the General Board was to devise plans which would employ United States naval forces to the best advantage, to organize in peace a proper defense for the coast, including the effective use of the naval reserve and merchant marine, and to develop an effective cooperation with the army. The development of detailed war plans, the selection of these sites, and the observation of foreign naval activities in relation to American planning and capabilities were among the important functions of the new board.[18] Throughout this period the General Board continued to provide guidance in war plans and recommendations for the growth of the American fleet. With the assistance of the Naval War College, the General Board was capable of broad reflection on the purposes, capabilities, and disposition of the United States Navy.[19]

Following the initial impetus of men such as Luce and Henry C. Taylor, committees such as the Moody Board and the Swift Board advised the Secretary of the Navy to reorganize the service. A tentative staff organization was established in 1909. It was strengthened in 1915 with the creation of the Office of the Chief of Naval Operations. With a centralized organization directly related to the General Board, the Secretary of the Navy, backed by responsible professional advisors, could ensure a continuity of policy, while still maintaining firm civilian control.[20]

Significant patterns developed at the Naval War College which paralleled the developments in naval organization in the Navy Department. In addition to the better-known reforming leadership taken by Admirals Luce and Taylor, which complemented the publicist and theoretical writings of Alfred Thayer Mahan, there were two additional factors: war gaming and the development of a philosophy for the military planning process.

A medically disabled navy lieutenant, William McCarty Little, living in Newport, R.I., lectured at the Naval War College, where he advocated the implementation of Sir Philip Colomb's concept of a naval war game which had been introduced into the Royal Navy in 1878. Neither Colomb nor McCarty Little were originators of the naval war gaming concept. As long ago as 1790 the Scottish merchant and etcher, John Clerk of Eldin, had publicly issued his famous work *An Essay on Naval Tactics*. In developing what became the standard text for tacticians in both the United States and Great Britain, Clerk used small ship models which he constantly carried in his pocket, "every table furnishing searoom" for his experiments. War games had been used much more extensively in the army. Both the British and American armies had been influenced by the German *Kriegspiele.* Major W. R. Livermore wrote the first American work on war gaming in 1879. The following year Lieutenant C. A. L. Trotten devised a series of war games for national guardsmen. At Newport, McCarty Little, then a permanent member of the Naval War College staff, perfected his system of naval war gaming. Under the presidency of Henry C. Taylor, the games became a regular part of the War College curriculum in 1894: As devised by Little, the war game became a valuable analytical tool which could readily be used by all ranks and could be made to represent any type of fleet or naval force. Despite its apparent limitations, the naval war game was an attempt by which theories of warfare could be tested in the light of contemporary and changing technology.[21]

At the end of the first decade of the twentieth century, the Naval War College borrowed another concept from the army: the "applicatory system." This method of teaching assumed that military principles were best learned by their application, rather than by the study of abstract principles alone. "Map maneuvers," war games in the tradition of the *Kriegspiele,* were used in conjunction with "rides" in which historical, tactical, strategic, and staff problems were solved on the actual terrain of the countryside. In the "rides," the troops were imaginary, but by using the physical contours of the land around them, students learned the relationship between the map and the terrain, a planning tool and an environment.[22]

The applicatory system consisted of three major parts: the estimate of the situation, the writing of orders, and the evaluation of the plan through war gaming or exercises. The "estimate" concept provided a structure to analyze a strategic problem. First, the mission of an operation, the position and strength of both sides were considered. Then a plan could be developed. The second step was writing orders to carry out the plan of action. It led to the establishment of a doctrine by which orders could be effectively passed from one level of command to another. This doctrine permitted the elimination of nonessential details from the orders of higher level officers to more junior officers. The result was maximum tactical initiative. In effect, this approach challenged the traditional demand for complete and absolute obedience from subordinates. It recognized the impracticality and inefficiency of attempting to control large and complex forces directly from head-quarters. This doctrine increased the responsibility of subordinate officers, by relying upon them as rational and capable men to further the known intentions of their superiors.[23] As Colonel G. F. R. Henderson put it in his 1905 work, *The Science of War:*

> ... no order was to be blindly obeyed unless the superior who issued it was actually present, and therefore cognizant of the situation at the time that it was received. If this was not the case, the recipient was to use his own judgment, and act as he believed his superior would have directed him to do had he been aware of how matters stood. ...[24]

The basic ideas of the applicatory system came directly from the German General Staff. In this country the army studied them first. In 1906 Major Eban Swift published his *Field Orders, Messages and Reports,* and in the same year, Major C. H. Barth published his translation of General Griepenkerl's *Letters on Applied Tactics.* In 1909 Captain Roger S. Fitch wrote *Estimating Tactical Situations and Composing Orders.*[25] These three works had a great influence at the Naval War College, where they were often cited as sources in lectures and studies by naval officers.

When Captain William L. Rodgers became president of the Naval War College, the course of study was reformed to include these new ideas derived from the army. The "estimate of the situation, the order form," and war gaming all intermeshed in a new direction for the navy. As one contemporary noted, "a great white light broke on the service, especially in 1912 when the War College first laid emphasis upon the importance of doctrine."[26]

Shortly after the innovation of these new concepts at the Naval War College, a dramatic change was seen in the war plans produced by the General Board. Previously war plans had consisted of charts and collected data on specific areas of strategic importance. In 1904 Army Chief of Staff Lieutenant General A. R. Chaffee proposed to the Joint Board that the army's General Staff and the navy's General Board prepare a series of war plans for joint use. The "Color Plans" developed from this proposal: *Blue* indicated the United States, while *Orange* meant Japan; *Black,* Germany; *Green,* Mexico; *Red,* Great Britain; *Indigo,* occupation of Iceland; *Tan,* intervention in Cuba; *Violet,* intervention in China; *Gray,* occupation of the Azores; *Brown,* maintenance of internal security in the Philippines, et cetera.

For the most part these plans were little more than abstract exercises and had little relation to international affairs and actual events.[27] Even so, both the Orange plan for war with Japan and the Black plan for war with Germany were frequently revised and kept current with the international scene. By 1913 the basic principles of this type of planning were being used in both the army and navy. The revised versions of the Orange and Black plans increasingly reflected the concepts of the "estimate of the situation," and the "order form." At both war colleges, war gaming had become more important as a testing device for these national strategic plans, as well as remaining an educational tool for officers. By these means, the services were developing broader conceptions of military and naval power. At the same time, they were creating methods by which these conceptions could be used to establish flexible control of military and naval forces. The use of the applicatory system and the naval war game, together with a growing understanding of the political and economic implications of warfare, helped officers to grasp the intellectual concepts pertaining to their profession.

Understanding a problem within its own context and in relation to other influences affecting it is not a concept unique to the systems analysts of today. It is an old idea in military and naval affairs. In 1916 Bradley Fiske wrote that

> ... a machine is in its essence an aggregation of many parts, so related to each other and to some external influence, that the parts can be made to operate together to attain some desired end or object. From this point of view, which the author believes to be correct, a baseball team is a machine, so is a political party, so is any organization.[28]

Strategy is concerned with all-encompassing direction. Its work is threefold: to design the "machine," to prepare it for war, and to direct its operations in battle. At the very outset, strategy must take account of all relevant aspects.[29]

Fiske described it this way:

> ... we must admit that as surely as the mind and brain and nerves and the material elements of man must be designed and made to work in harmony together, so surely must all the parts of any ship, and all the parts of any Navy, parts of material and parts of personnel, be designed and made to work in harmony together; obedient to the controlling mind, and sympathetically indoctrinated with the wish and the will to do as that mind desires.[30]

Such a notion was not unique to Fiske. McCarty Little in 1913 had even used the same imagery when he discussed the philosophy of the order form before the summer conference at the Naval War College. "We have noted that the order form was a complete plan of action. The different agencies are the different parts of a machine, and for the machine to work satisfactorily, every piece must do its part. Solidarity is the essential quality."[31]

Inevitably differences of approach developed. One approach was to emphasize the objective and then to tailor the means to fit it. The other approach sought to tailor the objective to the means available.[32] These two approaches to war planning were reflected in a criticism of the Black plan made by a staff officer in the Navy Department. In an undated memorandum signed only "McK." the officer protested that "this is not a Plan but an Estimate of the Situation upon which a Plan would be based. A preliminary study leading to a decision but not a Plan to carry out a decision."[33]

This divergence between those who claimed precedence for the overall concept and those who stressed the technical capabilities of the available resources was recognized early by Commander Vogelgesang in the earliest exposition of the "estimate of the situation" in its naval context. He warned that the two points of view were complementary, not opposing. "knowing the Art is common ground for us all," he wrote, "knowing our tools is our especial science; but each with his own tools may become better able to apply them to the tasks cooperatively, if each is well grounded in this knowledge of the Art."[34]

The blending of "art" and "science" in war planning can be seen in a variety of ways. The work of historians such as Mahan and Corbett had its own special place. The impact of their writings was more than esoteric, for they had a direct influence. The 1911 Orange plan, for example, contains a discussion of the possibility of a Japanese invasion of the American mainland. To support their contention that such an invasion would obviously be doomed to failure, the strategists cited "an established military maxim, that it is the weaker form of war to project the campaign into the theater where your enemy is strongest." A full understanding of military power "would seem to brand the conception (of invasion) as too fantastic to be seriously contemplated by Orange." The writers of the Orange plan felt that it was the historian, Sir Julian Corbett, who, in his *England and the Seven Years War,* had stated the principle most adequately. It was to him that they turned as an authority on this point.[35]

The degree to which the strategist was also believed to be a technician is difficult to gauge. As many naval leaders pointed out, the typical naval officer, totally involved in the technical details of his profession, failed to see the broader issues.[36] The opposite was also true: the strategists could not forget the tools which would be used. In lectures at the Naval War College, Mahan noted:

War is a tremendous game of skill and chance combined. The artist, to recur to my definition, may form the noblest conception, his skill may be of the highest order, and the refractory and uncertain character of his materials may defy all his efforts, a chance slip of his instrument may destroy the work of months.[37]

The painter and the sculptor, likewise in realizing their conceptions, must submit to the conditions—too often, alas, the limitations — imposed by the materials with which they work. These are the same for the veriest dauber as they are for a Raphael; they are stamped and branded by that stolid immutability of which Science boasts in the realm of Nature.[38]

The technical considerations with which strategists became concerned involved nearly every aspect of naval life. At the establishment of the General Board in 1900, Henry Taylor had carefully pointed out to Secretary Long and Admiral Dewey the dangers of becoming too engrossed in technical problems.[39] Yet, as other commentators have noted, technical considerations were necessary for the success of the broadest strategic outlook.

Dewey protested in 1909 to the secretary that a balance between designers and users had not been achieved. "The General Board believes it to be its duty," he wrote, "to invite the Department's attention to the fact that there is not ... anything that insures reference of the details of military features as they are developed in the elaboration of the designs and in the building of the ships to seagoing officers for their comment and recommendations." In order to ensure that all fleet ships were well built, Dewey recommended that details affecting the military nature and operational capability of the navy ship be submitted to a board of experienced men for review. Dewey was especially concerned with the development of ordnance, fire control, armor, torpedo installations, ammunition stowage, and anything else which affected the command and control of the ship such as steering gear, compartmentation, accesses, interior communication, coaling plans, ash handling, and small boat stowage.[40]

With any growing technology the problem of invention, research, and development naturally arises as a related function. However, in an international situation in which technology is an object of competition, the development of new machines becomes an area of prime concern. Admiral Sir John Fisher, while commander in chief of the British Mediterranean fleet in 1901, noted that the design of fighting ships *"must follow the mode of fighting instead of fighting being subsidiary to and dependent on the design of the ship."*[41] In other words, Fisher believed that the technology of ship design must be attuned to and directed by military requirements. The United States Navy, however, was not yet organized adequately to handle this sort of fundamental direction. The General Board recommended as late as 1909 that the details of ship design be submitted to a board of officers for precisely the reason Fisher gave. Research and development related to strategic concepts began rather slowly. For example, in 1903 the General Board discovered that no satisfactory method had been devised for mountings in undeveloped areas. The board's only recourse was to request that the Bureau of Ordnance be "invited" to investigate the problem and have the marine battalion in Annapolis make a practical test of prototype equipment.[42] A few months later the General Board reviewed the problem of obtaining proper optical glass for telescopic gunsights. Dewey lamented to the secretary:

> One of the serious difficulties in this matter is the lack of expert knowledge on the part of instrument makers in this country; the best of them being very hazy as to the actual power of telescopes which they supply. Quite recently a large contractor in buying a lot of telescopes for special purposes received one of them having a power of 4½ diameters when the contract called for 8, and the maker, one of our best opticians, seemed entirely unable to understand the criticism or to locate the cause of failure. It seems a fact that we must go to Berlin for expert opinions about this topic.[43]

The result of this organizational deficiency was that the United States did not have a research and development program which would be guided by the necessities of warfare. For example, in 1908 Commander A. L. Key, a former naval aide to President Theodore Roosevelt, reviewed the construction progress of the battleship *North Dakota* in the Fore River Shipbuilding Company at Quincy, Massachusetts. Horrified by the design defects, he wrote the secretary of the navy, pointing out the flaws he observed and recommended specific changes. At the instigation of the president's naval aide, Commander William S. Sims, President Roosevelt directed the secretary of the navy to convene an investigating committee composed of the General Board and the students and staff of the Naval War College to consider Commander Key's remarks. The final report of the "Battleship Conference" covered many problems. Two of the subcommittees specifically noted in their deliberations that American designs should never be allowed to fall behind the progress of other nations.[44] Only the president of the Naval War College, Rear Admiral Caspar Goodrich, expressed disappointment in the United States Navy's record in making an original contribution to battleship design:

> The evidences are unmistakable of the manner in which this design was reached. Its object is as plain as a pike-staff—to be just a little better than some particular foreign design—to see John Bull, for example, and go him one better . . . They preferred to ignore the plain teachings of naval history, they built along narrow and preconceived lines, they failed to deal with their task in a broad and enlightened manner.[45]

Bradley Fiske in 1907 charged that the navy's "ultraconservatism" retarded the adoption of new mechanisms. Although much of his discontent arose from the fact that many of his own inventions had not been accepted by the service, it was not unique. William S. Sims had experienced much of the same difficulty in the United States Navy as had Sir Percy Scott in the Royal Navy in his efforts to improve naval gunnery. Fiske's remedy was to establish an "experimental department" which would have the duty of improving old appliances, inventing new ones, and examining the schemes of others. He pointed out that such an organization had been used successfully by large business corporations. Such a department, as Fiske conceived it, would be a function of a general staff that directed the navy as a whole and guided the various components of the service.[46] As the Secretary of the Navy's Aide for Operations, Fiske several times urged establishment of a board of invention and development.

Shortly after Fiske left this post, Secretary of the Navy Josephus Daniels established the Naval Consulting Board.[47] Daniels wrote to Thomas Edison on July 7, 1915, to ask him to head the new board, the first duty of which would be to consider countermeasures for that "new and terrible engine of warfare," the submarine. "One of the imperative needs of the Navy in my judgment," Daniels wrote,

is machinery and facilities for utilizing the natural inventive
genius of Americans to meet the new conditions of warfare as
shown abroad . . . . With a department composed of the keenest
and most inventive minds that we can gather together, and with
your own wonderful brain to aid us, the United States will be
able to meet this new danger with new devices that will assure
peace to our country by their effectiveness.[48]

To an enthusiast such as Fiske, the application of new mechanisms was the navy's greatest glory. Writing in retirement at the
Naval War College in 1916, Fiske exulted, "The Navy more than
any other thing, will give opportunity for mechanisms and to
mechanism. Far beyond any possible imagination of today, it will
become the highest expression of the Genius of Mechanism and
the embodiment of its spirit."[49]

Not all naval thinkers were willing wholeheartedly to accept
Fiske's implicit assumption that technology per se was the ultimate measure of a navy. A controversial individual to begin with,
Fiske's penetrating and often unorthodox observations were not
always accepted. However, as Aide for Operations (1913-15) and
president of the United States Naval Institute (1911-1923), his
ideas were widely circulated and debated.

Some members of the General Board believed that naval technology should not be measured in absolute terms, but rather in
terms relative to other nations. The executive committee of the
General Board concluded in a confidential memorandum on 6 August 1915 that "the phenomenal and unprecedented progress in
naval development made by other powers, therefore, subordinates
consideration of the ultimate strength of the United States fleet
as recommended by the General Board to that of relative
strength." The committee felt that this conclusion was clearly illustrated by the fact that Germany's great merchant marine and
powerful navy had been driven from the seas because it was "inadequate" to cope with the navy of Great Britain.[50] Only the German
submarine had demonstrated the potential to operate effectively,
which meant the technology of the British opponent was less capable of meeting that particular challenge. The point of relativity
of naval technology was dramatically underlined in May of 1916
when a numerically superior British force faced a highly efficient
German battle fleet at Jutland and fought to a draw.[51] There was
little difference in the technological development of the two fleets.
Neither side had an advantage. If the balance were tipped either
way, it would be because of other factors. Professional thinkers

of the day began to realize that when opposing technologies had similar capabilities, the difference between victory and defeat lay with men, not machinery. Success would rest on the coordinated ability to manage an enterprise, to control specific weapons, and to develop a strategy.

Recognizing the importance of management and logistics in this problem, one officer detected in 1916 a change in the relative importance of the factors involved in war, a change not entirely realized by those vitally concerned with the problem. Before, it had seemed a question of generalship, and numbers of men that determined victory, but "now surely it is no disparagement to the skill of the strategist, to the vigilance of the tactician, or to the valor of the soldier in the ranks, to say that victory will rest with that side which can maintain the combat more vigorously and for the longest time."[52] While this opinion might not have met with total professional agreement among those who advocated moral courage as the determining factor in war, few would deny that the problem of logistics was crucial to the issue.

Commander Vogelgesang attempted to impress upon his lecture audience at the Naval War College the practical importance of this aspect of warfare. Logistics, he noted, had no direct relationship to tactics, but it is the dynamic force behind strategy. He felt that it was somewhat trite even to point out that "Material is soulless; it cannot be pushed to an endurance beyond that which the mind of man designs for it." Yet, Vogelgesang really wondered if naval men fully realized the obvious. Is the navy "prepared to say that the *being able to* is harmonized with the wishing ...?[53] The most artful strategy, supported by the highest order of valor and courage, but lacking a sound logistic understanding, "is only a phantom that lures *disaster, defeat,* and *disgrace.*"[54]

Others noted that modern warfare had developed into a national and an industrial undertaking rather than an undertaking of a specialized group of military experts. Warfare in this new era involved the organization of every detail and drew upon every resource in the nation.[55] Much of this organization would be in the realm of logistics and preparedness. Preparedness for war, the ability to mobilize military forces and equipment quickly and then to support them, is crucial to survival. The nation which has used peacetime to equip her fleet and to ensure its readiness as an offensive weapon at the outbreak of war has added materially to its chances for success, particularly if the enemy has been negligent.

Building a carefully balanced fleet demanded understanding a potential enemy's fleet and its capabilities. While navalists and their associates directed their attention to the international battle-ship-building rivalry, the strategists who planned for war knew very well the need for a strong and balanced naval force. Paymaster General T. J. Cowie noted that

> ... the auxiliaries of a fleet can truly be said to be as necessary to the battleship and cruisers, as Logistics is essential to Strategy. Embracing as they do, the colliers, fuel ships, transports, despatch boats, scouts, aeroplanes, etc. they represent the arteries that furnish and renew the speed and battling power of the fighting ship.[56]

Admiral Dewey wrote the Secretary of the Navy in 1910 that America's international commitments, her obligation to uphold the policies of the Monroe Doctrine, the Open Door, and the neutrality of the Panama Canal required an efficient and balanced fighting fleet with "fighting adjuncts" as well as auxiliaries. "The battleship fleet without its destroyers, repair ships, scouts, transports, supply ships, colliers, hospital ships, etc. is not complete, for it cannot keep to the sea continuously unless it carries its base with it and is accompanied by the train necessary for this purpose."[57] In the eyes of the General Board, strategists needed to understand the use and function of each type of ship and how these complemented one another. They needed to visualize the actual operational requirements of each type and to comprehend the technical basis of employment and support.

As naval officers dealt with the problem of coordinating technologies and bringing them into a complementary balance, they discovered that technology had intruded into the very execution of command. Communication by electromagnetic means threatened the efficiency of the command structure and the relations between men. In a letter to McCarty Little, Captain William L. Rodgers noted that "modern improvements in communications, typewriter, telegraph, telephones and radio all tend to centralization. We cannot dispense with any of them and yet ... both responsibility and unity of control and plan tend to disappear."[58] Rodgers went on to note that the Secretary of the Navy *thinks* he is in control since he is continually signing orders, but real control remained in the hands of an unknown clerk or junior officer who prepared the correspondence. With the delegation of this function to unrelated subordinates, each dealing with his own specialty, there appeared a loss of overall planning and a disorganized product. "No one is in charge of putting a given task through as a whole; and so we have the familiar order, counter order, dis-

order."[59] Rodgers was not alone in detecting the dangers of centralization and the detrimental aspects of long-range communication.
Secretary of the Navy Daniels himself noted that

> ...on one proposal there is another gesture about a system of
> communications which is capable of such large expansion, and
> that is that the temptation will be ever present to rely on such
> a system for momentary communication or orders instead of
> the development of doctrine and the reduction of the need for
> any system to a minimum.[60]

There were times, of course, when direct communication was useful and effective. Admiral Dewey remarked that "there is a psychological effect of direct personal communication between responsible officers which it is desirable to have the facilities for carrying
out in terms of great emergency."[61] Few observers recognized the
paradox of rapid, long-distance communication weakening the
command structure. The novelty and advantages of direct communication with the Navy Department and high-level commanders overshadowed a serious threat to efficiency. The vision of concentrating all decision making power in a single person or office
foreshadowed a faltering, inefficient executive and an uncontrollable bureaucracy. The unregulated centralization of command
would withhold initiative from subordinates, thus denying the full
exercise of judgment, expertise, foresight, and response in every
echelon. Although not designed specifically to handle the problem
of modern communications, the concept of the "order form" could
be easily adapted to maintain a decentralized organization and
still take advantage of the rapid exchange of information.

The Tampico incident illustrated another aspect of the problem
in command relations. At that time in 1914 Tampico, Mexico, was
in the throes of a revolution. On 9 April a whaleboat with an
officer and eight sailors was sent ashore from the U.S.S. *Dolphin*
to purchase gasoline for Rear Admiral Henry T. Mayo's barge.
While at the wharf, local guardsmen seized these uniformed men.
When the local military commander learned of the arrest of American sailors, he immediately released them and sent a personal apology to Admiral Mayo on board the *Dolphin*. Admiral Mayo, however, considered that the seizure of men from a boat flying the
American flag was a hostile and inexcusable act. He demanded
that a formal apology be issued, that the officer responsible for
the seizure be punished, and that the American flag be raised pro-
minently and saluted with twenty-one guns. In addition, the Mexi-

cans' reply was to be received and the salute fired within twenty-four hours. In Washington, President Wilson seized upon the admiral's ultimatum as an affair of national honor. The failure of the Mexicans to comply led Wilson to ask Congress for authority to use armed force against the Mexican forces under General Huerta. A minor incident had become a *casus belli.*[62] President Wilson and his cabinet completely supported Admiral Mayo's initiative. Although there was no question of improper conduct on Mayo's part, such incidents clearly raised the question of the level at which a particular type of decision should be made. Mayo had assumed responsibility for an area of policymaking that properly lay at the highest level of government. As a result of this incident and because modern communications were available, Secretary of the Navy Daniels changed article 1648 of Naval Regulations on 15 September 1916 to require a commander to communicate first with the Navy Department before issuing an ultimatum, "except in extreme cases where such action is necessary to save life."[63]

The dangers of overcentralization were matched by the other extreme of ineffectiveness resulting from fragmented control. "From all this we are rescued," wrote Captain William L. Rodgers, "if we appreciate the methods of problem solving, estimate of the situation and order writing."[64] In other words, to avoid the extremes which the new communications technology thrust upon the navy, it was necessary to understand the kinds of decisions which should be made at each level of command and to issue orders and commands on that basis. For the system to be effective, each level of command must display both an obedience to the direction it received and, at the same time, be able to exercise initiative within its own realm of responsibility. Good organization required a clear apprehension of a subordinate's area of discretion and the superior's sphere of action. As William McCarty Little put it,

> the expert is probably superior to the employer in ability to exercise the expert's art; but the employer does not feel in any way humiliated by employing him to exercise his skill . . . therefore there should be no squeamishness in giving to a subordinate all the latitude in execution which his capacity and the requirements of the problem permit.[65]

The problem arising from technology could be controlled through human leadership and discretion. It was a problem of men, not of machines.

The importance of men over machines was emphasized when

Professor Hugo Munsterberg lambasted "the world of newspaper readers" who were hypnotized by the naval machinery of the day. He told the students of the Naval War College in 1912,

> ... in the midst of this unquestioning enthusiasm for the material development of the physical progress of the battleship, you stand for the conviction that it is after all the man, man's thought, and man's emotion, and man's will which is of decisive importance. You do not submit to the popular prejudice which expects success only from the marvels learned of steel and power and electricity. You have learned too well the great lesson of history which demonstrates that throughout four thousand years the victory has been with the ships who were fit to win. It is not true that fate has been with heavy guns; it has been with the great minds. The knowledge of the ships and the armament becomes a living power only if it is embedded in the understanding of strategies and grand tactics, and they would be empty if the psyche of man were not acknowledged as their centre.[66]

Recognizing that even in a highly technological era it is human understanding that links together all the elements of a navy, professionals went further to ask what kind of individual man was required for this work. They dealt with the issues of proper training and the type of knowledge naval men should have.

In a highly technical society it seems natural that there would be a tendency for specialization among individuals. Even so, the General Board and other officers in the navy continually rejected recommendations for further specialization. It was evident to the General Board in 1909 that the navy would continue to need a large number of officers who were thoroughly trained and highly specialized in engineering to perform the duties of inspection and design. They agreed that the operation and care of machinery is different from its design and construction. Such tasks might be successfully performed by men not qualified as designers. The military advantage of having all the duties involving the management and control of the ships and their preparation for battle performed by one body of officers, the board felt, was so great that it should be regarded as fundamental and thus, should not be changed.[67] The General Board strongly believed that the determination of naval policy, fleet composition, and the strategic and tactical qualities of ships should always lie in the hands of the "military seagoing man." Control of the military features in warships could never be achieved if the seagoing man simply accepted what shore-based experts supplied him. Additionally, the board strongly believed that shipboard engineer officers should not be specialists in the single field of engineering. The advantage of discipline, military efficiency, and professional development was far greater if well-rounded officers of the line fulfilled this function.

Characteristically, Bradley Fiske wrote,

> ... he who sails the sea and braves its tempests, must be in heart and character a sailor—and yet he who fights the scientific war-craft of the present day cannot be merely a sailor like him of the olden kind, but must be what the *New York Times,* a few years ago, laughingly declared to be a combination quite unthinkable, "a scientific person and a sailor"[68]

W. B. Norris, an instructor at the United States Naval Academy, explored Fiske's argument. In his mind a naval leader should know more than just drills, parades, and cruises. He should be master of his calling. He should be at home with seamanship, electricity, engineering, and ordnance. Most important, "he should be able to put into operation and practical use all the principles of these subjects. In him the mastery of the sea which we associate with the old time seaman is joined with a professional attainment and a scientific attitude of mind that have hitherto flourished only ashore."[69] While the naval officer may not be able to perform every task done onboard ship, he should have a practical acquaintance with everything and understand its relation to the efficiency of the fleet. Such a goal was difficult to achieve because the entire atmosphere of shipboard life was permeated by mechanism. "Life on ship board is almost like spending one's days and night in an iron foundry," Norris admitted. The constant and overpowering presence of machinery tended to harden the mind and give everything a mechanical turn. In that kind of environment the concept of men acting as if they were machines grew stronger. "Personality then drops into the background and the necessity of man's being a source of inspiration to those he commands is forgotten."[70] Still, the knowledge of engine rooms and guns was important to the navy. After all, as Admiral Luce pointed out, "... every naval officer must be something of a marine engineer; and the better the engineer he is the better for the Navy. The point is: Why should his education stop there?"[71]

Education and training were the keys. Because wars are relatively rare situations, a man cannot learn about warfare on a day-to-day basis as he might learn about steam engines or seamanship. One cannot comprehend one subject by concentrating on another. As one officer remarked, "no one ever learned to handle an oar by swinging dumbbells."[72] The art and science of naval warfare can be learned only through continuous training operations at sea and extensive study of the principles in warfare. Fleet maneuvers and ship tactics are essential to this goal, and they can be augmented by war gaming. By employing "the applicatory system," students learned from actual practice the principles of their art that could not be gleaned from a textbook. On the game boards at the Naval War College, model ships moved over measured areas at a rate compatible with existing equipment. American ships were opposed by forces whose guns and capabilities conformed to the latest intelligence, thus testing American forces and strategics in a simulated crucible of war. When mock battles were played in this manner, the results were not always happy. One group of officers in 1903 reported that,

> ... the game has been played to solve the problems of what should be the proper tactics to be followed by our fleet in order to get the best results against the fleet of the enemy in the problem of the year. The game has been played as if making use of the means at hand. The result has been that we lose. In one game we tied and in every other we lost.[73]

Such work not only improved methods, but officer-students acquired skill in their profession by solving the kind of strategic and tactical problems that the use of their equipment involved. Politics, geography, and weather; logistics, engineering, and ordnance; command and control, planning, and decisionmaking—all joined on the game board to simulate actual situations. As McCarty Little expressed it, "the game offers the players the whole world as a theatre, and puts no limit to the forces either in numbers or kinds, any type of ship may be had for the asking, the only requirement being to state its qualities so they may be expressed in game convention."[74] The common purpose of war gaming and fleet maneuvers was to make the object so closely associated with the method that one suggested the other. Through continuous practice and repetition, art in naval warfare had to become instinctive.[75] The most perceptive students understood that when war did come, military and naval officers must rapidly respond to unknown forces. In the final analysis, they could not place their faith in machines alone: soldiers and sailors had only their own ability for reasoning and their own intuition and perception to fall back upon.

The brief span of years between the Spanish-American War and the American entry into World War I witnessed rapid changes in naval technology. Instead of engulfing professional naval men in the chaos between innovation and obsolescence, naval strategists and their articulate seagoing associates concentrated their efforts on developing the means by which men could logically control and direct this expanding technology for the purposes which they devised. Situations were avoided in which technology became its own object. Awakened by the teachings of Luce, Mahan, and the naval reformers of the late nineteenth century, the professional men of the early twentieth century were able to devise administrative structures, methods of operation, training procedures, and doctrine which contributed to a broadly based direction of naval power. The naval professional learned that a balance must be struck between the goals and principles of warfare and the realities, limitations, and characteristics of available technology. Neither the professional of the day nor the historian of the era can deny that an understanding of naval power derives from a clear vision of its vast scope, for it takes into account international politics, human nature, war principles, technology, strategy and tactics, and the national wealth and will, all at the same moment. The professional understanding which developed in the first decade and a half of the new century provided the background for naval operations in both World War I and World War II. It was in these years after the turn of the century that naval men learned to control the new technological environment which they, themselves, had created.

NOTES

Originally published in the *Naval War College Review,* November 1971.

1. Surgeon A. W. Dunbar, "The Medical Department in Warfare," typescript in Naval War College Lecture Collection, Naval Historical Collection, Naval War College, Newport, R.I., p. 1. (Henceforth abbreviated: NWC Lectures, NHC.)

2. Bradley A. Fiske, *The Navy as a Fighting Machine* (New York: Scribners, 1916). p. 129.

3. Richard Hough, *Dreadnought* (New York: Macmillan, 1964), pp. 15-23.

4. Elmer B. Potter and Chester W. Nimitz, eds., *Sea Power: a Naval History* (Englewood Cliffs, N.J.: Prentice-Hall, 1960), pp. 388-93.

5. Wilbur R. Van Auken, *Notes on a Half Century of United States Naval Ordnance* (Washington, D.C.; Banta, 1939), pp. 13-24.

6. Linwood S. Howeth, *History of Communications-Electronics in the United States Navy* (Washington: U.S. Govt. Print. Off., 1963), p. 518-27.

7. A study of the contributions of these men may be found in Donald M. Schurman, *The Education of a Navy* (Chicago: University of Chicago Press, 1965).

8. R. H. Spector, "Professors of War," unpublished Ph.D. dissertation, Yale University, New Haven, Conn.: 1967, p. 159.

9. Alfred T. Mahan, *The Influence of Sea Power Upon History, 1660-1783* (London: University Paperbacks, 1967), p. 7.

10. Alfred T. Mahan, "Lectures on Military Strategy," unpublished manuscript and typescript in NWC Lectures, NHC pp. 11, 77. Believed to have been originally written about 1889, these lectures were often repeated and later used as assigned reading at the Naval War College in the first decade of the twentieth century.

11. William McCarty Little, quoted in Frank Schofield, "Estimate of the Situation," lecture before the summer conference, June 1912, *Solution to the Problem 1912*, Naval War College Archives, NHC, pt. H, pp. 29-30.

12. William McCarty Little, "The Strategic Naval War Game or Chart Maneuver," lecture, Naval War College, Newport, R.I., 10 June 1911.

13. This brief review is based on an excellent summary of the beginning of U.S. naval war planning which may be found in D. J. Costello, "Planning for War: a History of the General Board of the U.S. Navy, 1900-1914," unpublished Ph.D. dissertation, the Fletcher School of Law and Diplomacy, Medford, Mass., 1968, pp. 1-22.

14. Luce to Mahan, 15 July 1907; original carbon typescript copy in Naval War College Archives, Ms. #184, NHC. Italics are Luce's. See Luce's articles "Our Naval Policy," *The United Service,* vol. 6, May 1882, pp. 501-21; "Annual Address, 1888," *United States Naval Institute Proceedings*, vol. 14, 1888, pp. 1-8; "Naval Administration," *United States Naval Institute Proceedings*, vol. 14, 1888, pp. 561-81; "Naval Warfare under Modern Conditions," *North American Review*, vol. 162, January 1896, pp. 70-77.

15. William R. Braisted, *The United States Navy in the Pacific,* 1897-1909 (Austin: University of Texas Press, 1956), pp. 21-22. The original plan may be found in the National Archives, RG 42, Records of the North Atlantic Station. A photocopy has been included in War Plans files, Records of the General Board, Naval History Division, Washington, D.C.

16. Kenneth Bourne and Carl Boyd, "Captain Mahan's 'War' with Great Britain," *United States Naval Institute Proceedings,* July 1968, pp. 71-78. Also, John A. S. Grenville and George B. Young, *Politics, Strategy, and American Diplomacy: Studies in Foreign Policy* (New Haven: Yale University Press, 1966), pp. 93, 171-72; Walter R. Herrick, Jr., *The American Naval Revolution* (Baton Rouge: Louisiana State University Press, 1966), pp. 78, 126 and 140; Ronald Spector, "Who Planned the Attack on Manila Bay?" *Mid-America,* Vol. 53, No. 2, April 1971, pp. 94-102.

17. Navy Department General Order 544, 13 March 1900, quoted in Costello, p. 25.

18. Long to Dewey, 30 March 1900, quoted in Costello, pp. 25-26.

19. Damon E. Cummings, *Admiral Richard Wainwright and the United States Fleet* (Washington: U.S. Govt. Print. Off., 1962), pp. 213-17; Mark A. deWolfe Howe, *George von Lengerke Meyer; His Life and Public Services* (New York: Dodd, Mead, 1920), pp. 466-69; Henry P. Beers, "Development of the Office of the Chief of Naval Operations," *Military Affairs,* Spring 1946, pt. 11, pp. 60-64.

20. Costello, pp. 2-3.

21. For an outline history of naval war gaming, see Francis J. McHugh, *Fundamentals of War Gaming,* 3d ed. (Newport, R.I.: 1966); Spector, chap. VI.

22. George P. Ahern, *A Chronicle of the Army War College, 1899-1919,* processed Washington, D.C., 24 July 1919, No. 21 of 32 copies, NHC, NWC, pp. 81-82. W. P. Cronan, "The Greatest Need of the United States Navy: Proper Organization for the Successful Conduct of War, An Estimate of the Situation," *United States Naval Institute Proceedings,* July-August 1916, p. 1153.

23. Charles W. Cullen, "From Kriegsacademie to the Naval War College: The Military Planning Process," *Naval War College Review,* January 1970, pp. 10-15.

24. Cullen, p. 11. Quote from George F. R. Henderson, *The Science of War* (London: Longmans, Green, 1905), p. 5.

25. Cullen, pp. 14-15.

26. Cronan, p. 1153.

27. Louis Morton, "War Plan Orange, Evolution of a Strategy," *World Politics,* January 1959, p. 227.

28. Bradley A. Fiske, *The Navy as a Fighting Machine,* p. 406.

29. Ibid., p. 193.

30. Ibid., p. 228.

31. William McCarty Little, "Philosophy of the Order Form," Lecture, Naval War College, Newport, R.I.: 12-13 August 1913, NWC Lecture, NHC, p. 14.

32. W. R. Shoemaker, "Strategy of the Pacific: an Exposition of the Orange War Plan," Lecture, Naval War College, Newport, R.I., 23 August 1914, NWC Lecture, NHC.

33. Typescript, "Notes and Comments on G. B. Plan Blue vs. Black, undated, signed "McK.," laid in Black Plan War Portfolio No. 1, Reference No. 5-4, Germany War Plan, Copy No. 1 General Board copy. Records of the General Board, Naval History Division, Washington, D.C. This writer believes "McK." to be Capt. Josiah Slutts McKean, USN.

A Naval War College graduate and former staff member, McKean served as assistant for material in the Office of CNO from 1915 to 1919. He remained on duty in the Navy Department for several years. During World War I he was promoted to rear admiral and, later, admiral. As assistant CNO he served as the acting chief of naval operations when Admiral Benson was naval adviser to the U.S. delegation at Versailles, 5 January to 20 June 1919 and from 5 September to 1 November 1919, between the retirement of Admiral Benson and the appointment of Adm. R. E. Coontz as CNO.

34. Carl T. Vogelgesang, "Estimate of the Situation," Report of the Conference 1911, pt. II, p. 2, NWC Archives, NHC.

35. Orange Plan, P.7, War Plans File, Records of the General Board, Naval History Division, Washington, D.C. (Henceforth abbreviated: GB Records, NHD.)

36. See for example, A. T. Mahan to W. L. Rodgers, 17 May 1910 quoted in Spector, p. 250.

37. Mahan, "Lectures on Military Strategy," p. 42-43.

38. Ibid., p. 8.

39. Costello, p. 26-27.

40. George Dewey to SecNav, 16 June 1909, General Board Letters, vol. VI, p. 0093, GB Records, NHD.

41. Quoted in A. J. Marder, *The Anatomy of British Sea Power* (New York: Knopf, 1940), p. 525.

42. Dewey to SecNav, 28 February 1903, General Board Letters, vol. II, p. 0210, GB Records, NHD.

43. Dewey to SecNav, 16 May 1903, General Board Letters, vol. II, p. 0261, GB Records, NHD.

44. "Report of the Board to Consider CDR A. L. Key's Comments on the Design of the Battleship North Dakota, July 1908," Report of Committee B, p. 4, and Report of Committee Z. NWC Archives, NHC. This controversy is discussed at length in Elting E. Morison, *Admiral Sims and the Modern American Navy* (Boston: Houghton, Mifflin, 1942), pp. 201-15.

45. Key Board, "Appendix H. Paper Read by Admiral Goodrich."

46. Bradley A. Fiske, "The Naval Profession," *United States Naval Institute Proceedings,* June 1907, pp. 570-73; Bradley A. Fiske, *Midshipman to Rear Admiral* (New York: Century, 1919), pp. 397-39; and Sir Percy Scott, *Fifty Years in the Royal Navy* (New York: Doran, 1919).

47. Fiske, *Midshipman to Rear Admiral,* pp. 580, 591-92. Fiske gives the impression in his autobiography that the Naval Consulting Board was seriously considered

only after the newspaper announcement on 5 July 1915 that Sir John Fisher had been appointed head of a similar board in the Royal Navy. There is evidence in E. David Cronon, ed., *The Cabinet Diaries of Josephus Daniels 1913-1921* (Lincoln: University of Nebraska Press, 1963), p. 102, that the 7 July 1915 letter to Edison was being drafted as early as 30 June 1915. See also Josephus Daniels, *The Wilson Era* (Chapel Hill: University of North Carolina Press; 1944), chap. 52, pp. 490-500. *The New York Times* interview with Edison which inspired Daniels to enlist the inventor's support appeared on 30 May 1915, pt. V, "Magazine Section," pp. 6-7, not in "early July" as stated by Daniels in his autobiography.

48. Daniels to Edison, 7 July 1915, quoted in Lloyd N. Scott, *Naval Consulting Board of the United States* (Washington: U.S. Govt. Print. Off., 1920), pp. 286-87.

49. Fiske, *Fighting Machine*, p. 63-64.

50. "Confidential Memorandum Adopted by the Executive Committee, 6 August 1915," General Board Study 420-2, 30 July 1915. GB Records, NHD.

51. See H. H. Frost, *The Battle of Jutland* (Annapolis: U.S. Naval Institute, 1936), pp. 505-18, and Arthur Marder, *From Dreadnought to Scapa Flow,* London: Oxford University Press, vol. 3, 1966, for an evaluation of the battle.

52. R. D. Gatewood, "The Industrial in Modern War," *United States Naval Institute Proceedings,* May-June 1916, p. 757.

53. C. T. Vogelgesang, "Logistics—Its Bearing upon the Art of War," lecture before the summer conference of 1911, NWC Lectures, NHC, pp. 6, 8.

54. Carl T. Vogelgesang, quoted in J. S. McKean, *Naval Logistics: A Lecture Delivered* ... at the Naval War College Extension, Washington, D.C., 10 March 1913 (Washington: U.S. Govt. Print. Off., 1915), p. 7.

55. Gatewood, pp. 757-59.

56. T. J. Cowie, "Logistics," Lecture, Naval War College, Newport, R.I.: 13 May 1915, NWC Lectures, NHC, p. 20.

57. Dewey to SecNav, 28 September 1910, General Board Letters, vol. VII, p. 0058, GB Records, NHD. Earlier letters on the same topic contain similar reasoning; see Dewey to SecNav, 9 February 1903, General Board Letters, vol. II, p. 0177 and 26 January 1904, vol. III, p. 0006.

58. William L. Rodgers to W. McCarty Little, 10 May 1914, pp. 3-4, manuscript letter in NWC Archives, Research file, "Little," NHC.

59. Ibid.

60. Josephus Daniels, SecNav, to W. H. Bullard, Superintendent, Naval Radio Service, 3 March 1916; letter (Second Endorsement) from Superintendent, Radio Service, 7 December 1915, GB Records, NHD.

61. Dewey to SecNav, Serial 467 of 19 January 1916, File 419, GB Records, NHD.

62. For a detailed account of the Dolphin incident, see Jack Sweetman, *The Landing at Vera Cruz: 1914* (Annapolis: U.S. Naval Institute, 1968), pp. 30-40.

63. Josephus Daniels, *The Wilson Era.* p. 191. Daniels indicates that the 1916 order was delayed for more than two years so that it would not be construed as a rebuke to Admiral Mayo.

64. Rodgers to Little, 10 May 1914, p. 4.

65. William McCarty Little, "Philosophy of the Order Form," Lecture, U.S. Naval War College, Newport, R.I.: 1913.

66. Hugo Munsterberg, "The Psychology of the Navy," Lecture, Naval War College, Newport, R.I.: 4 June 1912, NWC Lectures, NHC, p. 2.

67. Letter (Fourth Endorsement) on W. T. Culverinus' letter, 15 February 1909. Comments on the condition of the commissioned personnel, 23 December 1908, General Board Letters, v. V, p. 0433, GB Records, NHD.

68. Fiske, *Fighting Machine,* pp. 196-97.

69. W. B. Norris, "Leadership and Freedom," *United States Naval Institute Proceedings,* January-February 1916, p. 51.

70. Ibid., p. 61.

71. Stephen B. Luce, "On the Relations between the U.S. Naval War College and Line Officers of the U.S. Navy," *United States Naval Institute Proceedings,*

September 1911, p. 788.

72. H. G. Bergen, "The Principles of Training," Lecture, Naval War College, Newport, R.I.: 1909, NWC Lectures, NHC, p. 10.

73. "Solution to the Problem of 1903, Conclusions Deducted from the Use of the Game Board," p. 65, NWC Archives, NHC.

74. W. McCarty Little, "The Strategic Naval War Game."

75. W. McCarty Little, "Genesis of the Masterpiece of a Genius," unpublished typescript and notes for study of Napoleon's strategy, c. 1902, NWC Archives, Research File "Little," NHC.

National Interest in Imperial German Foreign Policy: Bismarck, William II, and the Road to World War I

Norman Rich

Editor's Note: *Norman Rich is Professor of History at Brown University. He is the author of* Friedrich von Holstein: Politics and Diplomacy in the Era of Bismarck *and* Hitler's War Aims.

A distinguished American historian, Raymond Sontag, has said of Bismarck that he was "one of the first great European statesmen of the nineteenth century who consciously and deliberately subordinated every ideal to the needs of the state .... Reason of state was his master, to be served with all his powers, by fair means or foul."[1] This is probably an accurate description of Bismarck's attitude toward politics, though whether his emphasis on reason of state was as novel in the nineteenth, or any other, century as this passage suggests is open to question. For surely even those leaders who profess to be guided by higher values, whether those be God, liberty, democracy, or even Nordic supremacy or the dictatorship of the proletariat, are generally convinced that they are acting in the interests of the state. The essence of the problem, of course, is not reason of state in itself, but what a statesman considers reason of state to be, and it is here that the most profound criticisms of Bismarck can be, and have been, made.

In a brief analysis of foreign policy, it is impossible to deal adequately with this crucial aspect of Bismarck's statecraft except to suggest that he was too much the egotist and too practical a politician to subscribe to the views of his more pedantic compatriots that the state was, or could be, an end in itself. The state might be his creation and the instrument of his personal power, but he was well aware that there was no line of demarcation between the welfare of the state and that of its people, that a state had responsibilities toward its citizens just as much as citizens had responsibilities toward their state.

The point should be emphasized that Bismarck's conception of reason of state did not automatically exclude considerations of right and wrong, humanity, truth, or justice, as some of his critics have maintained, if only because he understood how important moral forces could be in political life. The moral issue, however, went beyond mere political expediency. If the state had responsibility toward its citizens, so too did the statesman. Morality, Bismarck once said, was not an abstract conception standing outside political reality, but stemmed from within it and was expressed in a statesman's sense of moral responsibility for his actions. A sense of responsibility, then, was for Bismarck an integral part of reason of state.

It was on the basis of this combination of reason of state and moral responsibility, as he conceived them, that Bismarck selected his political aims.

A judicious selection of political aims is undoubtedly the most important task of any statesman, particularly in the field of foreign policy. How well that choice is made depends, of course, on the ability of the statesman in question or on the ability of the persons from whom he accepts advice. Bismarck himself insisted that politics was not a science but an art; it was not something that could be learned; one had to have a flair for it. In this judgment he was at least partially right. There is no substitute for talent.

The "flair" qualities of Bismarck's own statecraft, those talents that cannot be learned or copied, have often been enumerated: his ability to see the essential feature in a political situation; his timing, sense of proportion, fertility in expedients; his restraint combined with the instinct to choose the right moment to act.

He possessed other qualities, however, which did not necessarily depend on genius, qualities which had nothing to do with political virtuosity and which might be described as the fundamentals of diplomacy. These fundamentals played a greater role in Bismarck's diplomacy after 1871 than the flair he employed to such effect during the activist period of unification. The most important of these stemmed from his concern with reason of state and moral responsibility, and amounted to an awareness that the first task of the statesman must be to consider carefully and dispassionately what are, in fact, the vital interests of the state, to keep these always in the forefront of his political thinking, and to steer a political course accordingly. To make an accurate appraisal of national interests in itself demands political judgment and insight of a high order, but even more it requires a conscious effort to overcome prejudices and preconceptions, to put aside empty considerations of prestige or the temptation to score minor victories at the expense of major interests. It means having the self-confidence to adhere to a political course despite criticism and temporary political fluctuations; but it also means having the courage to face up to errors in judgment and rectify mistakes, and the mental resiliency to readjust ideas and policies when basic political changes are taking place. These qualities were in no way natural to a man of Bismarck's passionate and egotistic temperament, but his great strength lay in his recognition of the need for them and his disciplined effort to overcome weaknesses in his own character so as to live up to his own sense of moral responsibility.

Some critics have faulted Bismarck for his willingness to shift political direction, and adjust his policies to changing situations. On this score they have charged that Bismarck lacked principle. Bismarck's principle, however, was Germany's national interest. If the national interest was thereby served, he was willing to negotiate and conclude agreements with any state, any political force, or any person, no matter how great his previous hostility or prejudice against them had been.

Whether Bismarck's selection of political aims was sound, whether his consequent policies were necessary, desirable, or effective are questions that will be debated as long as history is studied. In the name of reason of state he accepted responsibility for the deaths of those who had fought in the wars of German unification; he sought to acquire a better strategic frontier for the state by annexing Alsace and Lorraine, thereby incurring the permanent hostility of France; he strove to eliminate subversive elements within the state by conducting vicious campaigns against the Poles, Catholics, and Socialists; and he ruined the life of Harry Arnim for undermining official policies.

Also for reason of state, however, he swallowed defeat at the hands of the Catholics and sought to regain their support for the state once the Catholic party had proved itself to be a stable political force; he quashed the love affair of the Princess of Prussia with Prince Alexander of Bulgaria because it might injure Germany's relations with Russia; he rejected appeals to come to the aid of stricken humanity in other parts of the world because he considered it irresponsible and dangerous to interfere in the affairs of other states when German national interests were not involved; and he ruthlessly suppressed military and chauvinist agitation to wage preventive war or to resume the paths of conquest. So long as he was chancellor, Bismarck would never condone a preventive war; war was the *ultima ratio* to be waged only when the most vital interests of the state were at stake. In his great Reichstag speech of 6 February 1888, he publicly denounced chauvinist agitators:

> Every great power which seeks to impose itself upon and influence the policy of other countries and to take the lead in areas outside its own sphere of interest is operating outside the area God assigned to it; it is conducting power politics, not the politics of self-interest; it is guided by motives of prestige.

Quite as important as Bismarck's attempt to identify German national interests was his corresponding attempt to understand the national interests of other great powers, an exercise that often gave him a clearer conception of the political possibilities and requirements of another state than that country's own leaders had. This practice saved him from the most common of diplomatic pitfalls, the pursuit of a policy which ran counter to the basic interests of another great power and thus pushed that power into the camp of his country's enemies. It was also the essential feature of one of his most effective diplomatic techniques, that of maneuvering other powers to defend their own national interests when these happened to coincide with the national interests of Germany.

At the center of Bismarck's evaluation of national interests was the problem of power, which his critics have often equated with military power and the use of force. The army, of course, played a crucial part in his political calculations, but for him the army was at all times a tool, not an end in itself. Far from furthering the army's position as a state within a state, he kept it under rigid political control and successfully warded off the attempts of army leaders to bring state policy into line with their concept of military requirements.

Bismarck never lost sight of the fact that a state's power depended on far more than military power, economic power, or similar material assets, important as those might be. Power depended on the wisdom of a state's leadership, on the morale of its people. Power depended on a state's relations with other states, on the strength of its alliances and the weakness of the alliances of its opponents. And, in a very significant way, power depended on a state's moral position, on its ability to claim that its critical diplomatic or military actions were taken in accordance with or in defense of that body of international treaties and conventions known as international law. Only from a strong moral position could a state appeal effectively to world, or even to its own, public opinion in time of crisis.

Bismarck's broad conception of the quality of power necessarily made him aware of the limits of power, both his own and that of the state he governed. It was this awareness that made him recognize the impossibility of further conquest and the futility of preventive war as a means of enhancing German security after 1871. Any German attempt to expand by force or to crush potential enemies would be certain to result in the formation of a European coalition which Germany could never hope to defeat.

These were among the considerations that determined Bismarck's selection of both the aims and methods of German foreign policy after 1871. His aim was the security of the state, which may indeed have been his basic objective after 1862. Only then, instead of trying to achieve security by broadening the base of Prussian power, he sought to do so by consolidating the gains he had made and by maintaining the status quo. Germany, he believed, was a satiated state which had little to gain and a great deal to lose by further territorial changes in Europe. As such changes could only be brought about by violent means, the most reliable method of safeguarding German security would be to keep the peace.

Peace, however, did not depend on Germany alone. In international affairs the satisfaction of one power is generally accompanied by the dissatisfaction of others. The unification of Germany under Prussia had frustrated the interests of several powers, so that from the moment of its creation the new German empire faced the hostility of those powers. While no continental European state has ever been immune to external threats, Bismarck's empire seemed far more capable of meeting them than the former state of Prussia or, indeed, any other German political organization of the past.

Bismarck saw no reason to fear any one of the great powers of Europe. It was the formation of a hostile coalition that he dreaded. The prevention of such a coalition therefore became the primary objective of his diplomacy. His method of achieving this objective was the most obvious one: to prevent the formation of hostile coalitions, he sought to form coalitions of his own. Bismarck's diplomatic axiom of seeking to be à trois in a world of five great powers has often been quoted, but his entire conduct of diplomacy suggests that he would have preferred more than anything else to be à cinq. As this was impossible owing to the hostility of France, he worked hard and on the whole successfully to be à quatre. This policy was at least in part the result of his recognition that Germany's relations with each of the great powers was closely connected with or even dependent upon her relations with all the others.

In seeking to retain the friendship of Austria, for instance, Germany was repeatedly faced with the demand to support Austrian national interests in Eastern Europe against Russia. As Bismarck had no desire to involve Germany in the disputes in Eastern Europe or to be blackmailed into fighting Austria's wars, he sought to maintain close diplomatic ties with Russia as well as Austria.

The greatest difficulty in winning the friendship of Russia was that many Russians believed Bismarck was supporting Austria against Russia, whatever he might say to the contrary, and that an alliance with France, the enemy of Germany, would be more profitable than one with Germany, the friend of Austria. Bismarck's only means for countering this belief was to convince the Russians that German friendship was more valuable and her hostility more detrimental to Russia's national interests than any advantage a French alliance could offer. To do this he not only proclaimed Germany's disinterestedness in Eastern Europe, but gave the Russians assurances of substantial support in that area. At the same time he allowed them to know that if they did ally themselves with France, Germany's only recourse would be an alliance—and no longer necessarily only a defensive alliance—with Russia's principal enemies, Austria and Britain, a grouping which would certainly attract Turkey and various Balkan states. Against such a combination, Russia, even with French support, would be powerless.

To make this threat convincing, it was essential that Germany maintain good relations with Britain, but Bismarck needed more than good relations with Britain. It was all very well to declare German disinterestedness in Eastern Europe and to promise the

Russians support there, but if Austria were to be preserved as a great power, she could not be left to defend her interests against Russia alone. Thus, it was necessary to secure support for Austria, and the most natural source of such support was Britain. The British had fought the Crimean War to keep Russia out of Constantinople and the Mediterranean, and their interest in the Near East had, if anything, increased since they had acquired control of the Suez Canal in 1875. So long as the British believed that Germany would support Austria against any Russian threat to vital Austrian interests, they could afford to stand aside and allow the Teutonic powers to stop Russia for them. By maintaining a German alliance with Russia, however, and by constantly restating that the fate of the Balkans and Constantinople in no way affected German national interests, Bismarck convinced the British that if they wished to keep Russia out of the Mediterranean they would have to assist in this task themselves. The German alliance with Russia was thus Bismarck's main lever to pry diplomatic commitments out of Britain.

Bismarck's game was a particularly delicate one, especially since he could not afford to expose the extent of Germany's dependence on any of the great powers. To camouflage this condition, he indulged in occasional demonstrations of hostility toward them all, always taking care to keep open his bridges for the restoration of amicable relations.

The policy of being à quatre was not only valuable in preventing the formation of hostile coalitions but it also allowed Bismarck to exercise some measure of supervision and control over the relations of his diplomatic partners to each other. Such supervision was important, for Bismarck not only wanted Germany to remain at peace; he wanted Europe, or at least the great powers of Europe, to remain at peace. Any major European war was certain to involve Germany, and the possibilities of advancing Germany's national interests in such a war were in no way proportionate to its hazards. By maintaining close diplomatic relations with the major powers, Bismarck was in a position to use his influence to prevent conflict between them. His system of alliances was thus one of his methods for preserving the peace.

The effectiveness of Bismarck's alliances as a method of preserving peace has often been questioned. There is a school of thought which maintains that secret alliances, far from preserving peace, are a major cause of war. Bismarck's alliances have been considered particularly sinister because of the devious tactics he used to create them and the dubious honesty of their occasionally contradictory terms. The peace of Europe, his severest critics contend, was preserved as much in spite of as because of Bismarck, and they offer the irrefutable evidence that peace continued almost a quarter of a century after his dismissal.

The peace of Europe was indeed preserved after Bismarck's dismissal, but that peace depended to a large extent on the successful operation of the balance of power, a precarious system at best, whose effectiveness during this particular period was due in no small measure to the diversion of great power rivalries outside Europe. Even then it was something of a miracle that a European war did not break out long before 1914. Bismarck, whatever else may be said for or against his policies, did at least try to impose some form of control and order on the European states system, to find more reliable guarantees for peace, and to make its preservation less dependent on the questionable good sense or goodwill of the statesmen who govern our destinies.

In a recent study of Bismarck, British historian Professor William Medlicott cites with evident approval Gladstone's belief that the rivalries on the continent could be neutralized and dissolved in the warm comradeship of a revived concert of Europe, and he condemns Bismarck for regarding Gladstone's opinions as both silly and perverse.[2] Professor Medlicott fails to mention, however, that a revival of the concert of Europe—not a liberal Gladstonian concert, to be sure, but an antirevolutionary conservative concert— was precisely what Bismarck sought to achieve through those loose agreements known as the First Three Emperors' League. This revival of a quasi-Metternichian system for maintaining the political and territorial status quo, and with it the peace of Europe, proved unable to cope with the first serious problem it encountered and was shattered in the Near Eastern crisis of 1876-78.

Bismarck's subsequent creation of a new European alliance system is one of the best known chapters of European diplomatic history, yet it is surprising how few British or American surveys of the period, or even specialized studies, have followed the lead of Professor William Langer in pointing out the unique quality of this system as it had developed by 1887 or in analyzing (whether favorably or unfavorably) its effectiveness as a mechanism for preserving peace.[3]

Bismarck's system was no revival of the balance of power or a balance of tensions, as it has sometimes been described. On the contrary, instead of dividing the powers of Europe into two hostile camps, which is the general result of the free operation of the balance of power, Bismarck brought them all, with the exception of France—and he tried hard to include France—into an interlocking network in which no single power would be assured of support in a war of aggression, preventive war, or in any aggressive gamble. If such a gamble were attempted, the aggressive power would find itself facing an overwhelming defensive coalition, either as a result of actual alliance treaties or of natural alliances that might be expected to form.

International agreements as such were unreliable instruments, as Bismarck well knew, but the strength of his treaties lay in the fact that they were all sufficiently advantageous to the powers concerned to give those powers a vested interest in adhering to them. The treaties were also sufficiently limited in time to prevent any power from growing restive under the terms of a particular agreement. When the time limit was up the treaty would lapse, or it could be negotiated anew to accord with changes in the international situation, for no power liked to be left without assurances of defensive support of some kind.

The Bismarckian system was not foolproof—no human institution is—but it was one of the most ingenious instruments for preserving peace in the anarchic world of sovereign states that has ever been devised.

Bismarck himself was well aware that his system offered no permanent solution to the problem of international anarchy, and that a constant readjustment of methods and ideas was required to meet changing political situations. Nothing in the world was permanent, he once said, neither peace treaties nor laws. A statesman could do no more than try to do his duty. Everything else was up to God.

This failure of Bismarck to offer Germany and Europe a permanent solution or an easily applied formula for international problems is deplored even by his admirers. His alliance system, they complain, was so complicated that it required a political genius to operate it. Perhaps this is true, and perhaps Bismarck himself would have found it unworkable if he had remained in office a few years longer. Nevertheless, the success of Bismarck's diplomacy—and I think it was on the whole successful—did not depend on any system but on his qualities as a diplomat. Of these the most important was not his genius but his attention to what was described earlier as the fundamentals of diplomacy: a dispassionate evaluation of national interests; care to avoid challenging the national interests of other great powers; and an awareness of the quality of national power and its limitations. It was the neglect of these fundamentals which, more than anything else, brought disaster to his successors, as indeed it brings disaster to most statesmen who disregard them.

Bismarck, of course, had the advantage of exercising exclusive control over the formation and execution of German foreign policy, a control which ensured unified direction of policy. Under his successors this unified direction, too, was lacking.

Emperor William II had both the right and the power to control German foreign policy, but among his many deficiencies he lacked the necessary capacity for work to carry this immense burden. Although he intervened decisively in affairs of state whenever events or mood prompted him, a large part of the responsibility for the formulation and execution of policy passed by default to the officials of his foreign office. Among these officials were intelligent and dedicated men, but the great weakness they all shared with the emperor was their failure to concentrate on the problem of Germany's national interests and to consider all their policies in the light of those interests. So frequently were considerations of pride, prejudice, and prestige allowed to determine their political course that it often seemed as though *raison d'état* had been displaced by *raison de moi.*

Other forces, too, began to exercise increasing influence on the conduct of German foreign policy. Courtiers, military leaders, and businessmen who had the support of the emperor, well-organized and well-financed pressure groups like the Navy League and the Colonial Society, and a variety of other social and economic interests began to bring pressure on the government which Bismarck's less powerful successors were unable to ignore. Perhaps the greatest problem faced by Bismarck's successors was the need to cope with these extragovernment forces, which the old chancellor himself had only held in check with difficulty. Foremost among the beliefs held by these pressure groups was that Germany was not, as Bismarck had maintained, a satiated state. German disunity, they argued, had prevented her in the past from acquiring her fair share of the world's spoils, but that disability had long since been overcome, and it was high time that Germany should take her place beside Britain, France, and Russia as a world, not just a European, power.

The German desire for empire was understandable enough in this heyday of European imperialism, and it may have been impossible for any German government to disregard the pressures of public opinion on this issue. The error in Germany's quest for empire was not so much the quest itself, but the means by which this policy was conducted. Neither in the foreign office nor in any other government department was a conscious effort made to determine where Germany might expand with maximum benefit to her national interests and minimum conflict with the interests of those states with which she hoped to maintain friendly relations. There were members of the imperial government who knew as well as Bismarck that Germany's vital interests lay in Europe, and that the maintenance of a strong diplomatic position on the continent had to take precedence over imperial ambitions. Although these men were in charge of German policy for extended periods, their policies could at any time be contravened by the emperor or by officials appointed by him to do his bidding. Unfortunately for Germany, this emperor gave way to every whim and pursued a variety of ill-conceived and contradictory imperialist objectives which were to bring Germany into conflict with every other great power in the world.

This problem was not apparent immediately. During the first years of his independent reign, William was content to move cautiously and leave most foreign policy decisions in the hands of his professional diplomats. In fact in these years the emperor and his diplomats were in substantial agreement as to the kind of foreign policy Germany should pursue. They wanted to put an end to the complications, the apparent dishonesties and inconsistencies of Bismarck's system, in order to follow a straightforward, honorable course to show friend and foe alike where Germany stood.

Instead of Bismarck's involved alliance system, they proposed to construct a coalition of Europe's peaceloving powers—by which they meant themselves, Britain, and Austria—which could then dictate terms to the perennial disturbers of the peace, France and Russia. They were especially critical of Bismarck's alliance with Russia, which they considered both useless and a threat to Germany's harmonious relations with her real friends. In accordance with these ideas, the first moves of Bismarck's successors were to drop the alliance with Russia and to begin an ostentatious courtship of Britain.

The dropping of the treaty with Russia left Russia isolated and virtually forced her into an alliance with France. German diplomats were undoubtedly correct in believing that Russia was an undependable ally, and that in the event of war she probably would side with France no matter what her treaty relationship with Germany might be. But they neglected to consider the enormous difference between an international situation in which Russia was linked to Germany, no matter how unreliably, and one in which Russia was definitely linked to France. As long as France was not absolutely certain of Russian support, she was not likely to risk a conflict with Germany. Once a solid Franco-Russian alliance had been formed, however, chauvinists in either country might be tempted to exploit it.

German diplomats also neglected to consider the effect that severing the link with Russia would have on their other allies. Once Germany had dropped Russia and taken her stand unequivocally at the side of Austria, Britain could safely withdraw from commitments in Central Europe, confident that Germany would now assume the tiresome responsibility of defending, not only the Habsburg monarchy itself, but what seemed to be Austria's vital interests in the Balkans and the Near East. By cutting Russia adrift, they had thrown away Germany's most effective diplomatic weapon for dealing with Britain. The change also left Germany in a weaker position *vis-à-vis* her remaining allies, for both Austria and Italy, now that Germany had made herself dependent on their support, were able to demand more for their friendship by threatening to defect to the Franco-Russian camp. This weakness was to grow increasingly obvious as the years passed and was to prove catastrophic in 1914.

German statesmen were annoyed by the growing independence and unreliability of Austria and Italy, but their greatest anger was directed against Britain, which did not leap at the suggestion of an alliance with the new, honorable German government.

What the Germans forgot was that the British, who had fought for centuries to prevent the domination of the continent by a single state and the consequent disruption of the European balance of power, were hardly likely to support a German diplomatic campaign for achieving this object. An Anglo-German diplomatic partnership would have cemented the Triple Alliance, it would have drawn Turkey and the smaller Balkan states into its orbit. In a power grouping of this kind, Germany, as the greatest military power in the system, would have been in a position to call the political tune, and the British had no desire to aid Germany in acquiring such a position. When the British made their famous bids for a German alliance at the turn of the century, it was to seek German aid against Russia in East Asia and to prevent the formation of a hostile coalition during the Boer War. Even then, however, they never made offers which the Germans considered adequate.

The Germans were not immediately conscious of the weakness of their international position after 1890 because the rivalry of the European powers was temporarily diverted to areas outside Europe, where Britain bore the brunt of international hostility. Intense as were these imperial rivalries, they never proved serious enough to provoke war between the European powers as the Germans confidently expected. They were not even sufficiently serious to force one of these powers to seek an alliance with Germany on German terms.

A wise German policy at this time would have been to sit tight, maintain cordial relations (if not treaty relationships) with all powers, and to develop German strength and influence through trade and economic expansion. Such a policy, however, was not positive enough for the professional diplomats of the German foreign office or spectacular enough for the German emperor or German public opinion. In the foreign office, frustration over the failure to gain a diplomatic alignment with Britain brought about a belated recognition of the importance of Russia as a lever to pry commitments out of Britain, and periodically strenuous efforts were made to restore closer diplomatic relations with the tsarist empire—efforts which only convinced the Russians of the beneficent results of their alliance with France. This was not, strictly speaking, a zigzag policy, but part of a desperate search for means of applying pressure on the British to convince them, if not of the desirability, then of the necessity, of German friendship. The Germans were to pursue this policy, not only through courtship of Russia, but by supporting all powers upon occasion, including France, in disputes with Britain, and by engaging in some vicious disputes with Britain on their own.

Thus the German foreign office officials, whose main objective was an alliance with Britain, did much to undermine their own policy. The policy was undermined further by the emperor's colonial ventures, especially by his ostentatious meddling in South Africa. It was finally scuttled beyond hope by the emperor's fleet-building program.

The emperor argued that a large navy was essential to protect Germany's colonies and trade, but his real reason for wanting a great fleet was to establish Germany as a world power. A great German fleet, he believed, in conjunction with the navies of other powers, would quickly compel Britain to make those colonial concessions which Germany had so long sought in vain through diplomatic means. The British, after all, had established their world empire largely on the basis of seapower, and what the British did, the Germans could do also.

Again the Germans forgot to consider the national interests of other great powers and their own. The fleet was for Britain what the army was for Germany: the main line of national defense. Any threat to British naval superiority was therefore a threat to British national security and absolutely decisive in determining British foreign policy. The Germans counted on French and Russian rivalry with Britain in the colonial field to secure the support of these powers against Britain. They neglected to consider that Britain, faced with a threat to her national security, might be willing to make massive concessions in the colonial field to prevent the formation of a naval coalition directed against her, or that France, which still remembered Alsace-Lorraine, might be far more willing to ally herself with Britain than with Germany. It was the fleet issue more than anything else that persuaded British leaders to make the 1904 entente with France.

Thus the emperor's great fleet, while draining large sums away from the army, the vital factor in Germany's national defense, at the same time added to the number of great powers Germany might some day have to fight.

Germany's Morocco policy of 1905-6 was primarily an attempt to disrupt the Anglo-French alignment, not a search for a pretext to crush France while Russian armies were tied down in East Asia in the war against Japan. If Germany had really been making a calculated bid for world power or even for continental hegemony, this would have been the moment to strike, but the German government had no broad aims of any kind. Its foreign policy was hand-to-mouth, shortsighted, and, for a country in Germany's difficult geographical position, disastrous. The Morocco policy itself was based on a set of false premises and never had a chance of accomplishing its object, though it might have won Germany some substantial territorial gains in Africa. A divided leadership, however, cost Germany even this chance of success. For while the German foreign office was applying the heaviest kind of diplomatic pressure against France in Morocco, the German emperor was making another bid to regain the alliance with Russia, and Russia would only agree to a renewal of the German alliance with the consent of France. William, delighted by the prospect of scoring a personal diplomatic triumph, now set out to win over the French by assuring them that he had no interest in Morocco whatever. Thus the German foreign office was undercut and the Morocco policy failed, but so too did the emperor's Russian policy, for France had no intention of allowing her most important continental ally to reenter the German camp.

Meanwhile, German diplomatic pressure on France had done

much to convince the British of the reality of the German menace. Far from disrupting the Anglo-French entente, German policy contributed to its consolidation and conversion into an actual military alliance. It also spurred French efforts to bring about an entente between Britain and Russia, which was concluded in 1907. Thus the lines were drawn for the events of 1914.

As the ring of alliances formed and tightened around Germany, her leaders became increasingly aware of their hazardous international position. The theory has been advanced that German statesmen, obsessed by the fear of encirclement, decided that their position was desperate, could only grow worse in the future, and that Germany's only chance to survive as a great power was to break the ring by going to war.

There is a second theory, which has recently been bolstered by the voluminous publications of the German historian Fritz Fischer, that Germany's leaders, far from fearing the power of the Triple Entente, were convinced of its impotence. They believed that neither France nor Russia was prepared for war, and that Britain, even if she did fight with her allies, was a negligible factor militarily. So certain were they of Germany's military superiority that they chose the opportunity offered by the Sarajevo incident to launch a European war in a bid to establish German supremacy in Europe and the world.

There are two major objections to Professor Fischer's thesis. The first of these is the quality of German leadership, and the second is the actual course of the 1914 crisis. The deliberate provocation of a major war requires a rare degree of foresight, daring, and nerve, but it was the very absence of these qualities that had characterized German policy since 1890. There is no evidence that the situation had suddenly changed in 1914. The only organization with anything like a long-range program was the army with its preposterous Schlieffen plan, but this was to come into operation only if a war broke out. It was in no sense a war plot.

Professor Fischer has fixed on Bethmann-Hollweg as his chief villain, and the German chancellor certainly played a sorry role in the 1914 crisis. Yet Bethmann was a man of decency and integrity, and in calmer moments he had a solid sense of political responsibility. What was more, he had the courage to back up his convictions. In the autumn of 1913, for example, the German crown prince, a man even more foolish than his father, submitted to the chancellor the bitter criticisms of a group of German chauvinists about the flabby conduct of German foreign policy, criticisms with which the crown prince obviously agreed. Bethmann replied on

15 November 1913:

> Our foreign policy is accused of striving to preserve peace at
> *any price,* of compromising the honor and dignity of the German
> Reich.... In no instance so far has the honor and dignity of
> the German nation been violated by another nation. Whoever
> wants war without such provocation must have vital national
> tasks in view which cannot be achieved without war. It was
> to accomplish such tasks and reach such goals that Bismarck
> desired and launched the wars of 1864, 1866, and 1870. After
> they were fought and won, he believed that "the most important
> political interest was the preservation of peace." This was stated
> by him so often and so clearly, this was so obviously the guiding
> principle of his entire policy after 1870, that one can only accuse
> today's warmongers of a consummate lack of political judgment
> or bad faith when they constantly appeal to the example of
> Bismarck and actually gain credence for such falsification of
> history. Every policy for the sake of prestige was condemned
> by Bismarck as basically un-German. Whither such policy leads
> he could, and we can, see from the example of Napoleon III.
>   In a future war undertaken without compelling reason, not
> only the Hohenzollern crown but the future of Germany will
> be at stake. Our policy must of course be conducted boldly. But
> to rattle our sabers in every diplomatic complication when the
> honor, security and future of Germany are not threatened is
> not only foolhardy but criminal.[4]

These are not the words of a man who is thinking in terms of
launching precisely the kind of war his critics seemed to desire.

As for the actual course of the 1914 crisis, the Germans may
indeed have decided that it was a case of now or never to break
the ring. There is considerable evidence that German leaders were
afraid that in a few years Russian power would be so great that
Germany could no longer hope to stand against her, especially
if Russia were supported by France. German historian Egmont
Zechlin has concluded: "The desire to remain a first-class power
in relation to modern world powers and to maintain its political
freedom of action was the main motive of German policy in the
July 1914 crisis."[5]

This, it seems to me, is a more tenable thesis than that of Professor Fischer, but it too presupposes long-range political thinking
on the part of the German government that was strikingly absent
in earlier crises.

There has never been much doubt that the German government was encouraging Austria to go to war in 1914. Any remaining doubt has now been removed by the research of Professor Fischer and the evidence contained in the recently discovered diaries of Tisza, the Hungarian prime minister, and the private correspondence of Tschirschky, the German ambassador to Vienna. The central issue, however, is not whether the Germans were inciting the Austrians to war, but what kind of war the Germans were trying to unleash. Were they, as Professor Fischer contends, coldbloodedly and deliberately intending to provoke a European war? Evidence that the German army had prepared for such a war and that German leaders speculated about future territorial gains is important, but it does not necessarily prove the correctness of the war-plot theory.

More plausibly, the documents suggest that the Germans sought a simpler solution to the entire problem and one far more in line with previous German diplomatic maneuvers, namely, that the Germans wanted Austria to exploit the horror evoked by the assassination of the heir to the Austrian crown at Sarajevo to eliminate the menace of Serbia, which was no longer merely a thorn in the side of the Habsburg Empire but seemed a threat to its very existence. A military campaign against Serbia had long been advocated by Conrad von Hötzendorf, the chief of the Austrian General Staff, but the Germans lacked confidence in the power of decision and determination of the rest of the Austrian government. They feared that the opportunity offered by the shocking crime in Bosnia would be frittered away through Austrian *Schlamperei.* These fears were perfectly justified because, despite German pressure and assurances of support, the Austrians allowed a full month to pass between the assassination of their archduke and their declaration of war against Serbia. By that time Europe had had time to recover from its shock, and public opinion, far from being sympathetic to Austria, had turned sharply against her.

The German government itself had not been exactly quick to exploit the Sarajevo affair, but six days after the assassination William II set the tone for the policy of his country: "It is essential to clean house in Serbia," he said, "and that very soon."[6] The German government was well aware of the danger of foreign intervention, but like the American government in its policies toward Korea, Cuba, and Vietnam, it took the calculated risk that other powers would not intervene in what was after all essentially an Austrian concern. "As things stand today," William assured the Austrians, "Russia is not yet in any way prepared for war, and will certainly think things over very carefully before taking up arms."[7]

The Austrians were less confident that an attack on Serbia would remain isolated, and to calm their fears the Germans assured them repeatedly that in the event of foreign intervention Germany would hold the ring on Austria's behalf. To make certain that the Austrians should have an excuse to deal firmly with Serbia, the Germans demanded an ultimatum so severe that the Serbian government would be certain to reject it. The Serbs, however, seeing their danger, accepted the most important points of the ultimatum and gave the Austrians the power to "clean house" in Serbia without firing a shot. It is therefore no wonder that the German emperor, impetuous as always, now declared that all reason for war had disappeared. He required only—and it was an immense only—that the Serbs allow Austria to occupy a part of their territory as a guarantee that they would fulfill the terms of the ultimatum. The German chancellor, Bethmann Hollweg, recognized the enormity of the emperor's qualification, and he was evidently doubtful as to whether the Serbs would accept Austrian military occupation peacefully. Still questioning Austria's ability to make a decision, he relayed the orders of the emperor to the German ambassador in Vienna with the admonition that these should not be interpreted as an effort to restrain Austria. It was solely a question of finding a way to allow Austria to achieve her desired goal "without at the same time unleashing a world war, but if this proved to be unavoidable in the end, to improve the conditions under which it was to be conducted to the greatest possible advantage to ourselves."[8]

Bethmann need not have worried about restraining Austria. By the time the German emperor's message, as diluted by Bethmann, had reached the Austrian foreign ministry, Austria had already declared war on Serbia. The Germans then found to their consternation that the Austrian army would not be ready for an actual invasion of Serbia for another fortnight. This was *Schlamperei* surpassing even their worst fears. Bethmann saw at once that the Austrian delay would furnish ample time for the other powers to intervene diplomatically and summon a conference to deal with the Serbian problem. At such a conference, as the Germans well knew from the experience at Algeciras in 1906, Austria and Germany, in a minority among the great powers, would be defeated. But if a conference were not accepted and a European war resulted, the odium for starting such a war would fall on Germany. The emperor made a desperate last-minute effort to draw back from this miserable position until finally the exigencies of the

Schlieffen plan propelled Germany into a war, not only with Serbia and Russia, but with France and Britain as well. Bethmann, moreover, was fully aware of how bad these circumstances were. If the German government had indeed planned to make the opening gambit in its bid for world power from an international position of this kind, then its long-range political calculations were even more foolish and irresponsible than its political maneuvers.

The basic flaw in the operations of the German government in 1914, as so often had been the case during the past quarter century, was that it ignored Bismarck's principle of taking into account the national interests and points of view of other powers. Again and again they repeated their confident belief that if Austria acted quickly, Russia and France would not intervene, that Russia was not ready for war, that the crisis would remain localized as it had always done in the past.

For France and Russia in 1914, however, their own international position could hardly have been more favorable. They were allied with each other and with Britain; they had successfully detached Italy from the Triple Alliance; and the Habsburg Empire seemed to be on the point of disintegration. But how long would these favorable circumstances continue? There were disquieting signs of a detente between Britain and Germany; the weak-willed tsar might succumb to German influences or be assassinated himself. Historians may yet have much to learn about what that shrewd Lorrainer and bitter foe of Germany, Raymond Poincaré, told the Russians in July 1914 or what was said in cabinet meetings in Paris and Saint Petersburg during those fateful days.

So far as the German government is concerned, it is possible to argue, as does Professor Zechlin, that vital German national interests were at stake in 1914—though this proposition in itself is very doubtful indeed. But vital national interests had not been at stake in Samoa, Kiaochow, the Transvaal, Morocco, Bagdad, Bosnia, the great battle fleet, the Kruger telegram, or in claims to a protectorate over the Mohammedan world. If German national interests were really at stake in 1914, it was because they had so frequently been transgressed in the past, and because of these same transgressions, Germany now found herself at war under the worst possible military, diplomatic, and moral circumstances.

NOTES

Based on a lecture delivered at the Naval War College, March 1973.

1. Raymond J. Sontag, *Germany and England: Background of Conflict, 1848-1894* (New York: Norton, 1969), p. 132.

2. William N. Medlicott, *Bismarck and Modern Germany* (New York: Harper & Row: 1965), p. 141.

3. William L. Langer, *European Alliances and Alignments, 1871-1890* (New York: Knopf, 1950), especially pp. 451-53, 504-5.

4. Hartmut Pogge-von Strandmann and Imanuel Geiss, *Die Erforderlichkeit des Unmöglichen. Deutschland am Vorabend des ersten Weltkrieges* (Frankfurt am Main, 1965), pp. 32-36.

5. "Die Illusion vom begrenzten Krieg," *Die Zeit* 21 September 1965, p. 5.

6. "Mit den Serben muss aufgeräumt werden, und zwar bald." Marginal note by the emperor on a report of 30 June 1914, from Tschirschky, his ambassador to Vienna, to Chancellor Bethmann Hollweg. *Die deutschen Dokumente zum Kriegsausbruch, 1914,* 2 vols. (Berlin, 1922), vol. 1, no. 7.

7. Szögyény, the Austrian ambassador to Berlin, to Berchthold, the Austrian prime minister, 5 July 1914 *Österreich-Ungarns Aussenpolitik,* 9 vols. (Vienna, 1930), vol. 8, no. 10058.

8. Bethmann-Hollweg to Tschirschky, 28 July 1914. *Die deutschen Dokumente,* vol. 1, no. 323.

Links Between World Wars I and II

Martin Blumenson

Editor's Note: *Martin Blumenson is currently on contract with the U.S. Air Force Office of History and he is President of the American Military Institute. He is a former member of the faculty, Army War College and sometime Ernest J. King Professor of Maritime History at the Naval War College. He is author of several works on World War II, including* The Patton Papers.

The striking similarities of World Wars I and II suggest that they were a single conflict. The farther we move away from them in time, the more they merge and appear to be essentially the same struggle. In the fifth century B.C., Thucydides considered the two wars separated by the Peace of Nicias to be a single conflict. The title of his history is *The Peloponnesian War*—singular. So, too, in the important aspects, are the two world wars in the twentieth century. They are distinguishable because they occurred at different times and out of different contexts. But together they were a continuing contest between coalitions.

Some of the details are quite dissimilar. For example, Italy fought on one side in the First World War and on the other during the Second, before switching once again. Turkey fought in the first war and remained neutral in the second. World War I was European—the vital action took place in the vital center of the world, with peripheral operations taking place elsewhere; World War II was far more global in scope—major campaigns were fought in Europe, but major operations also took place in Asia.

Despite certain differences, the conditions, the technologies, the strategies and policymaking, the nature of the wars and their outcomes are remarkably alike.

What is the point of such an examination? How is it relevant to our study of strategy? Let me go back for a moment to Thucydides. "What made war inevitable," he wrote, "was the growth of Athenian power and the fear which this caused in Sparta." Was the Peloponnesian War inevitable? It seems to me that the answer to this question depends upon one's view of the cosmos. In the ancient world, life was often seen as an unequal struggle between men and the gods. Everything was, therefore, foredoomed. Everything that happened was shaped by the gods, and all that men could do was to act out their assigned roles in a tragedy that unfolded inexorably. We see much the same thing today, but in modern terms we call it the struggle between human beings and historical forces. History today is concerned with the interaction of men and vast impersonal forces. But we believe that men's decisions have importance and impact on the developing scene. Otherwise, men have no roles except as robots carrying out foreshadowed actions, with foredoomed results, and inevitable outcomes. We might just as well submit to the cosmic forces. But I hope we do believe that our actions matter, that our decisions count, that we have at least some control over our destinies, that we do have choices and options, and that our selections will affect the course of our lives and of history. If we are of this persuasion, nothing is inevitable until it happens. Men do have a say in their future.

Having said this, I would like to add that men's choices are shaped by their assumptions, assumptions that grow out of their experiences, habits, upbringings, and outlooks. We are the creatures of our time and place. But as thinking persons, as future strategists and decisionmakers, we must try to understand which of our assumptions are outmoded and belong to another age and which are relevant to the world as it exists. What we are trying to learn is which assumptions about our world are valid. How can our choices be governed by reality rather than by prejudices, sacred cows, and cherished notions?

Both world wars were general wars. The belligerents mobilized and committed, so far as possible, the total means available to them. Huge armies were locked in land combat, large fleets fought at sea, and armadas of planes operated in the air. Behind them were enormous logistical systems organized to produce and deliver the supplies of war to the theaters of operation. Both times, the war developed a life of its own. The protagonists were overcome

by passion fueled by propaganda, and morality swept away considerations of power politics.

In both cases, except for Germany in the latter conflict, the
wars ended before the complete destruction of the defeated armed
forces, the occupation of the defeated nations' territories, and the
subjugation of the vanquished peoples. Even the unconditional
surrender concept was flexible enough to accommodate terms with
Italy and Japan.

The United States entered both conflicts late. Although the in-
fusion of American strength on the western front in 1918 provided
the margin of victory, the United States was a relatively minor
belligerent. In World War II the United States was one of the
principal members, if not the main member, of the Allied coalition.
One has only to contrast the positions of Pershing, who commanded American troops, and Eisenhower, who commanded Allied
forces. Russia, both times, was somewhat outside the Allied coalition: Britain, France, and the United States formed an alliance
within an alliance, and both times they were embarrassed on ideological grounds by their Russian partner.

Germany fought simultaneously on two fronts in both wars and,
although hampered by Austria and later by Italy, came close to
winning, both on land and at sea. In both wars, the Allies were
on the strategic defensive before going over to the offensive. Some
Germans tried to explain the defeat in World War I by the stab-in-
the-back theory: they said that the civilians, or at least some segments of society, had failed to support the military properly. After
World War II, many German generals blamed their defeat on
Hitler.

Both wars were fought with essentially the same technology,
the same weapons and equipment. The ground operations in World
War I were static, in the Second World War mobile. The difference
was the mastery of the technology by the military men. By the
Second World War, doctrine had caught up with technology.
Methodologies had been worked out for the employment of the
airplane, tank, motor vehicle, and other innovations that had been
revolutionary some twenty years earlier.

The causes of the conflicts were much the same. In Europe,
in both cases, a dynamic Germany with rising power and increasing
aspirations threatened the status quo. In World War II, that is
what Japan did in Asia.

The immediate results of the wars were much the same: the
growth of American power—a creditor nation for the first time
after World War I, a superpower after World War II; the tempo-

rary destruction of Germany both times; the rapid recovery of the defeated nations; the exhaustion of England and France; the dislocation of the European social order; the emergence of the Soviet Union from World War I and her growth to world power by the end of World War II; the emergence of Communist China from World War II. The first war spawned the League of Nations, the second the United Nations.

Both wars were, in turn, the culminating points of a period in history that started late in the eighteenth century with industrial, political, social, and intellectual revolutions. There was a new sense of individual worth and a new relationship between person and country. We call this patriotism, a sense of real attachment to the state, which no longer was the property of the ruler and his court, but was the possession of all the people. Governments were supposed to act as trustees for the benefit of everyone, not merely for the favored few.

Thus war became democratic, ideological, emotional, and as nearly total as possible in organization, mobilization, scope, and aim. Slogans and propaganda became powerful weapons: "Make the world safe for democracy," and "the Four Freedoms." The comparative abundance of men and goods, plus the unleashed emotions of waging a crusade, led to unparalleled destruction in both conflicts.

The periods before the outbreak of hostilities were somewhat similar. As preludes in both cases, the Balkan wars seem very much like the Spanish Civil War. The defeat of France by Prussia in 1871 planted some of the seeds of conflict in 1914. The defeat of Germany in 1918 planted some of the seeds of war in 1939.

The 1920s and 1930s were a time when people sought desperately and somewhat foolishly for peace. The First World War seemed to have produced only personal privation, financial inflation, and a widespread feeling that war was immoral. Vast feelings of antimilitariam and pacifism arose. There were several conferences to limit the size of navies. The Kellogg-Briand Peace Pact tried to outlaw war as an instrument of national policy. Many persons hoped that the League could keep the peace. Economic crises, particularly the Wall Street crash and the subsequent Depression, enhanced the attractiveness of socialism and produced totalitarianism in Italy and Germany to combat, not only economic distress, but also the evils of bolshevism. Dictators suppressed political and individual liberties, imposed strict controls on their states, and at great cost restored at home a sense of national unity and purpose. They turned Europe into two armed camps. When Mussolini invaded Ethiopia in 1935, he killed the League of Nations. When Hitler reconstituted Germany, he threatened to disrupt the general peace.

World Wars I and II were supposed to be local and short. The assassination at Sarajevo triggered a conflict that was expected to remain confined to Serbia and Austria. Instead it provided a sort of domino effect, quickly escalated out of control, and spread into a European conflagration. No one wanted general war, and no one knew how to avoid it.

So too in 1939, when Hitler's blitzkrieg into Poland was supposed to remain a local affair. He had neutralized the Russians by the Non-Aggression Pact with Stalin. England and France were far from Poland and Eastern Europe. No one wanted war, not even Hitler, who had managed to annex Austria and gobble up Czechoslovakia without resorting to force.

A good case can be made for the view that the nations drifted helplessly into both world wars because the leaders lacked the courage and the strength to avoid the clash of arms. The kaiser and his chancellor, the emperor and his foreign minister, the tsar and his court let things get out of hand, out of control. So did the politicians in the 1930s.

Perhaps the politicians in the 1930s had learned the wrong lessons of World War I. Perhaps they wondered whether the sacrifice of Serbia to Austria-Hungary in 1914 might have averted general war. They tried this technique at Munich and sacrificed Czechoslovakia to Hitler. But conciliation or appeasement of Hitler and Mussolini failed. Hitler gained bloodless victories. Mussolini seized Albania in the spring of 1939, and no one seemed to mind. Appeasement might have worked in 1914, but it did not work in 1939.

What triggered the assassination at Sarajevo in 1914 was the force of nascent nationalism. There was much agitation based on nationalism—or, as it was then called, self-determination. Ethnic groups were supposed to have the right to be self-governing. This feeling was very strong in the welter of nationalities living in the Austro-Hungarian Empire, but it was endemic in Eastern Europe. Slavs did not want to be ruled by Austrians or Hungarians. Poles insisted they were neither Russian nor German. Ruthenians and Macedonians were distinctly different sorts. So were Czechs and Slovaks. Religion, language, custom, and history had formed groups of people who were highly emotional in their national aspirations, who clamored for independence, and who sometimes engaged in intrigue and violence.

The settlement at Versailles legitimized this notion of self-determination. The peace treaty created new nations and restored some old ones—Poland, Czechoslovakia, Yugoslavia, Latvia, and others. But why not, for example, the Ukraine? Because it was difficult to define ethnic groups and their boundaries, difficult to decide which groups have legitimate nationalistic aims and can form proper national governments. The peace settlement fashioned at Versailles, somewhat arbitrary on this question, fragmented Eastern Europe.

Some resentments continued. For example, the Sudeten Germans found themselves in Czechoslovakia, and Hitler used this fact as an excuse to take over the country. In World War II, Germany and Russia again partitioned Poland, which disappeared temporarily as a state. The Soviet Union absorbed Latvia, Lithuania, and Estonia, and tried to do the same with Finland.

A rather fragmented Eastern Europe after World War I became somewhat reconsolidated after World War II in the Soviet satellite state system. The Warsaw Pact nations, a buffer between East and West, were tied earlier to the West. Now they seem tied to the East.

Nationalism continues to have force and to play a significant role in international politics, but nationalism, formerly centered in Europe has spread throughout the world under the guise of anticolonialism.

What of the planning and direction of the war efforts? The Prussian idea of the General Staff system had become part of all the major military establishments by the twentieth century, and the world wars featured the use of staff planning for movements of men and equipment, for allocation of supplies, and for the strategies to be put into effect. All the nations had war plans, and these indicated general strategic lines of action.

The greatest war plan was the Schlieffen plan, which was supposed to produce a short, lightning war. This was in accord with German strategic thinking, the search for the swift decisive act, the swift battle of annihilation. But the war quickly became a stalemate, a static war of attrition with enormous and senseless casualties on land. Serious attempts to stop the war failed. Civilians who called for a halt in hostilities were usually regarded as unpatriotic, or even as traitors. As the war of attrition ground on, to halt it short of total victory made less and less sense, for how could the casualties be justified without positive gains?

The overwhelming military problem was how to break the stalemate of trench warfare. The first solution was Gallipoli, a strategic outflanking movement, an indirect strategy. Fisher, First Sea Lord, suggested amphibious thrusts throughout the Baltic area. Churchill, First Lord of the Admiralty, advocated a thrust through the Mediterranean. The French had no wish to see resources diverted from the main theater, France. But they finally agreed to participate in what they regarded as a diversionary move.

Gallipoli turned out to be an Allied fiasco, and it failed to break the stalemate. But it divided the Allied strategists into two general groups: Westerners and Easterners. Westerners felt that the war could be decided only in France, the main arena. Easterners advocated a diversionary, indirect, or peripheral strategy.

The Germans tried to break the stalemate in France by introducing poison gas. Although chemical warfare was efficacious, the Germans lacked a doctrine that would permit them to exploit the surprise and the initial success they attained. Before long, the Allies had countermeasures—warning instruments, gas masks, and chemical agents of their own.

The Allies tried to break the stalemate on the western front with the tank. It produced a shocking effect on the Germans. But the Allies lacked a tactical doctrine or methodology for employing the new weapon. They were unable to exploit initial tactical success into strategic triumph.

Strategic theory and tactical doctrine in World War I foundered on technology. The proponents of land warfare, who continued persistently to try to destroy the enemy forces in consonance with what they believed to be Clausewitz' teachings, failed because the tacticians were not up to using the new weapons. The military technicians could not cope with the technology of their times. They were geared to operations tied to huge masses of men transported and supported by railroads and served by horses and mules. Only toward the end of the war would some tactical theorists begin to resolve the problems of how to use the new means of warfare available to them: Trenchard and Mitchell for airpower, Fuller for the tank, Monash, Hutier, and others for infantry attack formations.

The weapons in both wars were the same: the motor vehicle, tank, and the airplane. Not until the Second World War was their employment mastered. Curiously enough, it was the Germans who first put it all together.

Hitler's blitzkrieg astonished the world. The panzers smashed through defensive lines, roamed through lightly defended rear areas, and created fluid battle conditions that the Allies were not equipped mentally or materially to cope with. Hitler knocked out the Poles in less than a month, defeated the armies of France,

Belgium, and Britain in six weeks, forced the surrender of Belgium and France and the evacuation of British and some French troops from the Continent.

Britain in both wars put a professional army into France. However, the forced evacuation from Dunkirk and other ports in the summer of 1940, as well as the French surrender, prevented Britain and France from being bled white as in World War I.

The naval strategies of both wars were substantially the same. British sea strategy was dictated by familiar factors: the Royal Navy, a fleet in being; tradition; experience; and the geographical configuration of Northern Europe. As for the Germans, they had swallowed the thesis publicized by Alfred Thayer Mahan that great fleets made great nations. Imitating the British and hoping to emulate Nelson, they built a big-gun, big-battleship navy. Actually, a merchant-raiding navy would have suited them better.

Each nation blockaded the other: the British by bottling up the German fleet; the Germans by tying down and immobilizing the British and by using surface craft and U-boats to attack British shipping. The North Sea remained largely a British lake and the Baltic a German lake in both wars. The big-ship fleets stood in a state of equilibrium, and the single large naval engagement of World War I, the battle of Jutland, changed nothing.

In World War I, the British drove the German surface raiders from the seas by 1915, largely because radio permitted better tracking and stalking techniques. The British blockaded Germany both times and starved the country, although it took a long time to do so in both wars. The Germans launched a counterblockade in both wars by a *guerre de course*, and the merchant raiders, particularly the U-boats, had striking success. But German submarine production had low priority because of Germany's continental interests and because Mahan said that a *guerre de course* could not destroy enough shipping to win a war.

The German decision to institute all-out submarine warfare came rather late in World War I. It was designed to break the stalemates on the western front and at sea. By 1917, German submarines were sinking British ships faster than they could be built. The British were helpless. Jellicoe frankly said, "It is impossible to go on with the war if shipping losses like these continue." The solution was of course the convoy, which became the standard method of combatting the U-boat. Convoys were successful: more than a million American soldiers were transported to France without the loss of a single soldier's life from sinking at sea.

In World War II, Hitler ordered submarine warfare at once,

and the British, after an initial hesitation, adopted the convoy system. But Hitler enjoyed an advantage his predecessors had lacked. In a blitzkrieg at sea, he invaded and took posession of Denmark and Norway, which gave him favorable positions for U-boat warfare. After he obtained submarine bases on the Atlantic coast of France, he waged that war ruthlessly. Not until July 1943 did the Allies win what Churchill called the battle of the Atlantic. In that month Allied ship production exceeded shipping losses for the first time. It was that which allowed the Allies to take the strategic initiative.

The Germans were the first to employ strategic bombing, and they did so early in World War I. Zeppelins, later aircraft, dropped bombs on London. The Germans were the innovators of this type of warfare, but they were overtaken and outclassed by the British in World War II. The Germans failed to appreciate and therefore to develop the heavy, long-range bomber. The British did.

The British and the French were the first to develop and use tanks in World War I. But it was the Germans who brought tank warfare to its early perfection in World War II.

Does this tell us something about lessons learned? Do people learn from their own experience, because they understand it not only rationally but also emotionally? Can we learn from the experience of others? I think so, but only when we have digested that experience, so that it has rational meaning as well as emotional content. The British learned from their own experience as victims of strategic bombing during World War I. The Germans were profoundly struck by the danger as well as the promise of tank warfare.

By the end of World War I, Trenchard and Mitchell were planning to send fleets of bombers to strike at targets deep in the enemy rear. Had the war lasted into 1919, there would undoubtedly have been strategic bombardment in the style of World War II. But it was Hitler who launched terror bombing. The dive-bombing Stukas produced chaos on roads clogged with refugees in Poland and France, thereby disrupting ground movements by the military forces, which facilitated the advance of the panzers. The destruction of Rotterdam was a purely terroristic device, designed to overwhelm the will to resist.

The battle of Britain in 1940 was different. Germany attempted to gain air supremacy, regarded as the vital prerequisite for invasion of the British Isles. Control of the air might even give the German local superiority at sea. But the Luftwaffe never gained command of the air. Even had the Germans obtained it, it is likely that invasion would have been impossible because of the lack of surface craft. The airpower theorists believed that airpower is an offensive weapon. Yet the British defensive victory in the air battle of Britain was one of the great turning points of the war. Hitler's grand strategic design of conquering Britain had foundered on airpower and seapower. Germany, after all, was a land power. Thus Hitler turned to the east and invaded Russia instead.

To retaliate for the German bombing of British cities, Britain adopted strategic bombing, mainly for the psychological well-being of the British people. It was the only way to get back at the Germans. The targets were selected for terroristic reasons, and the prime objective was to give the British people a feeling of joyful revenge. Only incidentally were the bombers to knock out German industry and transport. That the British employed night bombing to reduce their losses in aircraft and that night bombing had to be area or saturation bombing rather than so-called pinpoint bombing—these underscore the essentially terroristic motivation of that campaign. In another sense, strategic bombing was blockade by different means.

Air bombardment raises all sorts of interesting and controversial problems and issues which are not limited to World War II; the selection of targets, the need for escorts, day versus night bombing, and the effectiveness of interdiction are only a few. What remains unclear is the question of the extent to which the executors of the Douhet thesis won World War II. Albert Speer says that Germany could not have stood a few more months of bombing. But the proposition that bombing alone would have completely destroyed the German ground forces appears dubious. It might well have paralyzed their movements, damaged their equipment and communications, disrupted their supplies, but probably would not have destroyed their will to resist. Americans who have never suffered from strategic bombardment have perhaps overemphasized the effect of bombing on the human will. Perhaps they have even misunderstood it. This area still remains controversial.

The direct relationship between strategic bombing and enemy surrender can be cited with assurance only in the case of Italy. It was no coincidence that the first bombardment of Rome, which had been spared because of the monuments, convinced the king to remove Mussolini from power and to start negotiating for surrender. The bombing of Rome was the straw that broke the camel's back. It was the crowning blow of a whole series of strokes that convinced the Italian people that continuing the war on the side of Germany would be a mistake.

Armies and navies played separate and independent roles in World War I, except for transport, supply, and one large amphibious operation. Even the air forces fought their own war. World War II saw the tri-service concept or the combined arms idea employed on a grand scale. The form that this integrated power took was amphibious assault. The best instance of a combat technique coming to maturity in the two wars is certainly this one. Contrast Gallipoli with the series of brilliant amphibious landings performed by the Allies in the European and Pacific areas during World War II. The failure of Gallipoli, which received intensive study between the wars, inspired the amphibious success of World War II. Here is an instance of lessons learned and technology mastered.

With hindsight, the sequence of amphibious operations that led the Allies toward victory seems inevitable and inexorable—but only in retrospect. The places where the amphibious assaults occurred were decided only after long and sometimes bitter debate and eventual compromise. The machinery that permitted this dialogue to take place was the Allied coalition command system. It had its roots in 1917.

For the Allies, 1917 was a year of mixed blessing. The good news was American entry into war. The bad news was a whole series of events—British exhaustion, French army mutinies, Italian disaster at Caporetto, and Russian revolution.

By instituting a variety of interallied committees, councils, and commissions, the Allies created a machinery designed to cope with the multiple national war efforts. Bodies met periodically on strategy—for example, in order to keep Italy in the war—on shipping, on war production, and on other like matters. There was even a group that discussed tank production, allocations, and doctrine. As a consequence, Allied cooperation and coordination developed in a variety of fields.

Perhaps the most striking development occurred in response to the spring offensive launched by Ludendorff in March 1918. The Russians having been eliminated from the war, German troops were transferred from the eastern to the western front to give Ludendorff numerical superiority in France. He hoped to crush the Allies before the Americans could field a large and well-trained army. Ludendorff came close to success, and he brought crisis to the Allied camp. This prompted the appointment of a supreme allied commander. In that position Marshal Foch made possible for the first time more than a semblance of cooperation to Allied arms. Lacking some of the ordinary prerogatives of command, Foch persuaded rather than ordered the French, British, and American commanders-in-chief, and to some extent the Italian, to act in conformance with a single battlefield strategy. This coalition command system was rudimentary. For example, Foch had a very small staff. Nevertheless, the idea of a supreme Allied commander became a reality.

In contrast, the Central Powers never had any system for the exercise of interallied strategy and command. Falkenhayn and Conrad, the German and Austrian military chiefs, occasionally consulted on timing for movements, but both countries fought little related, parallel wars until Ludendorff came to exercise the role of virtual dictator.

Almost the same thing happened in World War II. Hitler and Mussolini fought parallel wars and meshed their strategies at infrequent conferences, where the fuehrer spoke interminably and the duce listened uncomfortably. Beneath that level, the German and Italian military staffs were supposed to cooperate, but there was no real machinery for making strategic decisions and allocating strategic resources. Furthermore, the central direction of the German war effort below Hitler was fragmented: OKH (*Oberkommando des Heeres*), the army headquarters, ran the war in Russia and OKW (*Oberkommando der Wehrmacht*), theoretically a joint headquarters, ran the war everywhere else.

The Anglo-Americans in the Second World War built on their experience in the First. Even before the United States entered the war, military men from both nations met in Washington and laid the groundwork for a Europe-first strategy. They also laid the foundation for the Combined Chiefs of Staff structure that became a sophisticated coalition system to direct the global war. The early meetings in Washington are reminiscent of the Anglo-French conversations in the years before World War I. Although much attention has centered on the bickering that went on, the Combined Chiefs of Staff functioned effectively. The system featured the best characteristics of British command in committee and the American insistence on single or unified command.

In World War I, the military generally controlled strategy and policy. In World War II, the civilian leaders retained control. In the Combined Chiefs of Staff system, the prime minister and president determined policy and grand strategy. They were assisted by their principal military advisers, the British Chiefs of Staff and the American Joint Chiefs of Staff, who together formed the Combined Chiefs of Staff. Under this body were Allied theater commanders, who exercised authority and responsibility over all the troops and all the operations in accordance with directives received and resources allocated.

When the Combined Chiefs were unable to reach agreement on fundamental issues of strategy, they met with their political chiefs in the great periodic conferences of the war. There they hammered out their differences and reached agreement by compromise, for the British and Americans had different strategic concepts.

The Americans, favored by virtually unlimited resources, wished to execute a massive-thrust strategy. Highly conscious of the demands of the war in the Pacific, they desired to come to grips with the major enemy, Germany, as soon as possible, and this required a cross-Channel attack and a strike along the most direct path to the enemy homeland.

The British, with fewer industrial and human resources, proposed a peripheral strategy. They advocated making their main efforts in sea and air warfare while the Russians engaged the bulk of the German land forces. They wished to nibble at the periphery of German-occupied Europe, stretch the Germans to the point of collapse, and then invade the Continent.

To a large extent, this divergence in strategic thought, here grossly oversimplified, arose out of the debate between Easterners and Westerners in World War I. It was no accident that General Marshall, who had been closely associated with Pershing, was a Westerner who advocated the showdown battle with the Germans; or that Churchill, a leading Easterner, favored Mediterranean and peripheral operations.

Out of this came the compromise decision to invade North Africa, which set into motion a course of events. These events contributed an impetus and a momentum of their own. Because resources were concentrated in the Mediterranean area, because they could not be permitted to remain idle, because they would overburden sea transport if they were transferred elsewhere, and because they drew heavily on the global resources, the Allies had to postpone the climactic cross-Channel attack until the summer of 1944. Out of all this came the dual-thrust strategy in Europe, a drive in the Mediterranean region and a strike across the Channel, both moving toward Germany.

In the war against Japan, the American Joint Chiefs of Staff were acting as executive agent for the Combined Chiefs. Although the Joint Chiefs advocated a single-thrust strategy in Europe, they eventually implemented a dual-thrust strategy in the Pacific, one executed by Nimitz, the other by MacArthur. This strategy worked well, but the real motivation was the need to resolve service rivalry and ambition. The embarrassing question was what to do with General MacArthur.

Japan was a world power. She conquered Korea, defeated Russia, and acquired an island empire, formerly German, in World War I. When she invaded Manchuria in 1931, and later annexed that territory, then invaded China, she became too powerful in Asia, as Hitler in Europe.

American planners had concluded that Japan, an island empire like Britain, was vulnerable to blockade, and American submarines conducted unrestricted submarine warfare with great success. The Japanese were using convoys by 1943, but they were ill-equipped to protect merchant shipping because of deficient material and tactical formations. To a large extent, Japan was starved into defeat. This observation is not meant to degrade the operations of the fast carrier task forces, the fleet train, and the amphibious assault landings, which were superb operations because of men, equipment, and techniques.

The collapse of Germany in May 1945, the loss of Okinawa in June, growing shortages of all kinds in Japan, the severe bombardment of Japanese cities, all impelled Japan to seek an end of the war even before the release of the two atomic bombs and the Russian invasion of Manchuria. Despite the presence of large armies in Asia and the home islands, Japan had lost her strong defensive position by conquest or bypass. She had been deprived of control of the sea and of the air. She lost the means with which to continue the struggle. The kamikaze program that trained suicide pilots only showed how bankrupt Japan was, and her leaders should have had the sense to end the war long before August 1945.

Both world wars featured the expenditure of massive industrial resources, economic mobilization, and a highly developed science of logistics. In 1917, the United States lacked the economic base to produce materials of war. Americans used French and British material. For example, only two American tanks, imitations of the French Renault, reached France in 1918. They arrived after the armistice, too late for combat. The record of American economic mobilization in World War I is a sorry one. This chaotic effort prompted the postwar creation of the Army's Industrial College. Soldiers, as well as sailors and later airmen, would have to become experts in the highly technical field of managing the materials of war. That is to say, they would have to become knowledgeable in logistics, as part of an overall war effort. In World War II, their feats were prodigious.

The extent to which war in the twentieth century had come to depend upon industrial production can be seen in the case of

Italy. Mussolini embarked on a grand endeavor to restore the glory of the Roman Empire. He had large armies in the Balkans and in Libya, a respectable navy in the Mediterranean, and a good air force. After all, the Italians had been the first to use the airplane in war. Douhet, the prophet of airpower, was Italian, and Italo Balbo publicized the exploits of his country's airpower between the wars. But Mussolini soon discovered, as he should have known all along, that he lacked the industrial resources essential for success: arms, fuel oil, gasoline, guns, vehicles, and so on. The Italian fleet stayed in home ports, not because the naval commanders lacked courage, but rather because they lacked fuel oil.

So far I have talked about the wars between nations, conventional wars between states and combinations of states, which were fought by regular, uniformed forces of the state. It was this sort of war, fought by legitimate sovereign nations that Clausewitz, Mahan, and Douhet pondered, explained, and justified. At the same time, other wars were being fought, wars of revolution and guerrilla wars.

In East Africa during World War I, a force of 12,000 German troops under Lettow-Vorbeck carried on a guerrilla war and tied down 350,000 British troops. The military forces were conventional, and Lettow-Vorbeck's objective was wholly military in the conventional or nineteenth century sense of this word. Lawrence of Arabia had much the same military objective, tying down superior enemy forces, but he added another ingredient. He motivated his Arab guerrillas with the national political objective of gaining their independence from Turkey. The Russian upheaval growing directly out of World War I added another dimension, Marxism, to irregular warfare.

In World War II, the Chinese Communists supposedly fought the Japanese as they also fought the forces of the Chinese state. The guerrillas in Yugoslavia were in a similar civil war. And so too in France. The French Resistance operated eventually under the direction of de Gaulle and the Allied command, but the Resistance was also fragmented. Some Resistance groups fought the Pétain government, others the Germans, and still others fought among themselves. A substantial Marxist group inside the Resistance was dedicated to revolution in the Leninist sense.

In the world wars characterized by the massive use of equipment and weapons, combatants denied the use of sophisticated materials turned to the power of people and fought nonconventional wars featuring men against machines and existing institutions. Ideological conflicts in developing areas of the world remain a feature of the postwar world, and the roots of this kind of warfare are to be found in the nationalistic impulses of the two world wars. These were wars between nations fought according to the precepts of Clausewitz, Mahan, and Douhet. Along with that kind of war, there were conflicts according to the strictures of Lenin and Mao.

World Wars I and II were fought for political objectives that might be termed final solutions or final settlements to international problems. Victory was synonymous with panacea. Winning would solve all problems and set the world right. But this was quite different from what might be called the Bismarckian approach, a view of the world as a continuum, where an ongoing and uninterrupted series of events takes place. War in this kind of perceived world brings changes of less than gigantic or catastrophic proportions, and statesmen are motivated to maintain stability by taking measured and rational actions. The concept of total victory in the two world wars brought upheaval rather than peace. But impersonal historical forces and the power of certain ideas made it difficult for leaders in the twentieth century to act according to different rules and conventions. Their assumptions were outmoded, and they were unable to wage war as an instrument of national policy in small and limited terms. Clausewitz' inherent paradox of war was strikingly demonstrated both times. Reasonable national policy was swept aside by the urge to violence. Both world wars were ideological, emotional, and destructive. They went out of control, and the problems they solved only created new and greater ones. The fact is that total victory as a panacea became an illusion even as, paradoxically, the atomic bomb made a final solution, a final settlement, possible.

NOTE

Based on a lecture delivered at the Naval War College, March 1973.

Seapower in World Wars I and II

Stephen E. Ambrose

Editor's Note: *Stephen E. Ambrose is Professor of History at the Louisiana State University. He is the author of* The Supreme Commander *and* The War Years of General Dwight D. Eisenhower.

I

He who controls the sea controls everything—or nothing. It all depends on where he is and what use he makes of his control. He controls some, but not all, of the world's great commercial routes; but, except for the fisheries, he controls almost none of the earth's currently usable resources. In order to get the coal and iron and oil that make a modern industrial state go, he must be able to extend his control to one of the world's great landmasses. Obviously, then, nonexpansive nations that already occupy a large landmass do not need to control the seas, or at least they do not need to do so as badly as island empires do, a fact not often recognized by British and American naval strategists.

To continue for a moment in this heretical vein, it is possible that the purpose of a continental navy is not to destroy the enemy's navy in order to gain control of the sea. Perhaps France and Germany have followed the correct strategy in pursuing a *guerre de course*. Certainly for Napoleon, the kaiser, and Hitler, one of the keys to victory was denying the British access to their world market and sources of supply, but it is not at all certain that this required the destruction of the British battle fleet. There are enough *ifs* in the submarine campaigns of this century to lead one to suspect that it is theoretically possible to deny to the enemy the use of the seas without yourself controlling the ocean and, in an immediate crisis, the objective for continental powers is not so much to control the sea in order to use it as it is to deny its use to the British.

What I wish to suggest is that Mahan's concept that national greatness can come only through control of blue water is a limited one that must be examined with regard to a specific time and place. Surely the ancient Mongols, Napoleonic France, and modern Russia and China were, or are, great nations by any standard, yet none of them controlled the seas. German commerce-raiding in this century posed, potentially, a more dangerous threat to the Allies than Allied control of the water did to Germany. German submarines, by themselves, could have defeated England; English battleships, by themselves, could never have defeated Germany.

It is clear enough that had England lost control of the surface water at any time between 1914-18 or 1939-45, she would have lost everything. The same observation would apply to Japan, with even more force, for her relative paucity of resources at home, combined with the tremendous distances in the Pacific, made control of the seas vital to her if she wished to play the role of a great power. But it is not much more than a commonplace to say that island empires depend on control of the waters around them for their greatness.

What is necessary, it seems to me, is to realize the limitations inherent in any given situation; to be more specific, to recognize that it is well-nigh impossible for any one nation to control both the land and the sea. Only two nations in this century have really tried, Germany from 1900 to 1916 and Russia today. America does not challenge Russian control of the land in the Eurasian heartland nor China's domination in Asia. In Indochina, the United States has limited itself to contending for the periphery of China's sphere of influence. England has never by herself thought of challenging for control of the European landmass. For all the power of the combined British and American fleets in World War II, without the Red army the Western Alliance could not have won the war.

Clearly then, Mahan was wrong in intimating that control of Europe depended on control of the sea. In both world wars the Germans were brought down only by massive engagements on the land, brought about through alliances. Allied control of the oceans denied certain things to the Germans, to be sure, and therefore contributed to the victory, but the Allied navies, in the nature of the game, could not be decisive. By the same token, in Vietnam today, where the United States has total control of the sea, the navy has helped enormously in deploying and maintaining American power at a vast distance from the homeland, but it is able to give only limited help in achieving a tactical victory or, far more important, imposing a political settlement.

This rather long-winded introduction to seapower in World War I is meant only to suggest that Germany's naval policy ought not to be condemned out of hand. Insofar as Germany followed a *guerre de course* policy, I believe she had a correct strategy; insofar as she tried to challenge England on the high seas, she was mistaken. The geographical position of the two nations dictated certain rather obvious policies, of which by far the most important was that, in allocating resources, Germany had to put her major effort into the army, Britain into the navy. The more resources Germany put into the *guerre de course,* with its promise of a high return for a low cost, the better off she was.

But this was not so clear to the Germans, of course, and, in fact, they put their major naval effort from 1900 on into big ships. Great battleships brought great prestige, and the kaiser wanted his share of them. Realizing that the British would never allow Germany to outbuild the English fleet, Tirpitz came up with a theory to justify the construction of the High Seas Fleet, the so-called risk-fleet theory. Tirpitz argued that Germany's overseas trade and colonies could be effectively protected only by constructing a fleet so strong that even "the strongest naval power" could not fight it without seriously weakening its own naval power and leaving it helpless against a coalition of other naval powers. In other words, the German fleet did not have to be as strong as that of Britain, because England would never dare concentrate all its naval power against Germany. The cold calculation behind this doctrine was that England, rather than risk a clash with a powerful concentrated German fleet, would prefer to make concessions to Germany in the colonial field. In short, the new fleet would be used as an instrument of coercion.

There were a number of assumptions in Tirpitz' risk-fleet theory, none of which proved justified. Perhaps most important was the idea that big ships were the only way to challenge Britain on the high seas. Cruisers built for commerce-raiding and, of course, submarines would have worked much better. Tirpitz also assumed that it was important to Germany to protect her colonies and overseas trade—yet, in practice, Germany carried on for four years of arduous war without them. Germany's colonies were by no means as important to her as England's were to Britain. Finally, the risk-fleet theory was based on the concept that, if war with England came, Germany would have allies in possession of fleets that would be capable of taking on a weakened British fleet. This turned out to be not so, as German statesmen proved to be incapable of so arranging things as to bring about this desired political result. Germany's main ally, Austria-Hungary, was almost exclusively a land power. The risk-fleet theory proved to be a costly error.

Let me here just cover one highlight of German strategy, beginning with the observation that German naval strategy was governed in large part by the tools available at the beginning of the war. There was always a controversy over how to use these tools; to oversimplify, Tirpitz wanted the High Seas Fleet to accept risks, while the commanders of the fleet itself were cautious. Tirpitz virtually accused the commanders of cowardice. He argued that the High Seas Fleet was more at liberty to take risks than the British since Germany's fate did not completely depend upon the High Seas Fleet, whereas the fate of not only Britain but that of her allies depended on the Grand Fleet. There was some truth in his observation—Germany could have lost the High Seas Fleet and still won the war—but the commanders of the High Seas Fleet would have none of it. They were always weaker in capital ships, and their only hope of victory in an all-out encounter was luck— luck with destroyers, U-boats, or mines.

So the High Seas Fleet, built at such cost, both financial and political, contributed little to the German cause. Until 1917 submarines did not do much better, partly because of political limitations, more because there were not enough of them and their tactics were deficient. Finally, in early 1917, after the underwater fleet had been built up and following long discussions in which General Ludendorff seems to have taken the lead, the decision to introduce unrestricted submarine warfare was taken. It changed the nature of the war at all levels. Ludendorff knew it would bring America in on the British side; he reasoned that America could not make a contribution, however, until it was too late, and, given the information available to him at the time, it is hard to see how he could have reasoned otherwise. The decision gave Germany the initiative at sea, putting its navy on the offensive and challenging Britain in a way that had not been done since the Spanish Armada. Significantly, Germany made no bid to wrest control of the sea from Britain; the U-boats did not waste their effort in trying to get at the Grand Fleet. Instead, the sea war became an all-out *guerre de course,* with not only the submarines but also surface vessels switched to the attack on commerce, concentrating on traffic in the English Channel and the Mediterranean and against the Scandinavian trade.

To inaugurate deliberately a policy that would surely bring the world's greatest industrial power into the war as an enemy was a great gamble. The Germans realized this and regarded the decision as the most important of the war. Within weeks of taking it, they had reason to believe victory was in sight. Germany was on the verge of victory. Incapable of destroying her enemies on the ground on the western front, she had—in effect—successfully blockaded Russia and thereby contributed to the withdrawal of that nation from the war. Now she was blockading Britain, with startlingly effective results. One of every four ships that left England was sunk. Britain was replacing only one ship for each ten sunk. No pit props were arriving from Norway, which threatened to destroy the coal industry. Wheat supplies were down to six weeks (although there were piles of grain in France, belonging to the British, which Haig insisted on hoarding to feed the horses, so that when the breakthrough occurred his cavalry would be in good shape for the dash to Berlin).

How did the Royal Navy respond to this, the greatest crisis in Britain's history? Jellicoe, then First Sea Lord, admitted his helplessness by saying, "There is absolutely no solution that we can see." When Vice Admiral William S. Sims, USN, arrived in London on 9 April 1917, he was astonished at what he learned. Jellicoe told him, "It is impossible to go on with the war if losses like these continue." Yet Jellicoe had no solution nor could he even think of new methods to try. Britain was failing—and it is only a slight exaggeration to say that the Royal Navy decided it could do nothing about it.

There were other shocks for Sims. America had begun a great naval building program in 1915 and had naturally followed the British lead and concentrated on Dreadnoughts. Sims now learned that they were not needed, indeed, not even wanted. If they were brought over, they would just burn oil needed for destroyers. Destroyers were what was wanted, but America had only a few to offer, not nearly enough to save the day. It was quite a commentary on a whole generation of naval building, not to mention the way in which Germany, with a relatively small expenditure on submarines, had been able to change the entire nature of the war at sea.

The story of how Britain overcame the crisis is one of the most dramatic of the war; naturally, with so much at stake, there are a number of versions, with various people taking credit for the solution. The Americans claim that Sims was chiefly responsible. Actually, many contributed, but the key figure seems to have been Prime Minister David Lloyd George, that shadowy figure who reveled in the hatred of the entire British establishment and who was, according to A. J. P. Taylor, the greatest prime minister of the century.

Lloyd George first asked Jellicoe to devise a solution. Jellicoe said nothing was possible. Lloyd George then turned to the publisher Northcliffe, who suggested consulting Hankey, secretary of the War Cabinet and father of the Committee of Imperial Defense. Lloyd George discussed the situation with Hankey, who recommended the convoy system.

Lloyd George then returned to the Admiralty and demanded the initiation of the convoy system. He pointed out that the Grand Fleet never moved except in convoy. The Admiralty rejoined that merchant captains could not keep station, that the convoys would just offer larger targets to U-boats, that unloading facilities were inadequate to handle all the ships that would come into the ports at once. On 30 April 1917, nevertheless, on the only occasion in British history when a prime minister directed a great department of state in the teeth of the minister responsible, Lloyd George ordered the institution of the convoy. It was his greatest and most decisive achievement of the war. The first convoy left Gibraltar on 10 May. Others were organized from Canadian and American ports. Slowly but surely, the curve of sinkings went down. By 1918 over 80 percent of the shipping coming into Britain came in convoy. Less than 1 percent of ships in convoy were lost from all causes. By 1918 Britain was building more ships than she was losing. The convoy enabled England to survive and win the war.

Nothing illustrated quite so clearly how fully Germany had taken the initiative by launching unrestricted submarine warfare than the British decision to go to convoy. Because the destroyers' primary task became escorting convoys (as well as search and destroy missions through patrolling), the Grand Fleet was deprived of its screen and therefore, in effect, blockaded in its harbors. The effect was strikingly and tragically illustrated by Admiral Beatty's position as commander-in-chief of the Grand Fleet. At an Admiralty conference on 2 January 1918, Beaty said he no longer considered it wise to provoke a fleet action, even if an opportunity occurred.

This from the dashing Beatty, the man who had writhed under Jellicoe's cautious leadership at Jutland. Beatty argued that trade came first, that ships detached to protect convoys must be written off the strength of the Grand Fleet; that the German battle cruiser fleet was now more formidable than his own; that he had detached too many destroyers for the Grand Fleet to safely issue forth to take on the High Seas Fleet. Nelson must have turned in his grave as Beatty spoke, but there was no gainsaying that Beatty was correct.

What, then, of the Grand Fleet, that magnificent collection of gigantic Dreadnoughts and cruisers that were hardly smaller? It had been the Number 1 priority of Great Britain, built at enormous expense, and was regarded as the first line of defense. What was the strategy governing the use of this weapon? How successful was it? In the end, what contribution did the Grand Fleet make to victory? Did it justify the allocation of resources necessary to create it in the first place?

There are no clear-cut answers. Certain it is that the Grand Fleet kept German surface raiders under control and helped to keep the submarine menace from becoming worse than it did. The British blockade of Germany would hardly have been possible without the Grand Fleet, and there are scholars who argue vehemently that in the last analysis it was the blockade that brought the Central Powers to their knees. This, however, is conjecture and to my mind not valid. The German spring offensive in 1918 (the Ludendorff offensive) was an extraordinarily powerful one and came close—very close—to total success. That Germany could mount such an offensive so late in the war indicates that, great as the contribution the blockade made to reducing German strength was, it was not decisive.

As early as 1905 Admiral Wilson, the Channel commander in chief, considered the problem of what the British navy could do to tip the balance in a war that would be primarily fought by mass armies on the Continent. He believed that "no action by the Navy alone can do France any good," and declared that the best and most valuable contribution the navy could make would be to capture the mouths of the Elbe and Weser rivers through combined military and naval expeditions—amphibious assaults, in short, somewhat like what First Sea Lord Fisher would propose as the Baltic alternative in the early stages of the war. Wilson recommended that, when the serious possibility of war arose, he be placed in communication with the commander in chief of the expeditionary force in order that they could prepare plans for combined operations "on the largest scale possible," with the objective of drawing German troops away from the French frontier and threatening Germany's rear. He argued that all available small craft, as well as overage battleships, could be used to bombard the shore and prepare the way for the landing.

As noted, Fisher would later propose a similar idea as a proper use of seapower, but, unfortunately, the reforms he introduced during his first term as First Sea Lord, beginning in 1905, led to the creation of a navy ill-suited to combined operations. Fisher concentrated on Dreadnoughts; his critics at the time argued, among other things, that in weeding out the smaller ships of no great power and taking them out of commission he was concentrating his attention too exclusively on the fleet as an engine of fighting at sea, thereby ignoring its enormous possibilities for influencing operations ashore, especially through amphibious assaults. Fisher stuck to the Dreadnoughts, nevertheless, with results that are well known.

It is also true that the one great combined operation tried in the war was an unmitigated disaster. The reasons for the failure at the Dardanelles remain controversial; the list of mistakes is almost endless. Certainly, had the British used World War II amphibious methods the campaign would have been a success, but one can wonder if they should have tried it at all since they knew nothing of World War II methods. Had the overage battleships pushed just a little harder, they could have forced the Straits, but none of the commanders knew that at the time, and it is difficult to see how they could have known. Had the soldiers been more aggressive once they had landed, they could have carried the day, but it is much easier to be aggressive after the fact, when the enemy's strength and disposition are known, than it is when under fire.

I am not so foolhardy as to try to settle the Dardanelles argument; I would, however, like to make one observation on a broader aspect of the campaign. Almost everyone who writes about it seems to accept Churchill's basic justification for the attempt to force the Straits—that opening a pipeline to Russia would have had immeasurable effect on the war. Dr. Lundenberg suggests that if a supply route to Russia had been opened, the czar would have remained in control, the Russians would have fought on, and there would have been no Communist Revolution. Most Western writers seem to accept this idea, usually without thinking about it very hard.

It is time to call the idea into question. Great political upheavals do occur in a time and at a place to be sure, so that they are influenced by immediate events. But it seems to me to be questionable to assume that the overthrow of the czar, and later of Kerensky, could have been prevented by shipping some ammunition to Russia. Dramatic history and romantic historians to the contrary notwithstanding, world events do not turn on such small matters. More concretely, one must ask how many supplies the Western Powers could have shipped to Russia in 1917. Even had the Straits and/or the Balkan route been open, did England and France, in fact, have the ships and, more important, the guns and shells to spare? I doubt that they had anywhere near enough to supply the Russian army adequately, especially when one recalls that the Russian army needed everything—food, clothes, shoes, shelter, as well as implements of war. Finally, everything I have read about conditions among the officer corps in the Russian army leads me to believe that whatever was sent would have been sold on a black market for individual gain. More and more supplies cannot overcome ingrained corruption. They just add to it as shown in China in World War II.

The other great naval event of the war was a battle that, like Waterloo, has been analyzed *ad nauseam*. Jutland was the first great encounter between Dreadnoughts and the last of the gigantic surface actions in that war. Tactically, it is intensely interesting, and the personalities of the commanders on both sides add to the fascination. As with the Dardanelles, I intend to settle nothing here, but again some suggestions may be in order.

First, much of the criticism of Jellicoe for not being more aggressive seems out of touch with the realities he faced. That he was overly afraid of torpedoes, mines, and submarines is obvious now, but who was so sure then? He had, in any case, always made his position clear enough. As Arthur Marder writes in *From the Dreadnought to Scapa Flow* (London: Oxford University Press, 1966), 3:5,

Jellicoe would have liked nothing better than to take the offensive, strategic and tactical, and deal the Germans a smashing blow. But there were powerful reasons why he considered it his duty to handle the fleet at all times with caution. There was, in the first place, his cardinal belief that the overriding duty of the Grand Fleet was to stay alive and in superior force. . . . Of more immediate importance in explaining the defensive tone of the Grand Fleet Battle Orders was Jellicoe's determination not to hazard his capital-ship superiority to the risk of underwater damage from torpedoes, mines or submarine-and-mine traps.

Jellicoe's fears were exaggerated, because everyone was always telling him how important he was. As usual, Churchill put it best by saying Jellicoe was the only man who could lose the war in an afternoon, which was true enough but which, because everyone was saying it, had an unhealthy effect on Jellicoe's mind. One historian has pointed out that Jellicoe more and more saw himself as the focal point for the whole war and the Grand Fleet as the key to victory. Since Jellicoe also felt, as Hankey put it, that at any minute a German was going to jump through the Admiralty window behind him and hit him when he least expected it, he was quite naturally cautious.

But as Marder reminds us, one of the critics, Admiral Beatty, when he became First Sea Lord, changed nothing at all. For all his dash, Beatty would not dream of risking the Grand Fleet except under favorable circumstances, which meant north of the latitude of Horns Reef. Since the Germans would not fight except in waters comfortably close to their bases, the result was stalemate.

Now, everyone knows that neither of these two great fleets was willing to take risks, for reasons on both sides that were sound enough. Nevertheless, there is a feeling of frustration about Jutland. The two fleets that sailed through the misty night to their encounter at Jutland constituted the culminating manifestation of naval force in the history of the world, and they were unable to reach any decision. This was frustrating, especially for the British, who loudly demanded, "Was this the spirit of Nelson?" Nelson, Jellicoe's defenders rejoined, did not have to face torpedoes and mines. It is generally accepted today that Jellicoe was correct, perhaps not tactically, but strategically, for the maintenance of British control of the sea was even more vital than the defeat of the German fleet.

There is great force in this argument. I am compelled to ask, however, if it was the only factor in Jellicoe's, and later Beatty's, mind. The navies of World War I, on both sides, can with some justice be accused of sentimentally valuing things more than lives or even causes. The artilleryman's love of his guns and readiness to sacrifice his life to avert the disgrace of losing them is paralleled by the sailor's adoration of his ship. Liddell Hart suggests that this attitude may have its foundation in totemism, but it is accentuated by the military man's peacetime shortage of material and the penalties attached to any loss of it. The attitude hinders the soldier or sailor from adopting the commonsense view that a ship or a gun, like a shell, is merely a weapon to be expended profitably.

A very curious thing happened in Britain in World War I, and it happened twice. In early 1917 the Admiralty could think of no way in which the Grand Fleet, built at such an enormous national effort, could help overcome the submarine crisis. We have already covered the results. Then it happened again, in 1918. Ludendorff's spring offensive threatened the entire position in France. Another crisis was at hand. Again, the Grand Fleet could propose nothing.

I do not know of anyone who has studied this astonishing fact. I asked Arthur Marder, who by all odds is the expert to ask, about it last sprng. He said that Beatty made a couple of halfhearted proposals to Jellicoe which were turned down, and the fleet did nothing. It is astonishing to realize that while English soldiers were dying by the thousands, with their backs to the wall, and the fate of the empire trembled in the balance, the Grand Fleet felt it could do nothing at all to help.

Younger officers in the fleet disagreed at the time and urged action of some sort. The crux of the matter, as Marder emphasizes, was Beatty's conviction that there must be no gambling with the navy; the whole Allied cause was based on the latent power of the Grand Fleet. I am suggesting that Beatty was wrong; that even had the Grand Fleet remained intact, even had it defeated the High Sea Fleet in action in 1918, Britain and France still could have lost the war to Ludendorff's troops. Beatty's view of war was too narrow.

There is another disturbing element to naval warfare, 1914-18. Liddell Hart has said that a fundamental difference between the higher naval and military leadership in the war was that the admirals would not intentionally give battle unless reasonably sure of an initial advantage, whereas the generals were usually ready to take the offensive whatever the disadvantages. This is true, and one must wonder why. How did it come about that, while Beatty was carefully preserving his ships, Haig was spending tens of thousands of lives in absolutely useless offensives? England paid practically no attention when a hundred men died in the trenches because of a stray shell; England went into national mourning when a Dreadnought was lost. Why?

Let me make two highly tentative suggestions. First, the Dreadnoughts had been tied in with the whole idea of national prestige. In Germany the schoolchildren collected pennies to build the ships. No one had ever thought to collect pennies in the schools to buy the soldier a rifle. In World War II there was relatively little of this mystical nonsense about ships—aircraft carriers were seen as tools of war, expendable tools to be used profitably. Some flattops were lost, but they were used to advantage. They were not regarded as entities unto themselves, to be spared and protected for their own sakes. They were implements of national purpose, nothing more—and nothing less. Ships like *Lexington* are remembered today precisely because they did fight—who now remembers any of the Dreadnoughts?

The second tentative suggestion I should like to make as to why the Dreadnoughts did not fight, even in moments of supreme crisis, is this: it was a machine-oriented age. Social historians stress this point all the time. The industrial system of the time was geared to machines, not to men. As one quick example, if a machine worked most effectively by going twenty-four hours a day, seven days a week, then men had to adjust to it, and night shifts were invented. No one thought of adjusting the machine to the needs of men. So, too, with the armed services. Britain was willing to make any sacrifice in men's lives required to win the war, but she was unwilling to sacrifice her machines. Haig, Jellicoe, and Beatty all came from the same generation; all had comparable values, standards, and education. Yet Haig thought of nothing but attack, while the sailors thought of little but protecting their ships. There had to be a reason. Mine may not be the right one, but hopefully the question will at least provoke some discussion.

These criticisms of British naval strategy in World War I apply equally to the other powers, especially Germany. More important, I really do not see how Jellicoe, Beatty, and the others could have acted much, if any, differently. They were human beings, not computers, and they were the prisoners of their time and place. Their attitudes toward strategy were shared by nearly every important sailor. Their professional knowledge and experience were excellent for 1914-18. They all did their best, and one cannot ask humans to do more. It is the function of history, as I see it, to point to errors and make suggestions, based on hindsight, so that we can do better in the future, but who among us can say he could have done better at that time and in that place? Certainly I cannot.

II

It has long been my contention that there was no major technological breakthrough in land warfare between the beginning of the First World War and the conclusion of the Second. The major weapons of the 1914-18 period were also the major weapons of the 1939-45 period. There were improvements on basic designs, to be sure, and the tacticians of the Second World War used the weapons better than they were used in the First World War (tanks are an obvious example), but in basic essentials both wars were fought with the same weapons.

This was not the case at sea. World War I had inaugurated a new era, that of underseas warfare, which drastically changed the old strategies, especially that of the nature and extent of the *guerre de course*. Before the submarine, the ships that were capable of gaining command of the sea were also capable of destroying commerce raiders. After submarine development this was no longer true. Thus I would contend that the major breakthrough of World War I was the development and extension of underseas warfare. In World War II one sees refinement and improvement in submarine techniques, as well, of course, as in antisubmarine warfare, but no basic change. In essence, the *guerre de course* of World War II was similar to that of World War I. On the high seas, however, there were fundamental changes, which meant in practice that admirals in 1939 had to consider much more in the way of technological change than did the generals. The two most important changes were the revolution in amphibious warfare and the coming of age of the aircraft carrier.

There was also a change in attitude on the part of the British. In effect, the British armed services rejected the World War I experience totally. On the ground, the soldiers were determined to avoid the blood baths of 1914-18, and British strategy returned to the traditional practice of staying out of the mass warfare on the Continent, hitting at the enemy's periphery, and going onto the Continent only when the enemy was exhausted. At sea, British sailors were concerned with much more than just protecting the fleet in being, and British ships compiled an outstanding combat record, as they sought out the enemy at all possible opportunities. The British made especially great contributions in support of amphibious attacks, exposing the fleet in return for a measurable profit.

Throughout human history, navies have been used to transport soldiers to hostile shores, land them, and provide logistical support. In a sense, then, the United States and British navies of World War II only did what had been done before, albeit on a far larger scale. But the scale was so enormous that the difference was not just quantitiative but qualitative. Just as the aircraft carrier allowed navies to increase dramatically the area over which they could influence events, so did improvements in amphibious techniques make navies far more valuable by making it possible for them to project their power up to and beyond the coastline.

It was not just that the ships carried the men to the shores, although obviously that was the *sine qua non* of amphibious warfare. In nearly every amphibious operation of World War II, it was naval gunfire that saved the day. At Sicily, in July 1943, a German counterattack against the beaches by the Hermann Goering Panzer Division threatened to drive the Americans back into the Mediterranean. The troops had few antitank guns and practically no artillery ashore. The air forces were off flying strategic missions, for at that stage of the war they could not be bothered with close-in tactical support. The destroyers and cruisers, British and American, stepped into the breach. In one of the few actions in history that pitted tanks against ships, the ships demolished the tanks and thus secured the bridgehead.

At Salerno, in September of 1943, and again at Anzio, in January of 1944, the same story unfolded. Once again the size and accuracy of naval bombardment—mostly British—made it possible for the troops to hang on in the bridgehead. At Normandy it was ship-to-shore bombardment, much more than air strikes, that softened up the beachhead for Eisenhower's troops. Surprisingly, this story is seldom told and little known. One reason, I suppose, is that the air forces have better publicity departments than the navies. Another is that the airplanes are more spectacular, especially to the soldiers on the ground. Thus, in his memoirs, Eisenhower related how touch-and-go things were at Salerno, until the air force began to fly tactical missions and forced the Germans back. He did not mention the naval support fire. Yet the navies fired ten times more shells than the air force dropped, and I hardly need to remind this audience that the naval shells hit what they were aimed at while the free-falling bombs seldom did more than make large holes in the ground.

The navies' contribution to the revolution in amphibious warfare did not end with fire support; indeed, the scale of amphibious warfare could hardly have been possible had it not been for the enormous strides made in landing craft in World War II. Here I am not so much concerned with getting the men ashore—its importance is too obvious to belabor—as I am with the ability to supply them once there. The development of vessels that made it possible to bring supplies in over open beaches and the British development of artificial harbors and breakwaters were the chief innovations of World War II. I would go so far as to say that more than any other technological development of the war, the ability to supply troops over open beaches shaped the strategy in World War II.

Most of the great operations of the war, on both oceans, would hardly have been possible without this development. The Allies could not have invaded Sicily nor Italy nor Normandy, not to mention the Pacific islands, without it. Supply over beaches enabled the Allies to exert their power in areas previously denied to them and thus greatly extended the strategic scope of the war. Had it not been for the new landing craft and the artificial harbors and breakwaters, the Normandy invasion would have been a bloody failure. In fact, it would not have been tried, and since Hitler's defenses around the ports and harbors on the coast of France were so strong, it is doubtful if the Allies would have been able to return to the Continent at all.

Even after the capture of ports, most land campaigns would have failed had it not been for the navies' new-found abilities. In the French campaign, for example, the artificial ports (and Pluto) brought in by far the bulk of the supplies until the late autumn of 1944. The troops that overran France drew only a small percentage of their supplies from Cherbourg, the only working port available. It was not until Antwerp was opened and winter weather set in that the artificial harbors were overshadowed.

What the revolution in amphibious warfare meant was that no open coastline was safe from Allied power (the invasion of Casablanca in November 1942, may I remind you, was mounted in Norfolk, Virginia). This forced the enemy to protect all coastlines or face defeat. It is only a slight exaggeration to say that the Allies could strike anywhere with terrible swiftness (MacArthur's landing at Inchon is a later example of the effectiveness of this technique). It was all dependent, of course, on control of the sea, which is another way of saying that in World War II the Anglo-Americans used their control of the sea for positive purposes, as they had not done in World War I. The Grand Fleet made practically no contribution to the land battles in France in 1914-18; the Anglo-American fleet of 1942-45 was the decisive weapon in the European war. This is using resources effectively.

The success of Allied amphibious warfare was dependent on the ability to produce the necessary landing craft (more about that later), but an essential ingredient to the mix was men. Combined planning and control of operations reached new levels in World War II. If landing craft were the decisive factor in the strategy pursued in Europe and if the aircraft carrier revolutionized naval strategy in the Pacific, it was combined planning that made the

new tools usable. The achievement was especially impressive because, in Europe, it did not just involve getting the army and
navy to work together—a difficult enough task by itself—but rather
included the air forces plus officers of two distinct nationalities.
In effect, men from six different backgrounds had to be brought
together—British army, navy, and air officers, as well as American
officers from the three corresponding branches. The first time it
was tried, in the early days of planning for the North African
invasion, they "fought like cats and dogs."

Time and again Eisenhower said that his success all came down
to one word—the team. He always emphasized that he felt his
greatest contribution was getting everyone to work together
toward a common objective. He himself used the term *triphibious
warfare* to describe his operations, and he became a great advocate
of unification after the war. He thought the National Security
Act of 1947 did not go nearly far enough in unifying the three
American services and even went to the length of advocating a
uniformity of curriculum among the service academies and a single
uniform for all officers in the armed services. He also felt that
integration of the Anglo-American armed services was a desirable
goal.

Eisenhower's success did not come easily, but he did have certain
advantages that should not be ignored. There was, first of all,
the common language and heritage, something hardly ever found
in alliance warfare. Still, there was a certain amount of anglopho-
bia among the Americans which Eisenhower constantly fought.
Another great advantage was the relative absence of political bickering. The British and Americans shared the same general goal—
the total defeat of Nazi Germany; and because Eisenhower always
insisted on making his decisions on purely military, as opposed
to political, grounds, there was little bickering. There were, of
course, differences, the most important of which was British insistence on fighting in the Mediterranean as opposed to the American
desire to get into northwest France as soon as possible; but these
differences were ones of approach and method, not goals.

Eisenhower, in fact, had as much trouble in integrating some
American officers into the team as he did with the British. I am
glad to relate to this audience that it was the Army Air Force,
and not the United States Navy, that gave him trouble, although
the reason was not necessarily that the naval officers had a broader
vision. The air force, of course, had its own strategic doctrine and
fervently believed that it could win the war on its own, if only
the ground troops would stop bothering them with requests for

support. Eisenhower fought some momentous battles with the flyers before he could get them to cooperate, especially with those air force officers who believed the invasion of France was unnecessary and who maintained that they could bring Germany to surrender through massive air raids alone.

The navy was a different story. The admirals, like the flyers, had a strategic doctrine of their own, command of the seas, which might have led them to drag their heels in combined planning and to withdraw their vessels from support of the troops had there been a challenge to their command of the sea. But there was no such challenge, and since the navies already had command of the sea, they could willingly pitch in and give their all to supporting the troops. MacArthur's experience in the Southwest Pacific indicates that had the Germans maintained a large surface fleet, Eisenhower might not have enjoyed such full cooperation from the navies.

But the important point is that he did have it, most notably in the planning stages. British and American naval officers worked closely with soldiers and flyers, from the level of lieutenants up to admirals and generals, toward a common objective. In a way, however—to end the discussion on combined planning on a slightly sour note—the success may have been unfortunate for the future. It seems to me that the American and British armed services came out of World War II with a faith in the possibilities of combined planning in an alliance that was out of proportion to the reality. The only situation that I can envision in which an alliance could work so smoothly again would be to repeat World War II. That is, the alliance would have to be between Britain and America, the enemy a threat as obvious as Hitler was. This situation does not appear likely to be repeated. Even if something like it did come again, I doubt that the alliance could work as well because another essential factor has forever disappeared. I am referring to the relative equality of the contribution Britain and America made to the common cause. Throughout much of World War II the partners were more or less equally strong. After America became the senior partner, in late 1944, the British found that they were increasingly discriminated against in the strategic decisions—especially in the broad-front versus single-thrust controversy and the question of going into Berlin.

To return to the subject of cooperation between the United States Army and Navy in World War II, the story is not altogether one of easily achieved success. There were bitter fights, especially at the higher levels and in the Joint Chiefs of Staff, over worldwide strategy. To oversimplify, the army wanted to fight in Europe and take care of Japan after Hitler was finished, while the navy's war was in the Pacific. Alan-Brooke, chief of the Imperial General Staff, used to complain that Admiral King slept through Combined Chiefs of Staff meetings, awakening only when someone mentioned the Pacific. As I hope my account of the navy's contribution in Europe has made clear, that was not true, but it was the tendency.

This basic difference in emphasis led to problems all along the line. On the fundamental question of industrial priority, King wanted to build fighting ships, while Army Chief of Staff Marshall wanted the shipbuilding program to concentrate on landing craft. In effect, King won, which meant that the chief limiting factor in all strategic decisions of World War II was the relative absence of landing craft. Churchill once growled that history would always wonder at how it happened that the fate of two great empires was tied up in some god-damned things called LSTs. He was both right and wrong. Every amphibious operation of the war in Europe was delayed because of the shortage of landing craft, while in the Pacific some major operations had to be called off altogether for the same reason. There were never enough landing craft to go around. But Churchill was wrong in speculating that historians would not be able to explain this shortage for the reasons are clear enough.

First and foremost, King was faced with a challenge on the high seas in the Pacific. He reasoned, correctly, that the Europe-first decision, while basically sound, had to be modified in practice. The Allies could not concentrate everything in Europe and remain on the passive defensive in the Pacific, for that would allow the Japanese to build up their empire to such an extent that it could never be cracked. In order to undertake limited offensives in the Pacific, King had to have surface ships. If he were going to get them, the shipyards had to build them. In addition, the surface fleet program was not entirely a Pacific program, for many of the destroyers the shipyards turned out were vital to the antisubmarine war on the Atlantic. All the landing craft in the world would not have mattered had it not been for the victory in the submarine war.

The real culprit, I think, was the air force. Priorities got mixed up, not in the shipyards, but on a national level. To put it bluntly, the Anglo-Americans built far too many bombers. All the men and money and material that went into the Lancasters and B-29s would have been better used on landing craft. This is not to deny that the bombers made a contribution to victory, for of course they did, but it seems to me clear that any honest cost-effectiveness analysis would indicate that landing craft were a better buy than bombers.

In any case, there were not enough landing craft. The issue then became one of where to use those that were available. In this area Admiral King was playing a delicate game. The navy controlled the craft, and King wanted as many as possible for the Pacific war. He therefore kept the total number of craft a closely guarded secret. More to the point, he used his possession of the craft as a weapon to influence strategic decisions. In July of 1942, for example, when the Anglo-American struggle over whether to invade the Continent in 1943 or to go to North Africa in 1942 was being decided, King was willing to make sufficient craft available for a 1943 cross-Channel attack. When the British won, however, and North Africa was decided upon, King suddenly found that he did not have enough craft available for the operation. The issue could not be settled by the Combined Chiefs of Staff, and eventually President Roosevelt had to step in and order King to deliver the necessary landing craft.

Again, in 1944, worldwide planning on landing craft was impossible, since only Admiral King knew how many there were. He was willing to make more available to Europe if the British would promise to use them to invade the south of France, but he would not make them available if they were to be used for operations in Italy or against the Balkans. The British were furious, but nothing could be done about it. Once again Roosevelt had to step into the breach and order King to give up more craft when Eisenhower said they were necessary for the cross-Channel invasion. To my mind, by the way, King was correct in doing everything he could to prevent operations in the Mediterranean; his strategy, like Marshall's, with its emphasis on coming to grips with the Wehrmacht on the Continent as soon as possible, was the one with the greatest promise of a quicker victory.

The lesson in all this, I suppose, is that great events turn on comparatively little matters, or, to use Churchill's phrase again, the grand strategy of World War II turned on some god-damned things called LSTs.

No one ever called the other great development of naval warfare, aircraft carriers, those god-damned things, although in the early years of the war they too were in short supply. Like the landing craft, the most important contribution of aircraft carriers was vastly to extend the areas over which the navy could influence events. Fleets could see farther and hit farther. They could sail closer to enemy-held shorelines for they could provide their own protection in the air. Land-based fighter planes could not drive away a fleet that had sufficient aircraft carriers. In the Pacific this meant that landing craft could be used for the purposes for which they had been designed. It is doubtful that the amphibious operations in the Pacific could have been undertaken at all had it not been for the air cover provided by the aircraft carriers. It is notable in this regard that in Europe where, generally speaking, there were not enough Allied aircraft carriers, every invasion from 1943 onward was strictly limited to areas that could be covered by land-based fighter airplanes. In the Italian invasion, for example, Salerno was as far north as Eisenhower dared to go, even though the strategic rewards of going farther up the coast were obvious, because Salerno was as far north as his Sicily-based fighters could provide cover.

In listing the virtues of the carrier and its impact on naval warfare, it need hardly be added that the carrier was absolutely essential to gaining command of the sea. Navies without aircraft carriers were like babies still in the womb; they were tied to the short and inelastic umbilical cord of land-based air cover. They were incapable of challenging for command of the sea and were limited to sending submarines into blue water. Submarines, of course, could only carry on a *guerre de course*.

Which brings us back to the point at which I began the lecture on World War I—the value of the command of the seas. In World War II, control of the oceans was vital to England, the United States, Japan, and, to a much lesser degree, Russia so that she could receive lend-lease goods. Without the ability to move men and supplies across blue water, none of these nations could have carried on in the war, and, indeed, Japan was doomed when she lost that ability. For Germany the key was denial of the use of the seas to the enemy. In practice these distinctions in definition meant little except insofar as they applied to the manner in which the war at sea was waged. As in 1917-18, it was the war under the seas that counted, because no matter how great Allied superiority on the surface, no matter how many aircraft carriers and landing craft the Anglo-Americans had, they could only win the war by getting cargo vessels into the ports. (Incidentally, the navy's work in clearing demolished ports and keeping them working afterwards has always impressed me as one of the significant, although least noticed, achievements of the war.)

I cannot comment on the techniques of antisubmarine warfare as it is outside my field, but I would like to say a word or two on what did not work. All prewar, and to an extent postwar, claims by the advocates of strategic air forces to the contrary, it is clear that the submarine had to be met and defeated on the high seas. That is another way of saying that antisubmarine warfare had to be done the hard way—there were no shortcuts. The big bomber boys claimed they could knock out the submarines in their pens. The major effort came in the late summer of 1942 as the air forces concentrated on the pens in the Bay of Biscay. The campaign was an utter failure. Then the airmen said they would do the job by destroying the submarines in the manufacturing stage, at the factories. That effort, too, failed. The same was true, by the way, of the attempt to destroy the German fighter planes at their source; as with the submarine, the Allies discovered that the only way to do the job was the hard way—destroy the German fighters in the sky in combat. Airplanes were, of course, extraordinarily helpful in spotting submarines at sea, and fighters could do good work in attacking them, but the big bombers were practically helpless.

All of which points to the obvious conclusion, hardly original with me, that modern war is a team effort. No one service is capable of winning by itself. Victory in either world war would have been impossible without the navies, although both wars could have been lost by the Allies even though they retained command of the sea. Without the navies, the Allies could not have exerted their power on the Continent, but without the armies there would have been no power to exert. The chief responsibility of the strategist is to find a proper balance between the services in allocating resources. To reiterate my own assessment of the Anglo-American effort in World War II, I believe far too many resources were put into big bombers. The German error was not putting enough into submarines. But, of course, it is much easier to do better after the event than before it.

NOTE

Based on a lecture published in the *Naval War College Review,* March, 1970.

IV. Politics and Strategy in the Nuclear Era

The Rearming of Germany 1950-1954: A Linchpin in the Political Evolution of Europe

B. Mitchell Simpson III

Editor's Note: *Lieutenant Commander Simpson is a member of the faculty of the Naval War College and formerly Visiting Lecturer in International Politics at the Fletcher School of Law and Diplomacy, Tufts University, from which he holds the degree of Doctor of Philosophy. He is also Editor,* Naval War College Review. *He has also spent over ten years at sea in a variety of ships.*

I

Ten years to the day after the German surrender at Rheims, General Rommel's chief of staff stood beside the Supreme Allied Commander, Europe, as the German flag was raised at Allied headquarters. Germany, or at least the western part of it, had made the transition from vanquished enemy to rearmed ally.

The arming of the Federal Republic of Germany was not an isolated event. It occurred in a context of Cold War politics and military necessity, against a background of the Marshall Plan, the North Atlantic Treaty, and positive moves toward European integration. It closed an era which had started with the Allies and the Soviet Union triumphant at the collapse of Nazi Germany. The arming of the Federal Republic represented the establishment of an equilibrium of sorts in Europe.

In 1945 Germany ceased to exist; the territory of the Third Reich was conquered and occupied by the Allies, who then instituted military governments. At the Potsdam Conference, East Prussia was divided between Poland and the Soviet Union, and the provinces of Pomerania and Silesia east of the Oder and Neisse rivers also were given to Poland for "administration."

Ten years later, in 1955, Germany remained divided, but German military forces, wearing the uniform of the Federal Republic of Germany, were admitted to NATO pursuant to a treaty which provided specifically for the rearmament of the Federal Republic. By adopting a policy of rearmament, Chancellor Konrad Adenauer sought to weld the Federal Republic to Western Europe even at the price of postponing the reunification of all of Germany, which could only come about with the specific approval of the Soviet Union.

German rearmament is a condition of fact in any general European settlement. It plays a major role in the strategic considerations of the Atlantic Powers. German rearmament can best be described by two crucial facts: there has been no European war, and Germany has not been unified. While all men can rejoice at the former, opinion is somewhat less unanimous in regard to the latter. This division remains a sore point for Germany and a potential danger to the remainder of Europe, as well as to the United States and the Soviet Union.

In September 1955, only four months after the Federal Republic entered NATO, the Soviet Union established diplomatic relations with the Bonn government. Fifteen years later, on 11 August 1970, the Soviet Union and the Federal Republic concluded a nonaggression treaty. They not only renounced the use of force for the settlement of disputes but, significantly, the Federal Republic agreed to the inviolability of the European frontiers as they existed on that date. This meant the Federal Republic accepted the Oder-Neisse line and in effect renounced claims to the eastern territories lost in 1945.

The stabilization of Western Europe, including the phenomenal domestic success of the Federal Republic, has been accompanied by a containment of Soviet military power to Eastern Europe, outright violent rebellion against that power in some cases, and more subtle exercises of independence in others. Today, communism in Europe is no longer the monolith it once was. However,

many of the fundamental problems connected with the projection
of Soviet national power remain.[1] Whether there is a causal connection between the events antecedent to the arming of the Federal Republic and subsequent developments remains to be seen.

Fifteen years do not provide a vantage point for a definitive
historical perspective (if one is ever possible), but they do provide
a sufficiently good point from which to look back and analyze
some of the currents and elements which led to the phenomenon
of the Allies arming their late enemy in defense against their
former Soviet ally.

II

Following World War II, United States policy toward Europe
manifested itself in many ways. Perhaps the most obvious example
is the Marshall Plan. The premise of this policy was stated by
Secretary of State Marshall, who posited a faith in the vigor of
Western civilization to rise above the destructive effects of war
and to restore a healthy society.[2] The Communists openly predicted that such a restoration would not take place.

In 1949 Secretary of State Acheson noted how closely interwov-
en were United States policies toward Germany and toward
Europe. He saw clearly that the problems of Western Europe were
not compartmented and that Germany must share the obligations
as well as the benefits of the structure started by the free people
of Europe.[3]

European security could be ensured only if there were set in
motion in Germany those forces which would create a governmental system dedicated to upholding the basic human freedoms
through democratic processes. This assumption had been basic to
United States policy in Germany since the collapse of the Nazi
state in 1945. Acheson urged a radically new reciprocal approach
which, in effect, meant all nations in Europe, Germany included,
must come to realize that the benefits to be derived from community efforts would exceed by far those to be achieved by any individual efforts. He alluded to the paradox that the fruits of sovereignty
and independence could be best achieved by subordinating them
to measures of European integration, although he did not use that
term.

The theme frequently heard was one of American approbation
of a European community as the end result of the American-Euro-
pean efforts. However, the long-range purposes or results of such
a consummation were discussed less frequently. A Europe com-

posed of states closely cooperating in political, social, and economic
matters would no longer be either dependent on the United States
or fearful of attack from the East. Such a Europe would be a
stabilizing force with great influence in world affairs.

From the conclusion of hostilities in 1945 until the promulgation
of the Occupation Statute in September 1949, Germany was governed by military governors in their respective zones of occupation. When it became obvious that inter-Allied cooperation in regard to the occupation of Germany had become a chimera, the
Americans, British, and French coordinated their policies and
cooperated extensively among the three zones. The end result was
the Occupation Statute, which replaced the military governors by
an Allied High Commission, clothed with certain limited and defined powers. It also granted to the new Federal Republic of Germany a certain degree of internal autonomy and responsibility.
This step was highly significant in that it heralded the return
of a German government at least partially responsible for the fate
and interests of Germany, although the responsibility and powers
of that government were severely limited.

Against this background, Konrad Adenauer successfully negotiated the Petersburg Agreement of 1949 with the three Allied
high commissioners. The Germans sought to limit dismantling of
the German industrial complex and to obtain a relaxation of restrictions on certain industries, particularly shipbuilding. The
Allies were anxious to secure German participation in the Ruhr
Authority.

The net result was an agreement that, to a great extent, cur-
tailed industrial dismantling and permitted German shipbuilding
(thereby creating employment in the Socialist strongholds of Ham-
burg and Bremen to the benefit of the Christian Democrats). The
Allies sought and obtained German participation in the Ruhr Authority. In addition, the Federal Republic was permitted to establish consular offices abroad and to join international organizations,
such as the World Bank and the International Monetary Fund.
Germany was also free to join the Council of Europe. At the time,
all German political parties agreed that the Federal Republic
should remain demilitarized.

The significance of the Petersburg Agreement was precisely
what Adenauer intended: a turning point in the relations of the
Federal Republic with the occupying powers. It marked, not only
the return of a responsible government, capable and willing to
negotiate for German interests, but also the emergence of the Federal Republic into the international community, although with

powers less than those of a completely sovereign state. Part of the price was an agreement by the Federal Republic to remain unarmed.

One observer commented on Adenauer's policy and negotiating skill to the effect that Adenauer was able to strike a balance between German interests and those of the Allies and at the same time to shape events in a desired direction.[4]

In the months immediately following the Petersburg Agreement, John J. McCloy, the United States high commissioner for Germany, clearly stated United States policy in a series of speeches and reports. The first objective was a reunification of all occupation zones of Germany on a democratic and federal basis. Of course, by this time the Russians had established a rival Communist regime in their zone of occupation, and any lingering hopes for early reunification were fast fading. McCloy precluded any arrangement whereby Germany might be united and Communist.[5]

A leading principle of United States policy in Germany was that, when ready, Germany should share in the benefits and assume the obligations of participation in the economy of free Europe. American policy in regard to Germany neatly meshed with her policy toward Europe, to the extent that Germany should play an active part in the economic and political organization of Europe. In other words, German security would be protected by German participation in a closely knit Western European community.

In April 1950, McCloy saw that the fate of Germany was closely tied to that of Europe. There could be no solution to the German problem without fitting it into the larger context of a united Europe. Union was the best solution for Europe's economic problems, and such a union would go far in solving the political problem of restraining a revival of pernicious German nationalism. Perhaps more important yet, he pointed out the psychological benefits to be gained by widening horizons and focusing ideals for the war-weary and disillusioned people.[6]

In short, United States policy by May of 1950 was definitely committed to a healthy Germany in a healthy Europe, on the assumption that the two were mutually dependent.

On 9 May 1950, the French foreign minister, Robert Schuman, publicly proposed the pooling of both the French and the German steel and coal industries under a common higher authority, within the framework of an organization open to the participation of other nations.

The significance of the Schuman Plan was not lost upon Adenauer. It was not only designed to meet very real economic needs in industries basic to the economies of both France and Germany, but also it provided a revolutionary solution to a problem which had divided France and Germany so often in the past. This solution would tend to draw Germany into Europe and to further the ideals held by both Schuman and Adenauer of a larger European community as opposed to separate European nations.

From an American standpoint, the Schuman Plan was viewed as a European initiative to solve a European problem. It dovetailed with United States policy toward Germany and showed one way of eventual German integration into Western Europe.

On the eve of Korea, United States policy in Germany was essentially concerned with politics and economics. Military considerations were limited to stationing Allied forces in Germany as occupying troops. As late as 5 June 1950, Secretary of State Acheson denied before the House Armed Services Committee any intention of rearming the Federal Republic.[7]

III

The attack by the Communist North Koreans against the non-Communist Republic of South Korea in 1950 was a profound shock to Europe and particularly to Germany. The parallel of a state divided into Communist and non-Communist portions, with the former attacking the latter, was obvious for all to see. The year before, in 1949, the Allies had concluded the North Atlantic Treaty. This marked a radical change in American peacetime policy, which was motivated by the possibility of a Russian military move against Western Europe. Now, in many minds, the possibility had been raised to a probability. Even if the parallel were inaccurate, the weakness of Europe's defenses was a matter of grave concern to the West and particularly to the Federal Republic, which had no forces of its own and had to rely on occupation forces for external security.

Adenauer was particularly fearful of a situation arising in which Stalin would make the Grotewohl government of East Germany push the large and well-armed People's Police into West Germany to "liberate" the Federal Republic while the West Germans looked on passively, partly because the invaders would be their own compatriots and partly because they had lost faith in the strength of the United States. In view of the threatening and bellicose statements coming from East Germany, Adenauer felt that the government of the Federal Republic was shouldering an immense burden without the corresponding means of discharging its obligations. He requested the Allies to demonstrate their military strength more visibly, and he also requested permission to create a security force of the same strength and armament as the People's Police in East Germany.

At the end of August 1950, Adenauer sent a memorandum to the United States high commissioner in Germany in which he reviewed the lack of security of the Federal Republic. He repeated the declared readiness of the Federal Republic to make a contribution of a German contingent to an international army in Western Europe, but he rejected the idea of a remilitarization of Germany by means of creating a separate German national army.[8]

Simultaneously with this memorandum, he sent a letter to the Allied High Commission with a request that the contents of the letter be submitted to the forthcoming Foreign Ministers' Conference scheduled to meet in New York the next month, September 1950. Adenauer drew the political conclusion that a "reordering of relations" between the Federal Republic and the occupying powers was warranted. He pointed out that, not only had the government consolidated its position at home, but also that it had sought by every possible step to integrate itself into Western Europe. It was, therefore, necessary to "place the relationship between Germany and the Allied Powers on a new basis." The legal state of war must be terminated, and continued occupation should be for purposes of "security against external danger." The Occupation Statute should be progressively replaced by a "system of treaties or contractual agreements."[9]

Arming the Federal Republic was formally and seriously discussed for the first time at the September 1950 Foreign Ministers' Conference in New York. Acheson notified the French and British foreign ministers on the eve of their departures for New York that he would raise the question of German rearmament. Apparently Acheson's late notification of his colleagues was not because he wished to avoid a background chorus of adverse comment, which might have been the case if the French and British foreign ministers had had time to do adequate staff work. It was because the United States position had not become firm until shortly before the convening of the conference.

The idea of arming the Federal Republic or, put another way, permitting that nation to make a contribution to the defense of Western Europe on a basis of equality with the other Western European nations originated in the Pentagon as a logical answer to both a military and a political necessity. As one observer has pointed out, "The closer Germany came to sovereignty and the greater the attention paid to the task of defending Western Europe, the more difficult it became to leave out of calculation the military potential of a major European nation."[10]

After Acheson had raised the question of arming the Federal Republic, only the French steadfastly refused to accept even the principle of German rearmament. French objections were based on the dangers to France of German arms. At the 1950 Foreign Ministers' Conference, the United States, the United Kingdom, and France were able to agree only that the creation of a German national army, pure and simple and free of all restrictions, "would not serve the best interests of Germany and Europe."[11]

Finally, the French yielded to the pleas of their allies and proposed in October 1950 the Pleven plan, or European Defense Community. In so doing, René Pleven injected an entirely new concept into the politics of Europe by agreeing to German rearmament within the context of a European army, not subordinate to any nation, but to a supranational defense minister. After extensive and intensive negotiations, the Pleven plan was embodied in a series of treaties and protocols which provided essentially for a European Defense Community (EDC), sovereignty for the Federal Republic of Germany, and an extension of the North Atlantic Treaty protection to the territory of the Federal Republic. The agreements were contingent upon each other to be effective. In other words, if any one failed of ratification, none would be effective.

All the elements embracing cold war strategy—European defense, European integration, and the future of Germany—were drawn into this maelstrom, which was not resolved until after the French National Assembly failed to ratify EDC in 1954. The 1954 Nine Power Conference in London then produced a substitute series of protocols which finally achieved ratification by the signatory states. To understand how arming the Federal Republic was the catalyst of this series of events, it is necessary to analyze the underlying problem and how it was met.

IV

Nearly five years elapsed from the first serious discussion of rearming the Federal Republic in September 1950 until the Germans were finally admitted to NATO in 1955. During that time the ambitious, if not revolutionary, scheme of a European Defense Community was proposed by the French, accepted by all European

parties (except the British, who declined to participate), and finally, not without irony, killed by the French National Assembly.

At the start the question of arms for the Federal Republic was
a military problem born of necessity with very heavy political over-
tones. After the failure of the EDC, the political problem became
one of the first magnitude. Although the emphasis shifted to the
political aspects, many of the same considerations endured
throughout the entire period. These considerations were the important ones and were of immediate concern.

Logically, the first question to arise was whether an active military ground defense was both feasible and desirable. Some people
concluded that since the task of stopping the Red army was so
staggering, the West should rely on American nuclear weapons
to protect Europe and on the political venture implied in the North
Atlantic Treaty. They felt that since the Russians had not already
overrun Western Europe, they probably would not do so.

Following the attack in Korea, whatever merits European neutrality, or even German neutrality, may have had were lost in
a rising tide of anxiety over the deplorable state of Western European defenses. Not only were European defenses inadequate in
themselves, but the United States was then committed to a sizable
ground war, with sea and air support, in Korea. Considering the
limited size of the United States forces remaining after Louis Johnson's force reductions, the United States was doubly concerned
with doing something to bolster European defenses without making a dent in the forces available for Korea.

An early and important step was the agreement to establish
SHAPE (Supreme Headquarters Allied Powers Europe). This step
was significant, in a practical sense, because it provided for more
efficient utilization of forces available through coordination, cooperation, and some degree of command integration. Also, with an
American general at its head, it symbolized a positive American
commitment to the defense of Western Europe.

At this time American policy was based on the assumption that
the security of the United States was indissolubly linked with that
of Europe. The problem facing the United States was twofold:
first, how to keep Western Europe out of the Soviet orbit; and
second, how to defend Western Europe against Soviet attack. The
first part of the problem was being met by the European Recovery
Program, and the second part was under consideration. Some planners wanted a one-package deal in which the establishment of
SHAPE and German armament would be a part. However, the
United States finally adopted a position more in tune with political

realities, and SHAPE was established while Acheson continued negotiations for German armament.

The decision to arm the Federal Republic was not as easy as it might seem today. The first question was whether the North Atlantic powers—and particularly the Europeans in the light of the United States commitment in Korea—could raise sufficient forces to meet a possible Soviet ground attack. The price might have been to jeopardize the European economic recovery already achieved and to bankrupt the European economies, thereby sowing the seeds of domestic discontent and providing the Communists with new opportunities for mischief in Western Europe.

Economic considerations were not limited solely to the effects of military expenditures. One British writer raised the question as to the ultimate effect of a NATO German Army on European integration, and he felt that such an effect would be adverse. However, he agreed that integration was a necessary step in a return to multilateral trade and expanding worldwide exchanges.[12]

Aside from the adverse economic effects of Europe defending herself without the aid of Germany, the obvious fact remained that Germany would be the front line in a war with the Soviet Union. The possibility that the West might be forced to defend the Federal Republic against a "war of liberation" launched by the East Germans, while the West Germans looked on, was something to be avoided if at all possible.

Starting with the assumption that the means of defending Western Europe were inadequate, the solution was a choice between the Allies making a greater effort toward their own rearmament or finding some way of making a German contribution acceptable and possible. Military necessity demanded a choice, but only policy could make it.

At the time the United States, the United Kingdom, and France decided not to establish a German national army, free of all restrictions, because they felt that rearmament of Germany would be antithetical to the democratization program which had been pursued since the collapse of the Nazi state in 1945. Not only might another Wehrmacht have threatened democracy in Germany, but also a military establishment would have required the creation of an industrial complex capable of supporting it. This reasoning, coupled with fears of a revival of German adventurism and irredentism, underlay the decision of the foreign ministers to accept the Pleven plan.

One study has concluded that Western opinion in the early 1950s greatly exaggerated the importance of adventurism and irredentism in Germany and equally underestimated the German concern for external security.[13] Although Western opinion, including that of the policymakers, may have been guilty of such an exaggeration, it was an error *sans faute,* because consideration of German rearmament arose in a context of either a European army or an integrated NATO command. Furthermore, the Germans were intimately concerned with questions of their own security. A continuous theme of Adenauer's politics was that the security of the Federal Republic lay ultimately in a close association with Western Europe. This policy precluded an independent national German army.

National security is a prime concern of any state; and although the Federal Republic did not enjoy full sovereignty, that government was still concerned with security, particularly since the state was weak. There was also the danger that continued German weakness in the face of Soviet strength would lead the West Germans to believe that national security would be served better with the Soviet Union as a friend, no matter how difficult that would be, rather than as a foe.

From the standpoint of the Allies, a Federal Republic divorced from Europe would have been exceedingly vulnerable to subversion and eventual absorption into the Soviet bloc. Ultimately the Allies would have liked to have had a reunited Germany firmly allied to or integrated into the West, but since all of Germany could not be held, their policy was to hang on to what had already been gained, while trying to deny control of the remainder to the other side.

By renouncing neutrality and by joining Western Europe, the Federal Republic may have delayed the reunification of Germany, but Adenauer's point was that reunification could only come about from the strength and not from the weakness of the Federal Republic. He was also pursuing a course that would weld Germany firmly to Europe and would make impossible the former rivalries which twice in his lifetime had convulsed Europe. In general the Allies agreed with him, but for very different reasons: tying Germany irrevocably to the West would, by definition, preclude any future turning toward the East for strategic reasons or for communism.

V

And so it was by different routes and for different reasons that the feeling grew that the Federal Republic must be armed. Winston Churchill proposed to the Council of Europe that a European army be created. On 11 August 1950, the Council of Europe adopted the famous Strasbourg Resolution, which called "for the immediate creation under the authority of a European Minister of Defense, of a European army, subject to proper unified, democratic control and acting in full cooperation with the United States and Canada."[14]

When Acheson raised the question of arms for the Germans at the 1950 Foreign Ministers' Conference in New York, the French were in a difficult position. On the one hand, domestic opposition was partly based on the not entirely unreasonable fear of armed Germans. But on the other hand, they became subject to well-taken criticism that, for their own advantage, they were delaying European defense and thereby giving the Russians a diplomatic opening.

The Strasbourg Resolution was an invitation to proceed with German rearmament along the lines of the Atlantic Pact. Indeed, the United States and the United Kingdom assumed that a tightly knit Atlantic alliance would be strong enough to control and direct any German contribution to defense. This assumption went far in meeting the French position which was that, even accepting the ultimate necessity of some form of German rearmament, it was not a matter of immediate urgency, and an organization within the framework of the Atlantic Pact would provide the best answer.

The solution was the Pleven plan. The results as embodied in the treaties of 1952 differed only in degree from the original proposal, which essentially was for a European army under a supranational authority, headed by a European minister of defense. West Germany would contribute on a basis of equality with other states. The European army would be tied to the NATO integrated command. The protection of the North Atlantic Treaty would be extended to cover the territory of the Federal Republic. The occupation would end in Germany, and the Federal Republic would regain full sovereignty with the Allies retaining certain rights for emergency situations and without prejudicing Allied rights pending conclusion of a final peace treaty.

The advocates of the European army urged the view that the idea of European rearmament originated in Europe under such good Europeans as Churchill. They were highly disappointed when Churchill returned as prime minister for the second time and the United Kingdom followed the policy of the previous Labor government. In so doing it declined to participate in the European army on the ground that Britain's worldwide commitments precluded such a participation.

Schuman replied to the suggestion that Germany could be integrated into an Atlantic Pact force by pointing out that such a force would involve only a unified command and would allow the survival of national armies. He said, "The Atlantic Pact has a temporary aim. The European army in our view is a permanent solution, and must insure peace against all threats, internal and external, now and in the future."[15] Many of the supporters of the EDC hailed it as a prelude to a European federation which, paradoxically, turned out to be both its strength and its fatal weakness.

There was much dissent in West Germany over rearmament. While an analysis of the origins and forms of this dissent is beyond the scope of this essay, this widespread lack of enthusiasm for a military organization was important in itself. It was illustrative of a change from former Nazi militancy. The United States reframed the question from how the willing Germans could rearm to how best could a reluctant Germany be persuaded to accept her rightful position in the mutual defense system of the Western world. Adenauer accepted German rearmament as the price of German sovereignty. And here it should be remembered that in the 1949 Petersburg Agreement, he had accepted demilitarization as the price of internal autonomy.

From the conclusion of the EDC agreements in 1952 until their ultimate interment by the French National Assembly on a procedural motion at the end of August 1954, the substance of the issues was generally removed from the international scene, pending ratification by the various parties. However, Washington was constantly exhorting the signatory states to ratify the EDC treaty. This was particularly important since none of the agreements could come into force until final ratification of all the agreements. For the Federal Republic, ratification by all parties was especially important, since the Occupation Statute would remain in force and sovereignty would be delayed until the other agreements came into effect.

The reasons behind the failure of the French to ratify the EDC— which precipitated what might be described as a major diplomatic crisis—are multiple, complex, and somewhat obscure. This failure was indicative of the boldness of the EDC concept, which many Frenchmen were not willing to accept, rather than opposition to the concept of German rearmament per se.

French partisan politics played a large role in the defeat of the EDC. By early 1954 Bidault replaced Schuman in the Foreign

Office, which represented a slight but crucial shift in party alignment in the National Assembly. In fact, it was the first time in
several years that Schuman was neither prime minister nor foreign
minister. In the summer of 1954 Mendes-France was prime minister, and he was faced with serious problems in Indochina, brought
to a head by the fall of Dienbienphu. The Geneva Conference
by which France departed Indochina was concluded only the
month before the EDC was lost in the National Assembly.

In addition to the Indochina war and the shift to the left in
the government, both of which boded ill for the EDC, the Communists opposed it on general principles, and on the right the Gaul-
lists found it anathema for other reasons. The EDC was thus left
with only some center support. Previous governments had not
pushed it because they were uncertain of support and did not want
to fall on that issue.

Whatever else can be said about the EDC, it provided for a
supranational defense ministry without a corresponding foreign
ministry and other apparati necessary to a European federal government. This would have been an anomalous situation at best,
and at worst it might very well have proven unworkable.[16]

Lest all the blame be heaped upon France, it should be remembered that the British refusal to participate raised understandable
fears that Germany might eventually dominate the EDC.[17] Blame
has also been placed upon Secretary of State Dulles for both
threatening the so-called agonizing reappraisal of United States
policy toward Europe if the EDC failed and for other proddings
from Washington. United States anxiety, however, was understandable, particularly in the light of American worldwide commitments.

Juridically speaking, the demise of the EDC left the questions
of sovereignty for the Federal Republic and the defense of Western
Europe in an unchanged position. Relatively speaking, the
members of the Atlantic community were worse off than before,
if only because there was now no solution on hand to the complex
problems which would have been dealt with by the EDC package.
The Nine Power Conference met in London at the end of September 1954 in an attempt to resolve the crisis. On his departure
for London, Dulles clearly stated that the initiative rested with
the Europeans.

In London, Dulles spoke frankly and candidly. He said in effect
that, if arrangements were agreed upon for continuing the hope
of unity among the countries of Europe, then the United States
would be disposed to renew its pledge to maintain armed forces

in Europe. Dulles was careful to point out that the commitments of one president to a particular policy cannot constitutionally bind another president.[18]

The outcome of the London conference was the establishment of the Western European Union (WEU), achieved by a modification of the 1948 Brussels Treaty, which interestingly enough was originally aimed against Germany. WEU provided for a German military contribution to the defense of Europe. Although no European army was established, an integrated NATO command was established under SACEUR, (Supreme Allied Commander Europe) who would exercise operational control of the limited German military forces authorized by the treaty. The Occupation Statute was to lapse, and the Federal Republic was to obtain full sovereignty under essentially the same conditions previously agreed upon.

A particularly significant difference in this set of agreements was British participation in WEU, as well as Eden's pledge that the United Kingdom was willing to abandon her traditionally insular policy, join the Brussels Treaty powers, and maintain four divisions of ground forces and tactical air strength permanently on the Continent.

The protocols were rapidly ratified, although the French provided some suspense. By the spring of 1955 the Federal Republic was rid of the Occupation Statute and was free to engage in normal diplomatic intercourse. In ratifying these protocols, the French accepted a German national army within the framework of an integrated NATO command only a few months after they had rejected a German contribution within the context of a European army.

VI

Even though the protocols were ratified and came into effect, they were of such a profound nature that examination of the negotiations and of the main provisions of the protocols will fail to reveal their full import. Speaking for the State Department, Livingston Merchant stated three propositions in regard to Germany:

• No one can hold indefinitely in the status of an occupied country a proud and industrious people.

• Effective defense of Western Europe requires a German contribution.

• For Europe to be rid of the threat of internecine wars, Germany and her neighbors must be bound together in a new relationship, which weaves together their economics, their defense arrangements, and their institutions so as to make another war within the Western European family not merely unthinkable but actually impossible.[19]

While there may have been fairly general agreement in both Europe and Washington as to the correctness of these propositions, their application raised large domestic questions in Germany as to the policy of the Federal Republic. For the Federal Republic the issues involved in the EDC package and later in WEU were identical for all practical purposes. For this reason the debates on the EDC are pertinent to a consideration of German policy in regard to the arrangements which ultimately led to German rearmament.

Domestic opposition to Adenauer rested on the proposition that reunification should come first. Adenauer felt this was a rather shortsighted view, since reunification, if at all possible, could be had only at the price of neutrality and the loss of European integration. Reunification in that case would mean isolation, which could only exacerbate smoldering resentments in the rest of Europe and would do nothing to solve the larger problem of how to build a European community. No evidence has been found that indicates Adenauer deliberately chose joining Europe rather than pursuing reunification. Such an implication would be grossly unfair, as well as undocumented. Adenauer apparently pursued both goals and took the one that was closest to fruition, in the belief that the other could only be achieved through close association with Western Europe.

On 10 March 1952 the Soviet Union proposed a conference to meet within two weeks to discuss German reunification, the price of which would be German neutrality. The Allies and the Federal Republic refused this bait, not only because the time limit precluded proper staff preparation for such a conference, but also because they had every reason to believe it a transparent attempt to impede constructive Western development. While the Soviet proposal was superficially reasonable, they had everything to gain and very little to lose.

In the Bundestag debate on ratification of the EDC on 3 December 1953, Adenauer skillfully kept the question from becoming a choice between either arms or reunification. He presented the question as one of German security, which indeed had been a consistent element in German policy. German security could be had, not to the detriment of any European nation, but within a context of mutual advantage to all concerned. This approach was both original and novel, if not revolutionary. Adenauer's plea was essentially for Europe which, as a polity, could provide both physical security for Germany and for her neighbors, as well as the necessary moral strength which Germany so sorely needed.[20]

Adenauer's position was identical to that of the United States, as stated by McCloy, who insisted that Germany could not be set adrift without protection from aggression and that the best means of achieving German security was through the European Defense Force, built into the defense system of the Atlantic community. European integration and German reunification should be pursued simultaneously.[21]

VII

Perhaps in the long span of history the post-World War II period will be significant, not necessarily because of the cold war, but because the movement to end traditional European rivalries was removed from the realm of the theoretical. Dreamers were replaced by statesmen and politicians, who took concrete action to further European integration.

When the United States inaugurated the Marshall plan, she wisely insisted on dealing with Europe as a whole and not with individual countries. The Europeans were compelled to think of Europe as an entity. Economic recovery was more rapid than expected, partly because of intra-European cooperation in areas of mutual problems. The Schuman plan and the European army were logical developments of this trend.

United States policy was unambiguous in this area. The United States consistently pursued a policy of encouraging a strong and healthy Europe in an Atlantic community on the assumption that a strong and prosperous Europe would be a reliable friend and ally not only in a confrontation with the Communist bloc but also in meeting many of the other pressing problems in the world. There was a widespread conviction that Europe could not for long play a decisive role in world affairs as a congeries of independent states. The Schuman plan and the European army were looked on as steps toward obviating some of the age-old European problems of cartels, rivalries, and wars.

Adenauer pursued a policy which encouraged European integration and unity, because he realized that not only German security but also that of the rest of the Continent could be had only by authentic structural changes in Europe. He said,

We are certain that the narrow conception of the nation state which dominated the nineteenth and the beginning of the twentieth century has today altogether outlived its validity .... We must succeed, first of all, in re-establishing the unity of the European way of life in all its aspects and in all its fields.[22]

Adenauer spoke of the larger considerations, those that pertained to Europe as a whole. He spoke not only as the good European that he was but also as chancellor of a highly industrialized and organized society that suffered as great a defeat and collapse as any nation has known. He was speaking against a background of the threefold collapse of 1945: political, economic, and spiritual. The German state had to be built along lines and in accordance with policies that would ensure its continued development and prosperity, as well as its peaceful existence with its neighbors.

In regard to the economic and political strength necessary for a complete European recovery, it soon became obvious that there could be no prosperous Europe if the German economy remained shackled. After the Organization for European Economic Cooperation, the European Payments Union, and later the Schuman plan, there was little official doubt of the worthiness of these arrangements. Indeed, 1955 saw the beginnings of negotiations that eventually led to the Treaty of Rome and the establishment of the Common Market.

Any discussion of the vast movement and the deep currents flowing toward integration must ultimately be based on the intangibility of the ideal itself and the hopes that it expressed. General Eisenhower noted in his report as SACEUR that the central problem was one of morale.[23] The ideal of Europe was broad enough by definition to cover many shades of opinion and many interests. It was positive in that it worked to the detriment of no nation, and it offered hope that the errors of the past could be avoided in the future. Although the United States encouraged close German participation in an integrated Europe, this decision was one that the German people and Government had to make for themselves.

The immediate and most obvious mutual advantages of close German ties to Europe were fourfold:

· Europe would benefit from German industry and contributions to defense.

· The occupation of the Federal Republic would end, and that state would achieve full sovereignty.

· The fate of Germany would be so intertwined with that of Europe that Germany would be unable to turn on Europe again.

· The situation where either a weak Germany might be a prey of the Great Powers or a strong Germany might turn on Europe would be avoided.

One observer pointed out that in a strong Western European economic and political community in which the Federal Republic was an integral part,

> It will be very difficult for the Federal Republic either to accomplish reunification upon Russian terms or to drag the West into a revisionist war.... All her ties, military, political and economic will then be to the West. To sever these would result in a national catastrophe for her. Furthermore, she would almost certainly become a battlefield in any future war.[24]

In testifying before the Senate Foreign Relations Committee which was considering the 1954 protocols, Dulles pointed out that the treaty establishing WEU was no scrap of paper embodying promises, but that it established a viable, living organism. He said he had always attached more importance to creating unity in Western Europe than he had to the question of how many divisions would be maintained there. He said the basic problem to be solved was that "these constantly recurring wars ... must be ended if there is to be any salvation at all for the values that we believe in and call Western civilization."[25]

When asked about the binding effect of the protocols on a reunited Germany, Dulles disclaimed any practical application to such a situation, because the Federal Republic constituted such a large percentage of all Germany that, he said, "It is extremely unlikely that a unified Germany would adopt any course other than that which has been mapped out and adopted and committed to by the Federal Republic."[26]

The United States realized a Franco-German rapprochement was fundamental to a long-term assurance of security and vitality for Europe and, therefore, for the Western world. Such a unity would be the opposite of the disunity that had led to two world wars in this century.

While under the treaties that actually came into effect political ties may be less than originally intended, economic ties have assumed an increasing significance in Europe's postwar evolution. A Paris-Bonn entente is fundamental to any ties, economic or political. France, when confronted with Germany's economic resurgence and enlistment as a major party in European defense, had the good sense to join Germany. Germany needed France to realize her full opportunities as a member of the Common Market and to participate in the planning and direction of military affairs with the alliance. The result has been a new series of ties working against national separatism and in favor of regional integration.

VIII

A series of events involving such disparate elements as a cold war between the superpowers; recovery, reconstruction, and defense of Europe; creation of a new and democratic Germany; redirecting national energies from ancient rivalries and fears into more positive channels; replacing obsolete forms of thought and outmoded economic and political habits with structures more adequate to modern needs; the formation and execution of policy in a revolutionary era where at times change is the only constant factor—such a series does not lend itself to clearcut conclusions. Indeed, the outcome is not yet in sight. But in retrospect it can be seen that German rearmament was the linchpin of this series of events.

It can be observed how men of vision, goodwill, and political skill can boldly seize opportunities and bit by bit create the foundations of what may become a new political structure. It is worth noting that during World War I Schuman was a German, and shortly after that war Adenauer toyed with the idea of Rhineland separation. During the First World War their Italian colleague, DeGasperi, was a subject of the Habsburg Empire. These men were truly Europeans while in office, and they did much to create present-day Europe out of the postwar chaos.

Events have so far borne out the soundness of the overall United States policy, which went as far as it could to expiate the myopia and smugness of prewar American policy toward Europe. The assumptions upon which this policy was founded have in the balance been sound, and the programs that gave life to these assumptions have been generally well thought out and well executed. From the vantage point of 1970, the United States is entitled to a justifiable satisfaction as to the fruits of her European policies.

NOTES

Originally published in the *Naval War College Review,* May 1971.

1. Zbigniew K. Brzezinski, *The Soviet Bloc,* rev. ed. (New York: Praeger, 1961), passim.

2. George C. Marshall, quoted in Dean Acheson, "A Perspective on the Problems Facing the Council of Foreign Ministers," *The Department of State Bulletin,* 29 May 1949, p. 675, Vol. XX, No. 517.

3. Ibid.

4. James L. Richardson, *Germany and the Atlantic Alliance* (Cambridge: Harvard University Press, 1966) p. 15.

5. John J. McCloy, "Progress Report on Germany," *The Department of State Bulletin,* 6 February 1950, p. 197, Vol. XXII, No. 553.

6. John J. McCloy, "The German Problem and Its Solution," *The Department of State Bulletin,* 17 April 1950, p. 587, Vol. XXII, No. 563.

7. U.S. Congress, House, Committee on Foreign Relations, *To Amend the Mutual Defense Assistance Act of 1949,* Hearings (Washington: U.S. Govt. Print. Off., 1950), p. 22.

8. Paul Weymar, *Adenauer* (New York: Dutton, 1957) p. 332.

9. Ibid., p. 333.

10. Lawrence W. Martin, "The Decision to Rearm Germany," Harold Stein, ed., *American Civil Military Decisions* (Birmingham: University of Alabama Press, 1963), p. 658.

11. Ibid., p. 658.

12. David W. McLachlan, "Rearmament and the Shock of Korea," *Foreign Affairs,* January 1951, pp. 276-86.

13. Richardson, p. 5.

14. L. C. D. Onslow, "West German Rearmament," *World Politics,* July 1951, p. 456.

15. Ibid., p. 471.

16. Daniel Lerner and Raymond Aron, *France Defeats EDC* (New York: Praeger, 1957) pp. 2-24.

17. F. S. C. Northrop, *European Union and United States Foreign Policy* (New York: Macmillan, 1954), passim.

18. "Agreement on Restoration of German Sovereignty and German Association with Western Defense System," *The Department of State Bulletin,* 11 October 1954, pp. 523-25, Vol. XXXI, No. 798.

19. Livingston T. Merchant, "Progress toward European Security," *The Department of State Bulletin,* 6 December 1954, p. 844, Vol. XXI, No. 806.

20. Weymar, p. 448.

21. John J. McCloy, "U.S. Attitude toward Germany," *The Department of State Bulletin,* 10 December 1951, p. 943.

22. Weymar, pp. 287-88.

23. Dwight D. Eisenhower, "First Anniversary of SHAPE as an Operational Headquarters," *The Department of State Bulletin,* 14 April 1952, p. 574, Vol. XXVI, No. 668.

24. H. L. Trefousse, "Germany: Key to American Foreign Policy," *Antioch Review,* March 1954, p. 128.

25. U.S. Congress, Senate, Committee on Foreign Relations, *Protocol on Termination of the Occupation Regime in the Federal Republic of Germany. . .,* Hearings (Washington: U.S. Govt. Print. Off., 1955), p. 23.

26. Ibid.

Suez 1956:
Some Military Lessons

Henry E. Eccles

Editor's Note: In thirty years of active duty, Rear Admiral Eccles had extensive sea duty, including command of a battleship. Since his retirement in 1952, he has written and lectured extensively on military theory, strategy, and logistics. He is author of Military Concepts and Philosophy. *Currently he is a consultant to the president, Naval War College.*

I

From 1945 to 1956 the whole Near East was a welter of hatred and conflicting national and tribal interests intensified by religious differences. The State of Israel had come into being by a combination of terrorism, sabotage, illegal immigration, and the genuine legitimate aspirations of the long-suffering Jews. Western political society had a deep sense of guilt for the unspeakable horrors of the Nazi regime, but even so was unable to provide adequate reception and home for the suffering innocents. England was torn between her traditional friendship for the Arabs and the consequences of the Balfour Declaration and the Palestine Mandate. France was embittered by failure to reestablish herself in Syria, the tragedy of Indochina, and the Algerian revolt, all superimposed on the divisions and tragedy of the German occupation.

The United States was in the process of making so many treaties and agreements that a special effort was required merely to inventory them, let alone understand them. The Jewish political power center of New York was vigorous and very influential in the election year of 1956. The manner in which Russia had taken over Eastern Europe and the Chinese Communist policy of pervasive aggressive subversion posed the threat which created NATO. The United Nations was struggling to cope with intractable problems. Over everything there loomed the growing size and number of nuclear weapons, the grave controversial problems of "strategic warfare" and "deterrence."

Government leaders were worried, overworked, and worn down by incessant air travel. Ambassadors were downgraded by proliferation, and decisions were being pushed to the top of government. Desk men in the state department strove to gain access to their overworked superiors. The problems were almost always both equivocal and ambiguous. Thus at the very time that the problems demanded clear incisive thinking and clear communication between allies, circumstances combined to interfere with clarity of thought, and this led to inadequate communication. Hence the situation and conditions which made careful analysis more important also made it more difficult.

In this atmosphere, when the United States withdrew its offer of a loan to assist in the construction of the Aswan Dam, President Nasser of Egypt seized the Suez Canal on 26 July 1956. From then until mid-October, Secretary of State Dulles sought to reach a peaceful resolution of the problem. At the same time the British and French made plans and deployed forces in preparation for the use of military force. In mid-October the United States had lost touch with its close NATO allies France and Britain, who were collaborating with Israel in the planning for an attack on Egypt.

In late October the Hungarians revolted, and just before the Russians moved in with overwhelming force Israel attacked Egypt. In the next few days, as Russia crushed the Hungarian revolt, the United Nations called for a Suez cease-fire, Britain and France attacked Port Said, and the canal was blocked by the Egyptians.

In the midst of this extreme military-political confusion, there was a cease-fire in the Suez on 6 November, and on 14 November a United Nations peace-keeping force started to move into the area.

Since those climactic two weeks of 23 October to 7 November, dozens of commentators have examined the events, appraised the actions, and speculated on what might have been. Though another twenty-five or more years may pass before historians have access to most of the facts of the Suez crisis of 1956, and even though all interesting points will never be finally clarified,[1] there now is enough well-corroborated evidence to draw important even if limited lessons.

II

Political decision will always be an art that largely depends on how the immediate situation and operating factors are perceived by the responsible men at the time decisions are made. In great matters of state, particularly in the framework of an alliance, the manner in which politicians perceive their national interests and obligations is highly intuitive. I will not discuss what objectives should have been sought, what policies pursued, or what might have happened if these had been other than they actually were. I will emphasize those factors which I believe influenced the course of events in a decisive way and the relationship of these to some of the fundamentals of sound strategy and military decision. Since many of the principal leaders involved seemed to have been surprised by the manner in which events actually unfolded, I start by stating the truism: strategic realism requires the analysis of objectives, the challenge of assumptions, and the appraisal of expectations. These are not rhetorical terms, but terms of art, which are known, or should be known, to students of strategy and military decisionmaking. Their meaning and import are illustrated by the 1956 Suez fiasco. The lessons of Suez center on one fateful event—the decision to use force as made in a telephone conversation between Eden and Pineau on Friday, 27 July, the day after Nasser's seizure of the Canal. This intuitive decision was made without any major cabinet or staff discussion and with nothing that even approached an estimate.[2] Geoffrey McDermott, deputy to Patrick Dean who, in turn, was in charge of the political and military intelligence and planning of the Foreign Office, explained that the Foreign Office never doubted that Eden was determined to have his war. There might be subterfuges to show that every effort was made to reach accommodation before military operations started. But even the subterfuges failed.[3]

While the 27 July agreement was not a formal signed accord, it nevertheless was sufficient to set in motion a series of consequences that tended to blind the protagonists to facts later to be disclosed. We cannot expect political-military decisions always to be made by a process of rigorous logic. But all too often the process of rigorous logic is disregarded by men who feel that such major decisions should be reached on a purely intuitive basis or by a consensus of advisors.

The emotional commitment of a high-level politician brings many psychological forces into play. There is a difference between steadfast pursuit of a clear objective and stubborn adherence to a fatally defective decision or plan. When the situation is complicated by an aroused and angry public opinion, the psychosis of frustration, and an inner need to compensate or to live up to a fictitious image, the stage is set for a great disaster. Throughout history there are many instances in which a major wrong decision, once reached, acquired overriding momentum and led to disaster even though significant changes to the original situation clearly dictated a new estimate.

Since no formal Franco-British appreciations, staff studies, or major agreements are as yet available,[4] the primary and secondary political and strategic objectives must be deduced from the record of conversations and messages. The apparent major political objective of the Franco-British intervention was to bring about the fall of Nasser in order to install a government more sympathetic to their national interests and to forestall the development of an aggressive Arab power structure which could lead to a third world war. Israel had a simple, straightforward national objective: the preservation of the State of Israel.

Thereafter, the partners in the campaign had a variety of secondary or subordinate objectives which were generally, but not always, harmonious.

Israel sought:

1. Territorial realignment both to improve its military position and to provide economic viability,

2. The use of the Suez Canal and freedom of access to Elath on the Gulf of Aqaba,

3. Freedom from fellaheen raids and other acts of terrorism and sabotage in order to improve their political, social, and economic position.

The secondary Franco-British objectives and interests were more complex. Israel shared some of them. However, neither Israel, Britain, nor France attached the same order of importance to the secondary objectives, for example—to maintain freedom of passage of Suez in order to protect their commercial and economic interests.

In the case of Britain, to:

1. Protect their lines of communication to the Indian Ocean and Western Pacific,

2. Maintain the sanctity of formal treaties and agreements,

3. Reduce the growth of Communist influence in the Middle East. In the case of France, to reduce the Arab support of the Algerian revolt.

The United States government understood these interests and shared them to a high degree.[5] There were, however, several complicating factors. The earlier anticolonial attitude of President Roosevelt had created a sense of mistrust both in Britain and France. The French thinking was influenced by the disunity within France in World War II, by their major defeat in Vietnam, and by the extreme violence of the Algerian affairs. These combined to create a feeling of frustration which was not conducive to poised logical analysis. To some degree, an unfavorable physiological-psychological condition influenced Anthony Eden. Furthermore, the British government and people were unhappily aware of the decrease in Britain's stature as a world power. Again, this did not favor cold, clear logic.

Besides the Middle East oil reserves, the United States had two important interests: the strength and harmony of the NATO alliance and the preservation and useful development of the United Nations. Britain and France shared those interests. Yet their importance was blurred by emotional frustration or was pushed into a subordinate position by the Anglo-French intuitive evaluation of other interests. Also, the intense mutual dislike of Anthony Eden and John Foster Dulles created an element of mistrust which disastrously impeded vital communication nd greatly influenced Eden's decisions. Here we have the tragic situation that, at a time when the formulation of a good strategy made the analysis of objectives and interest imperative, such analysis was impeded, if not wholly prevented, by psychological pressures and personality conflicts. Thus, instead of there being anything remotely approaching a sound strategic concept, there was merely a series of haphazard improvisations in France, Britain, and the United States.

The consequences were that in the development of so-called strategic plans, the lack of conceptual unity produced a situation where the military commanders of the operation had no clear idea of the political aims of the campaign.[6] There was general confusion among the planners and operational commanders.[7] At this time Field Marshal Montgomery was deputy supreme commander of the NATO forces in Europe. His 1962 remark in the House of Lords is significant:

... The Prime Minister asked me if I would come over and see him. ... I said to him, "... what is your object? What are you trying to do?" and he replied: "To knock Nasser off his perch." I said that if I were his military adviser ... that object would not do. I should need to know what was the political object when Nasser had been knocked off his perch—because it was that which would determine how the operation was best carried out, what was the best disposition for our forces, and so on. In my judgment, it was the uncertainty about the political object of our leaders which bedevilled the Suez operation from the beginning.[8]

Here a specific lesson can be derived: when conceptual unity is missing, high command has the obligation to recognize its absence and must either take compensating measures or change the basic course of action. Again, from the standpoint of strategy, interests, and objectives, the uprisings in Eastern Europe in October created a new situation and changed the relative values of the basic interests previously mentioned. But by the start of the Hungarian revolt on 23 October, the Franco-British-Israeli plans were so far advanced and the British and French were so committed to them that no reevaluation of interests, objectives, or strategic decision was made. When the channels of communication to the United States were cut off on 16 October, the element of good faith which is vital to a successful alliance was destroyed.

III

A tactical critique of the Suez operation brings out a number of major features:

1. The striking success of the Israeli tactical concepts and their execution,

2. The difficulty of adjusting tactical plans to changes in the timing of the operation,

3. The difficulty of adjusting the tactics to the differing concepts of the British and French commanders,

4. The difficulty of adapting the tactical plan to the subterfuge of the Franco-British ultimatum and of overcoming the handicap imposed by the desire to minimize civilian casualties,

5. The enormous handicap imposed on tactics by the logistic limitations,

6. The exasperating handicap caused by the British planners not having a clear understanding of British political and strategic objectives.

Since in the last decade the Israeli Sinai campaign has been extensively explored in books and periodicals, it is not necessary to discuss it at any length. The basic Israeli strategic concept of a swift, decisive tactical operation was dictated by their national ethos, geography, and economy and by the size, quality, disposition, and political disunity of the enemy forces. This tactical concept depended on high morale and training, leadership which stressed aggressive initiative, and on a simple but technically excellent and austere logistic system. On this basis, and on excellent intelligence, a tactical doctrine of close air-ground coordination and high risk was developed and fully justified by the course of events. All in all, it was a superb illustration of the nature and virtue of "Weapon Morale."[9] To a high degree, Israeli doctrine was based on the theories of Sir Basil Liddell Hart, the British military historian and analyst. It depended heavily on excellent reconnaissance and thus was well suited to the special conditions of the area.

Commander-in-Chief, Allied Forces, General Sir Charles Keightly reported that the cumulative effect of lack of harbors, landing craft yards, and airfields in Cyprus, the limited landing craft and air supply resources together with necessity for much unloading and reloading

> ... was to make a requirement for a longer period between the executive order to start operations being received and the date it was possible to land on the mainland of Egypt. The period of notice which had been accepted for the start of operations was 10 days, although in the event we got little more than 10 hours.[10]

The Anglo-French tactical planning difficulties during the period 17 to 25 October were considerable. The initial plan of 10-14 September called for 8 to 10 days of bombing of troop movements and defenses plus propaganda after a 48-hour attack on the Egyptian air force. It was assumed that the Allied fleet could then land troops at Port Said with little opposition. But the French commanders opposed delay.[11] The situation was further confused by British reluctance to start bombing Egyptian airfields until 72 hours after the start of the Israeli attack.

By 4 November the tactical situation had been confused by the lack of clear-cut objectives. To make matters worse,[12] Eden began "to interfere in the detailed running of the planned operation ... the commanders cursed the speed of communications which made possible this kind of interference."[13]

Curiously, about 3 November the Israeli high command made a series of suggestions which would lead to the more rapid seizure of the tactical objectives and thus contribute to the better attainment of the supposed strategic-political objectives. These suggestions were turned down because they would be an admission of collusion![14] In other words, when at the critical moment it seemed possible to push the plan through to tactical success, the modification was rejected because the consequences as to cost were not acceptable. Thus, while the disadvantages of collusion were suffered, the advantages were not fully exploited.

The final irony of the Franco-British strategic-tactical planning was that even if all the physical objectives had been attained on schedule, the stated purpose of the operation would not have been accomplished. In other words, the plan failed the test of SUITABILITY.* Nevertheless, the plan was approved and executed.

The limited success that was achieved was due to the professional competence of the Allied leaders and troops at the level of unit tactics and was achieved in spite of the deficiencies of grand tactics and strategy. Nevertheless, the final decision to cease fire, induced by a variety of political and economic factors, was an example of failing to make a strategic exploitation of a tactical success. This principle was recognized in the most ironic and, to the British, the most fantastic comment of the whole crisis. When Selwyn Lloyd visited Dulles in the hospital in November he received a final blow, which was almost comic in its incongruity. "Why did you stop?" Dulles asked.[15]

At the highest level of political-military decision, considerations of strategy-economics and logistics tend to coalesce. Economic factors limit the combat forces one can create; logistic factors limit the combat forces one can employ. These fundamentals were clearly shown throughout the whole crisis.[16]

One of the British national objectives was to maintain the economic advantages of the continuing use of the canal. One of the major elements in the estimate of the situation should have been: what are the economic consequences of the proposed course of action? A full consideration of this element requires an understanding of the origins of the British strategic policy then prevailing.

After World War II the British were faced with a difficult, long-range strategic choice. Should they build atomic nuclear weapons and delivery systems? Their economic capabilities had been greatly

*The criteria of suitability, feasibility, and acceptability are discussed in detail further on.

reduced by the losses of the war, and a major effort had to be made to rebuild the cities and industrial facilities. There simply were not enough economic resources available to build even a small atomic weapons system and yet maintain large conventional warfare forces at a high level of operational readiness.

It is neither necessary nor feasible to examine all the complicated arguments and considerations which affected the final decision. The British chose to build a small but necessarily very expensive nuclear system. They accepted the reductions thus imposed on their other forces largely because of their concepts of strategic-military prestige and deterrence.[17] In effect, they adopted a "weapon strategy."

At the time this decision was made—with a few exceptions, such as Sir Stephen King-Hall—they did not appreciate the extent to which their strategic flexibility would be reduced. This became strikingly apparent on 27 July, the day after Eden and Mollet had mutually determined to take swift and decisive military action against Egypt. The British armed forces had absolutely no logistic capability to take such action in the eastern Mediterranean. While the deficiencies were widespread and included almost every logistic category, the single most decisive factor was tank landing craft. To make matters worse, even in cases where material support was available, the forces were not adequately trained. Because of economic stringencies imposed by the Algerian War, the French were in a similar position of impotence.[18]

It seems almost the ultimate irony that even after months of preparation, when every bit of evidence indicated that the United States would disapprove the Franco-British intervention, and when the mounting disagreement within the British government and the dissent of the opposition all showed that swift effective action was the only hope of strategic success, the British and French logistic capabilities were still not enough to provide for the coordinated close timing of the independent elements of the tactical operation. Thus, even though by the first of November the Israeli partner had performed brilliantly, the supporting airstrikes had been effective, and the British ultimatum had expired, the airborne assault was not launched until dawn of 5 November, and the seaborne force not landed until the morning of 6 November. The tactical operation followed Israeli success, which had been apparent on early 3 November, and it followed both Israeli and Egyptian acceptance of the United Nations cease-fire demand by the evening of 3 November. This inordinate delay in timing had been caused by the inexorable logistic facts of the seaborne assault. It allowed public dismay and world indignation and reaction to build up to such an intolerable degree that finally, on 6 November at midnight, when the invasion forces were on the brink of significant success, the Anglo-French forces ceased fire.[19]

One of the major factors in the British decision to desist was economic. In the face of American opposition to British policy, it was no longer possible to maintain the value of the pound sterling.[20] Logistics had dominated tactics, and economics had weakened logistics. But even when tactics had finally achieved partial success, it had fallen prey to economics, and strategy, prestige, and politics were then in chaotic shambles.

The relationships between strategy, logistics, economics, and tactics are in many cases relatively simple, quite clear, and, in some cases, tangible and quantifiable with considerable accuracy. In other cases, of course, they can involve more complex, intangible and subtle aspects. Moral values, prestige, credibility, and the integrity of command, however, are all intangible matters where opinions differ widely, and quantification is impossible. And yet these elements are the foundation for the structure of the tangible effective application of power and force in protracted human conflict. These intangibles form the basis for the aspirations and emotional attachments of men which, when they differ, create the conflict and, when they coincide, create the loyalties which make possible the force that is used in conflict.

A national strategy which is contrary to the moral values of the nation concerned is not likely to succeed. National values are represented not so much by the immediate feelings of the majority of the people on any particular day as they are by the continuing attitude of these people as expressed in their day-to-day behavior over the years.

The element of moral sanction is seldom clear and complete. In our harsh world of protracted violent conflict, many situations arise where the moral element is either uncertain or equivocal and the element of time does not permit a formal, deliberate estimate. Sometimes, in these cases the national interest may justify the use of military force in spite of a high degree of moral uncertainty. High political military command has the paramount obligations to appraise and be willing to accept the consequences of such use of force and to insure that the force is directed toward a clear purpose and is adequate to accomplish it.

In regard to a similar situation, the United States predicament at the Bay of Pigs, Hans Morgenthau noted a United States failure to understand the distinction between abstract principles (e.g., nonintervention) and national interests (e.g., ousting of Castro). He maintains that where they conflict, national interests must govern national action. This observation applies equally well to Suez:

> In consequence the United States failed thrice: The intervention did not succeed; in the attempt we suffered the temporary impairment of our standing among the new and emerging nations; and we lost much prestige as a great nation able to use its power successfully on behalf of its interests.[21]

A wholly professional military force made up of highly selected volunteers who are largely indifferent to domestic politics and who are motivated primarily by their loyalties to their flag or their king—to the traditions of their own organization and to their officers and military associates—can be used effectively in many ways where it may not be suitable to commit the full power of the nation. In particular, it can be employed to achieve a political purpose in special situations, usually small-scale, where the strategy-values relationship is either unclear or equivocal. In this connection we should appreciate the great distinction between swift overt action in a dangerous crisis and the long-range deliberate deception, subterfuge, and obvious absurdity of the Franco-British Suez intervention.

There is a great difference between the shock to one's sensibilities engendered by the former and the insult to one's intelligence by the latter.

One, as in the case of the Russian suppression of the Hungarian revolt, may produce anger, but it also induces respect and credibility. The other, as in Suez, produces nothing but disbelief and contempt. One may be considered to be in the national interest; the other defeats the national interest.

To the student of logistics there were no logistics surprises in the Suez crisis. Throughout the entire planning and conduct of operation the fundamental logistic factors exerted their influence almost precisely in accordance with the expectation of logistic theory based on historical analysis of World War II.

In Israel the logistic system was in harmony with the strategic and tactical concepts. It was based on technical excellence, the citizen-army concept, and the ability to improvise. It was completely responsive to the needs of tactical command. The logistic snowball was controlled by an austere exercise of discipline. Since the strategic and tactical concepts did not include a prolonged campaign, they were within the capability of logistic resources, and thus logistics factors did not exert their ultimate limiting effect. The flexibility and mobility of the defense concept and system, based on "weapon morale," permitted the strategic exploitation of tactical success. All in all, it was a striking illustration of the logistics aspects of operational readiness and combat effectiveness. Finally, since the Israeli strategic concepts were in harmony with French policy and since France was the chief source of Israeli logistic support, the relatively small logistics deficiencies of the Israeli forces disclosed in the early planning were readily made up by their ally.

The Franco-British logistics similarly confirmed basic concepts and principles. Logistics is a comprehensive, coherent process with its roots in the national economy and its payoff in the tactical operation of the combat forces. In its producer phase, economic factors limit the combat forces which can be created, and in its consumer phase logistic factors limit the combat forces which can be employed. The British economy could not support both an atomic weapon system and mobile flexible nonatomic combat forces.

Anthony Eden frankly admits that the extent and costs of defense preparations were "formidable and ever increasing." Accordingly, in order to maintain nuclear striking power the government reduced conventional forces, despite difficulties in reconciling the Treasury's view with that of the services as to what was essential.[22] The impossibility of an immediate riposte was known to the cabinet by midday on 28 July. A military movement could not be mounted for three or four months.[23]

Similarly, the French economy could not support both the strain of the guerrilla war in Algeria and mobile flexible forces suitable for the Egyptian campaign. Thus, the logistics aspects of operational readiness and combat effectiveness were clearly demonstrated by the deplorable state of Anglo-French preparedness, which Paul Johnson has ably described.

The French forces were in a grave state of unpreparedness. While part of the fleet could get under way from Toulon within forty-eight hours, the fleet itself could not be in the eastern Mediterranean within one week. Moreover, the sole French carrier had only twenty-five planes capable of meeting Nasser's Russian-built MiG 15s and 17s. Ground-based aircraft were not only unavailable for at least ten days, but also because they were so short-legged they would be useless if they were based in Algeria. Ground forces were in a similar state.

Johnson describes the news from London as even worse. The three British parachute battalions in Cyprus had received no training for months, because they lacked parachutes. There were no landing craft for the eight infantry battalions in Cyprus. Various infantry battalions in Aden and East Africa and parts of the Tenth Armored Division in Libya were stranded without transport. While the Mediterranean fleet was available, its carriers were not equipped with modern aircraft.[24]

Randolph Churchill mourned, "once again British political and strategic judgment had been found wanting." After recounting a series of errors, he concluded, "The state of military preparedness was staggering and humiliating." He noted the services tried to make good their deficiencies "with hasty improvisation."[25]

The operational aspects of the Suez crisis lasted too short a time and the documentation is not available to make any comments on the application of management techniques to the logistics problems. Obviously, systems analysis was not used in the strategic programming decision described by Mr. Eden. Under the circumstances it is doubtful how it might have been usefully applied. The overriding factor in the decision to build a "nuclear deterrent" obviously was wholly intuitive and based on a plausible but questionable assumption as to the utility of a small nuclear capability.

In addition to the manner in which logistic fundamentals dominated the Franco-British-Israeli intervention, they were a dominant element of the peace-keeping United Nations Emergency Force (UNEF). The United States Navy was given primary responsibility for the logistics of its organization and support. Since time was a critical factor in the political effectiveness of this force, its logistics assumed transcending political-psychological importance. While a fully documented story does not seem to be available, certain facts are known.

The normal legal, financial, and administrative rules and procedures of the United States Department of Defense were wholly ignored. The task was delegated to a captain in the office of the chief of naval operations who moved a cot into his office and stayed there for four or five days except to go to the head. He maintained frequent telephone contact with Dr. Ralph Bunche at United Nation headquarters in New York and with various four-star and other generals who controlled supplies, equipment, and air transport.

At first, all dispatches were highly classified, but after about forty-eight hours the communications system had become so clogged by the task of decoding and the physical exhaustion of the junior officers in the coding section that dispatches were shifted to plain English unclassified. It is estimated that about 95 percent of all dispatches dealing with UNEF were logistical, and most of the remaining five percent concerned command relations.

Thus again, in the crunch, we see another illustration of Ruppenthal's phrase, "the tyranny of logistics."

IV

All the elements and factors herein discussed come into critical focus in the major decision at the top level of political-military authority in each nation concerned. The day is long past, if there ever was such a day, when the political authority could make a political decision and then turn the problem over to the military authority for a military decision and subsequent action.

In some nations, such as the United States, the Constitution combines the chief political executive and the commander in chief in one office. In some countries a military dictatorship seizes and holds the chief executive office and power. In other countries parliamentary government provides essentially the same unity of authority.

Regardless of the circumstances of authority, the chief political executive now exercises military command, and thus it is essential that he view and understand the military problem from the perspective of command.

The political and military problems must be intuitively integrated in the mind of the one man who combines political and military authority. This is the essence of decision. The political authority must have the technique and take the time to explore the military aspects with the service chiefs themselves. No facade of agreement should interfere with the direct presentation of a blunt professional appraisal.

The military portion of this section, dealing with the problem of decisionmaking and control, has been divided into certain specific interlocking and overlapping parts in order to facilitate research and education. Each of these parts merits extensive specific study which can be effectively disciplined only if the military problem is seen as a coherent structure, with a body of substantive knowledge and a number of fundamental principles.

The first element in the classic approach to military decision is to identify the problem which requires a decision to be made.[26]

In the Suez crisis a specific problem was posed for Great Britain, France, Israel, and the United States by Nasser's seizure of the canal. Clausewitz observed that the first task of generalship is to decide the question, "What kind of war is it?" In this case the seizure posed a different problem for each of the four nations mentioned. The problem for no one of them could be separated from the context of their continuing problems of politics, economics, and military security. In the case of Israel the conflict with the Arab world was obviously the most urgent. In the case of Great Britain, France, and the United States, there was a common element of concern for collective security within the NATO pact, a concern for world order in the context of the United Nations, and a concern for the economics of world trade. Furthermore, each nation had its own special interests which varied somewhat from those of common concern.

At this point two major questions can be posed: To what degree must national sovereignty be sacrificed in order to deal successfully with the major problems of world affairs today? The old and rather romantic concept of untrammeled national sovereignty as being an absolute value or a viable, absolute entity is completely mythical.

Is the problem posed by the seizure a "puzzle" for which there is a specific solution, or a "difficulty" which must be surmounted or endured but for which there is no specific solution?[27]

In retrospect, and with some oversimplification, it appears that the British and French saw the crisis as a puzzle, the United States saw it as a difficulty, and the Israelis saw it as an opportunity.

From the recognition of the type of problem and the analysis of the overall situation, we pass on to the analysis of objectives. As previously mentioned, this derives from the national interests. But more than this, because of the interdependence of so-called sovereign nations, practical wisdom calls for considering the interests and objectives of one's allies and associates. It appears that in spite of protracted conversations, letters, and dispatches, this important element was inadequately accomplished in the period 27 July to 16 October. An important part of the analysis of objectives is to consider (1) what constitutes a satisfactory accomplishment of one's objectives, and (2) what change in the basic situation or in opponents' reaction will influence the objectives. This last is both subtle and important and constitutes more a part of the supervision of the planned action than an important part of the initial estimate. In the Suez crisis its importance was strikingly illustrated in the different reactions to the Hungarian revolt which broke out on 23 October.

The next logical step is to consider the means available and the means opposed. In the purely military part of the estimate, this includes relative fighting strength. The sad facts of time and distance related to logistic capabilities and state of training of forces as disclosed on 27 and 28 July should, at this point, have brought about a very thorough reevaluation of objectives.

It seems clear that the British military staff fully appreciated this point, but it is also clear that civilian political control which completely dominated the situation[28] chose to override these facts of life.

At this point, if they have not been considered earlier, the question of assumptions becomes important and should be treated with rigor. In a military estimate an assumption is not merely something believed to be true; it is rather a matter so critical to the success of a plan that the plan will fail if the assumption is not true. This matter is so important that for every explicit assumption there should be an alternate plan to be used should the assumption prove false. Otherwise, the planned operation should be canceled.

In the broader political sense, the assumption, while it need not be treated with equal rigor, still requires identification and challenge. For example, both Eden and Mollet assumed that, if unchecked, Nasser would develop the menace and the power of Hitler.

The British assumed that the Egyptians could not successfully operate the canal without Western assistance. The British seemed to have assumed that the canal could be secured before the Egyptians could block it.[29] The British apparently assumed that the invasion should bring about the fall of Nasser and that he would be replaced by a friendly government.

The British, the French, and the Israelis all seemed to have assumed that because of its presidential election the United States government would acquiesce in a *fait accompli.* There is no evidence of any alternate plan being prepared or even being seriously considered.

The United States assumed that Mr. Dulles' skill as a lawyer and negotiator would be sufficient to restrain Britain and France from attempting to use force. Implicit in this there seems to have been the further assumption that the British and French would take the same view of the NATO and United States interests and commitments as did the United States.

The next step in the estimate is to develop and compare various courses of action in order to make the basic decision. Many people who give lip service to the idea that this should be an orderly, logical process, nevertheless, in practice say in effect to their staff: "I have decided what I am going to do; now make a study to justify my decision." In effect, this is what Eden and Mollet did in their first conference in late July. This method certainly did not work well in 1956, and it is not recommended. But regardless of how high command reaches a decision, the classic tests of a military course of action should be applied: Suitability, Feasibility, Acceptability.

SUITABILITY: Will the action accomplish the purpose I have in mind? Will it accomplish the objective?

FEASIBILITY: Is it possible to carry out this course of action with the tactical and logistical resources that are available and in such a time frame that it will meet the test of suitability?

ACCEPTABILITY: Am I willing and able to accept the consequences as to cost involved in taking this course of action? In other words, is the accomplishment of the objective worth the price I will have to pay measured in terms of the values at stake?

Obviously, to make even a rudimentary evaluation of these basic criteria one must have a clear purpose in mind and must be able to express it in terms that are suitable for analytical evaluation. Here, precisely, is the central fault of the Franco-British collaboration, and Field Marshal Montgomery identified it in conversation with Prime Minister Eden on 20 September.[30]

The classic tests prove the objective. The evidence is clear that, regardless of how the Franco-British objective is deduced or interpreted, it fails to meet three of the classic tests of a course of action. If Operation Musketeer had been subjected to such a formal test by competent, responsible officers, its failure to pass any one of the criteria would have disclosed the fatal fault in the objective. If it was so tested, then the action in overriding the results of the test was an act of arrogant folly and a violation of the integrity of command.

V

It is impossible to draw any conclusion as to the merits of British and French action without considerable discussion of the position and action of the United States.

The American position and behavior during the summer of 1956 was, in the view of Mr. Eden, equivocal and unrealistic. While this is obviously less than completely true, his account of the course of events that summer in *Full Circle* does explain his reaction to the American action.

President Eisenhower was recuperating from a serious illness, and with his normal dependence on his staff and "completed staff work" it is unlikely that he was, in fact, following the course of events as closely as the situation demanded. His secretary of state, John Foster Dulles, is now dead. Dulles' legalistic attitudes and the close intuitive manner in which he reached his decisions have been commented upon by many who have admired his devotion and strength. The combination of these two aspects, however, seems in retrospect to have deceived Mr. Eden and led him on to expect positive action when in fact such action was never contemplated seriously.

It seems clear that delaying tactics of the United States in August and September laid the foundation for later adverse developments; particularly, it gave the British and the French governments the feeling that the United States could not be trusted. In the meantime England and France recognized that the course of events was more and more restricting their political freedom of action. This developed a sense of frustration which understandably contributed greatly to the irrationality of the final act in the tragedy.

Dulles in the summer of 1956 indulged in a haphazard series of improvisations aimed at an objective which was never clearly expressed to Mr. Eden. Without a clear common objective, there could be no unity of thinking and no clear communication between the British and American leaders. However, after Eisenhower's letter of early September, Eden had no reason to believe that the United States would support Musketeer.

When the Hungarian crisis arose, it presented opportunities for concerted diplomatic and political action by NATO and the United Nations in areas whose importance far transcended the immediate Middle East situation. The Franco-British-Israeli action obscured the Hungarian crisis and diverted the attention of the United States, its allies, and the neutrals from the major world issue in which the central issues of the cold war were crystal clear.

This, of course, does not excuse the United States behavior from 1 August to mid-October. It does explain why world and considerable British opinion was generally against Mr. Eden. Mr. Eden should have realized that the American election would influence American behavior in the Middle East; particularly, it would tend to inhibit decisive action at a time when Mr. Eden recognized the need for such decisive action. The American public had been deceived or lulled by Mr. Eisenhower's and Mr. Dulles' overoptimistic statements at press conferences.

It was not Mr. Eden's fault—he was helpless to change this. Very understandably, this created a sense of great frustration. However, Mr. Eden should have been experienced enough to recognize this vital if unfortunate fact, and he should never have expected Mr. Eisenhower and Mr. Dulles to have acted other than they did when he intervened. Therefore, he should not have intervened unless he had both the power and the will to move swiftly and decisively without United States acquiescence or support. One cannot use force slowly and gently in a situation such as this: one either does not use force at all or one uses it decisively.

Eden's great mistake was to undertake a project which could not succeed without United States support when he had no reason to believe he would have that support. To say that Mr. Eisenhower and Mr. Dulles should have supported him is beside the point. While Herman Finer is a strong, even violent critic of Dulles, the evidence he presents in his book, *Dulles Over Suez,* is consistent with other evidence and merits close attention.

Finer admits that if Dulles' diplomatic virtuosity shone at its brightest at the First London Conference (16-23 August 1956), his triumph came in the Eighteen Power Declaration to uphold British and French rights in Suez against Nasser. However, he concludes that Dulles' refusal to lead a mission to Cairo to present the proposals and subsequent misunderstandings and developments caused the Allies to "lose faith in his sincerity, friendship and clarity of mind."[31]

The Anglo-American disarray is further testified to by Winthrop Aldrich, then the American ambassador in London. Aldrich constantly advised the British against using force. This advice was not taken. Aldrich concluded that Eden reckoned that when presented with a *fait accompli* the United States would recognize vital British interests and would support him.[32]

In the climactic period of 5-6 November the threat of Russian volunteers; a series of Soviet atomic blackmail threats; the flight from the pound; the opposition of the Commonwealth nations; domestic opposition in the universities, among the clergy, in Parliament, and even in his own party, including the opposition of much of general public opinion; and the demands of the American government—all these combined to place intolerable pressure upon Eden.

Finer describes the circumstances in fascinating detail, pointing out that this pressure required a nervous and physical strength which Eden did not have and may never have had. Eden agreed to a cease-fire to take effect at midnight on 6 November.[33]

Finer further comments, "The British and French never came anywhere near to sensing the fearful degree of anger generated in the White House by Israel's entry into battle. They did not foresee the missionary zeal, efficiency, and speed with which the American leaders would press action in the United Nations. . . ."[34]

VI

There is a major overlap between the controllable and the uncontrollable areas of human conflict. Herbert Rosinski in his masterly short paper, "New Thoughts on Strategy," wrote: "It is the element of control which is the essence of strategy: control being the element which differentiates true strategic action from a haphazard series of improvisations."[35]

Almost to the last, Dulles thought he had control. It came as a great shock to learn that he had lost control. Any decision to use force demands an appraisal of the power available. The simple fact that Britain and France did not have the comprehensive military-economic political power to retain the initiative meant that they lost the element of control and were forced into haphazard improvisation. This was clearly shown by their maneuvers during the debates in the United Nations on and after 30 October.

One of the most fundamental attributes of an effective alliance is good faith. This essential element of good faith creates and demands as a further necessity that a country does not confront an ally with a *fait accompli* affecting the other country's vital interest. In particular, good sense would indicate that if such a desperate measure appears necessary, one's expectations as to the consequent behavior of one's ally should be modest. No statesman should assume that the ally will follow his lead when that ally has been deceived.

These elementary facts of statesmanship, diplomacy, and international politics should have been second nature to Anthony Eden. The fact that he ignored them in 1956 and has subsequently attempted to justify his conduct can be ascribed only to a deterioration of his mental capacity and moral perception.

This all emphasizes the importance of being able to identify the central issues in any complex problem. It, of course, cannot be done unless one has, first, had analytical experience and, second, understands the basic theory and principle of military decision in the area concerned.

From the foregoing it is evident that:

1. The American officials thought that the United States posi-

tion was clear, and some thought that it was consistent.

2. United States officials thought that this position was being adequately communicated to Eden and other foreign officials.

3. In early September some officials began to feel that the United States position was not completely understood.

4. Until the diplomatic blackout of 16 October, United States officials seemed to feel that the situation was under control.

5. The American position as expressed in public statements, official acts, and personal and official correspondence was in fact inconsistent, ambiguous, and equivocal in many points.

6. These elements derived from the great diversity and inner contradiction of American interests and from the unwillingness or inability of American officials to order these interests in specific terms.

7. These inconsistencies and uncertainties were frequently expressed in the various and, at times, almost parenthetical escape clauses that could have originated in the typical language habits of a clever lawyer, in personal uncertainty, or both.

8. The domestic political atmosphere of a presidential year was conducive both to uncertainty in policy and equivocation and ambiguity of language.

9. These facts and attitudes encouraged Nasser in his intransigence, or confused and exasperated British and French officials, and encouraged the Israelis to seize an opportunity. In other words, they encouraged the very qualities and stimulated the very events they were designed to prevent.

10. All in all, there was no identification and clarification of the central issues. Conceptual unity was not attained. It was all a matter of haphazard improvisation which in no sense could be called a national strategy.

The Middle East and Atlantic policy of the United States obviously failed to such a degree that a complete collapse was barely averted. The repercussions of this failure have influenced most of the United States actions and policy ever since. Such major failure poses some very difficult questions.

First, what were the causes of this failure?

Certainly it was not simply caused by the weakness or foolishness of one man or even one group.

In examining policy, do we ask the wrong questions? Do we underrate some forces and overestimate others? Do our government leaders argue for a position better than they analyze it? Certainly all these faults occur frequently and can be expected to continue.

Do we expect too much from policy? Do our attempts to do too much so clutter the minds of our executives and their staffs and so choke the channels of communication that even the major problems tend to be examined hastily, superficially, and with little consecutive thought by the senior responsible officials? Is our government so overcentralized that the inadequate delegation of authority further clutters the time and saps the energy of our senior officials in Washington?

Has the proliferation of small states so increased the requirement for highly qualified personnel in the foreign service and placed such a burden on communication as to introduce mediocrity and sluggishness into the diplomatic system?

These and similar questions will not be readily answered. But one in particular deserves comment. Do we expect too much from a policy? Hans Morgenthau has already pointed out the distinction between principles and interests and the need for policy to be guided by interests rather than by abstract principle. But even so, we should think further.

International policy is not formed by a political party and then carried out. Policy instead is dominated and almost wholly formed by the play of events as they are perceived and interpreted by the men in power in accordance with their own special concepts and habits of thought.

The methods and procedures used by the United States government in dealing with the events of 1956 were the usual conventional methods of thought and procedure that have been generally accepted as the best practicable way of doing the business of government. The men involved were as able, as dedicated, and as upright as we can expect to see in such position of authority.

But the formulation of policy is quite different from the overt use of military force. Policy can be changed and at times readily modified. Overt military force, particularly in the nuclear age, however, has its own special characteristics and sets special forces into play that cannot be changed so readily. Thus the decision to use military force in support of a policy poses an intellectual challenge of a higher order of difficulty than the normal demands of policy and the normal decisions of government. This is one of the major lessons of Suez just as it now is of Vietnam.

Consequently, when the issue of the use of military force is being discussed with an allied government, special care must be taken to keep the channels clear and the discussion unambiguous.

In passing, it is worth noting that many of the lessons of Suez eventually were reflected in subsequent United States policy and behavior; for example:

The strengthening of the so-called general purpose forces and the establishment of a stronger, ready, amphibious force and improved mobile logistic support,

The formation of the United States Strike Command,

The formal concept of prepositioning,

The establishment of a Special Assistant for Strategic Mobility to the chairman of the Joint Chiefs of Staff,

A more specific approach to the evaluation of Operational Readiness,

The great care that was taken to inform our allies of the situation and our position in the Cuban missile crisis of 1962.

Ironically, however, these improvements did not take place as a direct result of Suez because so many of the fundamental faults of Suez were repeated by the United States in the Bay of Pigs. So it can be said that some of the obvious lessons of Suez gradually sank in when they were reinforced by the comparably foolish and disastrous handling of that affair.

VII

The foregoing brings us to a group of concepts and ideas which have evolved over many years of military analysis, much of which took place before World War II and formed the heart of *Sound Military Decision* (published in 1936 by the United States Naval War College).

Regardless of how it be defined or organized in any particular nation, the highest level of military command is in reality vested in the highest political authority in the nation. This political-military linkage further combines with management to form a continuum of executive authority which must blend policy, strategy, logistics, tactics, and operations in coherent action devoted to the national interests and national security.

While the military aspects of the overall problem must be subordinate to the political, military considerations are a major factor in the political decision.

As a consequence of the thermonuclear threat, the level of tactical defeat that is acceptable to attain a higher strategic objective has been raised to a level never before visualized by military scholars. This and the resulting strict political control of all military action have placed a great burden on military command leadership to maintain combat morale and effectiveness under adverse political restraints.

The classic principle of military decision emphasizes the inter-weaving of thought as integrated in the mind of the responsible commander by requiring the test of each proposed course of action for:

1. SUITABILITY—Will it accomplish the mission? Attain the objective? This involves both strategy and politics.

2. FEASIBILITY—Can it be accomplished with the means available? This involves tactics, logistics, and economics.

3. ACCEPTABILITY—Are the consequences as to cost acceptable? This involves politics, economics, and logistics.

While it is not likely that in the contradictory environment of world politics the strict military meaning of the word *assumption* can always be applied, it is important for those who have the burden of decision to understand it.

Sound Military Decision comments:

> The word assumption, when used to denote a basis for a plan, signifies "the taking of something for granted." It does not mean a conjecture, a guess or a probability. The proposed action, resulting from a decision made under an assumption, is designed to be taken only upon the disclosure of the truth of the assumption. The fact that the assumption upon which the plan is based may prove false indicates the advisability of developing several plans based on various sets of assumptions .... *The visualization of valid and useful assumptions frequently makes the most serious demands on professional knowledge and judgment.*[36]

In political-military affairs, an assumption does not have to be formal or explicit in order to influence decisions and action. In some instances false assumptions seem to carry great authority even though after the fact they are clearly recognized as mere plausible, attractive myths.

The establishment of conceptual unity as to the purpose to be attained and of assumptions underlying the plan is of vital importance and is a primary responsibility of high command regardless of whether command is vested in an individual or a group. This requires the analysis of objectives, as well as their precise statement.

Military force should never be used except to accomplish a political purpose. That is, the ultimate objective must be political, although more immediate objectives may be categorized "military." The man who initiates, controls, and terminates the use of military force must have a clear idea of this political purpose. He must be alert for unexpected developments which invalidate the assumptions on which his plan is based or which alter the nature and primacy of the objectives sought.

At this point it is possible to define certain terms:

Strategy is the comprehensive direction of power to control situations and areas to attain objectives.

Tactics is the immediate employment of specific weapons and forces to attain the objectives established by strategy.

Logistics is the creation and sustained support of specific weapons and forces to be tactically employed to attain strategic objectives.

Strategy, tactics, and logistics are interrelated. For this reason each directly affects the others. A sound military decision requires all three to be in harmony.

It behooves policy to ensure not only that military strategy pursue appropriate aims but that the work of strategy be allotted adequate means and be undertaken under the most favorable conditions. Thus strategy and tactics are inseparable, and understanding between civil and military leaders is essential.

It is the duty of tactics to ensure results appropriate to strategic aim.

It is the duty of strategy to give tactics the power appropriate to the results demanded.

It is the duty of strategy to insure that the tactical struggle be initiated under conditions favorable for attainment of objectives.

The functions of command are threefold: to create combat forces, to support combat forces, and to employ combat forces.

Strategy governs the comprehensive employment; tactics governs the immediate employment; and logistics has the dual role of both creating the forces and thereafter providing their sustained support.

Command and management are not synonymous. The distinction is based on the difference in the responsibilities of command. The responsibilities of command are greater than those of management because command establishes the purpose for which military force is employed and involves ultimate questions of life and death. Command, however, must use a variety of management procedures and techniques throughout the military system.

As the link between the war front and the home front, the logistic process is at once the military element in the nation's economy and the economic element in its military operations. Thus there are two phases to the coherent process of logistics: the producer phase and the consumer phase.

Management is a group of procedures and techniques which enter the military system primarily as they are used to control the specific functions of the two phases of logistics.

Operations is a blend of tactical action and logistic action to attain the objectives set by strategy. The logistic action must take place before the tactical action becomes possible. Thus, the logistic system must be in harmony both with the economic system and with the tactical concepts and environment of the combat forces.

Economic factors limit the combat forces one can create. Operational logistic factors limit the combat forces one can employ. Thus, we can say:

Readiness = Degree of ability of a unit/ship to perform its designed mission. It includes status of personnel, equipment, supplies, maintenance facilities, intelligence, and training. It also incorporates "performance," "endurance," and "preparedness."

Readiness can be distinguished from Effectiveness, because Effectiveness = Performance Availability Utilization.

We now must ask a group of fundamental questions: What kinds of power and force can be used effectively to accomplish a political purpose? What kinds of power and force cannot be used to accomplish a political purpose? What changes in the basic political-military situation can shift a particular kind of power and force from one category of usability to the other? How does one measure, report, and evaluate combat and operational effectiveness and readiness?

An accurate appraisal of one's own operational effectiveness and readiness is a vital element in any decision to use military power and force. These questions will not be solved easily or quickly. They will best be achieved through a disciplined continuing exploration of military theory.

VIII

The evidence on the Suez crisis of 1956 is coherent, consistent, and has such an atmosphere of authenticity that any major contradiction or invalidation when the complete archives of Great Britain, France, and the United States are made available seems unlikely.

The pros and cons of the Aswan Dam controversy are beyond the scope of this paper. Nevertheless the student of military history and theory must understand how the cancellation of the proposed loan triggered events which had other causative components stretching far back into history. He should be particularly interested in the factors which caused the ineptitude of the political-military decisions made after the seizure of the canal.

The 28 July reports from the military staff to the cabinet that swift decisive military action would be impossible should have alerted Mr. Eden and Mr. Pineau to the dangerous realities of the problem. Thereafter a thorough military estimate of the situation should have been made before deciding the course of action. In partial extenuation of their action, we should realize that the equivocal attitudes and maneuvers of Mr. Dulles inhibited rather than encouraged such rigorous analysis.

Eden and Dulles each misjudged the strength of the other's commitment to opposing policies and the degree to which this opposition was supported, in one case by the momentum of a bad plan, and in the other by his associates in government. Neither seemed to recognize the nature and significance of his own assumptions and of the other's assumptions, concepts, and perception of his country's national interests. This misjudgment was accentuated by the use of the transatlantic telephone to discuss matters which are not susceptible to clarification by such an imperfect method of communication. We do not know the extent to which ill health, excessive workload, and the strain and readjustments of extensive travel by air influenced the thought process of individual men. We do not know the extent to which cancer influenced Dulles' emotions and thought process. We know that because of his two recent serious illnesses, Eisenhower's doctors and personal staff were solicitous in protecting Eisenhower from excessive mental and physical strain. We know that Eden's health was bad and that his illness was of a type associated with lack of poise and sound judgment.

The problem of Israel was clear and unambiguous. She considered that her national existence was at stake; she was constrained by circumstances to a relatively simple strategic concept. Her people, many of them recently freed from unspeakable misery, clearly understood the issues and the national interest, were inured to sacrifice, and were unafraid of risk.

On the other hand, the problems of Britain, France, and the United States were extraordinarily difficult. Their national interests were complex and diverse: the issues posed were uncertain and at times ambiguous. Both France and Britain were suffering from frustration and memories of past power. The United States, in an election year, was in effect trying to be all things to all people and thus had interests which were almost overtly contradictory.

The Israeli situation is unique: few, if any, nations have such a clear sense of purpose and interest. By contrast, the situation of the other powers is typical of the present and the foreseeable future. Contradiction and ambiguity in the face of equivocal threats are normal expectancy for these nations. Even though we cannot expect strict logic to govern high-level political military decisions, it certainly should influence the expectations of those who decide and plan. Because of the life and death aspect of command, this is particularly important for the military professional. When the politician exercises the authority of a military commander, he also assumes the obligation to know what he is doing and to understand the effect of his decision and actions on military operations.

The influence of the forthcoming United States presidential election permeated the thinking of all American politicians who were making policy during the summer and autumn of 1956. This influence also extended abroad, particularly to England, France, Israel, and Egypt. One can never know the precise manner and degree of its effect on the course and timing of events. It did affect the basic thinking of the dominant individuals.

The question of to what degree one can be frank and open with the leaders of an allied state is a difficult matter of intuition. It involves the analysis of one's own objectives, the evaluation of allied and opponents' objectives and intentions, and an evaluation of the degree of confidence one has in the allied leaders. This latter point has two aspects: confidence in their integrity and discretion, and confidence in their ability to control their own governments and nations.

This is an extraordinary combination of intelligence, information, psychological appraisal, and faith. Its very complexity emphasizes three major factors in top-level decision: the analysis of objectives, the examination of assumptions, and the vital importance of character and intuition. Neither organizational devices nor quantitative evaluations can help very much with this aspect of a major political military problem. Of all the lessons of Suez, this seems to be the most important and the most enduring.

Finally, these fundamentals should be studied and pondered so that they will be second nature to our commanders, be they civilian or military. Then when new crises inevitably arise they will be an integral part of their intuition, their professional judgment. When, under the pressure of events, the formal thought process must be telescoped, these factors and relationships will take their proper place and exert their proper influence. If anyone counters with the remark that it is not practicable to expect such leaders thus to study and meditate, that person must be prepared to accept the disastrous consequences of such ignorance and neglect.

In retrospect, the points made seem so obvious as to be almost trite. Yet it was the failure to understand them and their significance, the failure to apply sound long-established principles which produced one of the greatest military-political disasters of our time.

Strategic realism requires the analysis of objectives, the challenge of assumptions, and the appraisal of expectations.

NOTES

Originally published in the *Naval War College Review.* March 1969.

1. Hugh Thomas, *Suez* (New York: Harper & Row, 1967).

2. Paul Johnson, *The Suez War* (Hertfordshire, Eng.: Garden City Press, 1957), pp. 43-45.

3. Geoffrey McDermott, "Foreign Office—How We Planned the War," *The Spectator,* 7 July 1967, p. 6.

4. Anthony Nutting, *No End of a Lesson—the Story of Suez* (London: Constable, 1967), pp. 13-14. Nutting, minister of state in Eden's cabinet, kept no records of their discussions with France and Israel leading up to the attack on Egypt.

5. Herbert Nicholas, *Britain and the United States* (Baltimore: Johns Hopkins University Press, 1963), pp. 106-8.

6. Thomas, *Suez,* pp. 90, 111.

7. Ibid., pp. 111-13; McDermott, "Foreign Office," p. 6.

8. Thomas, *Suez,* p. 90.

9. Henry E. Eccles, *Military Concepts and Philosophy* (New Brunswick, N.J.: Rutgers University Press, 1967), p. 247.

10. Sir Charles Keightly, "Operations in Egypt, November to December 1956, "Supplement to the *London Gazette,* 10 September 1967.

11. Thomas, *Suez,* pp. 109-16.

12. Johnson, *Suez War,* pp. 102-3; Thomas, p. 140.

13. Thomas, *Suez,* p. 140.

14. Randolph S. Churchill, *The Rise and Fall of Sir Anthony Eden* (New York: Putnam, 1959), pp. 291-92.

15. Thomas, *Suez,* p. 149.

16. Henry E. Eccles, *Logistics in the National Defense* (Harrisburg, Pa.: Stackpole, 1959), pp. 30-41.

17. Anthony Eden, *Full Circle* (Boston: Houghton Mifflin, 1960), pp. 412-15.

18. Johnson, *Suez War,* pp. 43-45; Keightly, "Egypt"; Thomas, *Suez,* pp. 41, 42, 48.

19. Johnson, *Suez War,* pp. 92-103; Churchill, *Anthony Eden,* pp. 278-81; Keightly; Thomas, pp. 129-44.

20. Thomas, *Suez,* pp. 145-58.

21. Hans Morgenthau, "To Intervene or Not to Intervene," *Foreign Affairs,* April 1967, pp. 430-31.

22. Eden, *Full Circle,* pp. 414-15.

23. Thomas, *Suez,* pp. 41-42.

24. Johnson, *Suez War,* pp. 43-45, describes the state of French and British services.

25. Churchill, *Anthony Eden,* pp. 245-46.

26. I use the term *classic approach* to represent the "Estimate of the Situation" which had been issued from 1910 until 1936 by the Naval War College. This estimate, based on rigorous historical analysis, was then included in the War College publication, *Sound Military Decision,* and republished in 1942.

27. Eccles, *Military Concepts and Philosophy,* chap. IX, "Command Decision," particularly pp. 124-27.

28. Thomas, *Suez,* p. 158.

29. Johnson, *Suez War,* pp. 105-6.

30. Thomas, *Suez,* p. 90.

31. Herman Finer, *Dulles over Suez* (Chicago: Quadrangle Books, 1964), pp. 493-94.

32. Winthrop W. Aldrich, "The Suez Crisis," *Foreign Affairs,* April 1967, pp. 541-52.

33. Finer, *Dulles over Suez,* pp. 421-33.

34. Ibid., p. 372.

35. See Part I, pp. 63-65 above and Eccles, *Military Concepts and Philosophy,* pp. 36-46.

36. Naval War College, *Sound Military Decision* (Newport R.I.: Naval War College, 1942), pp. 155-156. Emphasis added.

The Cold War: Some Lessons for Policymakers

John Lewis Gaddis

Editor's Note: *John Lewis Gaddis is Professor of History at Ohio University. He is the author of* The United States and the Origins of the Cold War, 1941-1947, *winner of the Bancroft Prize for 1973.*

Historians frequently assert that one cannot draw lessons from the past. What has gone before, they tend to argue, is an infinite aggregation of variables; by their very definition, past events are unique, particular, and incapable of repetition. Some historians despair even of *describing* the past accurately, much less drawing lessons from it. And, in a way, they are right: one can never completely reconstruct the past; one can never discover everything that actually happened.

Historians who argue this way are also somewhat impractical, however, because they forget that selectivity in the perception and ordering of experience is a prerequisite for sanity. If human beings waited until they had all the facts before acting, no action would ever take place. The man who acts does so on the basis of selective evidence; invariably, and necessarily, past experience will make up the vast majority of the information upon which action is based.

In their concern to produce definitive accounts of past events, historians sometimes ignore these simple facts of life. Too often they define definitiveness in terms of bulk, failing to distinguish between the significant and the insignificant, producing big books on small topics which only other historians read. As a result, they have little practical effect on the shaping of government policy. It is not that policymakers ignore history, but that, for understandable reasons, they turn to people capable of summarizing, organizing, and analyzing evidence to interpret the past for them. These tend, unfortunately, not to be historians.

The historical profession thus has abdicated both responsibilities and opportunities, and the results have been pernicious. It is inevitable that policymakers are going to draw lessons from the past—it is not inevitable, or desirable, that it be left up to amateurs to help them do this. This essay is a modest effort to reverse the trend: to suggest, on the basis of some familiarity with the history of the cold war, a few practical lessons today's policymakers might legitimately derive from that experience. These lessons are neither original nor infallible. It does seem likely, though, that had they been applied more frequently than they were during the past quarter century, some of our worst mistakes in foreign policy might have been avoided.

One generally tends to focus on mistakes in discussing lessons of the past, and certainly many have been made in conducting United States foreign policy since the end of World War II. But the record has not been all bad. The ultimate objective of any nation's foreign policy is to create and maintain, by means short of war, an international environment congenial to the survival and prosperity of that nation's domestic institutions. There seems little doubt that our diplomacy has met this test: we have at least survived, without serious derangement of what we too imprecisely refer to as "the American way of life." But the test of a good foreign policy, as of an effective military strategy, lies in more than attaining ultimate objectives. It requires also an efficient adaptation of means to ends, and it is in this regard that our record in foreign policy has been uneven.

The main problem has been a lack of precision in four areas critical to the success of any foreign policy: the definition of interests; the perception of threats; the formulation of a response to threats; and its public justification. Much of what has gone wrong in recent American diplomacy can be traced to imprecision in one or more of these categories. This essay focuses on both the causes and consequences of this imprecision, showing how, in most cases, it arose at least in part out of misperceived lessons of history. It concludes by suggesting ways in which policymakers might use history better: guidelines by which men who wield power might determine what lessons of history are applicable to particular situations, and which are not.

I. *Definition of Interests*

What were the basic requirements for preserving a congenial international environment after World War II? George F. Kennan, in his typically succinct manner, has given us his view of what these requirements were: "Repeatedly, at that time and in ensuing years," he tells us, "I expressed in talks and lectures the view that there were only five regions of the world—the United States, the United Kingdom, the Rhine valley with adjacent industrial areas, the Soviet Union, and Japan—where the sinews of modern military strength could be produced in quantity; I pointed out that only one of these was under Communist control; and I defined the main task of containment, accordingly, as one of seeing to it that none of the remaining ones fell under such control."[1] Kennan acknowledged, of course, that protection of the four remaining non-Communist strong points would require control of surrounding and intervening areas: lines of communication across the Atlantic and Pacific, for example, and Western Europe. It ought also to be noted that when Kennan used the word *Communist* in this context, he had in mind primarily the Soviet variety. With these qualifications, his assessment of the irreducible national interest stands up, in retrospect, as at least plausible. Certainly it was consistent with the principal, if often obscured, thrust of American foreign policy in the twentieth century: control of the Western Hemisphere, together with preservation of a balance of power in Europe and the Far East.

The way in which we actually went about defining our postwar interests, however, was very different. Statements of war aims were frequent from the time of the Atlantic Charter on, but essentially they boiled down to five major objectives: (1) destruction of the warmaking capability of Germany and Japan; (2) preservation of the wartime Grand Alliance; (3) self-determination: the right of people everywhere to choose their own form of government; (4) multilateralism: the lowering of barriers to trade and investment throughout the world; and (5) collective security: creation of a new international organization which would assume eventual responsibility for maintaining world order.

Had these principles been put into effect, they might well have created the congenial international environment we so avidly sought. The problem was, though, that they could not be put into effect, given the configuration of power which existed in the world after the Second World War. We could not, for example, have both self-determination in Eastern Europe and cooperation with Russia because the Russians considered the denial of self-determination in that part of the world as vital to their security. Similarly, we could not destroy the warmaking capabilities of Germany and Japan without impairing prospects for multilateralism: the industrial base of both countries was essential to world economic recovery. Nor did we have the power, at least as far as the Russians were concerned, to compel compliance with our postwar plans. The atomic bomb was useless for such purposes, nor was our economic aid sufficiently valuable to the Russians to induce a more cooperative attitude. And, after all, adherence to principles like self-determination, multilateralism, and collective security cannot really be forced: it must proceed from mutual interests and mutual consent. These simply did not exist, so far as Soviet-American relations were concerned, in the postwar period.

Why did we proclaim war aims so far beyond our capacity to achieve? This happened, it appears, because we based our postwar planning, not on an informed estimate of what the postwar situation was likely to be, but on preventing the kinds of things that had led to World War II. Thus the destruction of German and Japanese warmaking capacity would correct the mistake of having left German industry intact after World War I; maintenance of the Grand Alliance would avoid the inter-Allied bickering which, during the 1920s, had allowed the defeated Germans to play the victors off against one another; self-determination would forestall irredentism of the kind which had allowed Hitler, until 1939, to cloak his aggressive intentions behind the argument that he was only righting the wrongs of Versailles; multilateralism would prevent a new global depression similar to the one which had stimulated German and Japanese militarism; and finally, the United Nations would atone for what most observers then saw as the "great betrayal" of 1919—the failure of the United States to join Wilson's League of Nations. There was thus an underlying logic to American postwar aims, but it was a logic more closely related to the past than to the real world in which these principles would have to be applied.

What our postwar planners did was to construct, on the basis of a single set of historical experiences, nothing less than a universal formula for the prevention of future wars. Such a sweeping generalization, it would seem, ought to be based on broader foundations than that, however shattering or intense the particular experiences in question. Lessons of the past are important in defining interests, but so too are careful assessments of national capabilities, the will to employ them, and the circumstances in which they are likely to be used. One is forced to the conclusion that Kennan's precise formulation of the irreducible national interest, based on a recognition of where power resided in the world, and of the need to keep it in balance, met these criteria better than did the millenial pronouncements with which we in fact greeted the postwar world.

Our definition of interests changed once it became apparent that bipolar confrontation, not great power unity, was to be the fact of life in the postwar world. For a time, in 1947 and 1948, we did define our interests much as Kennan had suggested: our policy was oriented toward keeping crucial power centers in Europe and Asia out of the hands of the Russians, without dissipating our energies in peripheral areas like China, Palestine, Korea, or Indochina, which we did not consider vital to our security. This proved to be only a transitory policy, however, for, as the dramatic events of 1950 showed, interests are as likely to be defined by emotions as by rational calculation.

Despite the fact that we had explicitly excluded South Korea from our security perimeter, the blatant nature of the North Korean attack in June 1950 made the defense of that country a vital interest, even if it had not been before. Analogies with the past proved too overwhelming to ignore: Truman specifically recalled the 1931 Japanese invasion of Manchuria; others harked back to the 1936 Rhineland crisis. Aggression, the argument ran, had to be nipped in the bud; otherwise, like cancer, it would grow until it engulfed the entire international organism. It followed from this that distinctions between peripheral and vital interests were unwise: international order was a seamless web which, if rent at any point, would imperil the structure of peace everywhere. Maxim Litvinov had been right all along: peace *was* indivisible.

But this again was a generalization based on limited, and in this case, misperceived historical evidence. It assumed that all aggressors have unlimited ambitions, something which was certainly not true of the Japanese, and may not have been true of Hitler either. Even if it had been true, the nature of power on the international scene is such that unlimited aggression could not long have been sustained: power is, after all, a function of both will and capabilities, neither of which is infinite.

The concept that peace is indivisible assumes much the same thing about interests: the security of peace-loving states, it implies, is best served by the proliferation of interests. But history does not sustain this argument either: the whole history of late nineteenth-century imperialism can be seen as a process by which great powers sought security through the expansion of interests, only to feel, as a result, less secure. One of the main reasons why the United States did not join the League of Nations in 1919 was the very fear that the indiscriminate proliferation of peace-keeping commitments would increase, rather than decrease, the danger of war. It is a classic principle of strategy that great power widely dissipated leaves one almost as vulnerable as if one had little or no power at all; certainly this would seem to be a logical consequence of the argument that peace and, therefore, interests are indivisible.

It is hardly necessary to point out the extent to which this belief in the indivisibility of peace has affected our foreign policy since 1950: the much criticized "pactomania" of John Foster Dulles grew out of it, as did the "domino theory." Certainly the United States has, until very recently, sought security far more often through the proliferation of interests, rather than through their stabilization or contraction. Even today, despite the Nixon doctrine, one gets the impression that our leaders still see us as bearing some kind of unique obligation, not shared by other nations, to maintain order in the world. It is an assumption marked more by national pride, one suspects, than by a precise calculation of where the national interest lies.

Precision in the definition of interests—the recognition that because power is limited, threats and responses to threats must be also—would, it seems likely, have resulted in a more efficient adaptation of means to ends in recent American foreign policy than was in fact achieved. It appears logical, therefore, to propose it as a first major lesson we might legitimately learn from the cold war experience.

II. *Perception of Threats*

A nation's perception of external threats is closely related to the way in which it defines its interests: as threats increase, interests tend to also, and vice versa. Because the two are so closely tied together, precision in the perception of threats is just as important as precision in the definition of interests. And as in the definition of interests, imprecision in the perception of threats has been one of the major difficulties in postwar American foreign policy.

Much of this imprecision arises from a widespread tendency after

1950 for American officials to employ ideology as an instrument with which to predict the behavior of Communist states. Convinced that ideology took precedence over the national interests of the states in which it existed, convinced that all ideologies serve, to some degree, as a blueprint for action, we came to view our antagonists as Communists first, Russians or Chinese or North Korean or North Vietnamese second. As a result we fell into the unwise habit of exaggerating the unity of our adversaries while neglecting some very profound divisions among them—divisions of which we have begun to take advantage, in a substantial way, only in recent years.

How did we come to focus so narrowly on ideology as a means of anticipating our adversaries' behavior? The tendency stems, it appears, from three separate experiences Americans have had in dealing with world affairs in the twentieth century:

1. First was a vague, almost unstated assumption, going back to pre-World War I days, that governments which feel obliged to be autocratic at home can be counted upon to be irresponsible, and quite probably aggressive, in their conduct of foreign affairs. Historians have yet to investigate adequately the origins of this belief—it may well have grown out of our concern over the ambitions of tsarist Russia and imperial Germany around the turn of the century. Whatever its origins, this conviction that there is a positive correlation between the internal structure of governments and their external behavior was well established by the time Woodrow Wilson set out to make the world safe for democracy. It also influenced, in turn, our attitudes toward Japan and Germany in the 1930s, and Russia and Communist China after World War II.

2. A second experience encouraging the tendency to see ideology as a blueprint for action grew out of what might be called the *"Mein Kampf* syndrome." The assumption had at first been made that Hitler's sole objective had been to correct the inequities of Versailles. It came as a great shock to discover, after Munich, that he had more in mind than simply bringing all Germans into the Reich. Because Hitler had been specific about his larger ambitions in *Mein Kampf,* it became an article of faith among statesmen of the period that, if only they had taken time to read it, they would there have discovered the complete program for Nazi aggression. How anyone could have made much out of the obscure pomposities which make up *Mein Kampf* is difficult to see: the signal was there, but it was pretty deeply buried in the surrounding noise. Still, the belief became widespread that all ideological writ-

ings ought to be taken literally as blueprints for action. As Russia, and later China, became areas of concern, policymakers sent their staffs burrowing through the ponderous writings of Marx, Lenin, Stalin, and Mao in an effort to find out what the Communists were going to do next. John Foster Dulles was particularly taken with this approach: he regarded Stalin's *Problems of Leninism* as nothing less than the Soviet equivalent of *Mein Kampf,* and, we are told, kept a well-worn copy of it at his bedside throughout his tenure as secretary of state. Nor did the tendency stop there: as late as 1967 Washington officials were citing the ideological pronouncements of the now unlamented Lin Piao in the same somber way.

This emphasis on ideology as a means of understanding our adversaries' behavior was by no means a useless exercise. Ideology obviously does play an important role in Communist societies. But the belief that by reading the ideological classics of communism one could predict how the Russians or the Chinese were going to behave seems to rest on a fundamental misunderstanding of what that role is. Ideology is a powerful instrument for justifying the actions of Communist regimes, both by invoking "laws" of history and the threat of a hostile outside world. It gives such governments a degree of influence they might not otherwise have in certain parts of the world by promising shortcuts in the development process. It also serves, consciously or unconsciously, as a perceptual filter, creating stereotypes through which Communist leaders perceive external reality. It does not, however, provide clear-cut blueprints for action; indeed, by the mid-1950s, ideology had been modified so many times in Communist societies that it is hard to see how it could have served as a guide to much of anything. Certainly it does not influence behavior with sufficient regularity to be reliably predictable from the outside.

3. The experience of watching the relationship between Moscow and the international Communist movement before and during World War II also reinforced the idea that ideology took precedence over the national interests of the states in which it existed. Americans noted the mechanical manner in which Communist parties throughout the world accommodated themselves to every twist and turn of the Kremlin's line; most saw no reason to anticipate that things would be different after the war. Yet there was some reason to expect the Communist monolith to become less monolithic. China's Communist party had maintained its independence from Moscow, as those few Americans familiar with its activities acknowledged. Moreover, before 1945, none of the major non-

Russian parties had had any experience with the practical business of running a government. American observers might well have anticipated that, once in power, Communist parties in areas like Eastern Europe would, where possible, begin to modify ideology to accommodate national interests. The Russians had done this, after all, time and time again. There were officials in the Truman administration who foresaw this: they quickly took advantage of Yugoslavia's defection in 1948, and hoped, during 1949 and 1950, to encourage a split between Moscow and Peking.

It proved difficult to get across to the American people, however, the idea that communism was dangerous only where clearly an instrument of Soviet foreign policy. The belief in ideology as a predictive instrument was too strong to overcome, and the administration's own imprecise rhetoric had done little to clarify the situation. Aside from Yugoslavia, there seemed to be little evidence that the monolith was about to crumble; certainly Mao showed few public signs at that time that he would eventually break with Moscow. Nor did the domestic atmosphere encourage differentiation between varieties of communism: the Alger Hiss furor was at its height, and Senator McCarthy had just begun his highly conspicuous search for subversives in government. As a result, this early anticipation of polycentrism within the Communist bloc had little practical effect. Most Americans remained firmly convinced that Communists everywhere followed the dictates of Moscow, and that therefore all Communist activity everywhere could be attributed to the machinations of the Kremlin. After the traumatic shock of Korea, almost all top officials of the Truman administration came to share this view, whether out of conviction or practical recognition of the domestic political realities.

This inability, or unwillingness, to distinguish between varieties of communism had the perverse effect of imparting to our diplomacy some of the worst characteristics of our adversaries. It caused us to take a rigid "us or them" approach to world affairs: ideological orientation, not pragmatic self-interest, became the chief criterion by which we distinguished friends from enemies. It reduced opportunities for negotiation: where absolute good confronts absolute evil, chances for an amicable resolution of differences seem small. It narrowed options open to policymakers, since every alternative considered had to meet the test of not being "soft" on communism. Finally, and most important, it got us into wars with the wrong enemies. Whatever the view at the time, it seems clear now that neither Communist China nor North Vietnam posed mortal threats to our security—certainly neither was capable of endangering it in the way the Soviet Union was. Yet, because we considered communism, not just Russia, to be our opponent, we managed to stumble into bloody and protracted conflicts with both.

The lesson in all this is clear: imprecision in the perception of adversaries can lead to devastating imbalances in the relationship of means to ends in diplomacy. While ideology has not been insignificant in shaping the behavior of Communist states, it has more often served as an instrument rather than a determinant of state policy. National interests have too often taken precedence over ideology, and ideology has too often been modified to reflect those interests, for the wise policymaker to rely very much on it as a means of anticipating how his adversaries are going to behave.

III. *Formulation of Responses to Threat*

Precision is also vital in formulating responses to threats. Such responses, it would seem, should be closely calibrated to the nature of the perceived danger. Too narrow a response may fail to deal with the problem in such a way as to deter one's adversary. Too broad a response may be seen by the other side, or by some third party, as a threat in itself, producing escalation and the possibility that resources may be dispersed in peripheral areas. The proper calibration of response in diplomacy is an extremely difficult thing to achieve, since both interests and threats are relative entities, not susceptible to precise standards of measurement. Yet such calibration must be made if a nation is not to perpetuate the very conflicts it is seeking to settle. The tendency in postwar American strategy and diplomacy has been to overrespond to threats, while underresponding to opportunities to resolve issues through negotiation.

Overresponse to threats stems largely from our leaders' proclivity for worst-case analysis. This phenomenon has been described so often that it seems unnecessary to go into it here in any detail: essentially it is a variant of the rule that "anything that can go wrong will go wrong," or, in its less abstract formulation, "the toast always falls on the buttered side." Worst-case analysis rests on two basic assumptions: (1) that an adversary's capabilities are likely to be less flexible than his intentions, and hence more predictable; (2) that by planning on the basis of an adversary's capabilities, one can therefore minimize risks. Nor is it necessary to trace the impact of this approach on our conduct of foreign affairs since the end of World War II. Its main influence, of course, has been in the area of strategic weapons policy, but it was also reflected in our tendency for a long time to see communism everywhere as an instrument of the Kremlin.

What has not been given sufficient attention, though, are the assumptions upon which worse-case analysis rests. Are capabilities really more predictable than intentions? Does planning on the basis of capabilities actually minimize risk? The history of the cold war suggests that both of these generalizations are questionable.

The problem with planning on the basis of an adversary's capabilities is that capabilities are not solely a function of physical resources: they are also the product of deliberate decisions within a government on resource allocation, and hence cannot really be separated from intentions. There is not much doubt that the Russians had, and probably still have, the physical capacity to invade Western Europe with relatively little difficulty. But what, at any stage of the cold war, has been the likelihood of their doing this, given the probable relationship of costs to benefits? There is no question that the Russians had, after 1957, ICBMs capable of reaching any point in the United States. But the fact was that they chose not to deploy enough of them, in the late 1950s, to achieve a first-strike capability. Emphasis on an adversary's capabilities as the basis for planning ignores one of the fundamental principles of strategy: that national power is as much a function of will as of capacity; that just because a nation has the power to do something does not mean that it will in fact do it.

Worst-case analysis is also a questionable device for minimizing risks, since there is nothing to prevent one's adversary from interpreting measures taken in self-defense as threats directed against him. An opponent's capabilities are likely to be the product, in part, of *his* perception of external threat. Much of the history of the arms race can be understood in terms of self-fulfilling prophecies brought about through the application of worst-case analysis: country A takes action because it expects country B to do something, but by taking that action it makes country B so insecure that it goes ahead and does precisely what country A had feared.

Finally, worst-case analysis is questionable because it violates the principle of concentration of force. Contingencies are infinite; one cannot arm against them all. Some calculations of probability in assessing threats, some selectivity in formulating responses, are necessary if a nation is not to spread its resources too thin, if the proper relationship of means to ends is to be maintained.

The American proclivity for worst-case analysis has not been the only tendency which has interfered with the proper calibration of responses to threat. Another difficulty has been the surprising reluctance of United States officials, until recently, to rely on negotiations as the primary means of resolving differences with adversaries.

Sincere, though frustrating, efforts were made to negotiate differences with the Russians during the early years of the cold war, but by 1949 the negotiating instrument had begun to grow rusty from disuse. Acheson refused to deal in a substantive manner with the Russians on the German question, despite evidence that the Soviet Union was prepared to make promising concessions in order to prevent the rearmament of West Germany. Reversing earlier inclinations, he refused to recognize the People's Republic of China, or to support admission of that state to the United Nations, despite the fact that he had foreseen the Sino-Soviet split and had hoped to take advantage of it. Dulles continued Acheson's policy by studiously ignoring gestures of conciliation emanating from the Kremlin after Stalin's death: whether these were sincere or not, they did reflect uncertainty and confusion in Moscow, and, for that reason alone, ought to have been pursued. This reluctance to negotiate also showed up in Dulles' notorious pessimism regarding summitry, his scarcely concealed contempt for the 1954 Geneva accords on Indochina, and his continued rigidity in dealing with China at a time when interesting opportunities had begun to develop to profit from that country's estrangement with the Soviet Union. Adam B. Ulam is not wholly exaggerating the situation when he writes that if Moscow had proposed a joint declaration in favor of motherhood during the Dulles period, it "would have called forth position papers from the State Department's Policy Planning Council, somber warnings from Senator Knowland, and eventually a declaration that while the United States welcomed this recognition of the sanctity of family life on the part of the Russians, it would require clear indication that the USSR did not mean to derogate from the status of fatherhood."[2]

Even Kennedy, who did initiate discussions with the Russians on disarmament and Southeast Asia, felt unable to enter into a dialogue with Communist China, even though he privately admitted the desirability of doing so. The Johnson administration's reluctance to negotiate on Vietnam, rhetoric to the contrary notwithstanding, is amply documented in the *Pentagon Papers*. Only with the advent of Nixon and Kissinger did negotiations again come into their own as the chief means of resolving differences with adversaries, and even in that administration there persisted a curious inhibition about normalizing relations with Cuba.

Why this reluctance to negotiate? For a nation which, at any stage in the past quarter century, has possessed physical power at least equal to and usually superior to that of its rivals, for a nation which has historically prided itself on the peaceful resolution of disputes between nations, this unwillingness to use conventional instruments of diplomacy seems odd indeed.

The explanation, it appears, is caught up in the ticklish problem of maintaining credibility: we have concerned ourselves so much with making our policies credible to our adversaries, our allies, and ourselves, that we have lost sight of the ultimate aim of diplomacy—the settlement of international conflicts through negotiation.

1. The problem of maintaining credibility with adversaries has been cogently discussed by Coral Bell in her 1963 book, *Negotiation from Strength*. As she demonstrates, there has been a widespread concern, based to some extent on the experiences of the 1930s, that too obvious a willingness to negotiate might be taken by the enemy as a sign of weakness; negotiations, to paraphrase Dean Acheson, ought never to take place until one is in a position to negotiate from strength. The difficulty, of course, is that strength is a relative concept which cannot be measured accurately short of actual combat. There will always be soft spots of one kind or another in one's armor; the nation which preoccupies itself with building impregnable positions may well never find the right time to negotiate.

2. An inhibition of equal importance has been the problem of maintaining credibility with allies. Alliances have an obvious value both in strengthening one's own position and in deterring irresponsible acts on the part of the other side. But they do multiply greatly the requirement of consultation, and this can delay negotiations indefinitely while positions agreeable to all members of the alliance are worked out. Negotiations can also be delayed if there is a constant necessity of reassuring one's allies that no sell-out to the enemy is contemplated. What all of this does is to make the progress of negotiations dependent, not on the skill of diplomats or the tractability of issues, but on the morale of allies. And if the morale of allies is so weak that it cannot stand negotiations with the adversary, one may legitimately ask how significant the assistance of such allies would be in time of war.

3. Finally, there is the problem of maintaining credibility with the American public. The problem here is twofold: the fear that

by engaging in negotiations one may lull the public into a sense of complacency, or even the isolationism which our policymakers have seen lurking, ever since the 1930s, just below the surface; and the concern, based on experiences like Yalta, that negotiations might cause a backlash, with the public rising up in wrath against what it might perceive as a sell-out. That the two fears seem mutually inconsistent has not caused them to carry any less weight in the view of Washington officials; together they have produced the curious conviction that popular support for containment is dependent upon the enduring credibility of the threat which that policy is supposed to contain.

It is impossible to say, of course, that a greater willingness on the part of American leaders to negotiate would have ended the cold war any sooner. The Russians too had problems in maintaining credibility with adversaries, allies, and, in their own way, domestic constituencies. But it is difficult to point to any very concrete advantages gained by our reluctance to negotiate; certainly there were some fairly substantial disadvantages, if for no other reason than that our inhibitions prevented us from taking advantage of the weaknesses and divisions which existed among our rivals. And it seems very likely that our "image," whatever that is worth, would have been better: too often the Russians and the Chinese were able to convey the appearance of wanting to negotiate, whether they were sincere or not, while the United States had to take the blame for continuing the confrontation.

Something is probably wrong, then, when a nation feels it cannot afford to negotiate. It may have taken positions which are untenable—nonnegotiability is often a good sign of this. It may be bogged down in bureaucratic inertia—serious negotiation is hard work, much more difficult than the unthinking defense of fixed positions. It may have exaggerated its own weaknesses and its adversaries' strengths. At the very least, it would seem that a nation which is interested in the preservation of peace but which finds itself unable or unwilling to negotiate has lost sight of the proper relationship of means to ends in diplomacy.

Precision in calibrating responses to threats, therefore, is all-important: worse-case analysis and excessive inhibitions about negotiations are two tendencies which can make such calibration difficult.

IV. *Justification of Response*

Precision in explaining policy, both within and outside the government, is as important as precision in formulating it. This is so because, in the final analysis, policy cannot be kept separate from the language which is used to explain and justify it. If the gap between them becomes too large, one of two things must happen: either rhetoric must be modified to bring it into line with policy, or, and this has more frequently been the case, policy must be altered to make it consistent with rhetoric. The consequences of this latter alternative can be serious indeed: policy can become the prisoner of rhetoric, with results far removed from those originally intended.

Why do gaps between policy and rhetoric develop? Why do our leaders' public rationales for policy not always coincide with their private ones? The chief enemies of precision in the justification of policy, it would seem, are the use of hyperbole and secrecy as a means of expanding freedom of action in the field of foreign affairs.

Now hyperbole has a long and distinguished tradition in American domestic politics. It is only fair to point out, though, that Americans seem more prone to take inflated rhetoric literally when it is applied to foreign affairs, and to demand explanations when policy fails to fall into line with it. Hence, many Americans really expected that the post-World War II settlement would implement literally the principles of the Atlantic Charter: much of our difficulty with the Russians over self-determination in Eastern Europe stemmed from Roosevelt's futile efforts to make reality coincide with rhetoric. Similarly, the Truman administration sold aid to Greece and Turkey on the grounds that it was in our interests to stop communism everywhere: it then found it difficult to explain why nothing was being done to prevent Mao's victory in China. John Foster Dulles had comparable problems with slogans like "liberation," "massive retaliation," and "agonizing reappraisal," all of which caused trouble when, inevitably, the audiences at whom Dulles had aimed these sweeping phrases took them too literally. American leaders have often had difficulty in sorting out short-term from long-term advantages: too often they have forgotten that while exaggeration may be an effective short-run technique for "selling" a particular policy, it may in the long run restrict rather than increase freedom of action by pledging the nation to unintended long-term commitments to which it may repeatedly be held.

In recent times, secrecy has more often been used than hyperbole to gain freedom of action in foreign affairs. The Vietnam War is full of examples in which the public was not given the whole

story, from the ambiguous 1964 Gulf of Tonkin incident and the
introduction of ground combat forces in 1965, to the secret bombing of Laos and Cambodia during the first years of the Nixon
administration. No one seriously argues that secrecy can be done
away with in foreign affairs. The purpose of secrecy, though, is
to keep essential information out of the hands of the enemy. In
each of these cases, the enemy already had the information: it
was the American public which was being kept in the dark. Leaving
aside moral and constitutional questions, this kind of secrecy is
debatable on purely pragmatic grounds: the simple fact is that
things rarely remain secret very long. One wonders whether the
relatively small advantages of being less than candid in explaining
these situations to the public outweighed the long-term disadvantages, in the form of the disillusionment, recrimination, and erosion
of trust in government which were bound to follow.

Credibility gaps are not, however, just a matter of information
being kept from the public. They can also result in information
which is available to the public not getting through to the policymakers. There is always a tendency in government to believe that
official, and therefore confidential, sources of information are more
likely to reflect what is actually happening in the world than the
information which appears in the newspapers or on the network
news programs. This tendency is intensified when the press and
the government are at odds with each other. Yet history simply
does not bear out the assumption that just because information
is secret, it is accurate. Roberta Wohlstetter has shown, for example, that President Roosevelt would have learned as much about
Japanese fleet movements prior to Pearl Harbor by reading *The
New York Times* as by relying on highly secret intercepted Japanese communications.[3] David Halberstam's reporting from Vietnam in 1963 is generally acknowledged to have conveyed a more
accurate picture of what was happening in that country than the
secret reports available to Kennedy from diplomatic and military
sources. The phenomenon by which intelligence is skewed to fit
official preconceptions is, or ought to be, familiar; nonofficial, and
even public, sources of information can be an effective safeguard
against this. But in order for government officials to benefit from
nonofficial sources, a certain amount of mutual trust must exist.
It cannot when the gap between policy and rhetoric yawns too
large.

The justification of policy, therefore, is yet another area in which
the absence of precision has caused us problems. Foreign policy
in a democracy depends, ultimately, upon public support if it is

to be effective. This, in turn, requires candor, a quality not enhanced by excessive hyperbole or secrecy. The lesson, then, is to level with the American people in discussing foreign policy. They will not be shocked to discover that our policy is designed to promote our interests—if this indeed is not its objective, then something is badly wrong. They will not learn many important secrets—in these days of instant journalism the real reasons why the government has acted are generally known anyway, whatever the official line has been. They may get a better sense of what is possible and what is not in foreign policy; certainly there will be less likelihood of disillusionment. And, finally, policymakers themselves may learn something by finding out what the informed public knows. Freedom of information is an admirable objective for the average citizen, but we need it for the men who run our government as well.

V. *Lessons of the Past*

One final lesson of the cold war may seem somewhat incongruous in the light of what has gone before: it is that excessive preoccupation with the past can be just as dangerous in its consequences for policy as complete ignorance of it. The philosopher Santayana once said, in a statement much repeated by teachers of history, that those who do not remember the past are condemned to repeat it. In the light of recent experience we might well modify that to read: those who oversimplify the past in an effort to draw lessons from it will live to regret it.

One does not have to look very far in the history of recent American foreign policy to see how the past has been oversimplified: Americans tried to stay out of World War II by passing neutrality legislation which might have kept us out of World War I; United States war aims during World War II were determined, not by the realities of the postwar situation, but by a determination to avoid mistakes which had led to that conflict; our response to Stalin in the late 1940s was shaped primarily by our view of what we should have done to contain Hitler in the 1930s; our response to the North Korean attack in 1950 was influenced largely by ideas of what we should have done to resist Japanese aggression in Manchuria in 1931; our response to Communist China in the 1950s was based largely on what had worked to contain Russia in the late 1940s; our abortive attempt to overthrow Castro in Cuba in 1961 was influenced to no small degree by our success in overthrowing communism in Guatemala in 1954; our response

to Vietnam was conditioned by the experience of successful counterinsurgency operations in Greece, Malaya, and the Philippines,
and, when these did not work, by the strategic experiences of World
War II. And it is quite likely that the foreign policy of the next
decade or so will be governed, in ways we cannot yet foresee, by
a determination to avoid the mistakes of Vietnam.

None of this is particularly surprising: it is difficult to know
what policymakers should base their decisions on if not, in large
measure, past experience. The trouble is not that our leaders draw
lessons from the past, but that they have done so in an oversimplified manner. As Ernest May has written, "Policy-makers ordinarily use history badly. When resorting to an analogy, they tend
to seize upon the first that comes to mind. They do not search
more widely. Nor do they pause to analyze the case, test its fitness,
or even ask in what ways it might be misleading. Seeing a trend
running toward the present, they tend to assume that it will continue into the future, not stopping to consider what produced it
or why a linear projection might prove to be mistaken."[4]

The problem, in a nutshell, is that our leaders have not been
very good at distinguishing recurrent from unique historical phenomena. Admittedly this is difficult to do, since the future always
has the potential of rendering the unique recurrent. Still, by paying attention to some elementary rules of generalization, rules one
might find in any basic handbook on logic or even on the use
of statistics, one can come up with a few practical guidelines which
might help policymakers use history better.

One such guideline would be to examine the number of experiences upon which the historical generalization is based. David
Hackett Fischer, a historian who has done much to prod his colleagues into thinking logically about the past, tells the story "of
a scientist who published an astonishing and improbable generalization about the behavior of rats. An incredulous colleague came
to his laboratory and politely asked to see the records of the experiments upon which the generalization was based. 'Here they are,'
said the scientist, dragging a notebook from a pile of papers on
his desk. And pointing to a cage in the corner, he added, 'and
there's the rat.' "[5] One gets the impression that all too many of
the generalizations American officials have made about aggression
and appeasement during the past three decades have been based
on the experience of dealing with one particular rat, Adolf Hitler,
and would not hold up well if applied to other authoritarian regimes in history. The soundness of any generalization, it would
seem, increases in direct proportion to the number of experiences

upon which it is based. No reputable statistician would make sweeping generalizations based on a single sample, yet our policy-makers, some of whom have prided themselves on their statistical abilities, have often done just that.

A second way to avoid the misuse of history would be to watch out for generalizations derived from dissimilar experiences. One cannot, in science, apply a hypothesis based on one set of phenomena to a completely unrelated set and expect it to explain very much. Yet American officials have frequently done this. A vivid recent example was their attempt to predict the effectiveness of strategic bombing in Vietnam on the basis of the World War II experience in Germany and Japan. What they failed to note was the difference between highly industrialized societies, whose factories, transportation networks, and distribution facilities were vulnerable to bombing, and a predominantly agrarian society like North Vietnam, where productive facilities were dispersed, transportation was largely a matter of foot power, and bombing could accomplish little more than to blow holes in the ground. Generalizations derived from one context but applied to wholly different ones are extremely hazardous enterprises, whether in comparative history or the realm of policy. They should be undertaken only with the greatest caution.

Yet another pitfall to avoid in generalizing about the past is the tendency to neglect relevant evidence. Selective inattention—the phenomenon in which the mind focuses on what it wants to perceive, filtering out all the rest—is a well-documented syndrome. Again, Vietnam provides the best recent example. In assessing the possibilities of a successful counterinsurgency operation in Vietnam, we ranged widely in search of precedents, finally concluding that the antiguerilla movements in Greece in the late 1940s, and in Malaya and the Philippines in the 1950s, were most relevant. But we neglected other less encouraging precedents which might have been instructive: the experience of the Japanese in China, for example, or the Dutch in Indonesia, or, most relevant of all, the French experience in Indochina itself. A good way to avoid this problem of selective inattention is to apply to each generalization the test of purpose: for what purpose is the particular historical analogy being made? Is it actually the basis upon which policy is being decided, or is it being advanced to justify a course of action already decided upon? If the latter, beware, because the body of historical evidence is sufficiently vast to provide the resourceful advocate with support for almost any generalization, provided he is willing to neglect other relevant evidence.

It is easy to suggest lessons; it is much more difficult to put them into effect. There are encouraging signs that under the Nixon administration several of the most important lessons of the cold war were taken to heart. The downgrading of ideology as a means of predicting adversaries' behavior, and the increased reliance on negotiations as a means of settling differences seemed in particular to reflect lessons learned. Whatever the Nixon administration's disasters in domestic affairs, its foreign policy record was impressive. Much of its success stemmed from a greater precision in thinking about world affairs than its predecessors demonstrated.

Imprecision remains a problem, however, in what is probably the most critical area of all: that of defining what our national interests are. The restraint promised by the Nixon doctrine has yet to be tested in a major crisis. Congress persists in defining our interests, not just in terms of protecting our own society, but of reforming others. Bureaucracies, civilian and military, continue to confuse their own interests with those of the nation as a whole. Nor are we wholly free from the danger that foreign policy may again, as it has in the past, become an instrument of domestic politics.

So, despite progress, much remains to be done. Increased precision in defining interests, together with continued precision in perceiving threats, formulating responses, and justifying them—these are likely to provide our best insurance that the mistakes of the cold war will not be repeated. The past is, after all, one of our most valuable resources. It is up to our policymakers, and ultimately, to the American people themselves, to see that it is used wisely.

NOTES

Based on a lecture delivered at the Naval War College in June 1974.

1. George F. Kennan, *Memoirs: 1925-1950* (Boston: 1967), p. 359.

2. Adam B. Ulam, *The Rivals: America and Russia Since World War II* (New York: Viking, 1971), p. 230.

3. Roberta Wohlstetter, *Pearl Harbor: Warning and Decision* (Stanford: Stanford University Press, 1962) p. 124.

4. Ernest R. May, *"Lessons" of the Past: The Use and Misuse of History in American Foreign Policy* (New York: Oxford University Press, 1973), p. xi.

5. David Hackett Fischer, *Historians' Fallacies: Toward a Logic of Historical Thought* (New York: Harper & Row, 1970), p. 109.

The Evolution of American Nuclear Thought

Robert L. Pfaltzgraff, Jr.

Editor's Note: *Robert L. Pfaltzgraff, Jr. is director of the Institute for Foreign Policy Analysis, Inc., and Associate Professor of International Politics at the Fletcher School of Law and Diplomacy, Tufts University. He is the author of* Contrasting Approaches to Strategic Arms Control, The Super Powers in a Multi-Nuclear World, SALT: Implications for Arms Control in the 1970s, *and* Contending Theories of International Relations.

Since the beginning of the nuclear age, American strategic thought has been based on the concept of deterrence. While the deterrence of conflict was of interest to policy analysts and practitioners before the advent of the nuclear age, one of the most important contributions to the study of military affairs since World War II has been the development and refinement of deterrence theory. In the last thirty years, a theory of strategic deterrence founded upon several general assumptions has evolved. First, the level of destruction that would result from resort to a strategic nuclear exchange outweighs the potential gains. Although the United States and the Soviet Union have had fundamentally different foreign policy objectives, both have striven to develop and maintain a strategic posture capable of deterring or preventing an attack by the other. Their respective strategic postures, while influenced by such factors as foreign policy goals, economic resources, technological capabilities, and governmental-bureaucratic

271

structures, have been designed to maintain the stability of the strategic balance by confronting a would-be nuclear aggressor with the threat of an unacceptable level of nuclear retaliation.

Second, and clearly related, is the assumption that a nation will deploy its strategic nuclear forces only in a circumstance where its national survival is at stake. And finally, because of the relatively rapid pace of the nuclear revolution in the years following World War II, the United States and the Soviet Union have developed second-strike forces capable of retaliating against a power that has already attacked.

The possession of invulnerable second-strike forces is crucial to the deterrence of nuclear conflict for several reasons. First, a power that might not have forces capable of surviving a first strike might conclude that it must launch a preemptive attack against an opponent who is perceived to be about to attack. This launch-on-warning theme permeates much of the study of strategic doctrine in the past generation and especially in recent years. Or, alternatively, an opponent who believes that he can destroy the retaliatory force of his adversary may be tempted to do so under certain conditions, such as during a crisis situation. In fact, much of the debate among United States strategic analysts over American strategic thought has focused on the question of to what extent, and under what circumstances, United States strategic forces are vulnerable to a Soviet first-strike attack. This, of course, touches on one of the most important issues in the current discussion of nuclear strategy in the United States: namely, whether to focus on one type of weapons system as opposed to another—land-based systems, mobile systems, sea-based versus mobile systems, or a combination of such systems in order to assure the survivability of United States strategic nuclear forces during a nuclear attack.

For more than a generation, the United States has sought to develop a deterrence doctrine based upon these overall considerations. While many of the same problems have faced United States defense planners since World War II, American strategic thought has evolved in response to changes in the international environment, the overseas commitments of the United States, and the growth of Soviet strategic forces. As a result, American strategic thought may be divided into several distinctive historical phases.

The first period, 1945-1949, was one of absolute nuclear monopoly by the United States. During that phase, the mission of the Strategic Air Command was to deter the Soviet Union from a land invasion of Western Europe and military expansion elsewhere in the world by threatening a retaliatory strike against the Soviet

Union itself.

The explosion by the Soviet Union in 1949 of an atomic device, however, ushered in a new phase in American strategic thought. This period, 1949-1954, was one of renewed appreciation by United States strategists of general purpose forces. Largely as a result of the North Korean invasion of South Korea in 1950, there evolved a general realization that strategy in the broadest sense depended upon a mix of deterrent and war-fighting capabilities, between nuclear and general purpose forces.

At the same time, the United States participation in the Korean War persuaded many in the United States that future Korean-type conflicts could only be deterred by a strategic posture emphasizing nuclear weapons. This view, enunciated in the Eisenhower New Look, or the strategy of massive retaliation, moved United States strategic doctrine into a new phase. The doctrine of massive retaliation called for a strategy of deterrence based on America's "special assets," particularly her atomic air power, to employ a selective range of actions "at places and times of our own choosing,"[1] should deterrence fail.

Between 1957 and 1961 there was another transition in American strategic doctrine brought about by the development and dissemination of new nuclear technologies, especially the attainment by the Soviet Union of a strategic launcher capable of carrying warheads the distance required to strike the United States. The Sputnik launch in 1957 thus encouraged broad debate, both in the United States and abroad, over the feasibility of a massive retaliation strategy in a period of increasing Soviet strategic power. Studies undertaken on American defense posture and strategic doctrine produced a growing literature in the late 1950s, especially in the civilian-academic sector, calling for greater attention to the problems of limited war, the use of tactical nuclear weapons, the development of insurgency capabilities and, in particular, counterinsurgency capabilities and greater flexibility in the available options for the United States in both the nuclear and nonnuclear areas. Their intent was to provide the United States with a capacity for controlled response in order to avoid the stark alternative of nuclear war or surrender.

The strategy of massive retaliation was valid only as long as the United States enjoyed clear dominance in nuclear weapons technologies and had the potential to destroy the warmaking capability of the Soviet Union without suffering a retaliatory strike from the Soviet Union itself. At the same time, however, the strategy of massive retaliation was of dubious utility, even in its heyday, since United States officials and the American public had eschewed the first-use of nuclear weapons. Thus, in the early 1950s during the Korean conflict, at a time of undoubted American strategic supremacy, the United States was not prepared, for a variety of reasons, to employ nuclear weapons.

One of the most important critiques of American strategy in the late 1950s was provided by Albert Wohlstetter, who questioned the stability of what he called the "delicate balance of terror."[2] The existing generation of strategic forces of the 1950s, based largely upon manned bombers, was vulnerable to a first-strike attack. By attacking an enemy's strategic forces, rather than his cities, one country could disarm the other country. Wohlstetter argued, therefore, for the development of a second-strike capability; that is, American forces that could survive a first-strike attack, because of their invulnerability, and then retaliate.

The strategy of the 1950s was criticized for other reasons. It was said to lack the flexibility to enable the United States to respond effectively to limited wars. Critics of massive retaliation called for a greater emphasis on conventional forces and, in the case of Henry Kissinger, the development of a capacity for limited war based upon the use of tactical nuclear weapons to provide additional options for American policy planners.[3] The growth of Soviet strategic forces led to an extensive debate both in the United States and Europe in the late 1950s about the adequacy of American strategic forces to deter conflict in Europe. Once the United States itself became vulnerable in the late 1950s to an attack from the Soviet Union, the question arose, especially in France, as to whether the United States would be prepared to risk the destruction of New York in defense of Paris.[4] If not, the Atlantic Alliance needed to evolve a strategy with greater options including, according to some analysts, European national nuclear capabilities or, as others put it, a European finger on the trigger of the American strategic force, together with an appropriate mix between strategic forces and conventional forces, deterrence, and war-fighting capabilities.

The Kennedy administration, shortly after it came to office in 1961, initiated a far-ranging review of defense policy, and it evolved a limited-counterforce or flexible-response strategy. The principal assumption of the Kennedy-McNamara strategy was that the United States needed a strategic concept, together with appropriate forces, that would provide the flexibility to respond in accordance with alternative conditions and at the same time ensure that weapons were closely controlled by the president and by the president alone, and that strategic forces were invulnerable to a pre-emptive attack by an opponent. As a result, in the period between 1961 and 1964 the United States evolved a strategy of flexible response based upon a mix of options to include countervalue targets, but emphasizing the counterforce option. Deterrence based on a counterforce strategy, as envisaged by Secretary McNamara in 1962, aimed at more than just the prevention of aggression; its main objective evolved toward what was called mutual assured destruction and damage limitation. In short, United States strategic capabilities would be maintained at a level where, even under the worst possible circumstances of a surprise attack by the Soviet Union, enough forces would survive to destroy singly, or in combination, the Soviet Union, China, and other countries in the Communist world. In addition, their remaining warmaking capabilities would be eliminated, while restricting, to the extent practicable, damage to the United States and its allies.

Weapons choices under this concept were to consist primarily of a high level of invulnerable missiles to guarantee the destruction of preplanned targets. The United States sought to maintain a secure second-strike capability based on a triad, even though the manned bomber component was reduced in importance. Missiles would be deployed at sea (Polaris) and on land (Minuteman I) at distances sufficiently remote from cities to lessen casualties. The mission of United States strategic forces, as set forth by Secretary of Defense McNamara, was "to serve as a maximum deterrent to nuclear war, while remaining visibly capable of fully destroying the Soviet society under all conditions of retaliation. In addition, in the event that such a war is forced upon us, they, that is, American strategic forces, should have the power to limit the destruction of our cities and population to the maximum extent possible."[5] According to the McNamara formula of the early 1960s, United States strategic forces should maintain simultaneously an assured-destruction capability and a damage-limiting capability, that is, the ability to limit damage to the United States and to inflict unacceptable levels of destruction upon the Soviet Union, if deterence were to fail.

Another objective of United States strategic doctrine in the early 1960s was to provide the Soviet Union with strong incentive to avoid the deliberate destruction of American cities. One of the most controversial aspects of the McNamara doctrine was the cities-avoidance doctrine, in which the principal goal of American strategic forces was to destroy an enemy's military forces, but not necessarily his civilian population. Soviet cities would be destroyed, according to McNamara, only if the Soviet Union attacked American cities. Furthermore, the McNamara strategy provided for a deliberate, selective, and controlled response. The United States sought to avoid the possibility of a spasm response by assuring effective command and control and the availability of as many options as possible in the event of nuclear crisis. At the same time, the United States engaged in a build-up of conventional forces, and the development of a capacity for counterinsurgency warfare. NATO's conventional forces were also designated to be increased and improved to provide a carefully controlled, discriminating response against a Warsaw Pact conventional thrust into Western Europe. At the same time, it was thought by the McNamara strategists that by employing a deliberate, selective option before resorting to a nuclear strike, an aggressor would have time to "pause" and reflect on the consequences that a further advance up the escalation ladder would bring. But the desired conventional buildup did not materialize as NATO's European members feared that the credibility of the nuclear deterrent would be weakened. Thus, by the mid-1960s, the strategic doctrine of the United States provided for strategic forces larger than necessary for a cities-only strategy, but less than would be needed for the full range of counterforce options.

The McNamara strategy thus evoked a storm of criticism in American strategic circles. It was argued that the Soviet Union would not accept a no-cities strategy. The American strategy of avoiding cities would be incompatible with a United States strategy against Soviet missile sites, or against Soviet military installations, since presumably the Soviet Union would have launched a large part of its strategic force against the United States if, in fact, we adhered to a second-strike capability. By focusing on Soviet strategic sites, the United States would be striking empty silos, or empty airfields, whatever would be the case. Therefore, a cities-avoidance strategy would mean that the United States might only be firing missiles against the empty silos or the empty weapons sites. This was one of the great problems of the counterforce strategy of this period.

The growing invulnerability of Soviet missile silos and weapons systems in the 1960s, as the Soviets developed hardened sites, made a counterforce strategy by the United States less and less feasible. The hardening and dispersal of Soviet forces, which took place in the 1960s, contributed to a gradual movement of American strategic doctrine in the Johnson administration from counterforce to "mutual assured destruction." But the principal intellectual rationale for a damage-limiting strategy was the belief in the defense community that a counterforce strategy was destabilizing because it threatened the deterrent capability of the Soviet Union. This issue has occasioned intense debate within the American strategic affairs community. To what extent is a United States strategic nuclear force which threatens Soviet strategic capabilities stabilizing or destabilizing? The argument has surfaced again in the discussion of the targeting options proposed by Secretary of Defense Schlesinger.

Instead, it was suggested by those who criticized the counterforce idea in the 1960s that the United States should maintain only a capability adequate to threaten massive destruction of an enemy's population and industry. If both the Soviet Union and the United States could destroy each other's population and industry, each would then be deterred from attacking the other, since the cities of each superpower would be hostage to the nuclear forces of the other. Carrying this reasoning one step further, analysts suggested that the United States should not undertake programs that might be perceived by the Soviet Union as endangering the Soviet strategic force because the Soviets, fearing an American first strike, might be more prone to launch a preemptive attack in a time of crisis. Thus, arguments were raised against an antiballistic missile system in the United States, in particular the Sentinel system, which was designed to protect American cities, and, later, the Safeguard, to protect American weapons systems.

Since the late 1960s, United States strategic doctrine has moved from mutual assured destruction and damage limitation to one of strategic sufficiency. Strategic sufficiency, the doctrine of the Nixon administration, sought to resolve the dilemma of whether a president of the United States, in a nuclear crisis, should be left with the single option of ordering an attack against Soviet cities. According to Mr. Nixon,

Our forces must be maintained at a level sufficient to make it clear that even an all-out surprise attack on the United States by the Soviet Union would not cripple our capacity to retaliate. Our forces must also be capable of flexible application .... A simple assured destruction doctrine does not meet our present requirements for a flexible range of strategic options. No President should be left with only one strategic course of action, particularly that of ordering the mass destruction of enemy civilians and facilities. Given the range of possible political-military situations which could conceivably confront us, our strategic policy should not be based solely on a capability of inflicting urban and industrial damage presumed to be beyond the level an adversary would accept. We must be able to respond at levels appropriate to the situation.[6]

Thus, strategic sufficiency rested on several criteria: first, on the maintenance of an adequate second-strike capability to deter an all-out surprise attack on our strategic forces; second, on providing no incentive for the Soviet Union to strike the United States first in a crisis, because the United States could strike more effectively second; third, on preventing the Soviet Union from gaining an ability to cause considerably greater urban industrial damage or destruction than the United States could inflict on the Soviet Union in a nuclear conflict; fourth, on defending against damage from small attacks or accidental launches. Narrowly construed, the sufficiency doctrine meant that there must be enough force to inflict a level of damage on a potential aggressor sufficient to deter him from attacking. In its broader political sense, it meant the maintenance of forces adequate to prevent the United States and its allies from being coerced or subjected to nuclear blackmail, especially in a period of rapid growth in Soviet strategic forces.

On January 10, 1974, Secretary Schlesinger announced "a change in the strategies of the United States with regard to the hypothetical employment of central strategic forces. A change in targeting strategy."[7] According to Schlesinger: "To a large extent the American doctrinal position has been wrapped around something called assured destruction which implies a tendency to target Soviet cities initially and massively and that this is the principal option that a President would have. It is our intention," he said, "that this not be the only option and possibly not the principal option."[8] Subsequently, Schlesinger suggesed that the key to understanding the modifications that the United States was making, rather than focusing on the issue of counterforce versus assured destruction, would be to recognize "that the emphasis is upon selectivity and flexibility. That does not necessarily involve what is referred to as major counterforce capabilities, however. The emphasis," he said, "is on the selection of targets. Nor does selectivity," he maintained, "necessarily require new force programs for that purpose alone. In order to have a strategy of selectivity and flexibility, one must consciously adopt that as a strategy and adjust plans to doctrine. And that," he said, "is a considerable change in American strategic doctrine."[9]

This change, the development of the flexible targeting option, is based on assumptions about the growth of Soviet strategic capabilities which he said have developed "ahead of rather than in reaction to what the United States has done, thus in this instance casting some doubt upon the action-reaction model which so many have used to discuss Soviet-American strategic relationships."[10] The selective-response option, as described by Dr. Schlesinger, seeks to assure that the United States possesses a strategic capability comparable but not necessarily equal in all respects to that of the Soviet Union.

The doctrine contains the assumption that the choice of targets selected by the United States would depend on the nature of the enemy's attack and his objectives. The idea of greater options has been one of the continuing themes of American strategic thought over the last generation. Thus, it has not been proposed that, for this purpose alone, the United States would increase its strategic forces, but rather that these forces be given greater flexibility in the future. We are entering an age in which new technologies are becoming available for the far more accurate targeting of strategic weapons as well as battlefield capabilities. New technologies, both at the strategic level and at the battlefield level, will have a considerable effect on deterrence and war-fighting capabilities available to nations in the next decade.

The Schlesinger doctrine is both broader and more limited than a major counterforce doctrine.[11] The operational objectives of a major counterforce strategy seek: (1) to defeat the enemy by destroying his offensive systems while still retaining sufficient offensive systems to induce a decision; (2) to limit the amount of damage an adversary can do to population and resources; and (3) to keep the weight of the attack on both sides away from cities and thus further reduce intended or collateral damage to populations and institutions. The Schlesinger concept, however, encompasses more than counterforce strikes; it seeks to deter attack against the United States and its allies by: (1) maintaining essential equivalence between the United States and the Soviet Union at both the strategic and conventional levels; (2) an ability to indicate clearly American intentions, capabilities, and resolve to adversaries; and (3) a capability to terminate any potential conflict at the lowest possible level consistent with United States objectives.[12] The ability of the United States to respond to any potential threat is seen to contribute to the deterrence of all threats. At the same time, the Schlesinger concept of a counterforce strategy is more limited than had been traditionally thought since his strategic initiative "can be abstracted from any change in the [United

States] force structure."[13] Moreover, he has even stated that the proposed changes in targeting options do not necessarily require the procurement of any additional weapons systems, although improvements in guidance techniques to achieve greater accuracies would facilitate the strategic objectives sought by the United States.[14] The United States has always included counterforce targeting in its Strategic Integrated Options Plan (SIOP); in fact, only one SIOP scenario involved attacks on cities.[15] Still, the counterforce options of the 1950s and the 1960s were limited by existing technologies to a massive-retaliatory response and did not include the selectiveness which is envisaged in the Schlesinger concept.

Critics of the Schlesinger doctrine have contended that it could be destabilizing by giving the United States a capability to launch a disarming first strike against Soviet land-based systems, the argument that was advanced against the McNamara strategy in the early 1960s. However, this argument ignores the fact that an increasing percentage of Soviet strategic capabilities over the next decade will be sea-based and, therefore, far less vulnerable to an American attack, and they may be based increasingly on mobile-launched forces. Both developments will make the targeting problems of the United States against Soviet strategic forces far more difficult. Moreover, Soviet military doctrine, while emphasizing the avoidance of nuclear war, provides for its possibility. Soviet strategic policies have consistently been directed toward the evolution of a force posture enabling the Soviet Union to wage war and to survive. This doctrinal emphasis on the attainment of victory requires the safeguarding of those elements considered by the Soviets to be necessary for their national survival. A change in the United States targeting concept to include Soviet military forces, industrial centers, populated areas, and administrative areas would provide an enhanced deterrent capability for the United States. Thus the Schlesinger doctrine, by its emphasis on a broad spectrum of strategic options and its reliance on the triad of strategic forces, marks a significant advancement in United States doctrinal thought.

Much of our discussion of strategic doctrine since the end of World War II has taken place in a largely bipolar nuclear world. However, we are entering, for better or for worse, a multinuclear world. The advent of strategic parity has had a major effect upon strategic thought. In addition, the emergence of additional nuclear powers will have important implications for the adequacy of existing deterrence theory. In other words, we must ask ourselves several questions about the adequacy of existing deterrence theory in a world which is unlikely to be strictly bipolar in the nuclear sense and instead will be increasingly multinuclear, even though there will remain major gaps, on the one hand, between the strategic forces of the United States and the Soviet Union and, on the other hand, the forces of the smaller nuclear powers.

The first question, of course, is how much strategic power will be enough or sufficient for the United States and the Soviet Union under conditions of nuclear multipolarity. Soviet analysts hold that the Soviet Union needs a margin beyond what is required by the United States because of the existence of additional nuclear powers such as China, whose primary emphasis will be upon targeting sites in the Soviet Union rather than the United States. What does this mean for the adequacy of forces as well as for strategic doctrine?

Second, does the development of additional nuclear powers make necessary the acquisition of major new systems, not just quantitative increases, but qualitative increases in the strategic posture of one or both superpowers? Third, is it necessary for a superpower to possess a capability to deter an attack from several other nuclear powers simultaneously? What kind of deterrence must exist in this kind of world? Alternatively, it may be hypothesized that nuclear multipolarity reduces the risks of nuclear confrontation by making it impossible for any single nuclear power to destroy the retaliatory power of all or maybe even several other nuclear powers. Will nuclear multipolarity enhance invulnerability, and hence the prospects for deterrence? Other hypotheses, of course, suggest that nuclear multipolarity increases the risks of nuclear war, simply by adding to the numbers of nuclear powers. What is statistically correct, however, may not be necessarily correct in the real world. We know very little about the stabilizing or destructive effects of additional nuclear powers, either upon political leaders' perceptions of their own defense requirements or their propensity to use such weapons. Conceivably, renewed attention will be given to theories of deterrence in a world which is changing in many ways from the world in which existing theories of deterrence were evolved. In addition, new generations of nonnuclear technologies may have profound effects on weapons for the deterrence of conflict and the development of war-fighting capabilities at the nonnuclear level. Thus, we need to understand far more clearly in the future than we do now the relationship between nuclear and nonnuclear forces in the deterrence of conflict, in preventing regional imbalances from developing, and assuring what has been the principal goal of deterrence theory—the prevention of the outbreak of conflict which could escalate to an all-out confrontation between the United States and the Soviet Union.

NOTES

Based on a lecture delivered at the Naval War College in December 1974.

1. "Evolution of Foreign Policy," speech by Secretary of State John Foster Dulles to the Council on Foreign Relations, Jan. 12, 1954 (Department of State Press Release No. 8).

2. Albert Wohlstetter, "The Delicate Balance of Terror," *Foreign Affairs*, January 1959, p. 211.

3. Henry A. Kissinger, *Nuclear Weapons and Foreign Policy* (New York: Harper & Row, 1957).

4. Pierre Gallois, *The Balance of Terror: Strategy for the Nuclear Age* (Boston: Houghton Mifflin, 1961). Gallois first suggested this thesis which later became a prominent theme of French President Charles de Gaulle's diplomacy.

5. Robert J. McNamara, "Address at the Commencement Exercises of the University of Michigan; June 16, 1962," *Department of State Bulletin,* July 9, 1962, p. 67.

6. *U.S. Foreign Policy for the 1970s: The Emerging Structure for Peace.* A Report to the Congress by Richard Nixon, Feb. 9, 1972, p. 158.

7. *New York Times,* Jan. 11, 1974, p. 1.

8. Ibid.

9. Ibid.

10. Ibid.

11. *Briefing on Counterforce Attacks.* Hearing, Senat Foreign Relations Committee, Subcommittee on Arms Control, International Law and Organization, 93d Congress, 2d session, Sept. 11, 1974. Released Jan. 10, 1975, p. 3.

12. Ibid., p. 8.

13. Ibid., p. 39.

14. James R. Schlesinger, *News Conference at the Pentagon,* Thursday, Jan. 24, 1974 (Washington, D.C.: Government Printing Office for the Department of Defense, 1974). Transcript.

15. William Beecher, "Major War Plans are Being Revised by the White House," *New York Times,* Aug. 5, 1972.

The Future of United States Development Assistance in the Insurgency Environment

Allan E. Goodman

Editor's Note: *Allan E. Goodman, formerly Chairman of the Department of Government and International Relations at Clark University, is currently with the Central Intelligence Agency in Washington, D.C. He is the author of* Politics in War—The Bases of Political Community in South Vietnam, The Lost Peace: America's Search for a Negotiated Settlement of the Vietnam War *and he is the editor of* Negotiating While Fighting: The Diary of Admiral C. Turner Joy at the Korean Armistice Conference.

I

Alexis de Tocqueville once wrote, "the most important time in the life of a country is the coming out of a war." The denouement of the decade of Vietnam suggests that America's coming out is likely to be all the more difficult from a war we did not win. Insurgency is here to stay. Its tactics are a new science of warfare. The social and economic conditions which give insurgents their cause have multiplied rather than diminished. The Vietnam experience has shown, moreover, that there are no counters to insurgency that military intervention by a democracy can provide. The era of relatively facile United States influence over world events, and the role that this has implied for United States foreign aid, is ending.

The decline in our influence abroad has stimulated a number of countries not to "rise from the ashes of the American system of world security"[1] but rather to seek alternatives entirely foreign to the American experience. China in Asia and the Pacific, Brazil and Chile in Latin America, Tanzania and Zambia in Africa, and India in the Asian subcontinent are not either regionally or on a worldwide basis trying to take the place of the United States. In an interview with the managing editor of Japan's *Asahi Shimbun,* Chou En-lai spoke for many Third World statesmen: "We are opposed to the 'major powers,' to politics and to domination. We will not become a major power under any circumstance."[2] Throughout the Third World, America's search for order and security, as the foundation for and, later, yardstick of socioeconomic change is being seen as antithetical to development. Brazilian economist Celso Furtado typifies this perspective when he observes that past development programs suggest that, while the United States is primarily concerned with security, Brazil's main concern is development.[3] The more conscious countries have become of the conflict between security and development, the less they have responded to the appeals of either the Democrats or the Communists, and sought, instead, solutions within the framework of their own national identity. This search follows Furtado's suggestion "that only the national framework and occasionally the regional one can serve as a basis for defining development value criteria." At a time when economic and environmental problems are becoming the common cause of all, the very notion that there is an identity of interests between the wealthy and the poor nations is under challenge.

As the United States role wanes, so also may that of its principal antagonists. The experience of one colleague, just returned from India, illustrates the case in point:

I found it impossible to work for our government and advise the Indians. We have such distinctive notions about development. But so do the Russians and the Chinese. Consequently, there are no clear choices here for India. Our theories and programs succeed and fail to just about the same extent as do those of our competitors.We are exporting development, allright, but it is rather like toothpaste: our brand is white, bright and does about the same thing as any other brand.[4]

The United States has made greater efforts than any of its competitors in development and security assistance, but, increasingly, leaders in developing countries have come to view all Great Powers in similar terms. The Third World views us and our antagonists as impediments to development. Why?

II

Clearly, no discussion of what John Kenneth Galbraith has called the "plain lessons of a bad decade"[5] could take place without reference to the experience of Vietnam. The principal lesson of the decade is that intervention—like world power—has limits; and this we knew before Vietnam, without having to experience the war. Intervention has limits, and among them the most prominent relates to our inability to bring internal stability and reform to countries which lack the political bases and institutions to sustain those processes. While we had accepted the notion throughout the 1960s that insurgencies were a profoundly destabilizing phenomenon, we failed to realize that our strategies designed to counter them were themselves profoundly destabilizing. Countering insurgencies required political reforms and institutional changes that most countries could not support. Insurgency need not have been synonymous with warfare, although the insurgencies in Southeast Asia and the Middle East in the 1960s became, in fact, major wars in scope, cost, and cruelty. A fundamental error in our doctrine of response was that we primarily viewed them as limited *wars* to which a limited *military* response was appropriate, rather than as political struggles that challenged the stability of governments and the viability of the systems of politics of the incumbent regimes we supported.

Apart from all the technological window dressing associated with counterinsurgency, the process required, fundamentally, governments and politics strong enough to compete with the insurgents. There was in Vietnam, for example, continuous talk of the need to transform the conflict from a military to a political one. But our approaches there consistently stressed the need for the government of South Vietnam (GVN) to develop military capabilities and not political ones. After our withdrawal, we found the GVN relatively well prepared to continue the war at least until 1975, but not so able to compete with the Vietcong politically. The prospect that the war would be permanent was very real. The capabilities for the GVN to emerge as a rival political force to the Vietcong were never adequately developed.

What went wrong? To Sun-tzu's classic dictum: "Know yourself; know the enemy. A thousand battles, a thousand victories," we forgot to add, "Know your ally." By turning the insurgency in Vietnam into a war of proxy between the United States and its Communist enemies, we failed to realize that the GVN itself was weak and that no amount of support to a weak government could substitute for one that could mobilize popular political support. We had continually sought to have the GVN decentralize power to the people as a means of increasing popular support for the regime. But the GVN had no power to decentralize. It barely had enough to maintain itself *vis-à-vis* elements in the military officer corps and religious groups that sought its overthrow. The GVN, in turn, made it easy for us to intervene in the war; but in so doing, we found ourselves virtually unable to influence the course of political reform.

Intervention, thus, was not the same as influence. The findings of the MIT study group in 1959 with regard to this aspect of American foreign aid doctrines are still pertinent:

> There can be no easy optimism about the consequences of American action. We must face the fact that our influence is limited. Our relationship to the newly emerging countries is not that of a 19th century European power towards its colonies, nor that of a modern Communist power towards its satellites. We exercise no direct control and can influence the course of events only marginally, largely by helping to provide some of the resources—skills, education, public utilities, capital—which countries must have for successful and stable modernization.[6]

The experience of the past decade has not substantially changed this assessment. Indeed, the conclusions of one Senate staff study of our assistance to the Greek junta can be taken as both a summary of past efforts in most countries as well as prologue. It pointed out that the policy of friendly persuasion to move the Greek junta towards a constitutional state clearly failed. The junta accepted the friendship, and the military assistance, but it ignored the persuasion. Indeed, the Greek regime seemed to have been able to exert more leverage on the United States with regard to military assistance than "we have been able to exert on the regime with regard to political reform. We see no evidence that this will not continue to be the case."[7] Such a state of affairs, of course, is not limited solely to the Military Assistance Program. Regardless of our goal (ranging from "friendly" persuasion to direct threats) and regardless of the vehicle by which it is advanced (ranging from military and development assistance to diplomacy), the results appear to be the same.

The more stable and secure the government establishment that we wish to influence, the less likely are our chances of doing so. The reasons for this are obvious. Strongly entrenched regimes have at hand the means to resist or selectively use American assistance and advice. Moreover, we are often inept in proffering aid and advice, and our overseas missions are frequently divided against themselves in ways that permit host governments to manipulate intrabureaucratic rivalry to their own advantage.

Ironically, however, our ability to exert influence through direct intervention or assistance is also very limited in countries where the ruling elite or the established government is weak. In such cases, regardless of the resources that we can provide to strengthen government, it may be inherently too weak to implement the kinds of reforms we suggest. Intervention, then, substitutes for political change rather than stimulates it.[8] Our support to weakly entrenched government elites tends to provide them with a level of confidence they have been unable to derive from their own politics. In the process of building such confidence, it often becomes unnecessary for the government to embark on the difficult task of fostering actual political mobilization by expanding opportunities for political participation. Regime survival depends upon the United States, not internal supports, and in a war by proxy we must appear to our foreign allies as more anxious to have their support than their reform. In fact, one distinct possibility suggested by past experience is that, if our goal is to influence a particular government, the probability that we shall succeed is much greater if it is clearly *not* in our national interest or a matter of national policy to do so.

In dealing with insurgencies, the broadening and strengthening of institutions of political participation are crucial, but such reforms are distasteful to the government we support. Democratic evolution requires that power be created and shared. The process implies, as most governing elites must view it, the likelihood that their position and influence will be eroded. One early study of the political significance of guerrilla warfare suggested that the confidence inspired by strong American backing might provide a temptation to defer the very reforms which the American aid was intended to facilitate, because the regime would be so firmly entrenched and supported by the United States that "inconvenient and distasteful changes" would no longer be necessary.[9]

This state of affairs is a result of two misconceptions about the efficacy of our development assistance. First, we tend to believe that when we support governmental establishments we are also supporting entire political systems or least the possibility of the former working to strengthen the latter. In fact, we fail to recognize that the two are not complementary but often opposing forces; we may, in short, close off the prospects for internal political reform by seeking to foster it within the governmental system. Second, we tend to regard insurgency as an external problem, generated by Communist subversion rather than as an internal conflict over the distribution of political power in a society. This is not to say that Communist states do not practice subversion, but that subversion rarely succeeds unless there are sufficient forces of internal discontent that predate the introduction of foreign arms, finances, or cadre. Because we view with alarm Communist influences in developing countries, we respond to communism and not to the bases from which it might draw support.

A well-balanced program designed to assist a developing country to meet some of the difficulties associated with modernization may very well be scrapped at the first appearance of even the most ambiguous signs of a Communist subversive presence. The host government realizes this and assumes that its interest in maintaining a grip on political power is identical with our preference for stable governmental and administrative systems to combat the Communists. Thus we end up providing the umbrella of sustenance under which the tenure of the governmental establishment is guaranteed. The result of this process has been that the Pentagon abroad transforms development assistance into civic action, insurgencies become limited wars that can be preempted by the development of police and paramilitary forces, and questions of political reform are relegated to an "after the war" concern.

III

But before the final collapse of the GVN we did not have a new policy either for Vietnam or for the rest of the developing world. Simply to do less in these areas, whether under the guise of searching for low-profile activities or under the mantle of isolationism, would not be a new policy. If Dean Rusk's fear that "one of the severe prices that we may be paying for Vietnam is that it may have stimulated a trend toward isolationism in this country" proves correct, then we shall not have any post-Vietnam policy. Indeed, if President Nixon's second State of the World

Report can be taken as a prologue, one critical analyst suggests that a low profile may ultimately mean no policy:

The American interest in the future of South Asia, which includes such large countries as India and Pakistan, is . . . reduced to three pages of banalities; the discussion of black Africa and its growing conflict with South Africa amounts essentially to a proclamation of American neutrality; and the analysis of Latin America does not address itself at any length to the dynamics, prospects, and implications of rising radicalism on the left and right, both exploiting and responding to popular anti-Yankeeism.[10]

Could the agony of the Vietnam experience fail to result in a new American foreign policy? It can, and the danger that it is already doing so is great. Vietnam was a disaster, but not to create new principles for foreign policy in its aftermath would be an even greater disaster.

The denouement of the Vietnam War, it is generally assumed, will precipitate substantial changes in American foreign policy. How could it be otherwise? The war itself was one of incredible scope, intensity, and cost. More young people were mobilized against this war than had been involved in the struggle for human rights of the late 1950s and 1960s; the protest appeared to coincide with the emergence of a new and alienated youth culture that exposed in sometimes beautiful but more often in bizarre ways the decay of the American social structure. One president sacrificed what would in all probability have been a second term of office out of the conviction that so doing would, in part, help to end the war, while another president ran for a second term on the record of his efforts ending American military participation in it. Countless government officials—at all levels—have left their posts as gestures of their opposition to the war; those who had upon leaving remained quiescent increasingly came forward to make their opposition known. Seven thousand pages of classified government reports were leaked in a dramatic gesture of despair to the public press, providing scholars with access to archival information (particularly from Defense Department and Joint Chiefs of Staff files) hitherto unavailable for scrutiny in the aftermath of any other war. All these features of the Vietnam War (to list only some of the most prominent) are bound to precipitate change in American foreign policy—or are they?

The very elements which have thrust this war so dramatically upon the political consciousness of Americans may be the ones which may make for the absence of any profound changes in the principles upon which American foreign policy is based. I suspect that we tend to overrate the lessons learned from unpopular or unsuccessful involvements abroad and, in the case of the Vietnam War, the very immensity of our involvement and failure makes it unlikely that its lessons will have much consequence.

It is commonly accepted among governmental officials now, as it was among concerned academics throughout most of the latter half of the 1960s, that the Vietnam War made little sense in the context of our foreign policy. As one government official suggested to me in an interview,

> This war has been blamed on the cold war mentality of supposedly cold warriors who were concerned about falling dominoes and stemming the red tide. But I do not think this is true, if I may speak as a cold warrior. Cold warriors *learn* from the past, and one of the most prominent of the lessons we have learned is that we should have no land wars in Asia.

The point here, of course, is not only that the level of intervention in the Vietnam War made no sense and could not be justified by reference to any contemporary United States policy,[11] but also that, because it has made no sense, the prospect that we can learn from it is greatly reduced. As horrendous and costly as the war has been, it has only marginally affected the bureaucracies and procedures which have participated in it. From the policymaking end of the involvement, ever since early 1965 the Vietnam War has been a special war, handled by special working groups within the diplomatic, security, and intelligence communities. Officials of high and low levels have gotten, as one put it, "stuck in the Vietnam thing," and many remained "with it" for almost a decade. Those who have staff and operational roles associated with Vietnam frequently report that they are warned, when they arrive at their next post, that nothing they have learned in or about Vietnam is relevant to their new assignment. One early Vietnam hand in the State Department, for example, described his mid-career transition in the following terms:

> I have spent three years in Vietnam and three in Washington working on Vietnamese affairs and I was, during the latter period, literally inundated with advice to get out of it. I finally did so by requesting a post in Latin America and the first thing I was told was that nothing I had learned in Vietnam would

be of help. I was amazed, in fact, at the intensity of the pressure within the [diplomatic] service to isolate the Vietnam experience.

Vietnam operations groups existed as self-sufficient entities (and sometimes as separate buildings) within the foreign policy bureaucracy, and in two agencies with which I am most familiar (the State Department and Agency for International Development), I was always struck by how little the whole of the institution had been affected by Vietnam. The remarks of one high-level official in the State Department (who was not working on Vietnam) made in response to a question about how he felt toward the students then protesting the Nixon administration's war policies serve to summarize the comments of many that I recorded over the past few years.

I do not think you should be amazed at how sympathetic we are towards the students. They have made getting to work for the mass of the Washington service difficult, but they have not really struck at what any of us are, in fact, doing in our work. We do not like, support, or believe in the Vietnam thing either. When the students speak, therefore, they are not speaking to us or to the way the government *as a whole* works. [Emphasis added.]

To the extent that this atmosphere was a pervasive one, the experience of the Vietnam War was effectively controlled and isolated, and so also was the impact of its lessons. The prospect is thus very real that we may be coming out of the Vietnam experience with our foreign policymaking institutions having learned very little and with those individuals who have learned something being in the least opportune positions to apply it.

IV

What should we have learned by now?

Insurgencies are political conflicts. They will increasingly focus on questions of political power and political participation. They will be launched by those who are denied adequate and effective channels of access to and participation in politics. They will not be wars of self-determination. As such they have often been political conflicts that began with rather than ended at the achievement of independence. Future insurgencies thus can be distinguished from wars of subversion, wars of proxy, and limited engagements between two or more countries.

Too often we have intervened to "preempt" insurgencies, and this has resulted in turning them into wars. Such a policy only delays or postpones either the insurgent or the incumbent coming to terms with the crisis of participation, that is, the conflict over who will participate in creating and exercising the political power. Insurgencies are conflicts about the distribution of power in a single country. The only way in which they can be preempted is by coming to terms with the issues of participation in politics that they raise, not by converting one side or another into a more effectively armed camp.

Insurgencies are also likely to become permanent wars. They will be characterized in their incipiency—whether it takes several years of a decade to play out—by intervention and withdrawal of either waning global or emerging regional powers. The second phase of the insurgency will be characterized by lower levels of violence than the first, but the basic issues of the conflict will remain the same. Phase two is the crucial stage. The Vietcong have demonstrated that insurgent movements can survive massive intervention. The real question is whether each side can sustain the conflict and transmit its goals over as much as several generations. If one side is successful in prevailing over the other in phase two, then the outcome will resemble the Mexican "success story": subjugation of the side least able to transfer the fervor of the conflict from generation to generation, class to class, and from political movement to political institutions. If neither side prevails over the other, the outcome is likely to resemble the Korean "success story": stable partition.

V

In the meantime, there is nothing on the horizon which could substitute for the American system of Security Development, for it is not unique from any of its present competitors. The great nations now emerging are not intent upon taking over the system we have created. There is little prospect of agreement and cooperation arising from the realization that we are, in the words of poet Archibald McLeish, all "riders on a tiny spaceship." The enfranchisement of a worldwide peasantry or the political triumph of the middle class is unlikely. The world will see a breakup into regional conflicts, perpetual conflicts, or insurgencies that current policies—much less current academic thought—will be unable to influence.

There will be cooperation on such things as the environment and possibly on the problems inherent in the specter of chronic poverty accompanying unparalleled rapid urban growth, but no fundamental agreement on war and peace. If anything, the once great global and the now-emerging regional powers will come to recognize that their ability to influence the world has greater limitations than anyone ever expected. Ironically, this realization—which will be a time yet in coming—may do more to end war and promote peace than anything that we could create, institutionally or politically, to do the job. The secret of riding the spaceship lies in the growing realization of shared perils, rather than in a burgeoning sense of efficacy and control, either over nature, ourselves, or the universe.

NOTES

Based on a lecture delivered at the Naval War College in October 1971.

1. Samuel Huntington, "Political Development and the Decline of the American System of World Order," *Daedalus,* Summer 1967, p. 928.

2. Chou to Moto Goto on 28 October 1971 and reprinted in the *New York Times,* 9 November 1971, p. 16.

3. Celso Furtado, *Obstacles to Development in Latin America* (Garden City, N.Y.: Doubleday, 1970), pp. 19-20.

4. See also Norman D. Palmer, "Foreign Aid and Foreign Policy: The 'New Statecraft' Reassessed," *Orbis,* Fall 1969, p. 775.

5. See his article on this subject in *Foreign Policy,* Winter 1970-71, pp. 31-45.

6. Center for International Studies, Massachusetts Institute of Technology, "Economic, Social, and Political Change in the Underdeveloped Countries and Its Implications for U.S. Policy," in Senate Foreign Relations Committee, 86th Congress, 2d Session, U.S. Foreign Policy (Washington: U.S. Govt. Print. Off., 1960), p. 1240.

7. Richard Moose and James Lowenstein, *Greece: February 1971, a Staff Report,* Prepared for the use of the Committee on Foreign Relations, U.S. Senate (Washington: U.S. Govt. Print. Off., 1971), p. 16.

8. See, for example, the discussion of this phenomenon contained in Amitai Etzioni, "Intervention for Progress in the Dominican Republic," in John D. Montgomery and Albert O. Hirschman, eds, *Public Policy,* XVII, 1968, pp. 299-306; Abraham Lowenthal, "The Dominican Intervention in Retrospect," *Public Policy,* XVII Fall 1969, pp. 133-48; and Peter A. McGrath, "The Style and Success of Counterinsurgency Foreign Aid: Some Determinants," ibid., 1968, pp. 307-31. A detailed analysis of the relationship between American policies and Vietnamese politics can be found in my *Politics in War: The Bases of Political Community in South Vietnam* (Cambridge: Harvard University Press, 1973).

9. James Cross, *Conflict in the Shadows: The Nature and Politics of Guerrilla War* (Garden City, N.Y.: Doubleday, 1963), p. 140.

10. Zbigniew Brzezinski, "Half Past Nixon," *Foreign Policy,* Summer 1971. p. 11.

11. See especially, Leslie N. Gelb, "Vietnam: The System Worked," *Foreign Policy,* Summer 1971, p. 245.

The Decline and Fall of the Joint Chiefs of Staff

William A. Hamilton III

Editor's Note: *William A. Hamilton III is a Lieutenant Colonel, U.S. Army. He is currently a Ph. D. candidate in international relations at the University of Nebraska.*

It may be years before historians will be able to judge the correctness of the policies pursued by the United States in Southeast Asia. Undoubtedly, that judgment will be tempered by the relative success of the venture. Even at this point in time, however, certain aspects of the war are already being debated. Inevitably some of the questions being raised center on the conduct of the war as a possible explanation for its excessive cost and duration. Was military force inappropriate to attain the national goals in this instance? Was force improperly used? Was our strategy correct? Were our tactics sound?

By law "... the Joint Chiefs of Staff are the principal military advisers to the President, the National Security Council, and the Secretary of Defense."[1] Did the JCS provide sound or unsound advice? Did the President listen to their advice?

The answer to the last two questions will be a long time coming. More presidential papers will have to be made available, volumes of documents will have to be declassified, and a number of books and memoirs will have to be written before the answers can be found. However, it is possible to examine the environment in which

the JCS operated during the Kennedy and Johnson administrations in order to assess their collective influence upon the formulation of policy involving the use of the armed forces.

Before initiating an inquiry of this sort, a normative model describing the relationship between a commander-in-chief and the
leaders of his armed forces must first be established in order to
set a standard by which actual interactions between past presidents and their military advisers can be measured.

The choice of a proper model is not difficult when so few exist.
In this case the selection is small because whatever the differences
between individual American military services over the years, they
have uniformly supported the concept of civil control over the
military. However, support of civil control was not held to mean
that the military would give up its advisory function in the policymaking process.

While the literature in this area is uniform, it is also scarce.
It is not clear whether this paucity is the result of oversight or
the general unanimity of opinion in this regard.

The model chosen comes from a book first published by the
United States Naval War College in 1936 called *Sound Military
Decision*. The book was used for years to enlarge the viewpoint
and broaden the basis of the professional judgment of officers.
Based on an enormous body of literature which included all avail-
able and pertinent military writings, *Sound Military Decision* be-
came a bible to students at the Naval War College prior to Pearl
Harbor and throughout World War II.

What influence the following passage from *Sound Military Decision* had upon the drafters of the act of Congress making the Joint
Chiefs of Staff "the principal military advisers to the President,
the National Security Council and the Secretary of Defense"[2] is
unknown, but given its general acceptance among the military
services, as well as the fact that it predates the National Security
Act of 1947, we may safely accept it as the model relationship:

The Advisory Function

Understanding between the civil representatives of the State
and the leaders of the Armed Forces is manifestly essential to
the coordination of national policy with the power to enforce
it. Therefore, if serious omissions and the adoption of ill-advised
measures are to be avoided, it is necessary that wise professional
counsel be available to the State. While military strategy may
determine whether the aims of policy are possible to attainment,

policy may, beforehand, determine largely the success or failure of military strategy. It behooves policy to ensure not only that military strategy pursue appropriate aims, but that the work of strategy be allotted adequate means and be undertaken under the most favorable conditions.[3]

Looking at the last decade (and particularly at the war in Southeast Asia) in light of the model relationship described above, one is moved to ask: What measure of understanding existed between the civil representatives of the State and the leaders of the armed forces? Was wise professional council available to the State? Were the policy aims of the United States such as to enhance the chance of success of the military strategy? Conversely, was the military strategy the correct one to accomplish the aims of policy? Were adequate means allotted to support the strategy, and was the strategy undertaken under favorable conditions?

While the temptation to address all these questions is strong, such an effort lies beyond the more limited constraints of time and space available here. Rather, examination will be limited to the degree of understanding or misunderstanding which existed between the commander in chief and the JCS during the Kennedy and Johnson administrations.

I

John Fitzgerald Kennedy became the thirty-fifth president of the United States on 20 January 1961. He brought to the nation his considerable talents, certain preconceptions about the military, and his brilliant and aggressive secretary of defense, Robert Strange McNamara. Before the first hundred days of his administration were over, President Kennedy came to rely upon Mr. McNamara for military advice. He also profoundly changed the relationship between the office of the commander-in-chief and the Joint Chiefs of Staff.

John F. Kennedy was raised in a home which placed high value on public service. There can be no doubt that Kennedy was proud of his own military service. He was also proud of his oldest brother, Joseph P. Kennedy, Jr., who was killed in a tragic military accident during World War II.

His own experiences as a naval officer left him unawed by generals and admirals. In 1944, while he was recovering from the injuries he received during his courageous exploit as the skipper of PT 109, he wrote to a friend about the

... super-human ability of the Navy to screw up everything they touch. ... Even the simple delivery of a letter frequently overburdens this heaving puffing war machine of ours. God save this country of ours from those patriots whose war cry is, "what this country needs is to be run with military efficiency."[4]

Kennedy's personal view of the military establishment did not lessen his interest in military affairs, however. Once Kennedy indicated to Sorensen that if he were ever to be a cabinet officer, the only two posts which he would consider were secretary of state or secretary of defense.[5] Later, as president, he took great interest in his role as the commander-in-chief, frequently inspecting the armed forces, examining military equipment, and discussing concepts such as "flexible response" and "counterinsurgency."

One of the major thrusts of Kennedy's presidential campaign was that we were falling behind the Russians in usable military power and that our basic strategy of reliance upon "massive retaliation" was unrealistic, leaving the United States only two options: "world devastation or submission."[6] Underscoring his concern for the state of national defense, he conducted an extensive talent hunt to find a man who would be a strong secretary of defense—a man who could unify the efforts of the separate services and put an end to the bickering among the JCS. The search led to the newly elected president of the Ford Motor Company, Robert S. McNamara. Characterized by the military as a "civilian on horseback," McNamara's approach with the JCS was one of "divide and conquer."

Losing no time, Kennedy directed McNamara to conduct a survey of the defense establishment and to report his findings. Shortly after Kennedy's inauguration, McNamara reported to the president that he had found in the Pentagon:

A strategic nuclear force vulnerable to surprise missile attack, a nonnuclear force weak in combat-ready divisions, in airlift capacity and in tactical air support, a counterinsurgency force for all practical purposes nonexistent, and a weapons inventory completely lacking in certain major elements but far oversupplied in others. ... Too many automatic decisions made in advance instead of in the light of an actual emergency, and too few Pentagon-wide plans for each kind of emergency. The Army was relying on airlift the Air Force could not supply. The Air Force was stockpiling supplies for a war lasting a few days while the Army stockpiles assumed a war of two years.[7]

President Kennedy's worst suspicions were confirmed. Even if the new president stopped to consider that the JCS had been merely carrying out the Eisenhower-Dulles strategy, making do with a budget ceiling imposed by a Republican administration, it is doubtful that he was favorably impressed with those aspects of McNamara's report which evidenced a lack of coordination and cooperation between the military services.

Surveying the shakeup of the JCS, President Kennedy regarded them as individuals "inherited" from the Eisenhower administration.[8] The Chiefs, however, had an apolitical institutional history and were equally loyal to Republicans and Democrats.[9] Nevertheless, Kennedy longed to have his own appointees make up the JCS, saying, "Any President should have the right to choose carefully his own military advisers."[10]

Prior to the Bay of Pigs, the president appeared content to allow normal attrition to change the membership of the JCS, because he had already arranged an interim solution by the appointment of former Army Chief of Staff General Maxwell D. Taylor as his personal adviser on military affairs until the time came when he could make Taylor chairman of the Joint Chiefs of Staff.[11]

That unfortunate event, the Bay of Pigs, was a turning point in the newly developing relationship between the president and his chief military advisers. Having lost confidence in the chiefs as a consequence of the Cuban disaster, President Kennedy chose to substitute Secretary McNamara and a number of *ad hoc* advisers in place of the JCS. A common pattern of poor communications between the president and the JCS was evident before, during, and after the Bay of Pigs and played a significant part in the deterioration of civil-military relations at the highest levels.[12]

From the early stages, the JCS were not happy about the CIA conducting large-scale military operations. The military chiefs held the project at arm's length, only providing their comments on the military feasibility of the plan when required to do so. Accordingly, in January the JCS commented in writing that the CIA plan to land at Trinidad had a chance of initial military success and ". . . that ultimate success would depend upon either a sizable uprising inside the island or sizable support from outside."[13]

Schlesinger criticized the JCS for the indecisive stance they took in the early preinvasion deliberations. He noted that the JCS paper "without restating the alternative conditions for victory, . . . concluded that the existing plan, if executed in time, stood a 'fair' chance of ultimate success."[14]

By March, however, the JCS noted that "... Cuban resistance was indispensable to success. They could see no other way short of United States intervention by which an invasion force of a thousand Cubans, no matter how well trained and equipped nor how stout their morale, could conceivably overcome the 200,000 men of Castro's army and militia."[15]

As time went on, President Kennedy insisted that changes be made in the plan to reduce evidence of United States involvement. As a consequence, new landing sites were sought. The Joint Chiefs were asked to comment upon the Zapata area, the Bay of Pigs, and one other area. "The Joint Chiefs ... on 14 March agreed that Zapata seemed the best ... but *added softly* that they still preferred Trinidad."[16] (Emphasis added.) On the other hand, Sorensen reports that the JCS failed to tell the president that they still preferred Trinidad.[17]

While the White House and the JCS felt that a revolt of the Cuban people was essential to the success of the operation, the CIA operatives in charge of the operation were prepared to go ahead without an uprising. Here was a communications breakdown between the CIA and the rest of the administration. "The invasion plan, as understood by the President and the Joint Chiefs, ... did assume that the successful *occupation* of an enlarged beachhead area would rather soon incite *organized* uprisings by *armed* members of the Cuban resistance."[18] But, after the disaster, Allen W. Dulles, the former CIA director, stated flatly that he did not know of any "estimate that a spontaneous uprising of the unarmed population of Cuba would be touched off by the landing."[19]

Unfortunately, the preparations for the operation moved inexorably onward, as if the project possessed a life of its own. Schlesinger describes meetings taking place "in a curious atmosphere of assumed consensus." While the CIA dominated, the Joint Chiefs seemed to be going along contentedly. The Joint Chiefs' preference for Trinidad was on the record. Even though they never formally approved the new plan, they at no time opposed it. The Joint Chiefs' collaboration with the CIA gave the White House the erroneous impression of wholehearted support.[20]

It is terrifying to think that a government could proceed on such a hazardous course on the basis of an assumed consensus or that the president could undertake to make such an important decision on the basis of an impression that his military advisers supported the plan and seemed to be content with it, when the JCS had repeatedly gone on record stating their preconditions for success. The point at issue is not whether the JCS should or should not be blamed for the abortive Bay of Pigs invasion: rather the question which must be answered is how such a state of affairs could come to pass. Could this situation have occurred if the National Security Council (NSC) machinery had been used as it was by President Eisenhower?

Research in this area has been hampered by an unwillingness of the military participants in this decision to discuss openly the subject.[21] The Joint Chiefs' side of the story can only be left to speculation. How could a group of dedicated and distinguished military officers and the commander-in-chief of the armed forces so misread the intentions of the others? The president was convinced that the JCS would not let him plunge into an unwise military adventure, and yet he seemed deaf to their warnings that to succeed the plan would have to be bold and its execution forceful.[22] Perhaps the JCS became convinced that it was the president who kept pushing the CIA's "covert" invasion project since it would not die a decent bureaucratic death even after all the preconditions and reservations raised by the Joint Chiefs. Or perhaps the JCS wanted to show the new president that they could get along with the CIA and were not just parochial nitpickers.

The CIA planners were so secretive in their approach that the JCS had to rely upon a patchwork of briefings "about" the invasion plans rather than receiving a formal operations plan which could have been subjected to minute scrutiny and to which the JCS could have appended formal comments. The changes urged by Kennedy's civilian advisers, which canceled forty to forty-eight planned air strikes, were unknown to the Joint Chiefs until the last moment. Attempts by the CIA and the military to restore the strikes were to no avail.[23] To say these changes doomed the proposed invasion and made disaster inevitable would not be an overstatement.

Lyman Kirkpatrick, former deputy director of the CIA and at the time of the Bay of Pigs episode the inspector general of the CIA, found no fault with the JCS in his postmortem of the entire affair:

> Throughout the rest of Washington, after the Bay of Pigs there was a general effort to try and move out of the hot seat and put somebody else in it. There were those that tried unjustly to blame the Defense Department and Joint Chiefs of Staff, whose participation had been limited.[24]

When it was all over and the president and the nation had been humiliated, it was clear to the president that many mistakes had been made, and many people shared in the blame. Publicly, he took all of the blame upon his own shoulders. Privately, he expressed to his intimates great disappointment in the performance of his advisers. He then slowly began to replace those whom he felt had failed him. For political reasons he could not move too fast, but eventually the errant (or thought to be errant) individuals were removed and/or their functions replaced by organs of his own design.

Despite President Kennedy's acceptance of responsibility for the invasion's failure, the controversy surrounding this ill-starred venture was just starting. Congress was the first to attack. Senator Gore wanted the JCS dismissed.[25] Senator Long wanted General Lemnitzer removed.[26] Secretary McNamara was painfully slow to defend the JCS, but President Kennedy had them pose with him in the Rose Garden for an official photograph which was accomplished with more than normal publicity.[27] Finally, in June, former President Eisenhower came to their defense,[28] for the most part ending the attacks coming from outside the administration.

Although the president made no public denunciation of his military and civilian advisers, he did, according to Schlesinger and Sorensen, make a number of comments about the JCS.[29] The comments he allegedly made about the Joint Chiefs and the military bear repeating because they reflect the attitude that was to carry on throughout his administration. Schlesinger speaks for the president:

> The President reserved his innermost thoughts and, in the end, blamed only himself. But he was a human being and not totally free of resentment. He would say at times, "My God, the bunch of advisors we inherited. ... can you imagine being President and leaving behind someone like all those people there?" My impression is that, among these advisors, the Joint Chiefs had disappointed him most for their cursory review of the military plans.[30]
>
> He felt that he now knew certain soft spots in his administration especially the CIA and the Joint Chiefs. He would never be overawed by professional military advice again.[31]

Sorenson concludes that, with the exception of General Shoup, the president was convinced, after the Bay of Pigs, that he needed military advice that neither Bundy's staff nor the holdover service chiefs were able to give him.[32]

A year and a half later, Sorenson reports, the president said,

"The advice of every member of the Executive Branch that was brought in to advise was unanimous—and the advice was wrong." Apparently, the advice was neither unanimous nor well-considered. Since the plan was the responsibility of another agency, the Joint Chiefs gave it only piece-meal consideration. Significantly, they did not subject it to the same scrutiny they would have applied had their forces been involved. While they still preferred Trinidad, they selected the Bay of Pigs as the best alternative, without informing either the president or secretary of defense of their continuing preference for Trinidad.[33]

The president and the White House staff felt that they had indeed learned some hard lessons and, according to Schlesinger the JCS learned also: "The Chiefs had their own way of reacting to the Cuban fiasco. It soon began to look to the White House as if they were taking care to build a record which would permit them to say that, whatever the President did, he acted against their advice."[34] When the question of intervention in Laos came up later, Schlesinger held the opinion that the Joint Chiefs, chastened by the Bay of Pigs, declined to guarantee the success of the military operations.[35]

Thus, if understanding, mutual trust, and respect are essential to achieve the proper relationship between a president and his military advisers, the JCS as an institution was now defunct for all intents and purposes. Under such circumstances the Chiefs could hardly perform their proper advisory role.

After making recommendations which led to the Bay of Pigs fiasco, the same set of advisers later recommended intervention in Laos. Not surprisingly, the president was skeptical of the experts, their analyses, and their recommendations. "Thank God the Bay of Pigs happened when it did," the president reportedly told Sorensen, "Otherwise we'd be in Laos by now and that would be a hundred times worse."[36]

Obviously the president of the United States cannot carry out his duties as commander-in-chief without professional military advice. President Kennedy recognized this. Having dismissed the advice of the JCS as unreliable, the president felt it necessary to search elsewhere for military counsel.

The president had long been an admirer of General Maxwell D. Taylor. Taylor's credentials were impeccable. He had a fine combat record. He was urbane, sophisticated, skilled in languages, and was regarded by many as an intellectual.

Under President Eisenhower, General Taylor was unhappy with the army's diminished role in the framework of the massive retaliation doctrine and hence he retired as army chief of staff to write a book, *The Uncertain Trumpet,* which expounded the virtues of flexible response. Kennedy had been impressed by Taylor's thinking and even before the Bay of Pigs he brought Taylor to the White House as his personal military adviser.[37]

This solution was only partially satisfactory because the president felt that he could effect the changes he wanted in the defense establishment faster if his own man was the chairman of the JCS. Further, General Taylor had good relations with the Congress. Clearly, bringing General Taylor out of retirement, although unprecedented, would satisfy both the Congress and the chief executive.

In January 1961, Khrushchev delivered a speech which made a significant impression upon President Kennedy. In an eight-hour oration, Khrushchev outlined three kinds of conflict between East and West: nuclear wars, conventional wars, and wars of national liberation. Dismissing nuclear war as too dangerous and the second type as possibly leading to nuclear war, he said that he saw wars of national liberation as an acceptable means of pursuing world communism. Kennedy immediately began to assess the capability of the United States to counter this type of warfare.

Following the president's request, Walt Rostow reported that the army's counterguerrilla training at Fort Bragg involved less than a thousand men in the Special Forces unit. Kennedy felt the instruction manuals were meager, and he directed the army to read Mao Tse-tung and Che Guevara.[38] He went on to examine the available training literature and the field equipment available to the army for counterguerrilla operations and decided that a major effort should be made to increase the army's capability in this area.[39]

The president called in the army chief of staff, General George H. Decker, and told him to expand the Special Forces and to change their mission from one of training to foster insurgencies behind enemy lines to one of putting down insurgencies within countries whose governments were friendly to the United States. Kennedy was convinced that counterinsurgency was the mirror image of insurgency, and since the Special Forces knew how to be insurgents by simply applying their expertise upside down and backwards, they should be best suited to lead the way to counterinsurgency.

There were those in the army who were reluctant to see the mission and capabilities of Special Forces altered. They preferred to see the army *in general* develop a counterinsurgency capability, leaving the Special Forces to practice its arcane skills unmolested. This faction felt that an expansion of the Special Forces on the scale proposed by the president would soon degrade its proficiency —a fact which special headgear (like the Green Beret) would be unable to mask.

Some in the army questioned the entire idea of counterinsurgency. Did the United States, the greatest revolutionary country in the world, really wish to line up on the side of the status quo and be classed by the Third World as the supporter of colonialism and imperialism?[40]

Nevertheless, if the commander-in-chief felt he needed a counterinsurgency capability to support national policy, the army would provide it. General Decker, in order to give the president's idea emphasis, appointed a rising general officer to oversee the expansion of the Special Forces.

General Decker was delighted with President Kennedy's interest in the army and the president's desire to increase the strength and capabilities of the Special Forces, but when the end of General Decker's first two-year tour as the army chief of staff came on 30 September 1962, General Decker made known his wish to retire. He was sixty years old, had served for thirty-eight years, and his office was weighing upon the general and his family. General Decker's desires were accepted by the president who was, at the time, opposing pending legislation which would have established the terms of the Chiefs at four years.[41]

On 30 September 1962 General Decker retired. On that same day General Lemnitzer turned over the chairmanship of the JCS to General Taylor and departed for Europe and NATO.

Now the president's own man was the chairman of the JCS. Of the Chiefs inherited from Eisenhower, only Kennedy's favorite, General Shoup, the commandant of the Marine Corps, remained.[42] With the Eisenhower Chiefs gone, President Kennedy now had his own team of military advisers.

General Curtis E. LeMay became the USAF chief of staff in June 1961. Admiral George W. Anderson, Jr., took over as chief of naval operations in August 1961. Although neither of these officers was inherited from Eisenhower nor were they on the JCS during the Bay of Pigs, both of them were soon to run into trouble with Secretary McNamara.

With a slate of officers appointed by the incumbent president, the relationship between the commander-in-chief and his principal military advisers would, hopefully, approach more closely the model prescribed by *Sound Military Decision*. Unfortunately, the events of the Cuban missile crisis did little, if anything, to improve the stature of the JCS.

The literature about the Cuban missile crisis is rich, for as President Kennedy later said, "Success has many fathers. . . ."[43] But even with the euphoria that one finds in this literature, the Joint Chiefs do not come out unscathed.

Early in his administration, President Kennedy admonished the JCS to ". . . base their advice not on narrow military considerations alone but on broad-gauged political and economic factors as well."[44] While our model recognizes the relationship between policy aims and military strategy, it does not license the military to attempt to determine national policy. Consequently, if the president were to ask the JCS about the propriety of the United States using force to accomplish its aims in Cuba, it would be improper for the military to answer.

Given the parameters of the model, the only question the military chiefs could legitimately respond to would be: What military means does the United States have to terminate the missile threat? What military courses of action does the United States have? Which course of action will have the greatest chance of success? What will each course of action cost in terms of lives and equipment? What military steps can be taken if the Russians intervene?

Perhaps the president's dictum to offer "broad-gauged" advice should not have been taken literally by the JCS. At the Bay of Pigs the JCS were condemned for not looking hard enough at, or not being vocal enough about, the pitfalls in the CIA plan, and the JCS were criticized after the Cuban missile crisis for not considering the implications of their recommendations.

It is interesting to note the impressions made by the Joint Chiefs on those who have written "inside" stories about what took place during the high-level deliberations. First, the president's brother Robert recalls:

> [The president] . . . was distressed with the [military] representatives with whom he met, with the notable exception of General Taylor, seemed to give so little considerations to the implications of steps they suggested . . . . President Kennedy was disturbed by this inability to look beyond the limited military field. When we talked about this later, he said we had to remember that they were trained to fight and to wage war—that was their life . . . . It was for these reasons, and many more, that President Kennedy regarded Secretary McNamara as the most valuable public servant in his Administration . . . .[45]

Schlesinger quotes the president as saying "an invasion would have been a mistake—a wrong use of our power. But the military are mad. They wanted to do this. It's lucky for us that we have McNamara over there."[46] Sorensen recounts a conversation with the president on 19 October 1962 as follows: "The President called me in, a bit disgusted. He had just met with the Joint Chiefs, who preferred an air strike or invasion . . . ."[47]

Historians will know someday whether or not it was correct to guarantee Cuba against invasion as the *quid pro quo* for the removal of the missiles.[48] The possible existence of a Soviet missile submarine base at Cienfuegos in 1970 argues against the president's 1962 decision. Would an invasion have led to a nuclear exchange? Doubtful, but, in all probability, it will never be known.

None of those who were there and who have written about the high-level conferences seemed disappointed with the performance of General Taylor, who had just assumed the chairmanship of the Joint Chiefs. Neither Robert Kennedy, Schlesinger, nor Sorensen reveal what General Taylor had to say, but, whatever it was, it satisfied the president. Most dramatic events must have villains as well as heroes. The press took Ambassador Stevenson to task for some of his conciliatory recommendations, but Robert Kennedy and Sorensen defended him. In a neat balance, the Joint Chiefs, except the chairman, were criticized for being too belligerent.

The Chiefs were praised for the manner in which the quarantine was conducted and the rapid response of all ground and air forces. Ironically, it was during the conduct of the naval blockade by Admiral Anderson that he had an encounter with Secretary McNamara which was, to some degree at least, to lead to Anderson's premature retirement.

When Admiral George W. Anderson joined the JCS on 1 August 1961, he was the "new boy." Generals Lemnitzer, Decker, White, and Shoup had been on board for some time, with General LeMay coming to the JCS at the end of June 1961. Capable, energetic, and outspoken, he developed a number of concerns which he wanted to discuss with McNamara and the JCS in executive session. The older members of the JCS had been having their problems with McNamara for some time. They were quite content to let the newcomer "bell the cat." Clearing these subjects with the other Chiefs, as it was protocol to do, he was encouraged by them to speak out.

Admiral Anderson made an issue of three individuals on the staff of the secretary of defense who were apparently hostile to the uniformed services either in approach or attitude, or evidenced a lack of understanding. One of these civilians had boasted that he could make or break any general or flag officer in the Pentagon. To Secretary McNamara's astonishment, Admiral Anderson asked him if this was so. Turning to one of his advisers, McNamara asked if such a thing could be true. To which the adviser is reported to have said, "No, he's too smart to be caught saying anything like that."

Admiral Anderson found it difficult to disguise his lack of enthusiasm for "whiz kids" and other nonprofessional military advisers in the Pentagon, and his willingness to bring up the subject of civilian officials allegedly throwing their weight around served notice on the fast-growing office of the secretary of defense that Admiral Anderson would bear watching.

As time went on it became clear that the basic problem between the secretary and the chief of naval operations was a personality clash. They were both able and strong-willed men. Neither was intimidated by the other. Admiral Anderson did not hesitate to dissent when he felt it proper. McNamara was Admiral Anderson's superior, and if the president had to choose between the two of them there could be little doubt as to which of them would have to seek other employment.

Admiral Anderson lasted two years, and his experience in the Cuban crisis of 1962 was perhaps the outstanding illustration of the low regard in which the service chiefs were held. First there was an incident on October 6. The defense officials decided they wanted to send a squadron of navy [carrier] fighters from Oceana, Virginia to Key West, Florida, and to put the squadron temporarily under air force control. Deputy Defense Secretary Gilpatrick, without going through channels, ignored the chief of naval operations, and called directly to Commander-in-Chief, Atlantic, Admiral Robert L. Dennison at Norfolk, Virginia, to give him the order.

As the crisis grew worse, the United States undertook a naval quarantine of Cuba. Secretary McNamara began spending time in the navy's Flag Plot, or operations center. This room, under Marine guard, contains visual materials locating the position of every ship. It also has communications links with ship commanders. McNamara insisted upon making decisions on the spot. He wanted to call ship commanders directly on the voice-scrambling, single-side-band radios. Admiral Anderson tried to dissuade the civilian official. The navy uses formal, stylized voice communications with coded names going through the chain of command. McNamara was inclined to ignore or belittle those techniques. He pointed to a symbol for one ship at sea and demanded of Admiral Anderson, "What's that ship doing there?" The chief of naval operations replied, "I don't know, but I have faith in my officers."[49]

In fact, Admiral Anderson did know what the ship was doing in that location. The ship, a United States destroyer, was sitting on top of a Russian submarine which had been detected by a highly classified means of detection. Present with Secretary McNamara were some of his civilian staff and with Admiral Anderson some of his own officers who were not cleared for this particular piece of highly sensitive information. Later, the CNO was able to get McNamara aside and explain the situation. This calmed the secretary, but as McNamara and his entourage departed the Flag Plot, Admiral Anderson said jokingly, "Don't worry Mr. Secretary, we know what we are doing down here." Apparently, McNamara took no offense at the remark at the time but later chose to conclude that it meant that the CNO did not need any civilian help and had little time to answer questions—even from the secretary of defense.

The final break took place when Admiral Anderson refused to endorse the TFX project after McNamara insisted that he support the all-service fighter plane.[50] Anderson may have been right, but he had crossed the secretary too often. As Sorensen related:

> Anderson had overstepped the bounds of dissent with Kennedy and McNamara on more than one issue, and the meaning of his departure was not lost on his fellow brass; but his many backers in the Congress were unable to make out a case of martyrdom when Kennedy put his considerable talents to use by naming him Ambassador to Portugal.[51]

Rocky as the relationship between Admiral Anderson and Secretary McNamara was, there is no evidence that Admiral Anderson and President Kennedy were ever at odds. Their relationship was always cordial and mutually respectful. Anderson never criticized President Kennedy and loyally carried out his wishes. The president and Admiral Anderson liked each other, but both were caught in a situation where the admiral had to do what he thought was right for his service and for the armed forces while the president had to back up his civilian secretary. And so Admiral Anderson became the second member of the JCS to retire after only one term. Later, President Kennedy would indicate his displeasure with General LeMay by extending him for only one year after his first two-year term instead of the normal two years.[52] At the time of President Kennedy's assassination, only General Shoup of the original group of Chiefs remained as a member of the JCS.

II

When Lyndon Johnson became the thirty-sixth president of the United States, his mental baggage included preconceptions of his own about the military. During the Johnson administration the JCS would be kept busy training and equipping troops and transporting them to Southeast Asia, but they would not be called upon to act as the president's principal military advisers. They would be called upon to carry out military and political decisions reached in the White House between the president and a small group of trusted civilian advisers.

Hugh Sidey, who covered the White House for *Time-Life,* provides insight into Johnson's ideas about military men in general in his book, *A Very Personal Presidency.* It is worth quoting at some length:

His deep suspicions of the military went back to his first days in the Congress . . . he was given a seat on Carl Vinson's powerful Naval Affairs Committee. There he watched the high brass parade, and he was disturbed. He found that too many military men grew arrogant behind the ribbons they wore on their chests. He found them contemptuous of new ideas, mean and thoughtless in dealing with those below them. He detected an alarming amount of sheer stupidity which was self-perpetuating because of the academy caste system. He found no companionship with military men. . . . In fact, the general level of competence which Johnson found among the admirals who came before the Naval Affairs Committee convinced him that the nation could not put its complete trust in the military in such hazardous times. How America met the threat had to be planned in detail, in Johnson's view, by the politicians.

This lack of confidence in the officer corps never really left Johnson. . . . he felt that the military men almost always were too narrow in their appraisals of a given problem, often ignoring the political implications in the United States or the reaction abroad. . . . Johnson could be merciless when he told about the generals. None got harsher treatment than the old bomber pilot Curt LeMay, chief of the Air Force under Kennedy and Johnson.

LeMay was credited with having offered the advice for the air war in North Vietnam. "We ought to bomb them back into the stone age." ... Johnson subscribed heartily to an axiom that Kennedy propounded before his death. One night in his office with friends, JFK said, "Once you decide to send the bombers, you want men like LeMay flying them. But you can't let them decide if they should go or not."[53]

Johnson's own military experience was limited to one tour as a lieutenant commander in the navy during World War II. This tour lasted only one month and five days.[54]

As President Johnson assumed office, he inherited a foreign policy formulating structure modified to meet the needs and desires of a predecessor keenly interested in foreign affairs and impatient with bureaucracy. President Kennedy had virtually scrapped the National Security Council. Instead of relying on this body, he relied on small groups of flexible composition for policy formulation and its execution.[55]

The Joint Chiefs of Staff had similarly been written off by President Kennedy. They had also been eclipsed by the rising power of Secretary McNamara. President Kennedy deliberately made the national policy structure loose and flexible, so it would be more suited to his style and interests. It was a Kennedy creation, designed for President Kennedy. However, it was a meager legacy for a new president, who was passionately interested in domestic affairs and who had little interest in foreign and military affairs.

Deliberations on Vietnam policy and the quality of President Johnson's decisions from the fall of 1964 onwards, showed itself in the structural weakness of the National Security Council and in inadequate attention to longer-range policy planning. The principal results were fragmented debate, loose coordination, and an excessive concentration on problems of the moment.[56]

Early in his administration, Johnson could have conceivably changed United States policy in Vietnam. His administration was new, and in Vietnam President Diem and his brother Ngo Dinh Nhu were dead.[57] During the next eighteen months, ten other South Vietnamese governments were to rise and fall.

It was a time of great instability. Many speculate as to what President Kennedy would have done about Vietnam had he lived. Some think that he would have replaced Rusk and Rostow.[58] But given Johnson's lack of expertise in foreign affairs, he chose to keep Rusk and Rostow, with Rostow eventually replacing Mc-

George Bundy in 1966 as the president's national security affairs adviser. Given the same set of advisers and his own uncertainty, there was not much chance that Johnson would set a different course in Vietnam. "Understandably, President Johnson's opening policy theme was 'Let us continue'; and just as he inherited the Kennedy Policies, so also the presidential elections still loomed ahead. Both considerations made it politically impossible for any change of course in Vietnam."[59]

As time went on Vietnam began to occupy more and more of the president's time. The Tuesday lunch was devised as a means of dealing with this problem. Each week the president and his senior advisers would gather in the president's dining room on the second floor of the White House to discuss Vietnam and related topics.[60]

Every war president has had his own way of conducting his war. Roosevelt dealt directly with General Marshall and the other Joint Chiefs and through his own military chief of staff, Admiral Leahy. Truman worked through the Joint Chiefs. When his field commander, MacArthur, started making political policy, Truman, backed up by the JCS, relieved MacArthur. Kennedy had little use for the JCS, but did keep General Maxwell D. Taylor close at hand. Significantly, no military man was regularly included at first in the Tuesday lunch, although major national security deliberations were held. Topics also included some relatively minor and purely military questions, such as scrambled eggs served to the men in the field. When special questions came up, the president would ask military men to dine.

Hugh Sidey concluded that Johnson felt that the consultative process was thorough enough and that all the military thoughts worthy of attention were brought to the Tuesday luncheon by McNamara, who was the man designated to speak for the entire defense establishment. Of course, the McNamara channel depended on the service chiefs' rapport with the secretary. There were other ways the military men could make their voices heard. For example, they could speak out at the National Security Council meetings, but that body had ceased to formulate policy and instead was simply a policy ratifying body. It is true the military men could seek audiences with the president whenever they wanted. However, this direct-channel approach meant putting McNamara on report. Retaliation could be severe, ranging from premature retirement to loss of funds for a service project or activity as demonstrated in Admiral Anderson's case.

But it was only under pressure from Congress in general and

Senator Stennis in particular that Johnson brought General Earle Wheeler, chairman of the JCS, to the White House more regularly. However, this step was apparently intended to appease the critics, rather than to alter the select group, with whom Johnson made his decisions.[61]

Professor Henry F. Graff, who was brought to the White House from time to time to work on a history of Johnson's handling of the Vietnam War, asked Bill Moyers about the advice received by the president: " 'President Johnson,' said Moyers, 'relies less on military advice than any President since Wilson.' (I understood 'military advice' to mean 'advice from the military.')"[62]

President Kennedy's sad experience at the Bay of Pigs, which was the result of vacillation and insufficient coordination fostered by his own informal method of conducting business, brought about the installation of a situation room in the White House itself from which the president could personally command and control the armed forces.[63] It was used during the Cuban missile crisis, and when President Johnson came to the White House that command and control of the war in Vietnam was exercised daily from 1600 Pennsylvania Avenue.[64]

To the dismay of the military, the president exercised extremely detailed control over the bombing of North Vietnam, including not only the target selection and the ordnance to be used, but also the execution of the strikes. Johnson and his civilian advisers conceived and pursued a strategy of "gradualism" in applying airpower, rather than accepting the JCS proposal that the bombing commence with the destruction of MIG airfields and air defense facilities in North Vietnam. The president was supported in his view by both McNamara and Taylor who ". . . wanted to test their theory of flexible response," which involved not a heavy bombardment but a series of attacks north of the demilitarized zone. Their theory was that if you twist someone's arm he can "cry uncle," but if you go for his neck from the beginning he does not get the chance.[65]

In essence, the commander-in-chief borrowed the means to make the strikes from the military but did not borrow or include the doctrine and tactics necessary to make their employment effective.

At the start of the bombing campaign in 1965, the JCS recommended destroying some ninety-four key military targets in the first two or three weeks. This campaign would maximize to the full the shock effect of airpower. Hanson Baldwin observes,

North Vietnam's air defenses then were weak; her gasoline

and petroleum storage, electric power, transportation, and other vital targets were concentrated and vulnerable; and the cumulative effect of destroying all these targets rapidly would, at the very least, have materially impeded Hanoi's aid to the Vietcong and might have shaken the North Vietnamese hierarchy.[66]

Undoubtedly the bombing as conducted by President Johnson made life more difficult for the North Vietnamese,[67] but it had little effect on the infiltration of men and supplies into South Vietnam.[68] The long and drawnout bombing episode provoked criticism of the United States both at home and abroad and was to prove to be a stumbling block rather than an inducement to negotiations.

The frustrations of the military became known to the Congress, who tried to intercede with the president. One senator telephoned the president during a bombing pause to offer some pointed advice.

"Mr. President," said the caller, "you've got to win this thing now. You've got to go for the jugular. I urge you to turn this war over to your military commanders. They are the men who know how to wage war, and they will win it."

"Not as long as I am President," Johnson replied. "As long as I sit here, the control will stay with the Commander-in-Chief."

The Senator persisted: "We've got to win it .... That's why Roosevelt and Truman were so great. They let their military leaders do the job."

"I was around in those days," Johnson said. "There were not many decisions made that Roosevelt did not know about. And Harry Truman watched everything closely. ... I'm not going to let the hounds loose."[69]

Paradoxically, while the president exercised minute control over the bombing, he was generally content to allow his commander in the field, General William C. Westmoreland and later General Creighton Abrams, to conduct operations in South Vietnam without interference.[70] Unfortunately Johnson's strategy of "gradualism" was not compatible with the strategy of "attrition" being pursued by the United States Saigon command.

Returning to the model relationship, *Sound Military Decision* cautions:

While military strategy may determine whether the aims of policy are possible of attainment, policy may, beforehand, determine largely the success or failure of military strategy. It behooves policy to ensure not only that military strategy pursue appropriate aims, but that the work of strategy be allotted adequate means and *be undertaken under the most favorable conditions.*[71] (Emphasis added.)

Apparently, Johnson had great admiration for his top commanders in Vietnam.[72] He was willing to provide them with almost anything that they wanted in terms of troops, material, and funds.[73] But he was not willing, despite repeated pleas by the JCS, to call up the reserves whose combat support and combat service support units were badly needed. As a result, the support structure for the war came "out of the hide" of the active forces. The mobilization of the reserves might have gotten the nation involved in the war and perhaps behind the war effort, but Johnson's rule was "guns and butter." Thus the war was fought by a small professional cadre of officers and noncommissioned officers leading a force of conscripts who, as time went on, became increasingly aware of the inequity of the nation's being involved in a major war while it was business as usual on Main Street. Johnson was willing to provide free mail service, ice cream, post exchanges—anything to make life in Southeast Asia more bearable—but he did not provide what was really needed—a war policy which would permit his commander to achieve the national aims.

Robert S. McNamara served longer as secretary of defense than did any of his seven predecessors. During his tenure, the military power of the United States rose to its highest point since World War II, while the influence of the Joint Chiefs of Staff sank to an all-time low. Prior to his military stint during World War II, McNamara spent most of his adult life in school either as a teacher or a student. After World War II he went to the Ford Motor Company and in fourteen years worked his way up to the presidency.[74]

Although McNamara's energy, dedication, and methods were impressive enough to result in his selection as the first non-Ford-family president in the history of the company, his reliance on numbers and measures sometimes led him astray. The demise of the Edsel is a case in point. One executive insisted, "It was killed not because of its repulsive front grill or because we were slow building a strong sales team, but because McNamara's charts showed there was no more market for a medium priced car." General Motors promptly disproved that conclusion. "Those charts," the executive dryly noted, "give you funny answers sometimes."[75]

While Mr. McNamara was working his way to the top of the Ford Motor Company, a number of changes were being made in the Pentagon which would someday allow Mr. McNamara to dominate the JCS just as he had his staff at the Ford Motor Company.

Paradoxically, the high-water mark of JCS influence occurred during World War II when the JCS did not officially exist. President Roosevelt reposed such trust and confidence in the Chiefs that "... he refused to issue a formal definition of JCS duties and functions, arguing that a written charter might hamper the Joint Chiefs of Staff in extending their activities as necessary to meet the requirements of the war."[76]

Beginning with the National Security Act of 1947, the role of the JCS began to be prescribed and circumscribed. As the threat posed by the expansionist policies of the Soviet Union grew, there were serious and honest disagreements among the armed services over the best method of containing the threat. This controversy was naturally reflected in the JCS as the Chiefs attempted to define the best military strategy. Fairly or unfairly, these deep concerns earned a bad image for the JCS, and it was said around Washington that "... The Congress debates, the Supreme Court deliberates, but the Joint Chiefs bicker." In an effort to minimize the effect of this bickering on defense policy, the Congress and the executive took a number of actions which greatly increased the authority and control of the secretary of defense over the service components.

In 1953 the JCS were taken out of the chain of command so that it ran from the president to the secretary of defense through the civilian service secretaries to the commanders in the field. In 1958 the service secretaries were taken out of the chain of command, and the JCS were given operational *responsibility* for the unified and specified commands but were specifically forbidden any executive *authority*. The scope of the chairman's duties was increased, thus giving him more influence over his fellow members, but at the same time a formal restraint was placed on easy communication between the JCS and the Congress. Free communication with the president was, of course, inhibited by the chain of command.[77]

By 1960 the stage was set for Robert McNamara. Seizing the initiative and armed with the requisite legal authority and the unqualified backing of President Kennedy, Secretary McNamara began to bring all activities in the defense department under his own control. Central to this effort was Mr. McNamara's conviction that, "... the direction of the Department of Defense demands not only a strong, responsible civilian control, but a Secretary's role that consists of active, imaginative and decisive leadership of the establishment at large, and not the passive practice of simply refereeing the disputes of traditional and partisan factions."[78]

The first step was to change the rules by which decisions about military strategy and procurement were made. To do this McNamara brought into his office a staff of systems analysts. McNamara and his staff felt that the generals and admirals relied too much on their judgment and experience as a basis for decisions. The generals and admirals felt that some things just could not be quantified and had to be decided on the basis of judgment and experience. Over the McNamara years the battle centered on just where this fine line lay.

The outcome of this struggle was vital to the future roles the generals and admirals were to play. For the systems analysts the contest was not as crucial. Systems analysis had proven itself to be a useful management tool, and its future was assured. The future was not so certain for senior military officers because, if almost everything could be quantified and rationalized mathematically, then generals and admirals were simply anachronisms in every regard except for holding command in the field. If intuitive judgment and professional experience were to be relegated to a minor role in the decisionmaking process, then general and flag officers were not needed anymore at the highest levels of the Defense Establishment because it is primarily for their judgment and experience that they hold positions in the defense staff.

Traumatic as the McNamara experience was, it was certainly not without benefit to the military. ". . . Probably McNamara's most significant contribution to military strength," said one veteran, was that "he forced the Services to get at the heart of their own basic logic on why they want things."[79]

It took the military services a while to adapt to the new rules in the Pentagon, and a number of new faces were brought in to cope with McNamara's "whiz kids." It was not long before each military service formed its own staff of systems analysts who were just as knowledgeable and bright as the ones from the office of the secretary of defense (OSD). The benefit of subjecting service originated plans and proposals to systems analysis had become obvious. At the same time the services learned that, by using certain assumptions, one could make the answer come out most any way that was desired.[80] The manipulation of these assumptions became, in fact, the basis for the fundamental disagreement between OSD and the services. Reports of this practice on the part of OSD began to circulate, and McNamara's honeymoon with the ever-watchful Congress began to end. Nowhere was this and the struggle for existence by the generals and admirals more clearly demonstrated than in the controversy over the TFX.

Both the navy and the air force were badly in need of a new attack aircraft, a new air-superiority aircraft, a new interceptor, and new reconnaissance aircraft. It seemed logical to McNamara that one airplane could be built to do all or most of these missions and that one airplane could be made suitable for use by both services. However, there were three obstacles to prevent the accomplishment of this worthy goal. First, the navy and the air force operated from entirely different environments. The navy airplane would have to be launched by catapult from the deck of an aircraft carrier and recovered by slamming onto the carrier's deck and catching its tailhook on a wire. The air force aircraft would have to operate from the ground and be subjected to dust and debris not found at sea. Second, the state of the art was not such to permit the combination of all the desired capabilities into one airframe that anyone could maintain. Third, and perhaps most serious, no secretary of defense had ever before told the services that they must combine everything into one airplane, told them how it was to be used, told them that they must all use the same aircraft, and told them just which aircraft manufacturer was going to produce it.

Before it was all over, the TFX issue became complicated by charges of intellectual corruption on the part of the analysts in OSD as well as political manipulation of the procedure whereby the contract was awarded to General Dynamics over Boeing. In the final analysis, however, the military view was vindicated when it turned out that the TFX could not do what OSD and General Dynamics said that it would do and when it cost more than twice what OSD said that it would.[81] The navy found that the TFX (or F-111 as it came to be called) was too heavy to land on carrier decks. The Air Force Tactical Air Command found that the F-111's performance was no match for what was known about Russian fighters already in mass production. Ironically, it was the Air Force Strategic Air Command that was made to take the F-111 as the FB-111 and put it in the inventory for a role not originally envisioned by McNamara—as a low-level nuclear bomber.[82]

If the TFX issue was a microcosm of the struggle for supremacy in the Pentagon, then its failure was an example of the consequences of ignoring the advice of the professional military. There was little solace in the TFX episode for anyone, and if it was a victory for the JCS it was clearly Pyrrhic.

McNamara and the JCS would continue to struggle, but in almost every case the secretary would be the winner as long as he enjoyed the strong backing of the president. "Never before had a Defense Secretary enjoyed such rapport with and unqualified backing from the White House. 'I couldn't accomplish anything over here without Presidential support,' he had once said. 'It is absolutely fundamental. I wouldn't and couldn't stay here one minute without it.' "[83]

When White House aides pointed the finger at the JCS after the Bay of Pigs, McNamara waited a week before he bothered to issue a halfhearted rebuttal. When General Lemnitzer pointed out that OSD had not given the JCS time to consider McNamara's directive on how developments in space would be pursued, he was ignored.[84] When McNamara and Admiral Anderson clashed, Anderson was sent to Portugal.

Despite difficulties, disagreements, and almost open warfare between the OSD staff and the JCS and service staffs, Mr. McNamara continued to meet with the JCS at almost every Monday afternoon meeting. As time went on, the discussions became less and the silences grew longer until, toward the end of McNamara's reign, Mr. McNamara and the Chiefs just sat around the table and looked at each other across a silent chasm that had grown too wide for any of them to bridge.

Mr. McNamara was and is a sincere and dedicated patriot. Much of what he did for the defense establishment was beneficial, but his abrupt managerial methods, his lack of understanding of the values prized so highly by his military subordinates, and his chilling personality prevented him from accomplishing all that he could have, and thus many of his changes failed to outlive his own tenure.

The lack of "understanding between the civil representatives of the State and the leaders of the Armed Forces" was manifestly evident from 1961 to 1968. Presidents Kennedy and Johnson, though different in many ways, shared a certain distrust of the views offered by the JCS. The McNamara secretaryship challenged the military on their home ground and placed them on the defensive.

Unfortunately this serious internal conflict took place at a time when decisions were made that pitted the might and prestige of the United States in a new and, in many ways, frustrating environment. While the intentions of the men involved were clearly the best, the result of the adversarial relationship which developed between the civilian and military leaderships of this country (particularly when viewed in light of the Vietnam experience) has had a most grievous effect on national security.

If genuine civil control over the military is the ideal, as most observers suggest, then the president and the Congress not only are obliged to define the role of the military, but also to protect the role of the military. The military can defend the nation, but it may not be able to defend itself.

The military will most likely play whatever role is allotted to it by civil authority regardless of how it sees its own role; however, when invited to enter the political arena, it becomes difficult for senior military officers to resist the siren call to become "soldier-statesmen."

There is little in the background of the average American president to prepare him for the awesome task of becoming the nation's grand strategist. The wise president seeks the counsel of his military leaders. He is not compelled to accept their advice, but it would seem that wisdom would dictate that he at least listen, and, further, wisdom would dictate that he insist that the military observe the precepts of their profession and offer "purely" military advice.

The civil-military environment in which the JCS operated during the Kennedy-Johnson era was marked by degrees of prejudice, pride, arrogance, and dillettantism. The attitudes and actions of both Presidents Kennedy and Johnson were affected by their prejudices regarding the military. The frictions that grew between Secretary McNamara and the Joint Chiefs found their roots in the seedbed of McNamara's enormous pride and intellectual arrogance. Dilettantism was practiced by all three men.

In the end it is the president and the Congress who should determine the role of force in each situation, but the military can best define the capability of that force to achieve the given policy objective. If it is the duty of the civil authorities not to misapply military power, then it is the duty of the military not to overstate the capabilities of its forces and to make it abundantly clear in a given situation just what the forces can and cannot be expected to accomplish.

Unfortunately, the Kennedy and Johnson administrations saw neither the need for, nor the virtue of independent, *professional* military advice on policy matters which were fundamentally military in nature.

There are exceptions to all rules, and there are times when it is better to operate outside the proven and traditional parameters. However, improvisation over the long term will eventually exact its price, and the price in the 1960s might well be called—Vietnam.

NOTES

Based on an article published in the *Naval War College Review,* April 1972.

1. JCS Publication Number Four, 1 July 1969.

2. Ibid.

3. U.S. Naval War College, *Sound Military Decision* (Newport: 1942), p. 9.

4. Theodore C. Sorensen, *Kennedy* (New York: Harper & Row, 1965), p. 18.

5. Ibid.

6. Arthur M. Schlesinger, Jr., *A Thousand Days* (Boston: Houghton Mifflin Co., 1965), p. 311.

7. Sorensen, *Kennedy,* pp. 603-4.

8. Schlesinger, *A Thousand Days,* p. 295.

9. President Eisenhower, according to a report in the *New York Times* of 12 January 1961, was satisfied with the performance of the JCS.

10. Sorensen, *Kennedy,* p. 608.

11. Schlesinger, *A Thousand Days,* p. 291.

12. In this examination a degree of reliance is placed on Mr. Schlesinger's and Mr. Sorensen's accounts as they shed some light upon President Kennedy's thoughts about the JCS; however, it should be kept in mind that Mr. Sorensen, and especially Mr. Schlesinger, are not generally regarded as objective reporters of events concerning President Kennedy and his administration.

13. Mario Lazo, *Dagger in the Heart* (New York: Funk & Wagnalls, 1968), p. 238.

14. Ibid., p. 238-39.

15. Ibid.

16. Ibid., p. 243.

17. Schlesinger's hearing may have been better than Sorensen's. In any event, the actual landing site was later changed to the Bay of Pigs, which was evidently the third choice of the JCS. It should be remembered that there was no uprising nor was any direct United States military support provided. (Sorensen, *Kennedy,* p. 305.)

18. Schlesinger, *A Thousand Days,* p. 247.

19. Ibid.

20. Schlesinger, *A Thousand Days,* p. 250.

21. In February 1971, almost ten years after the Bay of Pigs, the author, in a discussion with General Lemnitzer, tried to open the subject but was courteously refused any information other than the fact that the members of the JCS had great respect for President Kennedy's courage and, in keeping with their oath of office, the chiefs had remained silent.

22. Ibid., p. 290.

23. Lazo, *Daggers,* p. 285.

24. Lyman B. Kirkpatrick. Jr., *The Real CIA* (New York: Macmillan, 1968), p. 201.

25. "Gore Would Oust the Joint Chiefs," *New York Times,* 20 May 1961, p. 1:5.

26. "Would Oust Lemnitzer," *New York Times,* 5 June 1961, p. 3:4.

27. "President Poses with Joint Chiefs," *New York Times,* 28 May 1961, p. 39:5.

28. "I Pay My Personal Tribute to the JCS," *New York Times,* 2 June 1961, p. 14:5.

29. The author's investigations reveal a most cordial and respectful relationship between the president and the JCS. Whether President Kennedy actually said or believed the things which Schlesinger and Sorensen say that he said about the Joint Chiefs is open to debate. Either way, the impact of such thoughts within the administration served to undermine the prestige and influence of the JCS.

30. Schlesinger, *A Thousand Days,* p. 295.

31. Ibid., p. 290.

32. Sorensen, *Kennedy,* p. 607.

33. Schlesinger's account differs in that he says that the JCS "added softly" that they still preferred Trinidad. (Sorensen, *Kennedy*, p. 305.)

34. Schlesinger, *A Thousand Days*, p. 338.

35. Ironically, a political failure in Cuba, which was an area of vital interest to the United States, would later serve to undermine the credibility of the JCS, which had consistently carried Indochina much farther down on its list of priorities than Cuba and which was generally opposed to going ashore in Asia. (Schlesinger, *A Thousand Days*, p. 337.)

36. Sorensen, *Kennedy*, p. 644.

37. Ibid., p. 607.

38. Schlesinger, *A Thousand Days*, p. 341.

39. Ibid.

40. William F. Long, Jr., "Counterinsurgency Revisited," *Naval War College Review*, November 1968.

41. Sorensen, *Kennedy*, p. 608.

42. Air Force General White retired on 30 June 1961 after serving two terms. Admiral Burke retired on 1 August 1961, having served three terms on the JCS. (Sorensen, *Kennedy*, p. 608.)

43. Schlesinger, *A Thousand Days*, p. 289.

44. Sorensen, *Kennedy*, p. 605.

45. Robert F. Kennedy, *Thirteen Days* (New York: Norton, 1969), pp. 119-120.

46. Schlesinger, *A Thousand Days*, p. 831.

47. Sorensen, *Kennedy*, p. 692.

48. It should be noted that no physical inspection was even made to insure that the missiles had actually been removed.

49. Jack Raymond, *Power at the Pentagon* (New York: Harper & Row, 1964), pp. 285-86.

50. The TFX is now the ill-fated F-111 fighter, which the navy could not use on carriers and which the air force found was better suited for use as a low-level SAC bomber.

51. Sorensen, *Kennedy*, p. 608.

52. Ibid.

53. Hugh Sidey, *A Very Personal Presidency* (New York: Atheneum, 1968), pp. 202-4.

54. Robert Sherrill, *The Accidental President* (New York: Grossman, 1967), p. 28.

55. Townsend Hoopes, *The Limits of Intervention* (New York: Van Rees Press, 1969), p. 4.

56. Ibid., p. 2.

57. President Diem and his brother were deposed largely as the result of an uncoordinated message which President Kennedy released because he thought that Rusk and McNamara concurred with it. The message let it be known in South Vietnam that United States aid would continue even if President Diem were removed from office. The deaths of Diem and his brother Ngo Dinh Nhu were not intended by the Vietnamese generals. They were killed by a South Vietnamese Army major who had a personal grudge against them. Henry Brandon, *Anatomy of Error* (Boston: Gambit, Inc., 1969), pp. 25-26.

58. Henry Brandon, *Anatomy of Error*, p. 28.

59. Ibid., p. 31.

60. Henry F. Graff, *The Tuesday Cabinet* (Englewood Cliffs, N.J.: Prentice-Hall, 1970), p. 3.

61. Sidey, *A Personal Presidency*, p. 204-6.

62. Graff, *Tuesday Cabinet*, p. 50.

63. Hoopes, *Limits of Intervention*, p. 5.

64. Alfred Steinberg, *Sam Johnson's Boy* (New York: Macmillan, 1968), pp. 747, 771.

65. Brandon, *Anatomy of Error*, p. 41.

66. Hanson W. Baldwin, from his introduction to Jack Broughton, *Thud Ridge* (New York: Lippincott, 1969), pp. 10-11.

67. Peter Weiss and Gunilla Palmstierna-Weiss, *"Limited Bombing" in Vietnam,* Bertrand Russell Peace Foundation, n.p., n.d., acquired by the Naval War College Library on 17 June 1970, pp. 17, 27.

68. Hoopes, *Limits of Intervention,* p. 87.

69. Sidey, *A Personal Presidency,* p. 201.

70. Hoopes, *Limits of Intervention,* p. 62.

71. *Sound Military Decision,* p. 9.

72. Sidey, *A Personal Presidency,* pp. 202-3.

73. Ibid., p. 82.

74. Carl W. Borklund, *Men of the Pentagon* (New York: Praeger, 1966), pp. 207-8.

75. Ibid., p. 209.

76. Joint Chiefs of Staff Publication Number Four, p. 1-1-1.

77. Title 10, United States Code, chap. 5.

78. Robert S. McNamara, *The Essence of Security* (New York: Harper & Row, 1968), p. x.

79. Borklund, *Men of the Pentagon,* p. 218.

80. Curtis E. LeMay, *America is in Danger* (New York: Funk & Wagnalls, 1968), p. 301.

81. LeMay, *America is in Danger,* p. 237.

82. Ibid., pp. 285, 291.

83. Borklund, *Men of the Pentagon,* p. 224.

84. Jack Raymond, *Power at the Pentagon* (New York: Harper & Row, 1964), p. 283.

United States Military Roles in a Period of Resource Scarcity

John M. Lee

Editor's Note: *Vice Admiral Lee retired in 1973 after thirty-eight years of active duty, during which time he commanded a number of ships and served in NATO and United States politico/military billets. His most recent position was Assistant Director of the Arms Control and Disarmament Agency.*

I

Over the next decades, while resource scarcity is developing, the military environment will change, and the changes are less predictable the farther ahead we try to look. A few trends applicable to United States military forces, however, seem firmly enough set to guide thinking: the relative military power of the United States is declining; the resources devoted to our defense establishment will produce declining force levels; more debatably, the utility of military combat operations is eroding.

The relative decline of American military power is most obvious, of course, in the changing strategic nuclear relationship with the Soviet Union. The prospective situation, whether arrived at by agreement or by competition, is either parity ("political sufficiency") or sufficiency. The first may be understood as some sort of equivalence between United States and Soviet strategic forces, perceived by allies and others as well as the two superpowers; the second, sufficiency, based on the target system rather than the opposing force, being probably, as now, an assured destruction capability so redundant and so hedged as to provide a substantial surplus for military and other "flexible" targeting. In either case, the result is powerful mutual deterrence and debatable political advantage; at most, for either side, a great change from the situation a generation ago and a marked numerical change in the last ten years.

In addition, in the nuclear area, there are the three existing smaller nuclear forces, and a solid possibility of further proliferation, recently emphasized by India's test. Countries with deliverable nuclear weapons (or other weapons of mass destruction), even if very few in number, can pose unprecedented threats to hostile powers, even to superpowers. For force planning purposes, the United States has arbitrarily set a deterrence standard which requires substantial retaliatory forces. But comparatively minuscule capabilities should deter even the most powerful opponent, provided the question at issue is less than unequivocally vital to the greater power. McGeorge Bundy, with exceptional crisis experience at the center of power, has estimated real deterrence levels in the following often cited terms: "In the world of real political leaders— whether here or in the Soviet Union—a decision that would bring even one hydrogen bomb on one city or one's own country would be recognized in advance as a catastrophic blunder; ten bombs on ten cities would be a disaster beyond history; and a hundred bombs on a hundred cities are unthinkable."[1] By any such criteria, a smaller nuclear power has a formidable "equalizer." Robert Heilbroner conceives of even offensive use by lesser powers. He visualizes major undeveloped nations using small nuclear capabilities "as an instrument of blackmail to force the developed world to transfer large amounts of wealth to the poverty stricken world."[2] Whether or not Heilbroner's scenario is persuasive, American, and indeed Soviet, nuclear power, however large, declines relatively as other powers obtain and develop on any scale deliverable nuclear weapons or other weapons of mass destruction.

More generally, the size of nuclear forces, within broad limits, may come to be seen progressively as less significant. Today it is widely believed that American failure to maintain strategic parity or equivalence relative to the Soviet strategic force—however meaningless in military terms—would cause marked political effects: our allies and others would think us weaker and thus be more vulnerable to Soviet influence; the Soviet Union and we ourselves would think us weaker, making them more adventurous and us less staunch. Over time, however, one may hope for a clearer appreciation of the comparative insensitivity of strategic force levels, particularly as the irrelevance of nuclear weapons to actual operations—save as an overarching control on confrontations of nuclear powers—continues to be demonstrated, for example in Korea, the Congo, Vietnam, Bangladesh, and the Middle East.

In the area of conventional forces, United States military power appears to decline comparatively. In the East-West balance, the Soviet Union is spending heavily on research and development, is steadily modernizing, and is producing naval and amphibious elements which, together with her existing airborne forces, give her an increasing capacity for long-range force projection, once a near monopoly of the United States. Also, the Soviet Union is less vulnerable than the West to resource shortages. At the same time, our allies' vulnerability to threats to oil supply has been demonstrated, their cohesion has been shaken, and the probable resulting economic disruptions can be expected to affect their defense budgets. In the North-South relationship, strong regional military power centers are emerging, with large capabilities in their geographic areas in relation not only to local powers but to the projection forces of major external powers.

Trying to match these trends by major United States force increases would collide with budgetary realities. In the post-Vietnam climate, facing large and urgent domestic demands, threatened by massive economic dislocations stemming from the resource problem and needing certain levels of financing for international purposes, it is scarcely conceivable that this country will undertake great increases in defense spending.

The 1975 defense department budget request is an indicator. In a year when the defense budget is fortuitously and powerfully supported, by a need for pump-priming at home and arms control bargaining chips abroad, a strong defense secretary has asked to approximate the real spending of ten to twelve years ago, and Congress, while apparently sympathetic, will surely do some pruning.

Such stable budgets (in constant dollars), or even moderate increases, by no means imply increases in our military posture. The exponential increase in the price of weapons systems continues. A number of programs, now in research and development, will be major drains if they go into procurement. We face block obsolescence in vehicles and aircraft, among other items procured during Vietnam. Pay, and operations and maintenance, are taking much of current budgets; proportionately we spend about half as much for procurement, research and development, and military construction as we did ten years ago. As these latter elements grow, at expected prices, fixed budgets mean force cuts, even when they are adjusted for inflation.

But even fixed budgets are unlikely over the coming years. Defense spending will be under enormous pressure; progressive reductions are the much more probable outcome. This would mean severe force cuts.

The third trend is the declining utility of military combat for achieving national purposes, what Stanley Hoffman calls "a decline in the positive productivity of military force."[3] In the nuclear stalemate, reinforced by strategic parity, it is accepted that central war between the United States and the Soviet Union would be suicidal, and that even lesser conflict between them would pose risks of escalation disproportionate to rational objectives. Louis Halle carries "extended deterrence" a step further: "Any great war, extended in space and time, even though not fought with nuclear arms to begin with, would be too likely to spread and to escalate into a nuclear war to be hazarded even by a Caligula."[4] Marginal cases, are of course, debatable, but in any event both the United States and the Soviet Union are subject to a powerful deterrent in the application of major power.

The use of limited force is also subject to new doubts. First, of course, is the escalation effect: limited operations can lead to major confrontations. Second is the question of legitimacy; using military force, especially against lesser powers, is increasingly challenged, and the reaction to it may be severe and lasting. The political and internal costs of limited operations can be very great, as the Vietnamese experience makes clear. Third, there is the matter of simple effectiveness. Vietnam, Algeria, the Pakistani in Bangladesh, the Portuguese in Africa, the Bay of Pigs: all suggest that the requirements for success in "small wars" are exacting, and not often encountered in practice. These requirements seem to include overwhelming force, a divided and less than dedicated opposition, and a situation that can be military isolated, say Czechoslovakia or the Dominican Republic. Many more hypothetical cases appear infeasible than feasible.

As a speculative point in this connection, it may be that the vulnerabilities of modern technology and the capabilities of modern weapons have sharply increased the power of small groups relative to classic military forces. We have lately observed a surge of international terrorism, air piracy, kidnapping, and so forth, all of which are most difficult to control. If the military task were to seize and operate major resource or industrial installations in a hostile environment, similar difficulties would multiply. Such installations—large, concentrated, interconnected—present many critical vulnerabilities, and the destructive capabilities of comparatively small forces have been greatly enhanced by current tools.

On this general question of the utility of military force, the oil embargo is a vivid case in point. In brief, the oil embargo was an action by a group of militarily insignificant countries to obtain both political and economic objectives against the central interests of a large number of powerful states. Fifty years ago, perhaps even up to the Suez operation of 1956, a military reaction would have been an obvious measure. Today, while earnest staff officers have doubtlessly worked late into the night on the relevant mechanics, military intervention has not surfaced as a serious alternative. Why? Presumably because the feasibility and gains are doubtful at best, while the costs and risks are all too visible and entirely disproportionate.

In short, large operations are deterred and small wars are usually unpromising. This is not to say that military potential is insignificant; military capabilities clearly have a great political weight. Still, political weight rests, in the end, on a general conviction of ultimate usability. If and as that conviction erodes, the political weight—with due time lapse for human inertia—should erode also. In any case, the utility of military force has become more negative than positive, more in threat than in action. In Lawrence Martin's words: "... if military force remains useful, it will generally be much inhibited at all levels and will exercise its influence typically in latent ways."[5]

These trends—the relative decline in American military power, the increasingly severe budgetary restraints on our military posture, the declining utility of military operations—define the limits of the possible in adjusting militarily to a period of resource shortage. Further, the truly vital problems of the United States, and of the human race, over the coming years, are not susceptible to military solutions; indeed, military expenditures, and a fortiori military operations, are at best a drain on and at worst a barrier to solutions of these problems.

In brief, it is a time to reduce reliance on military power to achieve national purposes, and consequently to modify, restrain, or eliminate those national purposes which depend unrealistically on military action. In the military field itself, it is a time for retrenchment, for scrupulous economy of force, for careful reexamination of objectives, programs, tasks, and commitments, to eliminate the infeasible (or no longer feasible) as well as the inconsequential or marginal. It is no time for the grandiose; "solutions" to the problems or resource shortages that call for massive military operations, or cause exploding military requirements, or cheerfully add mission to mission for already fully committed forces, solve nothing. Samuel Huntington wrote in 1973: ". . . the preeminent feature of international politics at the present time is the relative decline in American power. American security policy and military strategy need to be reformulated to reflect this fact."[6] He wrote before the flowering of the oil crisis, but his words apply with force to planning for a time of resource shortage.

II

In speculating about the impact of resources scarcity on American military roles, it is useful to compare the effects of several possible general national military policies. This is not to suggest that this country does, in fact, embrace sweeping military policies single-mindedly, or pursue them to their implication. Probably fortunately, we are protected from dogmatic purity by changing people and situations, multiplicity of purposes, hedging, and confusion. Still, in theory, the United States could design its military structure, and conduct its deployments and operations, with the objective of strict self-defense, or of self-defense plus supporting key allies, or, in the oncoming concern about resources, of self-defense plus access to resources. There are other objectives which have their influence, from preventing aggression worldwide to supporting Israel, but we ourselves, our key allies, and the resources needed for our functioning, can be taken, for discussion, as central. They would suggest alternative military policies that could be called strategic disengagement, alliance support, and resource control. Strategic disengagement would imply military nonintervention abroad, dissolution of alliances, and restriction of military functions to the nations and its approaches. Alliance support would continue alliances with other major-resource-consuming countries, notably NATO and Japan, and would support the military ties and responsibilities incident thereto. Resource control would redirect military capabilities toward resource producing areas and their lines of communication. Each can be argued as, at least in part, a response to resource scarcity and its problem.

The rationale for strategic disengagement has been developed in a number of recent works.[7] Very briefly, strategic disengagement contemplates withdrawal from military intervention and military participation abroad (though not from political, economic, or social relations). It is based upon an appreciation of the effect of weapons or mass destruction, specifically, that the physical defense of this country itself, and with nuclear arms and geographically isolated, is secure against external attack and little affected by the existence or absence of allies, or the sympathy or hostility of others. There remains, of course, the possibility of nuclear attack, but this is deterred against rational action and is less likely to be stimulated by a noninterventionist United States than by a United States engaged in exerting control overseas by military means. In this situation, this country can accommodate to wide changes in the governments, policies, and adherences of other nations with no significant increase in the threat to our survival and with no need to develop a militaristic Fortress America.

Using our military weight around the world to influence or to control the actions of others is consequently unnecessary for our physical security. If unnecessary, it is highly undesirable because it involves us in critical situations, confrontations, and commitments with repeated risk of war, because it has high cost and diminishing utility, and because it stimulates hostility and counteraction.

The advocate of strategic disengagement therefore argues for a policy of toleration, neutrality, adjustment to change abroad, encouragement and use of international institutions, and the fostering of political, economic, and social interrelationships, without bringing military leverage to bear. To the objection that the military element is ultimately inseparable from the political and economic elements in international affairs, he replies that in the nuclear era this is no longer necessarily true, at least in the old sense, that the practical utility of military leverage has become low and the risk of its use is high and growing. To the objection that we risk isolation in a world under hostile hegemony, he replies that power is currently diffusing, not concentrating; that effective global, or even very widespread, hegemony is not feasible for anyone.

There remains the central question of resources. How does strategic disengagement approach access to resources, exerting leverage on resource sources, and supporting them against others? Essentially, it argues that, given American strengths, resources, and capabilities, we have powerful tools for obtaining resources by commercial and cooperative interaction with resource suppliers and others, and also for hedging against interruption of essential supply by developing alternate sources, alternate materials, and stockpiling. In Ravenal's words "... we must conduct a 'split-level' policy: of international cooperations as much, and as long, as possible;

but also of prudent and timely hedging and insulation, to decrease our vulnerabilities and dependencies, and insure the availability of noninterventionist options to protect the core of our national security."[8] Such a policy would bring us into the period of resource shortage with flexible access, minimum vulnerability, minimum hostility, and minimum involvement in conflict not our own.

Strategic disengagement is clearly a policy which would take years to put into effect. It calls for withdrawal from deployments and commitments in a deliberate, paced fashion, adjusted to the concerns and sensibilities of allies, adversaries, and neutrals.

It should be kept in mind that strategic disengagement has a large neutral constituency in the American public. Its support is by no means confined to xenophobic isolationists and radical peacenics; it includes many of those who feel internal problems and global nonmilitary problems merit priority, those who doubt the feasibility or ultimate efficacy of balance of power, those who deplore the size of military budgets or fear the extent of military influence in governmental decisions, and those who believe military intervention does more harm than good. With such broad backing, probably growing, strategic disengagement must be reckoned with even by those who find it unpersuasive.

Under strategic disengagement, the primary military role, is, of course, nuclear deterrence. Other substantial roles lose their rationale: there is no theoretical requirement for overseas garrisons in support of allies, or for projection or expeditionary forces and their air- and sealifts. Other roles would be reduced but not eliminated. There would be a requirement for sea control to protect continental approaches, peripheral sea resources, and some sea communications. While much of the present base structure would go, a limited and comparatively withdrawn pattern of bases for sea control would be needed. Finally, it would be essential to hedge to a degree against unforeseen developments and policy changes; there would consequently be a requirement for some strategic reserve and mobilization base at home.

To consider these points in sequence, take first the strategic nuclear problem. Strategic offensive forces—missile, submarine, and air—are little affected by a policy of strategic disengagement. Force level considerations and arms control positions would not change substantially. The chief current issue—call it combat capability or flexibility or hard-target kill capability—would still remain, though its European scenario would evaporate. Fundamentally that issue is a difference of conviction between those who support the highest possible firebreak against any use of nuclear weapons, and those who feel a need, even at some cost to the firebreak, for improved resources for controlled use in case deterrence fails, both to deter limited use against us and to build a series of graduated firebreaks within the nuclear zone which might stop even nuclear war short of catastrophe.

The question of strategic defensive forces would be raised anew. Strategic disengagement by the United States, in the form of withdrawing its commitment of nuclear support for our allies, would on balance encourage the development of national nuclear forces, though probably of relatively small-scale forces at least in the foreseeable future. Even very small forces, however, would pose a serious potential threat to the United States and the Soviet Union. Further, while deterrence between superpowers has been studied for years, no similar effort has been made on deterring small nuclear powers. We have a conception, even if it is arbitrary, of deterring the Soviet Union, but no one has explored whether similar criteria would control, or be feasible against, country X. For example, population dispersion in China makes it a much different problem of deterrence than that of the Soviet Union. Such factors would suggest a reconsideration of a missile defense system designed for nationwide population defense against small attacks (not for the point-defense of our own land-based missiles). Such systems are prohibited by the SALT Treaty, but since the problem would equally affect the Soviet Union, renegotiation would not be out of the question. A nationwide antiballistic missile system (ABM) would be an extremely expensive program, which would come out of other defense expenditures. More important, it would tend to destabilize, at least to a degree, the central United States-Soviet Union nuclear standoff. Nevertheless, if proliferation occurs, the population-defense ABM issue will be raised along with the issue of some level of continental air defense.

Strategic disengagement would produce its major reductions in general purpose forces. As Secretary McNamara stated, "The overall requirement for general purpose forces is related not so much to the defense of our own territory as it is to the support of our commitments to other nations. . . ."[9] Withdrawal from those commitments would exercise the basic rationale from the general purpose structure, requiring a largely new justification. For ground and tactical air forces, as well as for projection elements such as amphibious forces, air- and sealift, and overseas base structure, the justification would be the necessity to hedge against unforeseen contingencies, policy changes, and technological surprise. The end structure would presumably be a strategic reserve and a mobilization base, almost entirely located in the United States and at a fraction of present strength.

For sea control forces (other than naval projection forces) the justification would include, beyond hedging, the active tasks of defending sea approaches and sea resources and protecting lines of communication. Clearly there would be room for debate about the geographic extent of those tasks and the force levels required. However, a concept of strategic disengagement, which basically contemplates the use of alternative sources and materials as necessary in an emergency, would be inconsistent with readiness for full-scale, worldwide war at sea with the Soviet Union, or even an attempt to maintain all principal peacetime sea routes. At the core, the requirements would be to be ready to defend the sea against any anticipated opposition possibly as far as mid-Atlantic and Midway in the Pacific, and to hold open communications to Alaska, Hawaii, and to such convenient resource sources as Venezuela, as well as other useful and available resource sources when they were not blocked by major enemy submarine forces, heavy mining, or other extensive sea-air opposition. In short, sea-control forces would also be sharply cut.

In summary, the military problem that strategic disengagement would pose would be progressive reduction of other than nuclear forces in phase with reduction of commitments, to arrive, by the time that the disengagement policy was fully in effect, at a coherent and economical defense structure appropriate to the smaller missions.

III

The policy of alliance support rests on the belief that the independence and cooperation of the principal industrial/technological nations (at present non-Communist Western Europe and Japan, and perhaps others in time) are essential to the United States. Henry Owen writes, "Western Europe and Japan are where the power is. Outside the United States, only these areas of the non-Communist world have the capital and the technology to create great economic and military strength. Rifts between them and the United States could damage the attempt to meet important international needs beyond repair."[10] Frederick Wyle states, as a fundamental, ". . . the United States dare not under any circumstances permit the domination of the industrial and human resources of Western Europe by a potentially hostile power, most particularly including the Soviet Union."[11]

The advocate of alliance support thus views the security of NATO and Japan second only to that of the United States. He considers that American security policy and military posture must include necessary contributions to the defense of these allies. He regards other security demands as secondary, to be dealt with militarily, if necessary and if possible, but with minimum disruption to United States/NATO/Japan posture and readiness.

Both policies of alliance support and strategic disengagement would cultivate close relations with NATO and Japan, and have as these objectives successful cooperations and coordination with them. Neither policy would advocate abrupt changes in military relations. The essential difference between the two is in their ultimate objectives. Strategic disengagement, holding that, in the long run, our allies do not need military support, that close political, economic, and social relations with them are not dependent on military support, and that in any case providing military support is, over a period of time, so dangerous and so costly as to be unsound, would ultimately require withdrawal entirely from military alliance, commitments, and modifications of force structures. Alliance support, while usually recognizing that United States force adjustments downward are inevitable, holds that America must provide, not only nuclear support, but also a substantial conventional presence which gives nuclear support validity. This American support is essential indefinitely to the freedom of action of our irreplaceable allies, given their positions relative to the Soviet Union.

Alliance support approaches the question of resource shortage on these bases: First, the resource question is ultimately economic; the first essential is to hold together the chief resource-consuming nations to establish a workable bargaining structure for dealing with the resource-producing countries. Second, the military operations in response to resource shortages would be in some cases either realistically infeasible or not worth the cost of carrying them out; those that might be both feasible and desirable could be accomplished when needed by military forces designed for alliance support. For example, maintaining the flow of oil from the Persian Gulf—against some major combination of air, mine, submarine, missile, or gun opposition to the tankers, and ground, air, guerilla, or sabotage against the installations—would be infeasible. War to enforce resource access with a major regional country would be, on balance, unprofitable. On the other hand, providing a military presence, to show support for a resource country or to exert some leverage on it, or to establish that action by the Soviet Union or others aimed at dominating a resource source would involve confrontation with the United States, would be feasible under a policy of alliance support and could under certain conditions be executed. Alliance support can be defended on these grounds as a workable policy for dealing with the problem of resource shortages.

Alliance support is, of course, an approximation of the rationale for our existing military structure. Military roles would remain broadly as they are, perhaps hedged somewhat more toward maintaining access to Third World and oceanic resource sources. The chief changes to our military posture would be caused by the need to retrench, that is, to adjust to lower force levels and more severe budgetary constraints.

In strategic forces, the present trend for costs is up. Even a successful second SALT treaty covering offensive weapons cannot be expected in itself to reduce the present push for expensive programs. Savings of substance could only come out of these new programs, however, and the rationale for their slowing or cancelation has substance and support. Trident and B-1 are obvious current targets.

In the conventional area, there are also several expensive development programs subject to challenge, but in addition there will be a clear requirement for force reductions. Some of these drawdowns could follow from implementation of the Nixon doctrine in the Pacific, and some, relatively minor, from force reduction agreements negotiated between NATO and the Warsaw Pact. But for substantial results, more severe adjustments will be necessary.

A number of studies deal with reductions in Europe.[12] They examine concepts of relying more heavily on reinforcement, of shifting United States forces from front line to theater reserve, or of restructuring our forces in Europe to stiffen immediate defense capability at the expense of staying power. Their conclusions in general fall into two patterns: either a shift toward reserve and reinforcement, what Samuel Huntington calls the "Great Power Reinforcement" mission,[13] or a restructuring to maximize early defensive stiffness with reduced support.

Great power reinforcement contends that the probability of sudden major attack is low, and that the need to keep our forces in being and deployed is consequently reduced. The requirement is not to deter an attack now, but to be able to deter an attack in the future, after a serious deterioration of relations with the Soviet Union. This objective can be achieved with much reduced deployments, reduced force levels, and a capability to reinforce if and as relations deteriorate. Naturally, there will be reliance in good part on mobilizing reserve forces.

Restructuring argues a short-war thesis, that is, that the probability of a large-scale, nonnuclear, high intensity, East-West war, lasting more than a few weeks, is extremely remote. Such a war, if it lasted for any substantial period, would have a high probability of becoming nuclear; nuclear operations would quickly lead to escalation or cessation. Further, Soviet forces are designed to peak quickly and have relatively short support; stiffened immediate defenses would have maximum utility and effectiveness, and therefore maximum deterrent effect. For these reasons, our large investments in the support, line of communications, and reinforcement elements needed for a long war are dangerously wasteful, soaking up resources that could provide a higher level of short-run defensive combat potential and allow force reductions as well. Under the short-war thesis, reductions can be made in ground support forces, in late-arriving reinforcement elements, in deep interdiction aviation, and in the operation and defense of the North Atlantic sea lines of communication. Restructuring is conceived in a European context, but it would be combined, presumably, with Pacific drawdowns under the Nixon doctrine (Korea, Taiwan, Southeast Asia).

Under a policy of alliance support, aimed in substantial measure at cohesion of alliances, restructuring would appear a more promising approach than Great Power reinforcement, because it would maintain the visible structure of our deployments, while reinforcement would involve withdrawal of major elements. Properly negotiated and coordinated with our allies, restructuring should have little effect on their perception of our dedication. On the other hand, it would tend, comparatively, to lock us into alliance support. Adoption of Great Power reinforcement would move us toward a more flexible posture; our reserves could be employed in other than alliance support roles.

Insofar as access to resources is concerned, the limited operations contemplated under the alliance support concept—military presence, supporting reinforcement, some shipping protection—would not require any considerable additional forces, but they could be dealt with by redeployments if and when necessary. Some bases could be retained or developed for the purpose (e.g., Diego Garcia). Perhaps anti-submarine warfare, whose rationale would be weakened by the short-European-war thesis, would derive some support for southern hemisphere operations. In short, under alliance support, our military structure and roles would be a more austere version of the post-Vietnam structure.

IV

The concept of resource control sees the central strategic objective as guaranteeing access to, availability of, and the ability to move essential resources in a world where shortages of resource supply replace shortages of demand as the dominant force in world economics. This concept implies that, as the resource problem develops, the primary military task after physical defense of the homeland will be to support access to needed resources in the face of constraints, interruptions, or denials, whether imposed by military force, by governmental actions, or by economic effects. Resource control could include denial to hostile states of access to resource.

There are two distinct possible threats to our resource access. Each has quite different implications. The first is the resource states themselves, acting individually or in combination for their own economic or political ends. The second is the Soviet Union, acting against or in support of resource states, or directly against supply lines, with the objective of extending her control over resources essential to the United States and her allies. The first would raise the possibility of disruption of supply of specific resources, with greater or less impact on our national functioning, national strength, and freedom of action. The second, extending Soviet control over resources essential to us, would in addition affect the balance of strength between the superpowers and pose an immediate threat of United States-Soviet Union confrontation.

The period of resource shortages contains many other possibilities of conflict beyond direct manipulation of our resource supply. Oil, food, and fertilizer price rises are having graver consequences on developing than developed countries; India, for example, faces famine, and the relief of famine in sub-Sahara Africa is made difficult by the near exhaustion of food reserves. Such situations cannot help but produce hostility toward the resource producing countries which raises the possibility of conflict among Third World countries and powerful antagonism toward the developed countries as the only sources of excess food and essential manufactures. Further, the added economic power of resource countries, such as Iran, can lead to destablizing military buildups, with an accompanying potential for regional conflict. Threats to governmental stability of resource countries, with or without external stimulus and support, are matters of urgent concern to resource users. Other conflicts such as the Arab-Israel and black-white in South Africa affect resource areas. Ultimately, there is the possibility of competition among the resource consumers becoming acute; it is difficult to imagine this leading to hostilities with any of our chief allies, but not beyond conceiving that we could be lending active support to different sides. Conflicts growing out of such possibilities as these could affect access to resources in the same way as direct action by resource states themselves. And of course the distinction between Soviet involvement and noninvolvement would be equally significant in these cases.

The validity of the argument for resource control as a basic military policy depends on the degree of our vulnerability to these threats, and the necessity or utility of military force in countering them. The impact or denial or interruption of resource access could in theory be immediate or longer term, calling forth immediate threats which, carried into execution, would be quickly intolerable. Examples are food needed for subsistence, fuel enough to keep the combat forces in action, and in the longer term there are threats in a longer fuse: resource interruptions which would cause economic disruption, progressive national weakening, and major competitive disadvantage.

As far as immediate threats are concerned, the United States position is strong. Deprivation of a material, or several materials, or all resources from a given area, could produce severe economic dislocations, and the interconnected nature of the economy would spread them widely. But our self-sufficiency is such that even this would not quickly reduce us to starvation or impotence. For us, resource denial is not an instantaneous threat, like nuclear attack, or even a rapid threat, like invasion. Such measures as conservation, use of alternate materials, shift to alternate sources, perhaps selective stockpiling, will in many cases be effective indefinitely, or for a substantial period, over and above political, economic, or military countermeasures directed at the specific denial. Our allies, of course, are less autarchic, and, in some resources, especially fuel, much more vulnerable.

It is possible to conceive of a general, complete interruption of resource access: a general boycott by all significant resource producers, or a naval blockade by the Soviet Union. A collective boycott by the producers of many or all of the key imports, in effect a united economic war by the Third World, appears politically and operationally infeasible. For many of the participants it would be economically self-destructive. Short of a dominating and nearly global hostile hegemony, presumably under the Soviet Union, a general boycott is not a realistic possibility. Such hegemony, given present nationalistic and separatist trends, as well as nuclear deterrence, seems an even more remote contingency, to be achieved, if at all, on a step-by-step basis, and countered also step by step.

As far as a naval boycott of the United States is concerned, only the Soviet Union has the capabilities to undertake such an operation. Most of the relevant considerations were examined, in the 1960s, in analysing "War at Sea" (i.e., United States-Soviet or NATO-Warsaw Pact warfare conducted wholly at sea—combat at sea to the exclusion of fighting on land).[14] In brief, the possibilities of making a general blockade tight and enforcing it long enough to have a decisive impact on American supplies would be low. More important, the resource denial aspect would be submerged in more urgent considerations. Blockade would be a direct and unequivocal act of war, limited war to be sure, but unambiguous and combatant. To be decisive, it would have to be successful to an unlikely degree, to last for months, and to avoid major escalation. But it would immediately pose a high risk of escalation, and that risk would approach certainty if the blockade were to produce massive effects. From the Soviet standpoint, war at sea could conceivably be thought of as a relatively controllable way to engage in limited war with the United States, if their purposes required limited hostilities. A war at sea would, of course, be powerfully deterred by extended nuclear deterrence, as would any other direct combat between the United States and the Soviet Union. As a device for denying essential resources to the United States it would be a very high-risk and low-promise operation, and thus clearly less attractive than more manageable pressures on specific resources in concert with or through leverage on resource suppliers.

A number of allies, especially Japan and the United Kingdom would be more rapidly and critically affected by blockade than the United States, because their lines of communications to resource sources are more exposed. Considering the substantial probability of United States involvement, however, a blockade of an ally or allies is deterred, as a ground attack into Germany is deterred, although the blockade would be possibly more controllable since the blockade action would be physically separated from the general population and the effect would be slower.

While a blockade or a war at sea might be considered as a high-risk, probably short-term, combatant escalatory step in a critical East-West confrontation, overall neither one would be a reasonable course of action for interrupting resource inputs. From the resource control standpoint, its utility/risk ratio is very low.

Turning from general blockages of imports to interruptions or denials of specific resources, the United States is, overall, in a comparatively powerful and secure position, but not without important concerns. In the area of agricultural products, we are the world's largest exporter—a powerful source of national strength—and expect to remain a net exporter through the century. There are a few external dependencies, such as coffee, tea, cocoa, sisal, and bananas, which, however desirable, are certainly not essential. We are significantly dependent on Canada for timber and its products—important, but not a life or death dependency. We are entirely dependent on imports for natural rubber, largely from Malaysia and vicinity; natural rubber is essential for some purposes now, and could grow in importance in a petroleum shortage.

As far as minerals are concerned, this country has the resources to be self-sufficient in most essential minerals. In a number of them, however, self-sufficiency would be time-consuming and, by contrast with high-grade foreign sources, very costly, e.g., iron and aluminum. In some important minerals, we lack resources: chrome, manganese, tin, cobalt, diamonds. Overall, we now import some one-hundred minerals, some half of which have important uses, sixteen of which are imported in large quantities. The key resource areas of central importance to us for mineral imports are reasonably concentrated: in the western hemisphere Canada, Mexico, Brazil, Jamaica, the north coast of South America; southern Africa; and Australia.

In regard to energy, the United States is self-sufficient in coal, can make do with domestic uranium (we lead the world in nuclear power technology), and is launching an energy program which, among other measures, will develop alternative energy sources and methods to utilize currently unexploitable resources. Petroleum imports, however, remain a central concern. It is not yet possible to foresee how far Project Independence will take us toward self-sufficiency, but it seems generally agreed that we will in any case require substantial imports into the mid 1980s and perhaps well beyond, and that our allies will be dependent on external supply indefinitely. Further it is clear that dependence on imported energy can be a threat to the national economy and to political freedom of action. Even were we quantitatively self-sufficient, the existence of relatively cheap external oil would be a continuing threat to an economy based on high-cost energy. Theoretically, the key oil area is of course the Middle East. Venezuela, Nigeria, Canada, and Alaska are also significant. Of oceanic resources, the most important for our purposes is offshore oil, a rapidly growing source from the continental shelves of what, in a few years, could be as many as one-hundred nations, constituting an increasing proportion of global production.

In summary, we can see five areas of chief resource concern: first, North America, especially Canada and the continental shelf, second, parts of South America; third, southern Africa; fourth, Australia and Malaysia; and fifth, the Persian Gulf countries. The resulting key lines of communication are coastal North America, Caribbean, South Atlantic, South Pacific, and Indian Ocean. Of all the resources and all the locations, the oil of the Middle East is the most critical issue, because of the universal impact on energy requirements, the concentration of major oil reserves, the distant and exposed location of the Middle East oil producers and their relative accessibility for the Soviet Union, and the political problems of the area.

Resource control argues that maintaining access to the resources of these areas will, over time, become more essential to our security than supporting the defense of developed nations. Indeed, for alliance support also, resource control would contend that, as the danger of direct attack on the chief allies becomes progressively more remote, support of their resource access will be a more essential contribution to their real security than forces tied to their direct defense.

On the other hand, the applicability of military solutions to resource access problems is restricted. For some sources, e.g., Canada, military measures are inapplicable; for some, e.g., internal African suppliers, essentially infeasible; for some, e.g., because of a military build-up in Iran, disproportionately expensive; for all, there would be the shadow of extended deterrence. And the threats are not instantaneous or cataclysmic in individual cases. There is time and method for other types of measures.

The military roles that fall out of a policy of resource control, in addition, of course, to strategic deterrence, are intervention, that is, exerting leverage on resource sources; counterintervention, that is, exerting leverage to prevent domination of resource sources by hostile external states or externally supported internal factions; and protection of lines of communication.

Resource control would not greatly affect United States strategic deterrence. The basic United States-Soviet strategic nuclear relationship would not change and Third World operations would not require dedicated strategic weaponry. Proliferation might be encouraged among our allies as they felt a falling-off of American support and involvement, and perhaps among resource countries, which would feel more acutely threatened and have increased wealth for nuclear programs. Conceivably, in the resource pinch, whether or not the United States follows a resource control policy, some nonresource Third World countries could be drawn to nuclear programs to threaten or to deter resource countries; India is a recent concern. Such nuclear capabilities in our threatening resource areas would critically alter intervention and counterintervention operations, and in some cases protection of lines of communication. They would not, however, significantly influence our strategic retaliation forces except, as previously noted in discussing strategic disengagement, perhaps in time reraising the question of countrywide ABM defense against small attacks.

Pure intervention—using our military leverage against resource states to enforce access to resources—is powerfully deterred by the probable political consequences and by the limitations of military effectiveness. It is not inconceivable; Fouad Ajami writes, "It is an illusion for any Arab to think that a society willing to wage war in Vietnam, for a variety of intangible factors associated with the national interest, would never use its military might, overtly or covertly, to protect its prosperity and the only way of life its present generation has known."[15] This latent military threat, in combination with other elements of American strength, does produce leverage and can, in some cases and to some degree, be amplified by measures of deployment and alerting. One can envisage blockade as one riposte to boycott, perhaps productive in some circumstances. It is hard to conceive of a situation, however, where direct combat operations against a Third World resource country to obtain its resources would commend itself as feasible, effective, and, on balance, productive.

There is a wider range of scenarios for the role of counterintervention: the use or threat of military force to confront, defeat, or deter action against a resource country by an external power or an externally supported internal faction. Counterintervention, as Vietnam demonstrated, has its difficulties, and where it involves confrontation with the Soviet Union it would have extreme dangers. But a premise of the resource control policy is that our security would be impaired if a major hostile external power achieved dominance over one or more of the key resource areas; under resource control we would be strongly motivated to act to prevent such hostile hegemony. Also, under some conditions, we could become involved in supporting one side or another in regional conflict where access to essential resources appeared to be at stake.

V

The types of forces required for interventions and counterintervention are the same. These are the projection forces—ground, sea, and air, with their carriers, bases, and logistic structure—which can be brought to bear on the resource areas. Capabilities for military assistance are part of counterintervention strength, to stiffen friendly elements for "proxy war" or combined operations.

The general force levels of projection forces establish and communicate an important element of the country's overall military power. A great part of our military leverage, of course, comes from our strategic nuclear potential; in the days of the New Look we relied almost exclusively on nuclear weapons. Strategic nuclear potential, however, is visibly inapplicable, or only indirectly applicable, to resource control conflict situations. For them, a reasonably substantial capability to intervene—the fact and the general understanding that usable United States military weight exists—can be a substantial support for our influence.

It is neither necessary nor possible to build a force structure adequate for all contingencies. Substantial conflict with the Soviet Union in a resource area, for example, would be quickly subsumed in a direct United States-Soviet Union crisis dominated by strategic weapons; the local outcome would be peripheral. Forces for confrontation would meet the needs of the case. Adequate forces for large-scale United States wars against major Third World countries—invasion or occupation—would be very large indeed. Even were such force postures possible, the contingency is too remote to make them sensible.

Our general force levels for projectible forces, then, should be large enough to allow involvement and some build-up; we should be able to project minimum combat forces to key areas, to back them up sufficiently to give their presence weight—sufficient forces to be adequate for minor or balanced contingencies, and to allow us, if necessary, to produce or threaten a substantial confrontation with the Soviet Union. We do not, however, need standing projection forces adequate to fight large-scale wars ourselves; this is a course of action which the resource access problem does not demand of us, nor the overall military situation permit us. It is one of the conceivable missions which the prospective military environment requires us to drop. This overall posture produced by general force levels of projected forces would be enough to make the United States a useful friend and an undesirable enemy. It is consistent with the need to lower existing force levels.

As far as the stationing of forces is concerned, the variety, geographical spread, and rate of change of the nature of possible conflict is very great. Systems analysts like to specify the contingencies that we must be able to meet, and to calculate the needed forces and deployments. On the time scale of developing our force posture and adjusting overcommitments, however, with due respect to our analysts, contingencies are not that predictable. Versatility and freedom of action are force multipliers; the tying down and precommitment that are the effects of placing forces on a specific station or in a given area are intrinsically undesirable, and should be minimized.

On-station forces should be confined to those places where high readiness and irrevocable commitment are inescapably needed and justify the risk. On this basis, elements in Korea and Taiwan, for example, should probably be removed, and forces in Germany—where the precommitment remains but the need for readiness is eroding—should be drawn down substantially. New on-station forces should be considered only where, and when, a preemptive United States presence would powerfully ameliorate or control a situation critical to our interests. Generally, the trend of on-station forces should be substantially down.

In-area forces are justified on the grounds of shorter reaction time and the effect of military presence. The reaction time differential—in comparison to equivalent forces maintained at equivalent readiness at home—is essentially the difference in transit time, though there is also an effect of area familiarity. There could be circumstances in which the differential would be important, but the recent tendency, stimulated by the potential time scales of nuclear war or surprise attack into Germany, has been to overvalue reaction time, especially in connection with the short wars preceded by deteriorating East-West relations that are probable risks in Europe, and the limited United States operations contemplated in resource areas. Thus, it has been held that a footing in South Korea could not have been held had it not been for the divisions and support structure in Japan. On the other hand, a counterinvasion could have been mounted in due course if necessary, and maintaining in-area forces on such a scale adjacent to potential conflicts is out of the question. For a more recent example, consider the influence of the Sixth Fleet on the Yom Kippur War. If it had significant influence—an arguable point—it is unlikely that that influence was appreciably if any greater than the Second Fleet could have produced if, in the absence of the Sixth Fleet, the Second Fleet had sailed from Norfolk the same day the Sixth

Fleet moved toward support stations.

The utility of military presence, and the varying effects of different levels of military presence, are similarly somewhat ambiguous. How much more influence a force in the general area has than a force at a distance, how much more a force continuously present than one making an occasional visit, and how much more a larger force than a smaller one, are all debatable. Forces kept in area tend to sink into the local scene and become part of local orders of battle—sometimes with useful deterrent effect, but at a cost in precommitment and loss of versatility. On the other hand, periodic visits equally demonstrate potential and, being out of the ordinary, have more impact; in time of crisis, simple movement of forces to area can be disproportionately influential. Finally, the major political influence of military force on a situation is rationally less measured by a count of forces in area than by the overall capacity of the country to project forces to the scene in the time scale of the crisis and conflict.

As far as the size and composition of in-area forces is concerned, some forces have almost no military leverage; their function is contactmaking and area familiarization. Beyond a minimum combat level, proportioned in some degree to local forces and Soviet area deployments, the utility of additional force increments drops off rapidly. The reasonable function for in-area elements is not to conduct a campaign themselves but to provide, or threaten, a United States combat involvement, given weight by a prospective build-up coming in behind them. Versatile and mobile forces, notably tactical aircraft and ship—or airborne ground forces, perhaps surface-to-surface missile ships—are most useful and feasible constituents of in-area projection forces. These considerations suggest that in-area forces need not be large and that, like on-station forces, they should be held to a minimum, below current levels.

The bulk of projectable forces, then, should from a resource control standpoint be held in-being at home and available for deployment. The overall levels of projectible forces should be designed for prompt deployment of minimum combat forces and moderate follow-up reinforcements, capable of contributing United States combat weight to a conflict situation, and of producing, when needed, confrontation, but not for themselves conducting a large war. The nature of projectible forces should stress versatility.

Turning to the problem of protecting communications, the key sea lines of communication under a resource control concept were listed earlier as coastal North America, Caribbean, South Atlantic,

South Pacific, and Indian Ocean. In addition, alliance support would add concern for the sea lines to Europe and to Japan. On the open ocean, these routes are threatened primarily by the submarine, to a lesser degree by surface and air attack, the only large-scale threat being Soviet. Approaching the terminals, the relative weight of air, mine, and surface attack increases, and attacks on terminal facilities are added possibilities. Further, the potential of regional forces becomes serious.

Readiness to hold open all these routes against unrestricted opposition is a massive operation, requiring a very large commitment of resources. Even with such investments, some routes are instrinsically too vulnerable to maintain against full-scale opposition, e.g., the Persian Gulf. But such unrestricted global, full-scale opposition is an extremely remote contingency, and, if it were mounted, it would be a peripheral element in a primarily nuclear confrontation. Further, while these routes are significant over time, none of them would be decisive—as far as a flow of resource-carrying shipping is concerned—during a relatively short active combat phase. These points were made earlier, in discounting the probability of Soviet blockade of the United States.

The more realistic problem, then, is not global defense of all key routes, but defense—where feasible and to a degree measured by cost-benefit considerations—of those routes related to a specific conflict area, largely in and near the resource area themselves. Here the problem is more general: ground, air, surface, submarine, mine, and partisan operations could close, interrupt, or take a toll from ships or terminals. The outcome in any location would depend on the forces involved; relatively minor forces, if they are suitable and can be brought to bear, can have great impact on communications. But as far as the movement of resources is concerned, such interruptions would be largely confined to a conflict area, probably no more than one, or part of one, of the key resource areas, and would also, of course, be restricted to the phase of active combat. The resource problem would be manageable.

It follows from the foregoing that the focus of lines of communication protection should be on protecting projection forces, sea and air carried, and their reinforcements and logistic follow-up, leaving the protection of resource shipping largely to the incidental fall-out from protecting military elements. Further, the center of effort should be on local defenses, in and approaching sea and air terminals and in offshore support areas, and covering moving task forces, rather than concentrating on a global war of attrition against the Soviet submarine force. This thesis still leaves a formi-

dable challenge, and requires some redirection of force procurement and structuring. It does, however, allow reductions in the
present heavy antisubmarine warfare investments. A final point
of resource control is that the wide geographical spread of possible
conflicts emphasizes the utility of bases, where they can support
operations at key resource areas, and where they can be established
economically and without overriding commitments or political
problems.

To summarize briefly the military consequences of a resource
control policy: we would not need to prepare for global war, or
for conducting, ourselves, local war on a major scale. We would
need versatile projection forces, on a moderate scale, for counterintervention and confrontation, and need line-of-communication
projection for these forces and their support. We would minimize
forward deployment of these forces.

VI

The three most persuasive general military objectives for America are pure self-defense, support of our most powerful allies (or
collective defense), and, of increasing importance as resource shortages become more urgent, maintaining access to necessary resources on tolerable terms. Strategic disengagement, alliance support, and resource control have been discussed as though they
were alternatives. In practice, they will be pursued simultaneously,
with varying emphasis as the world military, political, and economic situation varies, and as men with differing views succeed in authority.

There are other possible objectives. The broadest was stated
six years ago by Secretary McNamara: to create "... a world in
which even the smallest state could look forward to an independent existence, free to develop in its own way, unmolested by its
neighbors, and free of fear of armed attack or political domination
by the more powerful nations."[16]

A somewhat less sweeping objective is to prevent hostile hegemony, globally or over critical areas, to prevent being isolated in
a hostile world, or subject to hostile dominance of areas vital to
our national well-being. Other objectives are specific: to ensure
the continued existence of Israel.

All these objectives, and many others, will be surging through
our political system, more or less explicitly and more or less influ-
entially. In an era of declining military power and effectiveness,
and of cataclysmic possible military consequences, however, the

objectives that we should contemplate pursuing by military means, even as a last resort, should be rigidly restricted.

Self-defense, support of *essential* allies, access to *necessary* resources are already very broad statements, upon which massive military programs and military operations could be hung. Our approach to even these central objectives should be governed by realism and scrupulous economy of resources and economy of force. Fortunately, as we have noted, working toward a satisfactory posture for one of these three key objectives tends to work for the others as well. For all three, we need an adequate strategic nuclear force. For all three, we must face reduced force levels, and can do so with capabilities that meet the needs if—we emphasize—versatile projection/reinforcement elements are held in-being at home in a condition of maximum freedom of action to employ them where and when needed, minimizing the locking in effect of in-area or on-station deployments.

The controlling element that makes possible a force structure that is both economically feasible and militarily rational is the enormous weight of strategic deterrence and its secondary effect on making major, long-continuing war, especially between superpowers, so remote a contingency that it would be unreasonable to invest heavily in readiness for it.

If we cut our large-scale, long-war preparations, if we avoid those expensive new military programs that are not justified by increased military productivity, we will be able to carry a solid structure of forces for nuclear deterrence, alliance support, and counterintervention, in balance with our needs. If, as soon as politically possible, we minimize the forces stationed abroad, and concentrate on versatile and deployable forces held uncommitted at home, we will maximize our ability to deal with actual contingencies as they develop, and minimize the risk of being involved against our interests.

Such reduced forces will not produce absolute security. There is, of course, no absolute security. Within the limits of economic feasibility, and within the boundaries of military possibility in a nuclear world of multiplying power centers, these reduced forces will give us the military tools needed to pursue our central and essential national objectives, including resource access, to the degree that these objectives must and can be pursued by military means.

NOTES

Based on an address delivered at the Naval War College, June 1974.

1. McGeorge Bundy, "To Cap The Volcano," *Foreign Affairs,* October 1969, p. 10.

2. Robert L. Heilbroner, "The Human Prospect," *New York Review of Books,* Jan. 24, 1974, p. 24.

3. Stanley Hoffman, "The Acceptability of Military Force," Adelphi Paper No. 102, Winter 1973, International Institute for Strategic Studies, p. 6.

4. L. J. Halle, "Does War Have a Future," *Foreign Affairs,* October 1973, p. 31.

5. Lawrence W. Martin, "The Utility of Military Force," *Adelphi Paper No. 102,* IISS, Winter 1973, p. 2.

6. S. P. Huntington, "After Containment: The Functions of the Military Establishment," *Annals of the American Academy of Political & Social Science,* vol. 406, March 1973, p. 5.

7. See, e.g., Robert W. Tucker, *A New Isolationism* (Washington, D.C.: Potomac Books, 1972); Earl C. Ravenal, "The Case for Strategic Disengagement," *Foreign Affairs,* April 1973.

8. Earl C. Ravenal, letter to the editor, *Foreign Affairs,* October 1973, p. 183.

9. Statement by Secretary of Defense McNamara before the House Armed Services Committee on the Fiscal Year 1969-73 Defense Program and the 1969 Defense Budget, Jan. 22, 1968, p. 3.

10. Henry Owen, ed., "The Next Phase in Foreign Policy," Brookings Institution, 1973, p. 310.

11. Frederick S. Wyle, "The United States and West European Security Interests, Forces, and Finances," *Survival,* February 1972, p. 8.

12. See, e.g., Horst Mendershansen "Revisiting the U.S. Force Posture in Central Europe," RAND R-972-ISA, February 1972 (Unclassified Section); Steven L. Canby, "NATO Military Policy: Obtaining Conventional Comparability with the Warsaw Pact," RAND R-1088-ARPA, September 1972; Kenneth Hunt, "The Alliance & Europe: Part II: Defense With Fewer Men," IISS, London, *Adelphi Paper No. 98.*

13. Huntington, "After Containment," p. 11 ff.

14. See, e.g., Lawrence W. Martin, *The Sea in Modern Strategy* (London: Chatto & Windus, 1967), pp. 81 ff.

15. Fouad Ajami, "Middle East Ghosts," *Foreign Policy,* Spring 1974, p. 108.

16. Robert S. McNamara, Statement before the House Armed Services Committee on the Fiscal Year 1969-73 Defense Program and the 1969 Defense Budget, 22 Jan., 1968, p. 2.

INDEX

ABM, 325, 333, 343
Adenauer, C., Chancellor, 203-204, 214-216
  domestic opposition to, 214
  European policy of, 215-216
  fearful of Stalin, 204
  negotiating skill of, 203
  on German security, 214-215
  on reunification, 209
Aircraft carriers, 187, 193-194
  on amphibious operations, 194
Airpower, 39, 41, 168, 192
Alliance
  Bismarck's system of 144-145
  British and American, 191
  good faith in, 240
  see also NATO, names of nations
Alliance support policy, 330, 334-338
American revolution, 84-86
Amphibious operations, 164-169
  Gallipole, 164-165, 169
  tri-service concept, 169
Amphibious warfare, 187-190
  and aircraft carriers, 194
  shortage of landing craft, 192-193
Anderson, Adm. G.W., 307-309
  conflict with McNamara, 308-309
Antisubmarine warfare, 183, 195
Applicatory system, 119-120
Aristocracy, 23, 25
Aswan Dam, cancellation of loan for, 246
Athens, 5-20
Athenian fleet, 16
Athenian naval power 8
Atomic bombs,
  in Japan, 172
  effect of threat, 243
  as final solution, 174
Austria
  Bismarck and, 144-145, 149

Germany inciting to war, 155
  and Serbia 155-156

Baggage trains, 23
Balkans, 41
Battle, 22, 23, 40, 45
Battle of Jutland, 126, 183
Battleship, 91, 124-125, 166
  battlefleet era, 92
  "Battleship Conference", 125
  building rivalry, 129
  design of, 124-125
  in German navy 166
  see also Dreadnought, Great Britain, High Seas Fleet
Bay of Pigs, 75, 230-231, 245, 299-303
Beatty, Admiral,
  on the Grand Fleet, 180-181, 185
Bismarck, 28, 139-157
  army as tool for, 142
  diplomacy of, 141
  European statesman, 139
  genius for diplomacy, 147
  identified others' interests, 142, 157
  network with great powers, 144-147
  on politics as art, 140
  reason of state, 140
  Reichstaag speech, 142
Blitzkrieg, 165
Bombers, 192-193
  too many built, 192
Bombing, see atom bombs, strategic bombing
Brotherhood of man, 93

Campaigns, 23
Centralization
  and communication 128-130
  dangers of 129-130
China
  Communist, 257-258

early seapower, 81
Churchill, W.R.
  and German rearmament, 206-212
  in World War II, 159-174
CIA in Bay of Pigs, 299-303
citizen-soldier, 26-27
Clausewitz, 8, 27-29, 32-38, 43, 44
  on generalship, 35, 36, 235
Cleon, 5, 6, 17, 19
Combined Chiefs of Staff 170-171
Commercial interests, 98, 104
Committee of Public Safety 51
Communications, 128-130, 346-348
  and centralization, 128-130
  protection of, 346-348
Communism, 257-260
  behavior predicted by ideology, 257
  perceived dangers of, 259
  U.S. opponent, 253, 259-260
Comprehensive control, 49, 64, 75
  strategy defined as, 64, 75
Comte de Guibert, 51
Comte de Saint Germain, 22
Conscription, 52
Convoy, 166
  combats U-boat 166
  Lloyd George demands 180-181
Corbett, Sir Julian, 122
  impact of writings, 122
Counterinsurgency, 285-292
  Special Forces in, 304-305
Credibility gaps, 266
Crowe, Sir Eyre, 93-94
Cuba, 267
  See also Bay of Pigs, Kennedy

Democracy, 16-17
  counterinsurgency by, 291
Dewey, Admiral
  on balanced fleet, 128
  on fleetships, 123
  on telescopes, 124
Dreadnought, 111, 112, 181, 185-186
Dulles, J.F., Secretary of State,
  and Stalin's writings, 258
  behavior in 1956, 238-239, 240
  ignores Russian gestures, 262
  misjudging Eden, 247
  on German rearmament, 212-213, 217
  on Suez, 228
  use of hyperbole, 265
Dynasty, 21-25, 26

Economic factors 21, 25
Economy of force, 64
Eden, Anthony, Prime Minister, 235-240

great mistake, 239, 240
  misjudging Dulles, 247
  on defense costs, 232
  Suez decision, 235, 237
  view of U.S., 237-238
Egypt, 4, 222
  Suez canal seized 222
  see also Suez Crisis
Eighteenth century, 21, 25, 50
  American revolution in 84-86
Eisenhower, D.D., 190-191
  in the Suez crisis, 238, 247
  on "the team", 190
Empire, 17-20, 148-149
Energy resources 341-342
England, see Great Britain
Enlisted men, 23, 24
  conscription of, 52
Envoys, 10-11
Europe
  peace of and Bismarck, 145-146
  U.S. policy towards, 201, 204, 207, 213-
    214, 215, 218
European Defense Community (EDC)
  206, 211-212
European Economic Community (Com-
  mon Market) 216

Fiske, Rear Adm. Bradley, 112
  on mechanisms, 125-126
  on "scientific . . . sailor", 132
Fleetships, design of, 123-127
Flexibility, 70
France, 40, 50
  and German rearmament, 206-212,
    217
  Anglo-French alliance, 152-153
  Franco-Russian alliance, 150
  in Suez crisis, 222, 224, 226-230, 232,
    234, 236
  in the world wars, 159-174
French revolution 15, 21, 25, 51

General Board of the Navy, 117-118
  Dewey and fleetships, 123
  investigate U.S.S. North Dakota, 125
  on specialization, 131
  recommend ship design, 124
Generalship, 35, 36
  Clausewitz on, 235
German foreign policy, 139-157
  and Russia, 144
  Bismarck and, 139-148
  British alliance bids, 150
  extragovernment forces and, 148
  Morocco policy, 152

peace in Europe, 145
Russian alliance broken, 150
William II and, 148
German navy 92
  and Great Britain's, 126, 152
  Battle of Jutland, 126
  emperor's fleetbuilding program, 151
  High Seas Fleet, 178-179, 184
  strategy of, 178-179
Germany, 143-157, 159-179
  guerre de course policy 177
  in the world wars, 159-174
  land and sea control, 176
  propelled into war, 157
  quest for empire, 148-149
  unification under Prussia, 143
Germany, Federal Republic of, 199-218
  arming of, 199, 205, 211
  participating in free Europe, 203
  reunification of 203
  U.S. policy toward, 208-209, 213-214,
    215, 218
Grand strategy, 32, 42-43, 45, 68
  controlled by civilians, 170
Great Britain 38, 46, 94
  and German fleetbuilding, 152
  and German rearmament, 206-212
  and the Near East, 221
  Anglo-French Alliance, 152-153
  as maritime state, 98
  Battle of Jutland, 126
  Bismarck and, 144-145
  courted by Germany, 149
  Grand Fleet of, 179-181
  in the Suez crisis, 222, 224, 226-230,
    233, 234, 236
  in the world wars, 159-174
  maritime policy, 101
  naval war game in, 118-119
  power of navy, 126
Greece, 3-20, 78
Guerilla warfare, 173, 304
  see also Counterinsurgency

Herodotus, 3-20
High Seas Fleet, 177-181, 184
Hitler, A., 41
  blitzkrieg effectiveness, 165
  bloodless victories, 163
Holland, 80

Ideology, 49-50, 257-262
Industrial bombing, 42-45
  see also Strategic bombing
Industrial Revolution, 22
Israel

attacks Egypt, 222
logistics at Suez, 224
national objective, 224
view of Suez crisis, 235
Italy
  detached from Triple Alliance, 157
  switching sides, 159

Japan
  as world power, 172
  battlefleet disappearance, 92
  cause of World War II, 161
  defeat of, 172
  security support, 335
Jellicoe, First Sea Lord, 179-181,
    183-184
  and Grand Fleet, 179-181
Johnson, L.B., 5, 310-314
  and the military, 310-311, 313
  and Viet Nam, 311-312, 313-314
Joint Chiefs of Staff, 171, 191, 298
  and Bay of Pigs, 299-302
  and Cuban missile crisis, 306
  and Johnson, 310-315
  and Kennedy, 297-310
  and McNamara, 316-319
  on Laos, 303

Kant, Emmanuel, 33, 34
Kennedy, J.F., 297-310
  and Bay of Pigs, 299-303
  and Joint Chiefs of Staff, 299-307
  and McNamara, 298-299
  and Taylor, 304
  biography, 297-298
  defense policy, 274-277
  on Laos, 303
King, Admiral, 192-193
  controlling landing craft, 193
Korea, 28, 204, 273
Korean War, 29
Kruschev, 305

League of Nations
  spawned by World War I, 162
  killed by Mussolini, 163
Lenin, 15
Limited force, doubts about, 328
Limited warfare, 22-25, 29, 50
Little, Capt. W. McCarty, 115-116
  introduced naval war game, 118
  on leadership, 130
  on order form, 122
  on war games, 133
Lloyd George, Prime Minister, 180
  demands convoy system, 180

Logistics, 72, 127, 231-133, 245
  Army Industrial College, 172
  consumer logistics, 72
  defined, 245
  in national strategy, 72
  in the Suez Crisis, 231-233
  in war, 127
  producer logistics, 72
Luce, Rear Adm. S.B., 114
  on Naval War College, 117
  on officer as marine engineer, 132
Ludendorff offense, 181
Luftwaffe over Britain, 167

Mahan, A.T., 77, 82-84, 95-106, 114-115
  at Naval War College, 82, 114-115
  concept of limited, 176
  impact of writings, 122
  information sources of, 82-83
  on international life, 103
  on naval history, 115,
  on power, 97
  requirements for free movement, 97
  six factors of, 81
  sudden insight of, 96
  warfare as Art, 115
Maritime power, 100, 105-106

  non-threat, 103
  purpose of battle for, 100
  structure of system, 100-101, 105
Maritime state, 98, 100
  Great Britain as, 98
Marshall Plan, 201, 215
Mayo, Adm. H.T., at Tampico, 129
McNamara, R.S., Secretary of Defense,
  298-309, 315-319
  and Admiral Anderson, 307-309
  and Bay of Pigs, 299-303
  and Johnson, 312
  and Kennedy, 298-299
  as Secretary, 315-319
  on general purpose forces, 333
Mechanized land forces, 39, 40, 41
Melian dialogue, 12-14, 19
Military decision, 234-236, 243-244
  integrated with political, 234-235, 243
  tests for effective, 244
Military structure, 22
Military targets, 22
Mineral resources, 341
  see also Resources
Mobility, 23, 39-40, 45
Monarchy, 25
Monroe doctrine, 87
Montgomery, Field Marshall, on Suez,
  225-226
Moslems, 79

Napoleon, 36, 50, 52-53
Napoleonic Wars, 28, 33, 56
Nation, 21, 26-28, 46
  "nation in arms" 52, 54
National policy, 100
  by civil and military leaders, 296
  navy as instrument of, 100
  see also names of nations
National power and seas, 81
National Security Council, 297, 298, 311,
  312
National strategy, 71-72, 230
Nationalism
  as force in international politics, 164
NATO, 206, 208, 209-210, 213
  German membership in 109, 210, 213
  threat which created, 222
  U.S. concern for, 225
  U.S. support of 335
Naval air power, 113
Naval communications, 113, 128-130
  detrimental aspects, 129
  Rodgers on improvements in, 128, 130
Naval Consulting Board, 125
Naval strategy, 121-122
Naval war
  sole end of, 101
  war plans, 120-121
Naval War College, 114
  "applicatory system", 119-120
  founding of, 114
  Mahan lectures, 114-115
  Munsterberg lectures, 131
  Vogelsgang lectures, 127
Navy, U.S., 87-99, 112-128
  design of ships for, 123-127
  erroneous views of, 102
  General Board of, 117-118
  nature of, 87
  need for strong, balanced, 128
  New Navy, 92
  Old Navy 87-90
  planning and coordination, 117
  policy, 92, 93
  seapower and seaforce, 97, 99
  Stimson on psychology of, 96
  technological advances, 112-114, 123-
  134
  war plans, 120-121
Nixon, R.M., 5
  foreign policy, 270
  negotiation, 262
  strategic sufficiency, 277-278
Nobility, 23, 25, 26
Normandy invasion, amphibious landing, 189

Objectives, 28, 31-47, 70, 235
  analysis of, 235
  attainment of, 70
  military, 31, 45
  multiple nature of, 70
  political, 31, 37
  U.S. military, 348-349
Office of Naval Intelligence, 117
Officer specialization, 131,134
Officers, 23, 24, 26, 54
Oil, 341-342
  embargo, 329
  maintaining flow, 335-336

Peace, 31, 45-47
  indivisibility of, 256
Peace of Niceas, 10
Peloponnesian war(s), 3-20
Pericles, 5, 6, 15, 16-17
Persians, 3-13
Plato's Lament, 74
Poland, 40
Policy, 29, 242, 252-268
  based on oversimplification, 268
  critical areas, 252
  formulation vs. use of force, 242
  freedom of information in, 267
Political decisions, 223-224, 234
  integrated with military, 234-235, 243
Political factors, 21, 25, 55
  in insurgency, 291-292
Power, 19, 39
  Bismarck's conception of, 143
  power politics, 12
  steam, 91-93
President, see Eisenhower, Johnson,
  Kennedy, Nixon, Roosevelt, Wilson
Prussia, 51
  defeated by Napoleon 53-54
  Germany united under, 143
Psychological factors, 49-59

Religious wars, 25
Research and development, 124
  Soviet spending on, 327
  U.S. budget and, 327
Resources, 23, 25, 325-348
  and military establishment, 325-348
  control of 330, 338-344, 348
  following Renaissance, 80
  geographical areas, 342
  in warfare, 127
  naval, 189
Roads, 23
Robespierre, 15
Romans, 78-79

Roosevelt, Theodore, "Battleship conference", 125
Russia
  Bismarck and, 144
  German alliance broken, 149-150
  land and sea control by, 176
  readiness for war, 154, 155
  see also Soviet Union

Schlesinger, Secretary of Defense, 277-
  280
  Schlesinger doctrine, 279-280
Schuman Plan, 203-204
Seaforce, 97, 99, 106
Seapower, 97, 99, 106
Second-strike forces, 272, 274
Secretary of Defense, see McNamara,
  Schlesinger
Secretary of State, see Dulles
Secretary of the Navy, 116
  Josephus Daniels, 125
Secretary of War, 96
Sicily, 5, 16
Society, 21, 27
Southeast Asia, see Viet Nam
Soviet Union, 13, 29, 41
  and German rearmament, 200-201
  atomic capability, 273, 276, 280, 326
  blockade by, 339-340
  non-aggression treaty, 200
  relation to U.S. changes, 325
  strategic posture, 271
  threat to U.S., 261
  see also Russia
Spain, 80
Spanish-American War, 111, 114
  plans for, 117
  technological developments after, 134
Sparta, 10, 13, 16
  Spartan, 5, 6,
Stalin, 15, 204
Steam power
  limiting effect of, 91
  underway replenishment and, 93
Strasbourg Resolution, 210-211
Strategic, two meanings for, 69
Strategic bombing, 42-45
  Germans first, 167
  role in World War II, 168
  role in Viet Nam, 269
Strategic disengagement, 330-334, 335
  nuclear deterrence in, 332-333
  sea control in 334
Strategic doctrine, 70-71
Strategic operation, 45
Strategic sufficiency, 277-278

Strategic war, 73-74
Strategist, 122-123
    as artist, 123
    technical considerations, 123
Strategy, 32
    definition of, 33, 71
    deterrence as, 271, 344
    inseparable from tactics, 71
    related to policy, 296-297, 314
Submarine, 112-113
    first commissioned, U.S., 112
    German 126, 166-167, 176
    underwater fleet, 178-179
    Thomas Edison and, 125
Suez crisis, 75, 222-241
Systems analysis, 121, 317

Tactics, 24, 26
    definition of, 33, 64, 245
    in Suez, 226, 229
    inseparable from strategy, 71
Tampico incident, 129
Taylor, Gen'l M. D., 303-305
    Chairman of Joint Chiefs, 305
    Kennedy's special advisor, 304
    under Eisenhower, 303-304
Thieu, 5, 311
Thirty Years' War, 37
Thracians, 12
Thucydides, 3-20, 159-160
Tirpitz risk-fleet theory, 177-178
Triple Entente, 153

Underway replenishment, 93
United Nations, 28
    in Suez, 222, 225
    spawned by World War II, 162
United States, 13, 28, 102-103, 252-267,
    271-290, 320-348
    alternative military policies for, 330-
    342
    and the Bay of Pigs, 230-231, 243
    and Suez, 235, 237, 240-241
    and the Near East, 221, 225
    and the Third World, 284-285
    boycott of, 339-340
    budget limits, 327-328
    consequences of actions for, 286-288
    declining nuclear power of, 326
    European policies of, 201, 204, 207,
    213-214, 215, 218, 335
    general forces of, 344-346
    hyperbole and secrecy in, 265, 266

    imprecision in diplomacy, 252-267
    in multinuclear world, 280-281
    in Viet Nam, 285-286, 288-291
    justification for policy in, 264-267
    late entry of into world wars, 161
    latent threat of, 343
    Middle East and Atlantic policy, 241
        lessons from, 243
    military objectives of, 348
    military role in, 320
    nuclear policies of, 271-281
    overresponse to threats by, 260-264
    perception of threats by, 256-260
    postwar interests, 253-256
    reluctance to negotiate by, 263-264
    simplification of history in, 267
    strategic posture of, 271-272
    vital problems for, 329
Unlimited warfare, 26-27

Victory, 29, 31, 38, 40, 45
    as illusion, 174
    result of teamwork, 195
Viet Nam, 5, 285-291
    conditioned response in, 268
    effectiveness of bombing in, 269
    Johnson and, 311-312
    lesson of, 283, 285-286, 288-291
    non-threat to security, 259

Western Europe, 22, 50, see also
    Europe, specific countries
William II, 139-157
    and German foreign policy, 148
    fleetbuilding program, 152
    on Serbia, 155
Wilson, W.
    Tampico Incident, 130
World War I, 38-40, 111, 159-174
    Germany propelled into, 157
    merged with World War II, 159-162
    military control of strategy in, 170
    strategy foundered on technology, 165
    technological developments before,
    134
    undersea warfare inaugurated in, 187
    Western and Eastern strategists, 165
World War II, 38, 41-45, 159-174
    amphibious warfare and aircraft car-
    riers in, 187
    civilian control of strategy, 170
    doctrine up with technology, 161, 165
    merge with World War I, 159-162
Worst-case analysis, 260-262